Walter William Skeat

A Moeso-Gothic Glossary

With an Introduction, an Outline of Moeso-Gothic Grammar, and a List...

Walter William Skeat

A Moeso-Gothic Glossary
With an Introduction, an Outline of Moeso-Gothic Grammar, and a List...

ISBN/EAN: 9783337091415

Printed in Europe, USA, Canada, Australia, Japan

Cover: Foto ©Thomas Meinert / pixelio.de

More available books at **www.hansebooks.com**

A MŒSO-GOTHIC GLOSSARY

WITH

AN INTRODUCTION, AN OUTLINE OF MŒSO-GOTHIC GRAMMAR,

AND A LIST OF

ANGLO-SAXON AND OLD AND MODERN ENGLISH WORDS

ETYMOLOGICALLY CONNECTED WITH MŒSO-GOTHIC

BY

THE REV. W. W. SKEAT, M.A.

LATE FELLOW OF CHRIST'S COLLEGE, CAMBRIDGE, TRANSLATOR OF 'THE SONGS AND BALLADS OF UHLAND', AND EDITOR OF 'PIERS PLOWMAN', 'THE ROMANS OF PARTENAY', ETC.

"If you should ever feel disposed to investigate the origin and structure of the "English language which you speak, you will find that Ulfila's version affords the "best and most valuable materials for the inquiry."
Palgrave's History of the Anglo-Saxons; London, 1867; p. 139.

LONDON:
ASHER & CO., 13, BEDFORD STREET, COVENT GARDEN
AND
BERLIN, 11, UNTER DEN LINDEN
1868

PREFACE.

The present book was undertaken with the view of providing English students with a useful handbook to the Mœso-Gothic language, free from the disadvantages which accompany most existing Glossaries of it. These are, for practical purposes, either too small or too large; either they give no references at all, or the page is crowded with references to every passage in which the word occurs. The former of these is a grave defect; the latter arrangement is, philologically, of great value, but makes a book all the more expensive to buy. Besides, the explanations are given in German, and, however 'improving' this may be to the reader, it gives him additional trouble and often leaves him in some uncertainty after all. It is high time, moreover, that Englishmen should have useful philological books written in their own language, to a much greater extent, that is, than is now the case.

The publication of Massmann's, Gaugengigl's and Stamm's editions of Ulphilas, and, in England, of Dr. Bosworth's cheap edition of the 'Gothic, Anglo-Saxon, Wycliffe, and Tyndale's Gospels' renders a good Mœso-Gothic text easily accessible, and this seems to make a small and convenient glossary, in English, the more necessary. The glossary is the only unsatisfactory part of Massmann's excellent book, a fuller notice of which will be given below.

The general plan of this volume is simply, then, to give English explanations of Mœso-Gothic words, and at the same time to give, in general, some three or four references to the passages in which the words occur. When only one or two references are given, it is because the word occurs only once or twice. It is precisely to these rarer words that the assignment of the passage in which they occur is most necessary; whilst, on the other hand, additional references can *often* be obtained (if required), in the case of more common words, simply by the use of any English concordance. Thus, under SLEPAN, *to sleep*, I give the references Mat. 8. 24; 9. 24; Mk. 4. 27. A concordance, s. v. *sleep*, gives also, for the New Testament, the references Mat. 26. 45: Mk. 14. 41; Lu. 22. 46; Jo. 11. 12; 1 Cor. 11. 30; 15. 21, &c.; and some more under *sleepest, sleepeth*, and *slept*. Of these, the passages in Matthew, Mark, and Luke are lost, but SLEPITH occurs in John 11. 12, and GAZAISLEP in the verse preceding. *Cæteris paribus*, my references are chiefly to the Gospels.

Those who want, however, to know all about a word that is known, will of course consult Schulze, or Gabelentz and Löbe, or Diefenbach.

The present glossary being a mere compilation from the labours of others, I desire here to indicate my sources of information, that the student may know precisely what he is dealing with, and may more easily be enabled to detect any mistakes, which I may not, I fear, have always avoided, though I have done my best to do so.*

The list of words is copied from Massmann's Glossary, in which the words are all arranged in alphabetical order, *as well as* under root-words. I did not at first detect that his list is incomplete, and hence, unfortunately, I have had to add a short Appendix of words missed, to which I beg to refer †

---

* Any reader who discovers a mistake will greatly oblige me by informing me of it.
† See p. 279—282.

the reader, if he does not find the word he wants in its right place. During the revision of the proof-sheets, Schulze's new smaller Glossary was published, and this has enabled me to correct the list of words with tolerable certainty. It gives the *fullest* list of words of any glossary yet published, including even a few imaginary ones which I have not cared to retain.

The genders of the nouns are taken from Massmann, misprints being corrected by comparison with Schulze and (very often) with Gabelentz and Löbe also. The principal parts of the verbs are also from Massmann, compared with Gabelentz and Löbe.

The meanings of the words are either taken from these glossaries, or, *in nearly every instance*, from actual inspection of the passages in which they occur in Massmann's edition. I have taken particular care, when suitable, to use the English words which occur in our Authorized Version, and have sometimes added the letters A. V. to denote this rendering.

The references are taken, some from Schulze, some from Gabelentz and Löbe, corrected by *actual reference* in a very large number of instances. By this process I discovered a few misprints in Gabelentz and Löbe, but their edition is, on the whole, surprisingly correct. I hope I have made no new mistakes of my own. The corresponding words in German, Dutch, and English (or Anglo-Saxon) — given within square brackets — are mostly taken from Gabelentz and Löbe, where the etymology of the words is treated very fully, with examples also from Swedish, Danish, Old Norse, &c. Of the Dutch words, however, I had to supply a large number myself (for which I used the small 'Tauchnitz' Dictionary), since they have made less use of the Dutch, than of German or English. Yet it is, perhaps, the most important of all, as coming nearest, in many cases, to the Gothic. The List of derived words, &c., is partly from Gabelentz and Löbe, but with several additions and corrections, though I have purposely inserted some words that seem to be wrongly derived, that the reader may consider them for himself.

To Gabelentz and Löbe's Glossary I am therefore, as it thus appears, very largely indebted, and it is a book which I should advise all who can to consult, and which is not to be superseded. But to the beginner it must always be rather a distressing book, owing to the highly philosophical, but practically most unwise, arrangement of the words. Not only are they arranged under their roots, so that a student must know the etymology of the language in order to look out a word, but the folly (as I consider it) is adopted of arranging them according to the order (not of the Roman, but) of the *Mœso-Gothic* alphabet, so that in looking out LAGGA-MODEI, for instance, one must first of all remember to look under MOD..., and must further bear in mind that MO comes after MU. The derivations given in the present volume will be found often to serve a double purpose. When SOKEINS, for example, is described as being '*from* SAKAN', the reader who consults Gabelentz and Löbe will save time by looking under SAKAN at once. In fact, he will not otherwise find SOKEINS there at all; the nearest approach to it will be 'SOKJAN; *v.* SAKAN'.

A few practical remarks as to how the reader may make the best use of the volume now before him will be found at the end of this preface.

I now proceed to give an answer to the question — what is Mœso-Gothic?

A carefully-written answer to this will be found in Bosworth's Anglo-Saxon Dictionary, ed. 1838; pref. pp. CXII—CXX. It would appear that Mœso-Gothic is a term rather conventional than correct, and must be taken to mean the language of the Visigoths who at one time dwelt in Mœsia; and it must not at all be taken as signifying that this dialect was formed in Mœsia. The Visigoths are the West-Goths, as distinguished from the Ostrogoths, or East-Goths. We also meet with the term Suio-Gothic, which is applied to mean the language of the Goths of Gothland in Sweden, and which may be looked upon as Old Swedish. Of the Mœso-Gothic dialect all that has come down to us are certain fragments of a translation of the bible by Ulphilas (of whom more presently), a fragment of a commentary on St. John by the same author, a fragment of a Gothic calendar, and two very brief documents known as the *Neapolitan* and *Arezzo* documents. Of the language itself, the best account is in Professor Max Müller's Lectures on the Science of Language, 1862; p. 187. He says: — "The "language of Ulfilas, the Gothic, belongs, through its phonetic "structure, to the Low-German class, but in its grammar it is, "*with few exceptions*, far more primitive than the Anglo-Saxon "of Beowulf, or the Old High-German of Charlemagne. These "few exceptions, however, are very important, for they show "that it would be grammatically, and therefore historically, im- "possible to derive either Anglo-Saxon, or High-German, or "both, from Gothic...... It is because Gothic is the only "one of these parallel dialects that can be traced back to the "fourth century, whereas the others disappear from our sight "in the seventh, that it has been mistaken by some for the "original source of all Teutonic speech." This is well said; at the same time, it must not be lost sight of that Anglo-Saxon and Mœso-Gothic being both of a *Low*-German type, it would be a far less error to look upon Mœso-Gothic as an older form of Anglo-Saxon than of High-German; and we may certainly go as far as to say this — that to study Mœso-Gothic is, practically, more the business of Englishmen than of any one else — excepting perhaps the Dutch — and further, that though Mœso-Gothic is not strictly an older form of Anglo-Saxon, it comes sufficiently near to it to render a study of it peculiarly interesting and instructive to *us*, and a thing by no means to be neglected. The resemblance to English is, indeed, often very striking, as in the instances adduced by Dr. Bosworth, such as: *Ik im thata daur*, I am that (the) door; *nauh leitila hweila*, now a little while; *hardu ist thata waurd*, hard is that word; *wheitos swe snaiws*, white as snow. For the first and last of these phrases we find, in a Dutch bible: *Ik ben de deur, wit als sneeuw*, but in a German bible: *Ich bin die Thür, weiss wie der Schnee*; from which we at once see that the Low-German forms *daur, deur, door, wheitos, wit, white*, must suffer transliteration before they can agree with the High-German forms *Thür* and *weiss*. And what is true in these special instances will be found to hold generally, with not many exceptions; so that an Englishman can often catch at the meaning of a Mœso-Gothic word at once as it stands, without need of changing any of the letters to adapt it to our own peculiar spelling. One exception to this is especially deserving of remark. There are some Gothic words which require the change of *s* into *r* before we perceive their meaning. Change the words *auso, hausjan, basi, leisan*, into *auro, haurjan, bari, leiran*, and the meanings *ear, hear, berry, learn*, become more obvious. Yet this is not a general rule, for we find *kiusan*, to choose, *lausjan*, to loosen. A thorough investigation of words of this kind would probably be found to be not without profit.

Ulphilas is the usual Græcized spelling of a name which is also found in the forms Ulfilas, Urfilas, Urfilus, Gulfilas, Hulfilas, and several others.* The true spelling is almost certainly *Wulfila*, i. e. a little wolf, formed from *wulfs*, a wolf, like *magula*, a little boy, from *magus*, a boy. Wulfila was a bishop of the Mœso-Goths, of Cappadocian parents, born, as generally stated, in A. D. 318, and who died in A. D. 388; but there are reasons for altering these dates to 311 and 381 respectively. The chief of these is that, according to Philostorgius, he was consecrated as bishop at the age of forty in the year 341 by Eusebius of Nicomedia, who died in that same year. Wulfila's death took place at Constantinople, when he was seventy years of age. He is said by ancient authors to have translated the New Testament into Mœso-Gothic, and also the whole of the Old Testament except the book of kings. It would also appear that he is the author of a 'Skeireins áiwaggeljons thairh Iohannen', or 'Explanation of the Gospel by John', a fragment of which has come down to us. He was an Arian†, and it is because he is mentioned both by Arian and Athanasian

---

* See Gaugengigl's Gothische Studien; 5te Ausg.: München, 1864; p. 1.
† This statement is doubtful, and has often been warmly controverted.

writers that the accounts concerning him are contradictory. For further information I must refer the reader to the article 'Ulfilas' in the English Cyclopædia; to Max Müller's Lectures on the Science of Language, 1st Ser. 2nd ed. pp. 179—184; to Bosworth's larger Anglo-Saxon Dictionary, p. cxvi; to G. Waitz, über das Leben und die Lehre des Ulfila, Hannover, 1840; and to Bessel, über das Leben des Ulfila, Göttingen, 1860.

The New Testament he translated from a Greek text, not wholly agreeing with the one we now have; of this, all that we possess are fragments of the Four Gospels, and of some of the Epistles of St. Paul. The Old Testament he translated from the Septuagint, but only the slightest fragments of it are extant, viz. pieces from Genesis, Ezra and Nehemiah. The fragments of verses of other books of the Old Testament which appear in some editions are merely made up from *quotations* of those verses which occur in the New Testament.

The MSS. (or sets of MSS.) now extant are all fragmentary, and may be classed in five classes. These are:

I. The Codex Argenteus, written on mulberry-tinted vellum in letters of gold and silver, formed with such regularity that Ihre (wrongly however) imagined that they must have been stamped on to the vellum. (See Bosworth's Gothic and Anglo-Saxon Gospels, pref. pp. v—vii.) It contains portions of the Gospels, including (not without many *lacunæ*) Mat. V. 15—XI. 25, XXV. 38—XXVII. 66; Mk. I. 1—XVI. 12; Lu. I. 1—X. 30; XIV. 9—XX. 46; Jo. V. 45—XIX. 13. An excellent facsimile of this beautiful MS. will be found in Bosworth's Gothic Gospels, and there is one also in Uppström's edition. It is now preserved in the Royal Library, at Uppsala (Upsal). It first came into notice at the end of the sixteenth century.

II. The Codex Carolinus, discovered by Knittel in a palimpsest MS. at Wolfenbüttel, in the middle of the eighteenth century. It is a mere fragment, containing parts of the 11th, 12th, 13th, 14th, and 15th chapters of the Epistle to the Romans. It was named after Charles, duke of Brunswick.

III. The Milan MS. (or, rather fragments of MSS., with the classmarks G. 147 and I. 61). "In 1818", says Max Müller, "Cardinal Mai and Count Castiglione discovered some more "fragments in the Monastery at Bobbio, where they had pro- "bably been preserved ever since the Gothic empire of Theodoric "the Great in Italy had been destroyed." They are palimpsest MSS., and contain Ezra II. 8—42, and parts of Nehem. V—VII; parts of Mat. XXV, XXVI, and XXVII, and fragments from the Epistles to the Romans, 1st and 2nd Corinthians, Galatians, Ephesians, Philippians, Colossians, 1st and 2nd Thessalonians, Titus, Philemon, and 1st and 2nd Timothy. Also here was found the 'Skeireins' above mentioned, and a fragment of a Gothic calendar. They are sometimes called the Ambrosian MSS., as belonging to the Ambrosian library.

It may be observed that of Romans XII. 17—XIII. 5 there are *two* copies, viz. in MSS. II and III.

There are also *two* copies of parts of the 2nd of Corinthians, Galatians, Ephesians, and other of the epistles, *both* at Milan. At Milan were also found fragments of the 25th, 26th, and 27th chapters of S. Matthew, so that there are two copies of Mat. XXVI. 70—XXVII. 2, viz. at Milan and Upsal.

IV. The Salzburg MS., now (I believe) at Vienna: This preserves mere fragments, but they satisfactorily shew that Ulphilas actually did translate much of the Old Testament, for here we find a portion of the 5th chapter of *Genesis*; portions of *Ezra* and *Nehemiah* existing, as already mentioned, at Milan. Among the fragments is also a scrap of the first chapter of St. Luke.

V. The Vatican MS. (marked No. 5750). This contains part of the 'Skeireins'.

A complete list of the contents of the several MSS. will be found in Massmann's Ulfilas, pp. LVIII—LXII.

It remains to say something about the various editions of Ulphilas.

In Gaugengigl's 'Gothische Studien', 5te Ausg., München, 1864, a list of 45 authors is given, who have written upon

Mœso-Gothic, including a careful and critical notice of the various editions. He justly praises Gabelentz and Löbe, and Massmann, but he casts rather too severe strictures upon the patient labours of Uppström.

Dr. Bosworth's preface to the Gothic Gospels describes 11 editions; see p. VII—IX. It is hardly necessary to transcribe his words; I therefore merely enumerate the editions as briefly as I can, with notes of my own.

1. *Junius and Marshall*; 4to. Dordrecht, 1665; Amsterdam, 1684. The 4 gospels; Mœso-Gothic and Anglo-Saxon texts in M.-G. and A.-S. letters; notes by Marshall; a glossary by Junius.

2. *Stiernhelm*; 4to. Stockholm, 1671. The four Gospels, in 4 languages in parallel columns: 1. Gothic (Roman type); 2. Islandic; 3. Suethic (Suio-Gothic); 4. Latin. At the end, a 'Glossarium Ulphila-Gothicum', *not always found with it.*

3. *Benzelius*, published by *Lye*; 4to. Oxford, 1750. The 4 Gospels; Gothic (in Gothic characters) and Latin; notes and a grammar by Lye.

4. *Ihre.* A book with the title 'I. ab Ihre scripta, versionem Ulphilanam et linguam Mœso-Gothicam illustrantia, edita ab A. F. Büsching, Berolini, 4to. 1773', contains some valuable criticisms on the 4 Gospels, grammatical notes, and specimens of a Glossary, from A—Atdriusandei. [A book entitled 'Specimen Glossarii Ulphilani primum. J. Helsing. Upsaliæ, 1753' contains words from A to Afthwoh; a second specimen, by O. Norrström, has the words from Afthwoh—Anameljan; a third, by O. Granlund, words from Anananthjands—Atdriusandei. These were prepared under Ihre's direction, and he doubtless revised and corrected them for his own use. I may mention here a 'Dissertatio academica de linguâ codicis argentei,' by N. Thenstedt; Upsaliæ, 1754; also 'Ulphilas Illustratus,' by E. Sotberg; Holmiæ, 1762 (containing Matthew and Mark), and an older volume, Upsaliæ, 1755, by the same (containing Luke and John).]

5. *Knittel.* The title is 'Ulphilæ versionem Gothicam nonnullorum capitum epistolæ Pauli ad Romanos ..... eruit, commentatus est, datque foras F. A. Knittel', &c.; no place or date. (It seems to have been published at Wolfenbüttel in 1762.) It contains all the fragments of the Codex Carolinus, with notes, and a glossary of the words occurring in these fragments.

6. *Fulda, Reinwald,* and *Zahn.* 'Ulfilas, ... ausgearbeitet von F. K. Fulda, das Glossar umgearbeitet von W. F. H. Reinwald, ... herausgegeben von J. C. Zahn; Weissenfels, 1805.' It has the 4 Gospels with an interlinear Latin translation, and the fragment of Romans from Knittel's edition; also a grammar and a glossary, which seem better than most of the previous ones. It is generally known as *Zahn's* edition.

7. *Henshall's* St. Matthew, London, 1807. 8vo.

8. *Schmeller's* St. Matthew (Zahn's text); Stuttgart, 1827. 8vo.

9. *Angelo Mai,* 'Ulphilæ partium ineditarum', &c.; Mediolani, 4to. 1819. See Bosworth's A.-S. Dict. p. cxix. It contains extracts from the Milan MSS.

10. *Castiglione,* 'Ulphilæ Gothica versio, &c.; edidit C. O. Castillionæus'; Mediolani, 4to. 1829; also 'Gothicæ versionis... quæ supersunt, &c.; edidit C. A. Castillionæus'; Mediolani, 4to. 1834. See Bosworth, as above.

11. *Massmann's* 'Skeireins'; 4to. München, 1834. This is a facsimile edition of the 'Skeireins', in Gothic types, the lines arranged as in the MS. It contains much other information, and is a thoroughly satisfactory book.

12. *Gabelentz and Löbe.* 'Ulfilas'; 2 vols. 4to. Lipsiæ, 1836—1843. A very valuable and complete work, containing *all* the Gothic texts, and a complete and careful glossary and grammar. Of this book I have made large use. Taken altogether, it is the best edition of all.

13. *Diefenbach.* Diefenbach has issued no edition of Ulphilas, but only a Gothic Glossary, published at Frankfort-on-the-Main, 1846—1849. It discusses etymologies very fully, and is a most elaborate and valuable work, but somewhat confusing; nor is it free from unreasonable guesses.

18. *Gaugengigl.* 'Ulfilas, Urschrift, Grammatik und Wörterbuch', by I. Gaugengigl; Passau, 1849. 8vo. The text follows that of Gabelentz and Löbe. A second edition (Passau,•1849) contains 65 emendations. A third edition (Passau, 1853) contains several more; and a fourth edition appeared at Passau in 1856.

14. *Schulze.* This is a glossary only, a very good one, published at Magdeburg, without date. A smaller edition, without the references, was published at Züllichau in 1867, at a low price. I have frequently consulted both editions.

15. *Uppström's* Codex Argenteus, Upsaliæ, 1854—1857. 4to. This, of course, contains the four gospels only. It is intended to represent the MS. *exactly*, being printed line for line, with the words divided just as they often are in the MS. It is a most important work, the result of much patience, and does not seem to deserve the severe strictures of Gaugengigl (Gothische Studien, 5te Ausg. p. 19). Pages 87—100, including Mk. I—VIII, were afterwards cancelled, and a more correct edition of them substituted. It appears that ten leaves of the Codex, including Mk. I. 13—37, II. 15—III. 7, and V. 42—VII. 32, were some time ago stolen, and were missing for many years; they were afterwards restored to Professor Uppström (who tells the story in his second preface), and replaced by him in the Codex. These folios were numbered 58, 59, 62, 63, and 21—26 inclusive. But Uppström's improved edition contains scarcely any differences of reading: the only variation, for instance, in foll. 58 and 59 is the substitution of *leitilata* for *leitil* in Mk. I. 19. Yet the MS. has not *leitilata*, but *leita*; and though he supposes this to have been written for *leitilata*, it is quite as probable that it meant *leitil*, as that is the usual form. Indeed, my own opinion is that it may even have meant *leita*, i. e. exactly what it says, and that the wisest course is, in general, to accept the MS. as it stands; for it is to be expected that such a writing would contain variations of spelling, and even occasional false concords and colloquialisms, whilst, on the other hand, it is not to be expected that a modern editor can tell,

with certainty, whether a given word was or was not used by the Goths in the year A. D. 360. In a case like this, emendations should be made with the greatest caution. I would illustrate this by remarking that, in Old English, the form *lyte* is quite as usual as the form *lytel*; and one wonders what would be thought of an editor who assumed that only the latter form can be right. Uppström's real reason for cancelling the old pages is clearly because, in them, the words are often *divided quite wrongly,* which rendered the printed copy no longer a facsimile of the MS. He adopted the wise course of using Roman types.

16. *Massmann's* Ulfilas, Stuttgart, 1857. 8vo. Dr. Bosworth says, justly, that "it is a most useful and comprehensive book, "containing in one moderate 8vo-volume the whole of the Gothic "translation of the Old and New Testaments hitherto discovered, "and all that is known on the subject". It contains, an introduction, texts in Gothic, Greek, and Latin in parallel columns, glossary, grammar, and notes. The grammar is very good, but the glossary is not quite useful enough, from its want of references. This and the next are the the texts I have constantly used and referred to.

17. *Stamm's* Ulfilas, Paderborn, 1858. 8vo. This is founded on Gabelentz and Löbe. As it omits the Greek and Latin texts, it is a still cheaper and more compact book for general use than Massmann's, and its form is very compact and portable. The type is clear, and the text complete; a good grammar and brief glossary are added. It reached a third edition in 1865.

18. *Uppström.* 'Fragmenta Gothica selecta, ad fidem codicum Ambrosianorum, Carolini, Vaticani, edidit Andreas Uppström. Upsaliæ, 1861.' The preface contains a defence of his former work (No. 15).

The documents at Naples and Arezzo are title-deeds. Their chief use is, that they prove the language and writing of the Codex Argenteus to be genuine Gothic. The Arezzo document is now either lost or mislaid. Here is a copy of the whole of the Gothic part of it, the rest being in Latin and to the effect that Gudilaib, a deacon, sells to Alamoda a farm with some buildings.

Ik Gudilaib 'dkn' tho frabauhta; boka fram mis gawaurhta thus, 'dkn' Alamoda; fidwor unkjana hugsis Kaballarja jah [s]killigans 'RLG' andnam, jah ufmelida.

"I, Gudilaib, deacon, sold these things; an account (of them) from me I have made over to thee, deacon Alamoda; four *unciae** of the farm Kaballarja and 133 shillings I have received, and have subscribed my name."

The punctuation of this is uncertain. Massmann seems to make 'frabauhta-boka' all one word (if I rightly understand him) with the signification, *a deed of sale.*

The document at Naples contains five similar subscriptions, all nearly in the same words. One of these may suffice as a specimen. For the rest, see Massmann's Ulfilas, p. 810.**

Ik Sunjaifrithas diakon handau meinai ufmelida, jah andn[-emum] skilliggans .J. jah fau[r]this thairh kawtsjon, mith diakona [Ala]moda unsaramma jah mith gahlaibaim unsaraim, andnemum sk[il]liggans .RK. wairth thize saiwe.

"I, Sunjaifrithas, deacon, with my hand have subscribed, and we have received 60 shillings; and, before this, as a caution, with our deacon Alamoda and with our companions, we have received 120 shillings — the worth of these seas (i.e. lakes)."

The name of the deacon Alamoda occurs in *all* the subscriptions, and it is probably to him that we owe them in the first instance.

The fragment of a Gothic calendar was found among the Milan MSS. It merely gives the numbers of the days of the month for the whole of November, and for the 23rd to the 30th days (inclusive) of some other month, with a few entries against some of them. The method of counting the days throughout the month is by these letters: — a, b, g, d, e, kw, z, h, th, i, ia, ib, ig, id, ie, ikw, iz, ih, ith, k, ka, kb, kg, kd,

---

* *Uncia* sometimes means the twelfth part of an acre.
** Or see Gabelentz and Löbe's Ulfilas; vol. 1. p. xiii.

ke, kkw, kz, kh, kth, l — which is easily followed, and clearly imitated from the Greek. Against *kth* (it should have been against *l*) is the entry — *Andriins apaustaul[a]us*, of Andrew the apostle. But the most interesting entry is against a day in the other month, viz.: *Kg. thize ana Gutthiudai managaize marytre [martyre?] jah Frithareikeis;* i. e. 23. 'of the many martyrs among the *Gothic people*, and of Frederick.' Here is exact evidence that they called themselves the *Gutþiuda*, i. e. Gothic people, for *thiuda* is the A.-S. *peód*. Hence, too, the Gothic name for a *Goth* was, in all probability, *Guta*, pronounced *Goota*.

In a sort of magazine entitled 'Germania; herausgegeben von P. Pfeiffer — zwölfter Jahrgang, zweites Heft — Wien, 1867,' there is (at p. 232) a paper by Gabelentz on a MS. of Ulfilas found at Turin. The MS. is nearly illegible. All that can be made out is that the characters are Gothic — and the fragments of the words — 'Amen ..... Paul ... ia ... fa' — are nearly all that can be read. The words *Amen* and *Paul*... shew that the MS. probably contained one of St. Paul's epistles, and I should guess that *fa* is part of the word *Aifaisium*, i. e. that the MS. contained the epistle to the *Ephesians*.

As specimens of the language, I here transcribe the 'Lord's prayer', and one of the fragments of the 'Skeireins', with the closest possible translation:

Swa nu bidjaith jus: Atta unsar, thu in himinam, Weihnai
So now bid (=pray) ye: Father our, thou in heaven, Be sanctified

namo thein. Kwimai thiudinassus theins. Wairthai wilja theins,
name thine. Let-come kingdom thine. Be-done will thine,

swe in himinam, jah ana airthai. Hlaif unsarana, thana
so in heaven, and on earth. Loaf our, the

sinteinan, gif uns himma daga. Jah aflet uns, thatei skulans
daily, give us this day. And let-off us, in-that debtors

sijaima,   swaswe jah weis afletam thaim   skulam   unsaraim.
(we) are,   so-as   also we   let-off   the   debtors   our.

Jah ni briggais uns in fraistubnjai, ak lausei uns af thamma
And not   bring   us into temptation, but loose us off   the

ubilin; unte theina ist thiudangardi, jah mahts, jah wulthus,
evil;   because thine   is   kingdom,   and might, and glory,

        in   aiwins.   Amen.
        unto æons.   Amen.   Mat. VI. 9—13.

Old English would supply us with *worth* for *wairthai*, *ac* for *ak*; and *frayning* for *fraistubnjai*. A.-S. would help us to *peóden*, a king, as the root of *thiudinassus* and *thiudangardi*; also to *wuldor* as an equivalent to *wulthus*. *Weihnai* is connected with the German *weihen*, and the A.-S. *wig*, holy.

The seventh fragment of the 'Skeireins' or 'Explanation' runs thus:

... *hun kunnandins   fraujins   maht jah andthaggkjandans*
    of-one-knowing the-Lord's might and   bethinking

sik   is   waldufneis;   nih   Stains,   ak jah Andraias,
himself of his power; nor (was it) Stone[Peter], but even Andrew,

saei kwath: Ist   magula ains her, saei habaith fimf hlaibans
who quoth: There-is lad   one here, who hath   five loaves

barizeinans, jah twans fiskans; analeiko swe Filippus gasakada,
of-barley, and two fishes; likewise so   Philip reproved (him),

ni waiht mikilis   hugjands,   nih   wairthidos   laisareis
no   whit of-mickle considering, nor the-dignity of-the-Teacher

andthaggkjands;   thairh   thoei   usbar   kwithands,   Akei
thinking-on;   through which he-answered, saying,   But

EXTRACT FROM THE 'SKEIREINS.'

thata	*hwa*	*ist*	*du*	*swa*	*managaim?*	*Ith*	*frauja*
that,	what	is-it	to	so	many?	But	the-Lord

andtilonds   *ize*   *niuklahein*   *kwath:*   *Waurkeith*
serving (helping) their weakness-of-faith, quoth: Work (cause)

thans mans anakumbjan; ith eis, at hauja managamma
the men to-recline; but they, since hay(grass) much

wisandin in thamma stada tho filusna anakumbjan gatawidedun,
being in the stead, the multitude to-recline made,

fimf thusundjos waire inuh kwinons jah barna, swe at mikilamma
five thousands of-men, without women and bairns, as at a-mickle

nahtamahta anakumbjandans, at ni wisand[e]in aljai waihtai
night-meat reclining, at not being other whit

ufar thans fimf hlaibans jah twans fiskans; thanzei nimands jah
over the five loaves and two fishes; these taking and

awiliudonds gathiuthada, jah swa managai ganohjands
giving-thanks he-blessed, and (with) so much satisfying

ins wailawiznai, ni thatainei ganauhan thaurftais im
them (with)-food, not only a-sufficing of-need to-them

fragaf, ak filaus maizo: afar thata matjan so managei,
afforded, but of-much more: after that to-eat the multitude,

bigitan was thize hlaibe twalif tainjons fullos, thatei aflifnoda,
acquired was of-the loaves twelve baskets full, that remained,

samaleikoh than jah thize fiske, swa filu swe wildedun. Nih
equally then also of-the fishes, so much as they-willed. Not

than ana thaim hlaibam ainaim seinaizos mahtais filuzna
then on the loaves only of-his might the-magnitude

ustaiknida,   ak jah in thaim fiskam;   swa filu auk swe ganauthida
he-tokened, but also in   the   fishes;   so much also as   needed

ize   wairthan,   swaei ainhwarjamme swa filu swa   wilda,
of-them to-become,   even   for-each-one   as   much as   he-willed,

andniman is gatawida, jah ni in waihtai waninassu thizai
to-receive he caused,   and not in   any-whit   a-waning from-this

filusnai   wairthan, gatawida; akei nauh   us   thamma filu
quantity   to-become, he-caused; but   yet out-of   that,   much

mais siponjans fullafahida jah antharans gamaudida gaumjan,
more his disciples he-satisfied and the-others he-reminded to-perceive,

thatei is was sa sama, saei in   authidai   .m. jere   attans
that he was the same, who in the-wilderness   40 years the-fathers

ize   fodida. Thanuh, bithe   sadai   waurthun,   kwath
of-them fed.   Then,   whilst satisfied they-became, quoth-he

siponjam   seinaim, galisith thos aflifnandeins drausnos,   ei
to-disciples   his,   collect   the   remaining   fragments,   that

waihtai   ni frakwistnai.   Thanuh   galesun   jah
in-any-whit it-may-not-perish. Then-however they-collected and

gafullidedun .ib. tainjons gabruko   us   thaim .e. hlaibam
filled   12 baskets with-fragments out-of   the   5   loaves

barizeinam jah .b. fiskam,   thatei aflifnoda at   thaim
of-barley   and   2   fishes,   that   remained   to   the

[matjandam] . . . .
eating-ones.   *See* Massmann's Ulfilas, p. 586.

I trust the reader will forgive the baldness of this translation, the object being to shew the force of each word as closely as possible.

It may be remarked that there is *no* authority for the use of *accents* in Mœso-Gothic. The accents adopted in some editions are purely imaginary.

I have purposely omitted all proper names, with a view to making the glossary more compact. Every one must know how to translate them; whilst, on the other hand, any one wishing to see how any name is spelt in Gothic, can find the place where it occurs by help of a Concordance to the English Bible. A list of them all will be found in Massmann, pp. 763—769; or in Schulze (see pp. 225—229 of the smaller edition). In Gabelentz and Löbe they are mixed up with the other words. They enable us to compare the Gothic orthography with the Greek.

ON THE GRAMMAR. This is a mere outline intended as a general guide for practical use. There are many words of which the gender and declension are uncertain. These are set down in the dictionary as of that gender which seems most probable. Exceptional forms the student must do the best he can with. Long lists of exceptions are not of much practical value in a case like the present, where we have but fragments of a language to deal with.

ON THE 'LIST OF WORDS', &c. Many of these English words connected with Gothic are to be found in Gabelentz and Löbe. Some are given in Diefenbach. Many are discussed by Mr. Cockayne in his book entitled 'Spoon and Sparrow'. I have collected all that seemed most suitable (omitting remoter analogies), and have added a few more to the list. This 'List' may also serve in some measure as an *English-Gothic* dictionary, as it gives the Gothic for nearly all the words of most interest and importance.

EXPLANATION.

The words are arranged in alphabetical order, and in precisely the same order as in Massmann's glossary. Thus words beginning with the letter *th* will be found between *te* and *ti*.

Massmann's *v* has been changed into *w*; his *hv* into *hw*, and his *kv* into *kw*; but this does not affect the order of the words.

The *q* used by some editors is represented by *kw*; see the Remarks on the Alphabet at the beginning of the Grammar.

In general *three* quotations are given except when the word occurs only *twice* or *once*.

Words marked with a star(*) are *supposed root-words*. Often, we feel sure they must have existed. Thus, the occurrence of *af-agjan, in-agjan, us-agjan* shew that there was a simple verb *agjan*.*

At the end of all the principal root-words, a list of derivatives is subjoined, with the heading *Der.* Thus under BALTHS* is given '*Der.* balthaba, balthei, thrasa-balthei, us-balthei, balthjan'.

Conversely, to find the words with the same root as *us-balthei*, look under *baltheis*, where again a reference is given to *balths*, only the second word below, where the list (containing the five words just mentioned) is found. This arrangement will be found in practice to be nearly as convenient as Massmann's, who explains every word twice over, once under its root, and once in its proper place.

When the derivation is obvious, it is not given. Thus, *faura-gameljan* is of course from *gameljan*, where again *ga* is the common prefix, and the root-word is *meljan*.

The knowledge of the root-word is necessary for any one one consulting Gabelentz and Löbe. Thus, against *bandja* I have written '*From* bindan'; and only under BINDAN will it be found in that work.

The words within square brackets are words connected etymologically with the one in question. Thus, *bagms* is connected with the Dutch *boom*, German *baum*, English *beam*.

ABBREVIATIONS. A.-S. Anglo-Saxon; D. Dutch; G. German; O.E. Old English; Sc. Scottish; M. Massmann; G. & L. Gabelentz and Löbe; S. Schulze; A. V. Authorized Version of the English Bible.

Also, *str. sb. f.* strong substantive feminine; *wk. sb.* weak substantive; *pt. t.* past tense; *pp.* past (or passive) participle; *pl.* plural; &c.

Also, *Skeir.* 'Skeireins'; *Neap.* Neapolitan; *Arezz.* Arezzo. Such abbreviations as *Mk.* for Mark need no explanation.

The references to the 'Skeireins' are to Massmann's complete edition of Ulfilas. Thus 'Skeir. 1. 3' means 'Skeireins; fragment 1, line 3'. In any other edition, fragment 1 must be read through to find the word. But the fragments are all of them *very short*.

A few words, accidentally omitted in their right places, will be found in an Appendix, after the letter Z.

Cambridge, April 1868.

MŒSO-GOTHIC GLOSSARY.

CONTENTS.

PREFACE. — Sources whence the present volume is compiled. — Some account of Mœso-Gothic. — Wulfila, Ulphilas or Ulfilas. — Mœso-Gothic MSS. — Editions of Ulphilas. — The Neapolitan and Arezzo documents. — The fragment of a Gothic calendar. — The Lord's prayer. — Fragment of the 'Skeireins', or Explanation of St. John's Gospel. — On the Grammar and List of Words . . . . pp. I — XX
EXPLANATION OF THE GLOSSARY . . . . p. XXI
GLOSSARY . . . . col. 1
OUTLINE OF GRAMMAR . . . . p. 287
LIST OF ENGLISH WORDS, &c. . . . . col. 311
ERRATA . . . . p. 341

A.

A, the first letter of the Gothic alphabet. It is, apparently, generally short in pronunciation; and can be lengthened into *e*, as *lag, legum;* or into *o*, as *giba, gibos*. It helps to form the diphthongs *ai, au*, which occur especially before *h* and *r*, as in *taihun, bairan; nauh, baur*. As a numeral, 1. [It is convenient to pronounce *a* like *a* in *father; ai* like G. *ei* or E. *i* nearly, or perhaps, more broadly, like *ah-ee;* and *au* like E. *aw*.]

ABA, *sb. m.* a man; or, rather, a husband, Isa. 54. 1; Mk. 10. 12; Lu. 1. 34; 2. 36; *gen. pl.* Ab'ne, 1 Cor. 11. 3; *dat. pl.* Abnam, Eph. 5. 22, 24. *Cf.* MANNA, WAIR, GUMA.

ABBA (ἀββᾶ), father, Gal. 4. 6.

ABRABA, *adv.* strongly, excessively, very much, Nehem. 6. 16; Mat. 27. 54; Mk. 16. 4. *See* Abrs.

ABRJAN*, *used in the comp.* bi-abrjan, q. v.

ABRS, *adj.* strong, mighty, excessive, Lu. 15. 14. *Der.* abraba, bi-abrjan. Cf. A. S. *abal*, strength.

AB-U: *see af and uh.*

AF (Ab-u, Jo. 18. 34), *prep. with dat.* of, from, out of, by. *Cf.* Afar, Fram. It enters into numerous compounds, for which see below. [A. S. *af, of;* G. *ab;* D. *af.*]

AF-AGJAN, to strike with awe, terrify, 1 Thess. 3. 3; Phil. 1. 28. *From* agjan.

AF-AIKAN, to deny vehemently, imprecate curses on oneself, Mat. 26, 72; Mk. 14. 68; Jo. 18. 27; to deny, Mat. 10. 33; 2 Tim. 2. 12; *refl.* to deny oneself, Lu. 9. 23; 2 Tim. 2. 13. *From* aikan.

AF-AIRZJAN, to lead astray, to deceive, 1 Cor. 15. 33; Mk. 13. 22. *pass.* to go astray, 1 Tim. 6. 10; to go away, Jo. 7. 47. *See* Airzis.

AFAR, *prep. with dat. and acc.* after (both of place and time), according to, Mat. 26. 2; Lu. 1. 59; &c. Afar thata, thereafter; afar thatei, after that; afar leitil, after a little while; afaruh than, but after, Mk. 16. 12; Lu. 18. 4.

AFAR(A)? *sb.* ns afar' Abijins, of the course of Abiab, Lu. 1. 5.

AFAR-DAGS, *str. sb.* the next day, day after, Lu. 7. 11; Mat. 6. 30.
AFAR-GAGGAN, *vb.* to go after, follow, Mat. 8. 23, Mk. 5. 37; to follow after, Phil. 3. 12.
AFAR-HUGJAN, *vb.* to think after, think upon, trust in, Mk. 10. 24? [M. *gives this verb, but* S. *and* G. *and* L. *ignore it.*]
AFAR-LAISTJAN, *vb.* to follow after; *with dat. case,* Mat. 8. 10; Mk. 10. 32; 1 Tim. 5. 10.
AFAR-SABBATUS, *sb.* the week following, Mk. 16. 2.
AF-DAILJAN, *vb.* to distribute, set apart; afdailja taihundon dail, I give tithes; Lu. 18. 12.
AF-DAUBNAN, *vb.* to become obtuse, to grow dull, 2 Cor. 3. 14.
AF-DAUJAN, *vb.* to tire, vex, harass; Mat. 9. 36. *See* diwan.
AF-DAUTHJAN, *vb.* to kill, put to death, Mat. 27. 1; Mk. 14. 55. *pass.* to die, Mk. 7. 10; to be dead, Rom. 7. 4. *See* diwan.
AF-DOBNAN, *vb.* to become dumb, to hold one's peace; Lu. 4. 35. *See* daubs.
AF-DOMEINS, *str. sb. f.* condemnation, Skeir. 8. 7.
AF-DOMJAN, *vb.* to condemn, Lu. 6. 37; to judge, Jo. 16. 11; to curse, Mat. 26, 74.
AF-DRAUSJAN, *vb.* to cast down, precipitate, Lu. 4. 29.
AF-DRUG(G)EJA, *wk. sb. m.* a drunkard, 1 Cor. 5. 11.
AF-DUMBNAN, *vb.* to hold one's peace, Mk. 4. 39. *See* dumbs.
AF-ETJA, *wk. sb. m.* a glutton, Mat. 11. 19; Lu. 7. 34. *See* itan.
AF-FILHAN, *vb.* to hide, Lu. 10. 21.
AF-GAGGAN (*pt. t.* af-iddja), *vb.* to go away, depart, Lu. 2. 37; Mat. 11. 7; Jo. 6. 15.

AF-GIBAN, *vb.* to give away; afgab sik, *lit.* gave himself away, *hence,* departed, Philemon. 15.
AF-GRUNDITHA, *str. sb. fem.* an abyss, Lu. 8. 31; Rom. 10. 7.
AF-GUDEI, *wk. sb. fem.* godlessness, iniquity, Isa. 59. 20; Rom. 11. 26; ungodliness, 2 Tim. 2. 16.
AF-GUDS, *adj.* godless, impious, Skeir. 4. 26. *Cf.* gudalaus.
AF-HABAN, *vb.* to keep oneself from, abstain from, 1 Thes. 5. 22.
AF-HAIMS, *adj.* absent from home, absent from, 2 Cor. 5. 6, 9. *See* ana-haims.
AF-HAMON, *vb.* to strip off (clothes), to unclothe oneself, 2 Cor. 5. 4.
AF-HLATHAN, *vb.* to load, 2 Tim. 3. 6. [*The* Ms. *reading is* aflathana; M. *proposes* uflathana.]
AF-HOLON, *vb.* to deprive of unjustly, defraud, Lu. 19. 8.
AF-HRAINJAN, *vb.* to cleanse from, Skeir. 1. 3.
AF-HRISJAN, *vb.* to shake off, Lu. 9. 5; 10. 11.
AF-HUGJAN, *vb.* to make senseless, stupefy, bewitch, Gal. 3. 1.
AF-HWAPJAN, *vb.* to quench, Eph. 6. 16; 1 Thess. 5. 19; to choke, Mk. 4. 7; Lu. 8 7.
AF-HWAPNAN, *vb.* to be quenched, Mk. 9. 44; to be choked, Mk. 5, 13; Lu. 8. 14, 33.
AF-IDDJA: *see* AF-GAGGAN.
AF-KWITHAN, *vb. with dat.* to renounce, forsake, Lu. 14. 33.
AF-LAGEINS, *str. sb. fem.* a laying aside, remission, Mk. 1. 4.
AF-LAGJAN, *vb.* to lay down, Jo. 10. 18; to put away, Eph. 4. 25; 1 Cor. 13. 11.
AF-LEITHAN, *vb.* to go away, depart, Mk. 3. 7; Lu. 20. 9;

to leave, Lu. 5. 11; (*see* afletan.
AF-LETAN, *vb.* to leave, Mat. 5. 24; to depart, Mat. 7. 23; to let one have, Mat. 5. 40; to put away (a wife), Mk. 10. 4; Mat. 5. 31, 32; to send away, Mk. 4. 36; to let off, forgive, Mat. 6. 12, 14, 15; afletan ahman, to expire, Mat. 27. 50.
AF-LETS, *str. sb. m.* forgiveness, remission, Luc. 1. 77; Skeir. 3. 19.
AF-LIFNAN, *vb.* to be left remaining, to remain over and above, Lu. 9. 17; Jo. 6. 13; to survive, be alive, 1 Th. 4. 17. *See* leiban.
AF-LINNAN, *vb.* to depart, Lu. 9. 39.
AF-MAINDS, *adj.* (ἐκλυόμενος) faint, growing faint, Gal. 6. 9.
AF-MAITAN, *vb.* to cut off, Mk. 9. 43; af-maitan haubith, to behead, Mk. 6. 16, 27; Lu. 9. 9.
AF-MARZEINS, *str. sb. fem.* deceitfulness, Mk. 4. 19; Eph. 4. 22.
AF-MARZJAN, *vb.* to offend, Jo. 16. 1; 2 Cor. 11. 29.
AF-NIMAN, *vb.* to take away, remove, Mat. 9. 15; Lu. 1. 25; Jo. 11. 39; Rom. 11. 27; to take away from, Mat. 9. 16; Mk. 2. 21; 4. 25.
AF-SATEINS, *str. sb. fem.* divorcement, Mk. 10. 4.
AF-SATJAN, *vb.* to divorce, Mat. 5. 32; Mk. 10. 2; to dismiss, Lu. 16. 4.
AF-SKAIDAN, *vb.* to sever from society, treat as an outcast, shun, Lu. 6. 22; *refl.* to depart from, Lu. 9. 33; to separate oneself, 2 Cor. 6. 17; Gal. 2. 12.
AF-SKIUBAN, *vb. with dat.* to put away, 1 Tim. 1. 19; to reject, Rom. 11. 1.

AF-SLAHAN, *vb.* to slay, Lu. 20. 14; Eph. 2. 16.
AF-SLAUPJAN, *vb.* to strip off, renounce, Col. 3. 9.
AF-SLAUTHJAN, *vb.* to vex; *pass.* to be in despair, to be vexed to death, 2 Cor. 4. 8; to be in great doubt or difficulty about, Gal. 4. 20.
AF-SLAUTHNAN, *vb.* to be beside oneself, to be amazed, Lu. 4. 36; Mk. 10. 24.
AF-STANDAN, *vb.* to recede, revolt, fall away, Lu. 8. 13; to keep aloof from, 2 Cor. 4. 2; 2 Tim. 2. 19.
AF-STASS, *str. sb. fem.* divorcement, Mat. 5. 31. Deut. 24. 1.
AF-SWAGGWJAN, *vb.* to make one despair; af-swaggwidai weseima *is another reading for* skamaidedeima uns *in* 2 Cor. 1. 8.
AF-SWAIRBAN, *vb.* to wipe away, blot out, Col. 2. 14.
AFTA, *adv.* behind, backwards; tho afta, that which lies behind, the past, Phil. 3. 14. *See* aftana, af-aftaro, aftuma, aftra, afar, af.
AFTANA, *adv.* behind, from behind, Mk. 5. 27. *Cf.* afta.
AFTARO, *adv.* from behind, Mat. 9. 20; Lu. 8. 44; behind, Lu. 7, 38.
AF-TAURNAN, *vb.* to be torn away from, to make a rent, Lu. 5. 36.
AF-THAURSJAN, *vb.* to be thirsty, Mat. 25. 42, 44.
AF-THLIUHAN, *vb.* to flee away, Jo. 10. 13.
AF-THWAHAN, *vb.* to wash off, to wash oneself, Jo. 9. 7, 15.
AF-TIUHAN, *vb.* to draw away, push off, Lu. 5. 3; to take, draw aside, Mk. 8. 32.
AFTRA, *adv.* back, backwards; again, once more, Mk. 2. 1.

AFTRA LEITIL, again a little while, Jo. 16. 16.
— anastodeins, *str. sb. fem.* a renewing, Skeir. 1. 22.
— atwandjan, *vb. refl.* to return, Lu. 19. 15.
— gabotan, *vb.* to restore, Mk. 9. 12.
— gagawairthjan, *vb.* to be reconciled, 1. Cor. 7. 11.
— galathon, *vb.* to invite again, Skeir. 1. 25.
— galeithan, *vb.* to re-enter, Jo. 3. 4.
— gasatjan, *vb.* to restore, heal, Mk. 8. 25.
— gawandjan, *vb. refl.* to return Lu. 2. 43.
— haitan, *vb.* to invite in return, Lu. 14. 12.
— timrjan, *vb.* to rebuild, Gal. 2. 18.
— usfulljan, *vb.* to fill up, consummate, gather together (A. V.), Eph. 1. 10.
AFTUMA, *adj.* the hindmost, the last, Mk. 10. 31.
AFTUMISTS, *adj.* the last, Mk. 9. 35; aftumist haban, to lie at the point of death, Mk. 5. 23.
AFUNGASTOTHANAIM: *see* ungastothans.
AF-WAGJAN, *vb.* to move away, Col. 1, 23.
AF-WAIRPAN, *vb.* to cast (stones) at, Lu. 20. 6; Jo. 11. 8. *Cf.* wairpan, Jo. 10. 31; to cast away, put away, Eph. 4. 31.
AF-WALWJAN, *vb.* to roll away, Mk. 16. 3, 4.
AF-WANDJAN, *vb.* to turn away, turn aside, Isa. 59. 20; Gal. 1, 6; Rom. 11. 26; 2 Tim. 1. 15; Tit. 1. 14.
AGAN*, *vb. (from this root, meaning* to fear, *comes the Present* ik og, *and the verbs* ogan *and* ogjan, q. v.). *Der.* un-agands, un-ageins, agis, agjan, af-agjan, in-agjan, us-agjan, ogan, ogjan.
AGEINS*, *in comp.* un-ageins, q. v.
AGGA*, *wk. sb. m. in comp.* halsagga, q. v.
AGGELUS: *see the following.*
AGGILUS (*also* aggelus, aggillus, *pl.* aggiljus *and* aggileis), an angel, Mk. 1. 13; 8, 38; &c.; a messenger, Mat. 11. 10; Mk. 1. 2. *Der.* ark-aggilus.
AGGWITHA, *str. sb. fem.* anguish, distress, Rom. 8. 35; 2 Cor. 6. 4. *From* aggwus.
AGGWJAN*, *vb., in compound:* ga-aggwjan, q. v.
AGGWUS, *adj.* narrow, strait, Mat. 7. 13, 14. [Lat. *angustus;* G. *eng;* D. *eng.*]
AGIS, *str. sb. neut.* fright, fear, terror, awe, Mk. 4. 41; Lu. 1. 12, 65; 2. 9; 5. 26; &c.
AGJAN*, *vb. in* af-agjan, in-agjan, *and* us-agjan. *See* agan.
AGL: *see* aglus.
AGLAITEI, *str. sb. fem.* lasciviousness, Mk. 7. 22; 2 Cor. 12. 21; Gal. 5. 19; Eph. 4. 19. *From* aglus.
AGLAITGASTALDS, *adj.* covetous, greedy of filthy lucre (A. V.), basely greedy, 1 Tim. 3. 8; Titus 1. 7.
AGLAITI, *str. sb. neut.* wantonness, unchastity, Rom. 13. 13. *From* aglus. *See* aglaitei.
AGLAITIWAURDEI, *str. sb. fem.* unclean talk, filthy speaking, Col. 3. 8. *From* aglus.
AGLITHA, *str. sb. fem.* agony, anguish, tribulation; aglitha winnan, to suffer tribulation, 1 Th. 3. 4. *Cf.* aglo.
AGLJAN*, *vb. in comp.* us-agljan, *with dat.* q. v.
AGLO, *wk. sb. fem.* anguish, tribu-

lation, Mk. 13. 24; Rom. 12. 12; Jo. 16. 21; 2 Cor. 2. 4; aglo winnan, to be in distress, 1 Tim. 5. 10.

AGLUBA, *adv.* hardly, with difficulty, Mk. 10. 23; Lu. 18. 24.

AGLUS (*also* agls?), *adj.* difficult, hard; aglu ist, it is hard, Mk. 10. 24; agl' ist, it is hard, it is a shame, 1 Cor. 11. 6. *Der.* agluba, us-agljan, aglitha.

AHA, *wk. sb. m.* understanding (νοῦς), Phil. 4. 7; 1 Tim. 6. 5; 2 Tim. 3. 8; Tit. 1. 15. *Der.* inahs, inahei, ahjan, ahma.

AHAKS, *str. sb.* (*fem. or m.?*) a dove, Mk. 1. 10; Lu. 2. 24; 3. 22. *Cf.* dubo.

AHANA, *str. sb. fem.* chaff, Lu. 3. 17.

AHJAN, *vb.* to think, Mat. 10. 34. *Cf.* aha.

AHMA, *wk. sb. m.* the spirit, the Holy Ghost, Mk. 1. 8, 10, 12; &c. *Der.* ahmeins, ahmateins. *Cf. also* hugs, muns, moths, anan. *Cf.* ἆημα.

AHMATEINS, *str. sb. f.* inspiration, 2 Tim. 3. 16.

AHMEINS, *adj.* spiritual, Rom. 7. 14; 1 Cor. 10. 3, 4; Gal. 6. 1; Eph. 1. 3, &c.; *from* ahma.

AHS (*gen.* ahsis), *str. sb. neut.* an ear of corn, Mk. 2. 23; 4, 28. Lu. 6. 1. [G. *ähre*; E. *ear*; D. *aar.*]

AHS(A)? *See* amsa.

AHTAU, eight, Lu. 2. 21; 9. 28.

AHTAU-DOGS, *adj.* on the eighth day, Phil. 3. 5.

AHTAU-TEHUND, eighty, Lu. 2. 37; 16. 7.

AHTUDA, the eighth, Lu. 1. 59.

AHWA, *str. sb. f.* a river, Mk. 1. 5; a flood, Mat. 7. 27; Lu. 6. 48; a stream, Jo. 7. 38.

Cf. saiws, flodus, wato. [W. *afon*; A. S. *œ.*]

AIAIK, said; *pt. tense of* aikan, *vb.* q. v.

AIALTH: *see* althan.

AIAUK, increased; *pt. tense of* aukan, q. v.

AIBR, *str. sb. neut.* a gift, an offering (for the altar), Mat. 5. 23.

AIGAN, AIHAN, *vb.* (*of which are found the principal forms* aih, aig; aihum, aigum; aihta, aigands), to have, own, possess, Lu. 15. 4, 11; 17. 7; 20. 28; &c.; *with a double acc.*, Lu. 3. 8. *Der.* fair-aihan, aigin, ga-aiginon, aihts, aihtron, aihtrons. [A. S. *agan*; A. H. G. *eigan*; O. E. *owe.*]

AIGIN, *str. sb. neut.* possessions, property, substance, Lu. 8. 43; 15. 12; 19. 8; *from* aigan.

AIGINON*, *in comp.* ga-aiginon, q. v.

AIH, I have; *from* aigan.

AIHAN, to have, 2 Cor. 6. 10. *See* aigan.

AIHTA, *vb.* I had, he had. *See* aigan.

AIHTRON, *vb.* to desire, beg for, pray, Eph. 6. 18; Col. 1. 9; to beg, Mk. 10. 46; Jo. 9. 8. *Cf.* aigan.

AIHTRONS, *str. sb. f.* prayer, supplication, Eph. 6. 18; 1 Tim. 2. 1; Phil. 4. 6.

AIHUM, we have. *See* aigan.

AIHUN, they have. *See* aigan.

AIHUTH, ye have. *See* aigan.

AIHWA-TUNDI (βάτος), *str. sb. fem.* a bramble-bush, Lu. 6. 44; a bush (βάτος), Mk. 12. 26; Lu. 20. 37.

AIKAN*, *vb.* (*pt. tense* aiaik) to say. *Der.* af-aikan.

AIKKLESJO (ἐκκλησία), *wk. sb. f.*

a church, Rom. 16. 23; Col. 4. 16; the church, Eph. 3. 21; Eph. 5. 23; 1 Cor. 10. 32; 1 Cor. 15. 9; 1 Tim. 3. 5. *The pl. occurs in* 1 Cor. 7. 17; 16. 1; &c.

AIN, once; *in the comp.* thatain. *See* ains.

AINA, one. *See* ains.

AINA-BAUR, *adj.* only-born, Skeir. 5. 21.

AINAHA (μονογενής), *adj.* only, Lu. 7. 12; 9. 38; *fem.* ainoho, Lu. 8. 42. *See* ains.

AINAI (μόνοι), *pl. adj. See* ains.

AINAKLS, *adj.* lonely, left alone, desolate, 1 Tim. 5. 5. *See* ains.

AINA-MUNDITHA, *str. sb. fem.* unanimity, unity, Eph. 4. 3, 13; *from* ains *and* munths.

AINANAN: *see* ga-ainanan.

AIN-FALTHEI, *str. sb. f.* simplicity, 2 Cor. 1. 12; 11. 3; Col. 3. 22.

AINFALTHABA, *adv.* singly, simply, only, Skeir. 3. 18.

AIN-FALTHS, *adj.* single, Mat. 6. 22. [*Lit.* one-fold; *see* falthan.]

AIN-HWARJIZUH, *adj.* (εἷς ἕκαστος; ἕκαστος; πᾶς), every single, every one, Lu. 4. 40; 16. 5; 1 Cor. 12. 18.

AIN-HWATHARUH, *adj.* each of two.

AINNOHUN, AINOHUN; *see under* ainshun, ains.

AINOHO, *fem. form of* ainaha, q. v.

AINS, *adj.* (*fem.* aina; *neut.* ain *or* ainata?), one, single, only; seina ainis = seina silba (ἑαυτοῦ); ainamma sintha, once; *for* aina baurga, aina thiujo, aina anabusne, *cf.* baurgs, thiuda, anabusns; ain wisan, to be one, *see* Jo. 10. 30; ains jah sa sama, one and the same, 1 Cor. 12. 11; ains — jah ains, the one — and the other, Mk. 10. 37; ains — anthar, one — another; ni ains, no one; *also used with pronouns, as:* is ains, he by himself, Jo. 6. 15. [E. *one;* G. *ein.*]

AINS-HUN, *adj.* (hun *being a suffix*); *only used with* ni *preceding*; ni ains-hun, not any one, none; Lu. 1. 61.

AIN-LIF, eleven; *dat.* ain-libim, 1 Cor. 15. 5.

AIPISKAUPEI (ἐπισκοπή), *str. sb. fem.*, a bishopric, 1 Tim. 3. 1.

AIPISKAUPUS (ἐπίσκοπος), *sb.* a bishop, 1 Tim. 3. 2; Tit. 1. 7.

AIPISTAULE, AIPISTULE, *sb.* an epistle, a letter, Col. 4. 16; Neh. 6. 17, 19.

AIR (πρωί), *adv.* early, Mk. 1. 35. *Cf.* airis, airiza. [E. *ere;* G. *eher.*]

AIRINON, *vb.* to be a messenger, to be an ambassador, 2 Cor. 5. 20; Eph. 6. 20. *See* airus.

AIRIS, *adv.* earlier, long ago, Lu. 10. 13.

AIRIZA (ἀρχαῖος), *adj.* of old time, ancient, living formerly, Mat. 5. 21, 33. *It is a compar. form, from* air.

AIRKN(I)S, *adj.* good, holy, sincere, 1 Tim. 3. 3. *Cf.* unairkns.

AIRKNITHA, *str. sb. fem.* goodness, genuineness, sincerity, 2 Cor. 8. 8.

AIRTHA, *str. sb. fem.* earth, region, land, Ps. 19. 5; 24, 1; Mat. 27. 51; Mk. 4. 5. *Cf.* mulda, malma, stubjus. [A. S. *eorðe;* G. *erde;* D. *aarde.*]

AIRTHAKUNDS, *adj.* earthy, earthly, born of the earth, Skeir. 4. 15.

AIRTHEINS, *adj.* earthly, 1 Cor. 15. 49; 2 Cor. 4. 7; 5. 1; Phil. 3. 19.

AIRUS, *str. sb. fem.* a messenger,

Lu. 7. 24; 9. 52; *also* a message, Lu. 14. 32. *Der.* airinon. *Cf.* aggilus.

AIRZEI, *str. sb. fem.* error, deceit, Eph. 4. 14; Skeir. 5. 5. *Cf.* airzis.

AIRZITHA, *str. sb. fem.* an error, Mat. 27. 64; 1 Tim. 4. 1. *Cf.* airzis.

AIRZ(E)IS, *adj.* astray, going astray; airzeis wisan, wairthan, to go astray, be deceived, Gal. 6. 7; to err, Mk. 12, 24. *Der.* airzei, airzitha, airzjan, af-airzjan.

AIRZJAN, *vb.* to lead astray, deceive, Mat. 27. 63.

AIS, AIZ, *sb.* brass, coin, money. *See* aiz. [Lat. *æs.*]

AISTAN, *vb.* to heed, regard, Lu. 18. 2, 4; 20. 13. *Der.* ga-aistan.

AITHEI, *str. sb. fem.* a mother, Mat. 10. 37; 27. 56; Mk. 3. 32; &c.

AITHIS: *see* the following. Lu. 1. 73.

AITHS, *str. sb. m.* an oath, Mat. 5. 33; 26. 72; Mk. 6. 26. *Der.* uf-aithis. [A. S. *áð;* G. *eid.*]

AIW, *adv.* ever, aye; ni aiw, aiw ni, never; aiw hwanhuh, at any time; ni aiw hwanhuh, not at any time; ni aiw ainshun, no one ever; ni thanaseiths aiw, never for ever. [E. *aye;* G. *je.*]

AITHTHAU, *conj.* or.

AIWAGGELI, *str. sb. n.* evangel, gospel, 1 Cor. 15. 1; Gal. 1. 7; 2. 2; Eph. 1. 13.

AIWAGGELJO, *wk. sb. f.* evangel, gospel, Mk. 1. 1, 14; Rom. 10. 16.

AIWAGGELJAN, *vb.* to preach the gospel, to preach, Gal. 4. 13. *Cf.* wailamerjan, thiuthkwithan.

AIWAGGELISTA, *wk. sb. m.* an evangelist, Eph. 4, 11; 2 Tim. 4. 5.

AIWCHARISTIA (εὐχαριστία), *sb.* thanksgiving, 2 Cor. 9. 11.

AIWEINS, *adj.* eternal, Mat. 25. 41, 46; Mk. 3. 29; &c. *See* aiws. [G. *ewig;* D. *eeuwig.*]

AIWISKI, *str. sb. n.* shame, 1 Cor. 15. 34; 2 Cor. 4. 2.

AIWISKON, *vb.* to treat shamefully, to behave unseemly, 1 Cor. 13. 5. *Der.* ga-aiwiskon.

AIWJAN*, *in comp.* us-aiwjan, q. v.

AIWLAUGIA (εὐλογία), *sb.* 2 Cor. 9. 5.

AIWS, *str. sb. m.* time, a long time, an age, eternity, the world, Lu. 1. 70; Mk. 10. 30; an age of the world, Gal. 1. 4; life, Lu. 20. 35. *Cf.* mel, alds, witoth, aijukduth. Du aiwa (dage), du aiwam, in aiwam, *or* in aiwins, for ever, Gal. 1. 5; Mat. 6. 13; fram aiwa, *or* aiwam, from eternity. *Der.* aiweins, us-aiwjan, ajukduths; *and cf.* aiw, halis-aiw, sunsaiw. [G. αἰών; Lat. *ævum.*]

AIZ, AIS, *str. sb. n.* brass, coin, money, Mk. 6. 8.

AIZA-SMITHA, *wk. sb. m.* a coppersmith, 2 Tim. 4. 14.

AJUKDUTHS, *str. sb. fem.* an age, eternity; *in phrase* in ajukduth, for ever and ever, Jo. 6. 58; Lu. 1. 33.

AK (ἀλλά, δέ, γάρ), *conj.* but; *gen. used after a negative, as:* ni thatanei — ak jah, not only — but also; ne — ak; ak niu (ἀλλ' οὐχί); ak jah (ἀλλὰ καί); ak ei (ἀλλ' ἵνα. [A. S. *ac;* O. E. *ac.*]

AKEI (ἀλλά), but; *used for* δέ, *once only,* 1 Cor. 14. 20; akei ni (ἀλλ' οὐδέ), but neither, Gal. 2. 3.

AKEIT, AKET, *str. sb. n.* vinegar, Mat. 27. 48; Mk. 15. 36. [Lat. *acetum*.]

AKRAN, *str. sb. n.* fruit, Mat. 7. 20; Lu. 1. 42; Gal. 5. 22.
— matjan, to eat fruit, Mk. 11. 14.
— niman, to receive fruit, Mk. 12. 2.
— giban, to bear fruit, Mk. 4. 7.
— bairan, to bear fruit, Mk. 4. 28; Jo. 15. 2; Col. 1. 10.
— waurkjan, to bring forth fruit, Lu. 3. 8.
— gataujan, to bring forth fruit, Mat. 7. 17. 18.

AKRANA-LAUS, *adj.* unfruitful, Mk. 4. 19.

AKRS, *str. sb. m.* a field, Mat. 27. 7, 8, 10; Mk. 15. 21; Lu. 15. 25. [E. *acre*; G. *acker*.]

AKWIZI, *str. sb. fem.* an axe, Lu. 3. 9. [G. *axt*.]

ALABASTRAUN (ἀλάβαστρον), *sb.* an alabaster box, Lu. 7, 37.

ALA-BRUNSTS, *str. sb. m.* a holocaust, whole burnt-offering, Ps. 40. 7; Mk. 12. 33.

ALAKJO, *adv.* together, collectively; allai alakjo (πάντες), all together, Mk. 11. 32; Lu. 4. 22; managei alakjo (ὁ λαὸς ἅπας), Lu. 19. 48; alakjo managei (ἅπαν τὸ πλῆθος), Lu. 19. 37. *See* alls.

ALAMANS, *adj.* individual, every; in allaim allamannam, in every man, in all men without exception, Skeir. 8. 11.

ALA-MOD, *a proper name; occurs in* Neap. *and* Arez. *documents.*

ALAN, *vb.* to nourish; alans (ἐντρεφόμενος), nourished, 1 Tim. 4. 6. *See* althan, aljan. [Lat. *alere*.]

ALATHARBS, *adj.* very needy, very poor, Lu. 15. 14. *Cf.* thaurban.

ALDOMO, *wk. sb. n.* old age, Lu. 1. 36. [*The nom. may be* aldomo, aldoma *or* aldums. E. *eld*; G. *alter*.]

ALDRS*, *adj.* old; *in comp.* framaldrs, q. v.

ALDS, *str. sb. fem.* an age, a generation, Lu. 1. 50; Eph. 2, 2; life, 2 Tim. 2. 4; *see* altbs.

ALDUMA, *perhaps another form of* aldomo, q. v.

ALEINA, ALLEINA, *str. sb. fem.* a a cubit, Mat. 6. 27. [E. *ell*; G. *elle*; D. *el*.]

ALEW (ἔλαιον), *str. sb. n.* olive oil, Lu. 7. 46; 16. 6; Mk. 6. 13.

ALEWA-BAGMS, *str. sb. m.* an olive-tree, Rom. 11. 17, 24.

ALEW(E)IS, *adj.* belonging to the olive-tree; fairguni alewi (ὄρος ἐλαιῶν), the Mount of Olives, Mk. 11. 1; Lu. 19. 29.

ALHS, *str. sb. f.* (*dat.* albai *and* alh) the temple, Mat. 27. 5; Mk. 12. 35; &c.

ALIDS, fatted, Lu. 15. 23, 27, 30. *See* aljan.

ALIS (ἄλλος, ἕτερος), *adj.* other, another; ni waiht aljis (οὐδὲν ἄλλο), nothing else. *Der.* alja, aljakuns, aljaleikos, alja-leikon, alja-leikoths, aljar, aljath, aljatbro. [O. E. *ellis*; E. *else*.]

ALJA (εἰ μή, ἐὰν μή), *conj.* than, except, unless, Lu. 4. 27; 10. 22; *prep. with dat.* (πλὴν), except, Mk. 12. 32.

ALJAKUNS, *adj.* born in a strange country, foreign; sa aljakunja, this stranger, Lu. 17. 18; aljakunjai, foreigners, Eph. 2. 19.

ALJALEIKOS (ἑτέρως), *adv.* otherwise, 1 Tim. 5. 25.
— laisjan (ἑτερο-διδασκαλεῖν), to teach otherwise, 1 Tim. 6. 3. [Lit. *else-like*.]

ALJALEIKON*, vb. to set forth an allegory (?). See next word.

ALJALEIKOTHS, adj. allegorical, Gal. 4, 24.

ALJAN*, vb. to fatten, whence alids, q. v.

ALJAN, str. sb. n. jealousy, Rom. 11. 11; zeal, 2 Cor. 7. 11.

ALJANON, vb. to have zeal for, to zealously affect (A. V.), Gal. 4, 17, 18. Der. in-aljanon.

ALJAR, adv. elsewhere; aljar wisands (ἀπών), absent, 2 Cor. 10. 1, 11.

ALJATH, adv. other-whither, in another direction; hence afleithan aljath, to go away, Mk. 12. 1.

ALJATHRO, adv. by another way, Jo. 10. 1; when absent, 2 Cor. 13. 2; Phil. 1. 27.

ALL-ANDJO, adv. altogether, 1 Th. 5. 23.

ALLATHRO (παντόθεν, πανταχόθεν), adv. from on all sides, Mk. 1. 45.

ALLA-WAURSTWA, wk. sb. m. all-worker; hence, one who does all one's duty, one who is perfect, Col. 4. 12.

ALLEINA. See aleina.

ALLS, adj. all (πᾶς, ἅπας); whole (πᾶς, ἅπας, ὅλος); much (πολύς), in Mk. 12. 37; and all, everywhere (πανταχοῦ) ufar all, above all, Eph. 3. 20. Der. allis, allathro, all-andjo, all-swerei, all-waldands, alla-waurstwa, ala-brunsts, ala-mans, ala-tharbs, ala-mod, alakjo.

ALLIS, adv. wholly (ὅλως); for (γάρ); for, as in allis than, for when (ὅταν γάρ), Mk. 12. 25; allis (μέν) answered by ith (δέ); ni .... allis (μή .... ὅλως); nih allis, for neither, for not (οὐ γάρ, οὔτε γάρ).

ALL-SWEREI (ἁπλότης), str. sb. f. simplicity; or lit. without respecting of persons, Rom. 12. 8. Cf. sweran.

ALL-WALDANDS, adj. all-ruling, almighty, 2 Cor. 6. 18.

ALTHAN*, vb. (pt. t. aialth), to grow old; in comp. us-althan. Cf. aljan, alan, alds, altheis, aldomo, aldrs. Der. us-althan. [G. altern.]

ALTHEIS, adj. old, Jo. 3. 4; sa althiza, the elder, Lu. 15. 25.

ALTHS, ALDS, str. sb. f. an age, Eph. 2. 7; 3. 5, 21; Col. 1. 26; life, world, 2 Tim. 2. 4. Cf. althan.

AMEN, amen, verily, Mat. 5. 18; &c.

AMSA, wk. sb. m. a shoulder, Lu. 15. 5. [Perhaps it should be ahsa. Cf. G. achsel.]

AN, adv. used in asking questions, like an in Lat. an hwas (τίς καί); an hwa (τί οὖν); an nuh (οὐκ οὖν), Lu. 3. 10; 10. 29; 18. 56. [Lat. an.]

ANA, (1) prep. with dat. and acc. to, upon, on, in, over, towards. Cf. in; (2) adv. as in atlagjan ana, to lay on, Mk. 8. 23; galagjan ana, to lay on, Mk. 11. 7; ana dag (τῆς ἡμέρας), in the day, a-day, Lu. 17. 4; ana andaugi, face to face, 2 Cor. 10. 1. The comp. are very numerous. See below. [G. an; E. on; D. aan.]

ANA-AUKAN, vb. to add, Mat. 6, 27; to go on (to do), Lu. 20. 11, 12.

ANA-BIUDAN, vb. to command, Nehem. 5. 14; Ps. 91. 11; to give commands to, instruct, Mat. 11. 1; 1 Tim. 6. 13.

ANA-BUSNS, str. sb. f. a command, commandment, Isa. 29.

13; Mat. 5. 19; Lu. 15. 29; 1 Tim. 6. 14. *See* biudan.
ANA-DRIGGKAN, *vb. refl.* to get drunk, be drunk, Eph. 5. 18. [G. *antrinken.*]
ANA-FILH, *str. sb. n.* a tradition, Mk. 7. 3, 5; 2 Thess. 3. 6; commendation, 2 Cor. 3. 1; a thing committed to one, 2 Tim. 1. 12.
ANA-FILHAN, *vb.* to hand down as tradition, Mk. 7. 13; to deliver up, Mat. 27. 2; to commend, 2 Cor. 10. 12.
ANA-FULHANO, *sb.* a tradition, Mk. 7. 9.
ANA-GAGGAN, *vb.* to come after, be future, Eph. 2. 7. [G. *angehen.*]
ANA-HABAN, *vb.* to possess, take hold upon; *in pass.* to be taken (by fever), Lu. 4. 38; to be possessed, Lu. 6. 18. [G. *anhaben.*]
ANA-HAIMS, *adj.* at home, present with, 2 Cor. 5. 8. 9.
ANA-HAITAN, *vb. with dat. and acc.* to call on, to call upon, 2 Cor. 1. 23; 2 Tim. 2. 22.
ANA-HAMON, *vb.* to put on (clothes), 2 Cor. 5. 4.
ANA-HNAIWJAN, *vb.* to lay, rest upon, Mat. 8. 20; to stoop down, Mk. 1. 7.
ANA-HWEILAN, *vb.* to give rest to, to refresh, 2 Cor. 7. 13.
ANA-INSAKAN, *vb.* to add to, Gal. 2. 6.
ANA-KAURJAN, *vb.* to overload, bear hard upon, 2 Cor. 2. 5.
ANAKS, *adv.* suddenly, Lu. 2. 13; 9. 39; Mk. 9. 8.
ANA-KUMBJAN, *vb.* to lie down, recline, sit at meat, Mk. 2. 15; to sit down, recline, Mk. 8. 6. *Der.* mith-anakumbjan.

ANA-KUNNAN, *vb.* to read, 2 Cor. 1. 13; 3. 2.
ANA-KWAL, *str. sb. n.* rest, quietness, 1 Thess. 4. 11.
ANA-KWIMAN, *vb.* to come to, approach, Luc. 2. 9.
ANA-KWISS, *str. sb. f.* blasphemy, Col. 3. 8; 1 Tim. 6. 4.
ANA-KWITHAN, *vb.* to blaspheme; *hence pass.* to be evil spoken of, 1 Cor. 10. 30.
ANA-KWIUJAN, *vb.* to rekindle, excite, stir up (A. V.), 2 Tim. 1. 6.
ANA-LAGEINS, *str. sb. f.* a laying on (as of hands), 1 Tim. 4. 14.
ANA-LAGJAN, *vb.* to lay upon, Lu. 4. 40; 10. 30.
ANA-LATJAN, *vb.* to let, to hinder, 1 Thess. 2. 18.
ANA-LAUGNEI, *str. sb. f.* secretness, Jo. 7. 4. *Cf.* liugan.
ANA-LAUGNIBA, *adv.* secretly, Jo. 7. 10. *Cf.* liugan.
ANA-LEIKO, in like manner, Skeir. 7. 4.
ANA-MAHTJAN, *vb.* to use one's might against any one, to be violent against, Mat. 11. 12; to defraud, Mk. 10. 19; to maltreat, Lu. 6. 28; 18. 32; to do wrong, 2 Cor. 7. 12; *pass.* to suffer wrong, 2 Cor. 7. 12; suffer violence, Mat. 11. 12.
ANA-MAHTS, *str. sb. f.* injury, ill-treatment, 2 Cor. 12. 10.
ANA-MELJAN, *vb.* to be enrolled for taxation, to be taxed, Lu. 2. 5.
ANA-MINDS, *str. sb. f.* a supposition, surmising, 1 Tim. 6. 4.
ANAN*, *vb.* to breathe out; *in comp.* us-anan, q. v.
ANA-NANTHJAN, *vb.* to have courage, to dare, to be bold, Mk. 15. 43; 2 Cor. 11. 21; Skeir. 4. 27.

ANA-NAUTHJAN, *vb.* to constrain, compel, Mat. 5. 41.
ANA-NIUJAN, *vb.* to renew, 2 Cor. 4. 16; Col. 3. 10.
ANA-NIUJITHA, *str. sb. f.* a renewal, renewing, Rom. 12. 2.
ANA-PRAGGAN, *vb.* to harass, worry, 2 Cor. 7. 5.
ANA-SILAN, *vb.* to be silent, grow still, Mk. 4. 39.
ANA-SIUN(I)S, *adj.* evident, visible, Skeir. 2. 22. *Der.* un-anasiunaba.
ANA-SLAWAN, *vb.* to become silent, Lu. 8. 24.
ANA-SLEPAN, *vb.* to sleep, fall asleep, Lu. 8. 23. [G. *entschlafen.*]
ANA-STODEINS, *str. sb. f.* beginning, Mk. 1. 1; 10. 6; first fruits, 1 Cor. 15. 23.
ANA-STODJAN, *vb.* to begin, Gal. 3. 3.
ANATIIAIMA, anathema, Rom. 9. 3; 1 Cor. 16. 22.
ANA-THIWAN, *vb.* to keep in subjection, 1 Cor. 9. 27.
ANA-THRAFTSJAN, *vb.* to refresh, 2 Tim. 1. 16; Philem. 20.
ANA-TIMRJAN, *vb.* to build upon, Eph. 2. 20.
ANA-TRIMPAN, *vb.* to press, throng round, Lu. 5. 1.
ANA-WAIRTHS, *adj.* about to come, future, Lu. 3. 7; Jo. 16. 13; Col. 2. 17.
ANA-WAMMJAN, *vb.* to blame, 2 Cor. 6. 3.
ANA-WILJEI (σεμνότης), *str. sb. f.* discretion, gravity (A. V.), 1 Tim. 3. 4.
AND (είς), (1) *prep. with acc.* to, towards; (2) to, according to, upon, at, (είς, κατά, επί); and all (πανταχοῦ), every-where. *For the numerous compounds see below. It also takes the form* anda *in comp. Cf. also* and, andis, andizub, andeis, all-andjo.
ANDA-BAUHTS, *str. sb. f.* a price, price of redemption, 1 Tim. 2. 6. *See* bugjan.
ANDA-BEIT, *str. sb. n.* reproach, reproof, 2 Cor. 2. 6.
ANDA-HAFTS, *str. sb. f.* an answer, 1 Cor. 9. 3.
ANDA-HAIT, *str. sb. n.* confession, acknowledgement, profession, 2 Cor. 9. 13; 1 Tim. 6. 12.
ANDA-LAUNI, *str. sb. n.* a recompence, 2 Cor. 6. 13; Col. 3. 24.
ANDA-NAHTI, *str. sb. n.* twilight, gloaming, evening, Mat. 8. 16; Mk. 1. 32.
ANDA-NEITHS, *adj.* contrary, 1 Th. 2. 15; Col. 2. 14.
ANDA-NEM, *sb. n.* a receiving, Phil. 4. 15. *See* niman. [G. *annahme.*]
ANDA-NEMEIGS, *adj.* holding fast, Tit. 1. 9. [G. *annehmlich.*]
ANDA-NEMS, *adj.* pleasant, acceptable, Lu. 4. 19, 24; 2 Cor. 6. 2; 1 Tim. 2. 3. [G. *angenehm;* D. *aangenaam.*]
ANDA-NUMTS, *str. sb. f.* a receiving up, Lu. 9. 51; acceptation, 1 Tim. 1. 15. [G. *annahme.*]
ANDA-SETS, *adj.* abominable, Tit. 1. 16. *See* sitan. [G. *entsetzlich.*]
ANDA-STATHJIS, *str. sb. m.* an adversary, Lu. 18. 3; Phil. 1. 28.
ANDA-STAUA, *str. sb. m.* an adversary, Mat. 5. 25.
ANDA-THAHTS, *adj.* thoughtful, prudent, vigilant (A. V.), 1 Tim. 3. 2; 2 Tim. 4. 5; Tit. 1. 8; reasonable, Rom. 12. 1. *See* thaggkjan.
AND-AUGI, *str. sb. n.* the face, 1 Thess. 2. 17.
AND-AUGIBA, *adv.* openly, plainly, Jo. 7. 26; 16. 29.

ANDAUGJO, *adv.* openly, Mk. 1. 45; Jo. 7. 10; 18. 20.
ANDA-WAIRTHI: *see* and-wairthi.
ANDA-WAURD, *str. sb. n.* an answer, Lu. 20. 26; *unless we read* anda-waurdeis, *from the next word.*
ANDA-WAURDI; *the same*, Lu. 20. 26; Jo. 19. 9. [G. *antwort;* D. *antwoord.*]
ANDA-WIZN, *str. sb. n.* need, want, necessity, Rom. 12. 13; Phil. 4. 16. *See* wizan.
ANDA-WLEIZNS, *str. sb. m.* the countenance, face, Mat. 26. 67; Lu. 17. 16; 2 Cor. 11. 20. [G. *antlitz.*]
AND-BAHTI, *str. sb. n.* service, ministry, 1 Cor. 16. 15; 2 Cor. 8. 4.
AND-BAHTJAN, *vb.* to serve, minister, Mat. 8. 15; 25, 44; Mk. 1. 13, 31.
AND-BAHTS, *str. sb. m.* a servant, minister, Rom. 13. 6; Mk. 14. 54; an officer, Mat. 5. 25.
AND-BEITAN, *vb.* to reprove, rebuke, threaten, Mk. 1. 25; to perplex, to harass, 2 Cor. 4. 8.
AND-BINDAN, *vb.* to unbind, loosen, Mk. 1. 7; to explain, Mk. 4. 34.
AND-BUNDNAN, *vb.* to be unbound, to be loosened, Mk. 7. 35; 7. 6.
ANDEIS (*and* ANDS?), *str. sb. m.* an end, Mk. 3. 26; 13. 27; Rom. 10. 18; 1 Cor. 15. 24; &c. *Der.* andi-laus, all-andjo. [G. *ende;* D. *einde.*] .
AND-HAFJAN, *vb.* to reply, Mat. 8. 8; 11. 4.
AND-HAITAN, *vb.* to profess, confess, Mat. 7. 23; 10. 32; to profess, witness (A. V.), 1 Tim. 6. 12.
AND-HAMON, *vb.* to take off (clothes), to spoil, Col. 2. 15. *Cf.* af-hamon.

AND-HAUSJAN, *vb.* to listen, to hear (a prayer), Lu. 1. 13; Jo. 11. 41; to hear, 1 Cor. 14. 21.
AND-HRUSKAN, *vb.* to ask questions, 1 Cor. 10. 25. *Cf.* 1 Cor. 10. 27.
AND-HULEINS, *str. sb. f.* uncovering, illumination, Lu. 2. 32; revelation, 2 Cor. 12. 1; Eph. 1. 17; 3. 3.
AND-HULJAN, *vb.* to uncover, Mk. 2. 4; to reveal, Lu. 2. 35; 10. 22; Eph. 3. 5; Phil. 3. 15; Mat. 10. 26. [G. *enthüllen;* A. S. *unhélen.*]
ANDI-LAUS, *adj.* endless, 1 Tim. 1. 4. *From* andeis.
ANDIS, ANDIZ-UH, *adv.* otherwise, Lu. 16. 13.
ANDJO*, *in* all-andjo, q. v.
AND-KWITHAN, *vb.* to bid farewell to, Lu. 9. 61; to approach; Lu. 8. 19.
AND-LETNAN, *vb.* to get oneself free, to depart, Phil. 1. 23.
AND-NIMAN, *vb.* to receive, take, Nehem. 5. 17; Mat. 10. 40, 41; Mk. 6. 11. [G. *entnehmen.*]
AND-RINNAN, *vb.* to compete in running; *hence*, to strive, dispute, Mk. 9. 34.
ANDS?, *another form of* andeis?, q. v.
AND-SAIHWAN, *sb.* to regard, Lu. 20. 21. [G. *ansehen;* D. *aanzien.*]
AND-SAKAN, *vb.* to speak against, Lu. 2. 34. *Der.* un-andsakuns.
AND-SATJAN, *vb.* to attribute, Skeir. 5. 21.
AND-SITAN, *vb.* to regard, Gal. 2. 6; to inquire into, 1 Cor. 10. 27. *Cf.* and-hruskan.
AND-SOKS*; *in* un-andsoks, q. v.
AND-SPEIWAN, *vb.* to reject, Gal. 4. 14.
AND-STALD, *str. sb. n.* a supply, Eph. 4. 16; ministration (ἐπι-

χορηγία), Phil. 1. 19. *See the following.*
AND-STALDAN, *vb.* to produce, set forth, minister (A. V.), 1 Tim. 1. 4.
AND-STANDAN, *vb.* to oppose, withstand, resist, Mat. 5. 39; Jo. 19. 12.
AND-STAURRAN, *vb.* to murmur against, Mk. 14. 5. *Cf.* staurran.
AND-THAGGKJAN, *vb. refl.* to consider, Lu. 16. 4; Skeir. 7. 5.
AND-TILON, *vb.* to serve, cleave to, Lu. 16. 13.
AND-WAIRTHI, *str. sb. n.* presence; *esp.* the face, Lu. 9. 51, 53; a. withra a. face to face, 1 Cor. 13. 12; in *or* faura andwairthja, in presence of, before, Nehem. 5. 15; Mat. 5. 16; Mk. 9. 2; in managamma andwairthja, in presence of many, 2 Cor. 1. 11. *See* wairthan.
AND-WAIRTHI, *sb.* worth, price, Mat. 27. 6, 9. [*The MS. has* anda-wairthi *in* v. q.]
AND-WAIRTHIS, *prep. with dat.* over against, Mat. 27. 61.
AND-WAIRTHS, *adj.* present, 1 Cor. 7. 26.
AND-WASJAN, *vb.* to uncloth, take off clothes, Mk. 15. 20.
AND-WAURDJAN, *vb.* to answer, reply to, Rom. 9. 20. [G. *antworten.*]
AND-WEIGAN, *or* AND-WEIHAN, *vb.* to strive against, oppose, Rom. 7. 23.
ANNO (ὀψώνιον), *wk. sb. f.* charges, cost, 1 Cor. 9. 7. *Cf.* ansts.
ANS (*gen.* anzis), *str. sb. m.* a beam, Lu. 6. 41, 42.
ANSTEIGS, *adj.* favourable, gracious, Eph. 1. 6.
ANSTS, *str. sb. f.* favour, grace, Lu. 1. 28, 30; 2. 40; 1 Cor. 10. 30; &c. *Der.* ansteigs. [G *gunst.*]

ANTHAR, *adj.* another (ἄλλος, ἕτερος); second (δεύτερος); the rest, (λοιπός), Jo. 15. 24; Mk. 12. 21; Mat. 27. 49; anthar, the one, antharuh, the other; anthar antharis, anthar antharamma, anthar antharana, one another; anthar fruma (δευτερόπρωτος), Lu. 6. 1; thata anthar (τὸ λοιπόν), the rest, Eph. 6. 10. *Der.* antharleiko, antharleikei.
ANTHARS, *prob. for* anthar s(a), Skeir. 4. 27.
ANTHARLEIKO, *adv.* otherwise, 1 Tim. 1. 3.
ANTHARLEIKEI, *wk. sb. f.* diversity, Skeir. 5. 15; 6. 14.
APAUSTAULEI, *wk. sb. f.* apostleship, 1 Cor. 9. 2; Gal. 2. 8.
APAUSTAULUS, APAUSTULUS, *str. sb. m.* an apostle, messenger, Lu. 9. 10; 17. 5; Jo. 13. 16. *Der.* apaustaulei, galiuga-apaustaulus.
AR, *or* ARA, *wk. sb. m.* an eagle, Lu. 17. 37. [G. *aar.*]
ARBAIDJAN, *vb.* to work, toil, Mat. 6. 28; Eph. 4. 28. *Der.* bi-, mith-, thairh-arbaidjan. *Cf.* arbaiths. [G. *arbeiten.*]
ARBAITHS, *str. sb. f.* work, toil, labour, 2 Cor. 6. 5; 11. 27; 1 Thess. 3. 5; pressure of business, 2 Cor. 11. 28; work (κανών), 2 Cor. 10. 16; (in) arbaida winnan, to labour, 2 Th. 3. 8; in arbaida briggan, to vex, 2 Cor. 11. 20. [*M. gives only* arbaiths, *gen.* arbaidais, *acc.* arbaith. *But why not nom.* arbaids? *See* 1 Cor. 15. 58.]
ARBI, *str. sb. n.* a heritage, inheritance, Eph. 1. 14; arbi niman, to inherit, Gal. 4. 30. *Cf.* arbi-numja, arbja, ga-arbja, arbjo. [G. *erbe;* D. *erf.*]

ARBI-NUMJA, *wk. sb. m.* an inheritor, heir, Mk. 12. 7; Lu. 20. 14; Gal. 4. 1. [G. *erbnehmer.*]

ARBJA, *wk. sb. m.* an heir; arbja wairthan, to inherit, Mk. 10. 17; Gal. 4. 21. *Der.* ga-arbja.

ARBJO, *wk. sb. f.* an heiress; arbjo wairthan, to inherit, 1 Cor. 15. 50. [G. *erbinn.*]

ARHWAZNA, *str. sb. f.* an arrow, dart, Eph. 6. 16.

ARJAN, *vb.* to plough, Lu. 17. 7. [A. S. *erian;* Lat. *arare;* O. E. *ear.*]

ARKA, *str. sb. f.* an ark, *i. e.* a box; *hence* a money-bag, Jo. 13. 29.

ARK-AGGILUS, *str. sb. m.* an archangel, 1 Thess. 4. 16. *From* aggilus. *Cf.* ark-ippus, taitrarkes, areist-arkus.

ARMAHAIRTEI, *wk. sb. f.* pity, mercy, Lu. 1. 78; Rom. 15. 9. *From* arms *and* hairto.

ARMAHAIRTITHA, *wk. sb. f.* the same, Mat. 9. 13; alms-giving, Mat. 6. 4.

ARMAHAIRTS, *adj.* pitiful, merciful, tenderhearted, Eph. 4. 32.

ARMAIO, *wk. sb. f.* mercy, 2 Tim. 1. 2; alms, Mat. 6. 2, 3. *Cf.* armahairtei.

ARMAN, *vb. with acc.* to pity, have mercy on, Mat. 9. 27; Mk. 10. 47; to shew mercy, Rom. 12. 8. *Cf.* bleithjan, infeinan. *Der.* ga-arman.

ARMS, *adj.* poor, miserable, wretched; *sup.* armosts, most miserable, 1 Cor. 15. 19. *Cf.* halks, unleds, us-haista. [G. and D. *arm.*]

ARMS, *str. sb. m.* the arm, Lu. 1. 51; ana armins niman, to take up in the arms, Mk. 9. 36; ana armins andniman, *the same,* Lu. 2. 28.

ARNEIS*, ARNIS*, *adj.* certain, sure. *See* arniba.

ARNIBA, *adv.* surely, safely, Mk. 14. 44. *From* arneis(?).

AROMATA (ἀρώματα), sweet spices, Mk. 16. 1.

ARWJO, *adv.* without a cause, Jo. 15. 25; freely, gratis, 2 Cor. 11. 7.

ASANS, *str. sb. f.* harvest, harvest time, Mk. 4. 29; Lu. 10. 2; summer, Mk. 13. 28. *Cf.* asneis.

ASILUKWAIRNUS, *str. sb. m.* a millstone, Mk. 9, 42. *Cf.* asilus. [G. *esel,* an ass; E. *quern.*]

ASILUS, *str. sb. m.* an uss, an ass's foal, Jo. 12. 14, 15. *Der.* asilu-kwairnus. [G. *esel;* D. *ezel.*]

ASNEIS, *str. sb. m.* a servant, hired servant (A. V.), Mk. 1. 20; a hireling, Jo. 10. 12, 13.

ASSARJUS (ἀσσάριον), *sb.* a coin, called in A. V. a farthing, Mat. 10. 29.

ASTATHS, *str. sb.* truth, certainty, Lu. 1. 4.

ASTS, *str. sb. m.* a bough, a twig, a branch, Mk. 11. 8; 13. 28. [G. *ast.*]

AT, *prep. with dat.* at, by (πρός, παρά, ἐπί, *with acc.*); to (πρὸς, *with acc.*); from (παρὰ, *with gen.*, *and* ἀπό); at (*of time*), (ἐπὶ, *with gen.*), *and Greek gen. abs.* Also *with acc.* Gal. 6. 9; Lu. 2. 41, Mat. 27. 1; at ist, is near. *Cf.* du, bi. *For compounds see below.*

AT-ATHNI, *str. sb. n.* a year, Jo. 18. 14. *See* athns.

AT-AUGJAN, *vb.* to bring before the eyes, shew, Mat. 8. 4; Mk. 1. 44; *refl.* to appear; *pass.* to appear, Mk. 9. 4.

AT-BAIRAN, *vb.* to bring, offer, Mat. 8. 4; to bring, Mat. 8. 16;

9. 32. *Der.* inn-atbairan, us-atbairan.

AT-BAIRHTJAN, *vb.* to make manifest, display, Tit. 1. 3.

AT-DRIUSAN, *vb.* to fall, fall into, 1 Tim. 3. 6, 7; 6. 9.

AT-FARJAN, *vb.* to fare, journey, sail towards a place, Lu. 8. 26.

AT-GAGGS, *str. sb. m.* access, Eph. 2. 18. *Cf.* gaggs.

AT-GAGGAN (*p. t.* at-iddja), *vb.* to go to, come; *hence* to descend, come down, Mat. 8. 1; Mk. 1. 10; to enter, Mat. 9. 25. *Der.* du-atgaggan, inn-atgaggan, un-atgahts, at-gaggs.

AT-GAHTS*, *in comp.* un-atgahts, q. v.

AT-GARAIHTJAN, *vb.* to set right again, direct, Tit. 1. 5. *From* raihts.

AT-GIBAN, *vb.* to give over, deliver up, Mat. 5. 25; 26. 2; to give, Mk. 4. 11; 2 Cor. 8. 5.

AT-HABAN, *vb.* to have at; *hence, refl.* to come towards, Mk. 10. 35.

AT-HAFJAN, *vb.* to take down, Mk. 15. 36.

AT-HAHAN, *vb.* to let down, Lu. 5. 4; 2 Cor. 11. 33.

AT-HAITAN, *vb.* to call to one, Mat. 10. 1; Mk. 3. 13; 6. 7; Lu. 19. 13; &c.

ATHNS, *str. sb. m.* a year, Gal. 4. 10. [*Athns* = *atnus* = Lat. *annus. Cf.* Greek ἔτος.] *Der.* at-athni.

ATHTHAN, *conj.* but, Mat. 5. 28; 6. 16; 8. 11; &c.

ATJAN*, *in* fra-atjan, q. v.

AT-KUNNAN, *vb.* to afford, render, give, Col. 4. 1.

AT-LAGJAN, *vb.* to lay, lay on, Mat. 9. 18; to put on (clothes), Mk. 15. 17; to lay out (money), Lu. 19. 23; at-lagjan faur, to lay before, Mk. 8. 6; to cast, Mat. 7. 19.

AT-LATHON, *vb.* to call (*lit.* invite), Eph. 4. 4.

AT-LIGAN, *vb.* to lie close to, be present with, Rom. 7. 18.

AT-NEHWJAN, *vb. refl.* to draw near, be at hand, Mk. 1. 15; Lu. 10. 9, 11; to be nigh to, Phil. 2. 30.

AT-NIMAN, *vb.* to take to, adopt, Col. 1. 13.

AT-RINNAN, *vb.* to run to, come to, Lu. 16. 21. *Der.* du-atrinnan.

AT-SAIHWAN, *vb. with gen. and acc.* to take heed, Mat. 7. 15; Lu. 20. 46; give heed to, 1. Tim. 1. 4.

AT-SATJAN, *vb.* to present (in the temple), Lu. 2. 22; to present (to God), Col. 1. 22.

AT-SNARPJAN, *vb.* to taste, Col. 2. 21.

AT-SNIWAN*, *vb., in* du-atsniwan, q. v.

AT-STANDAN, *vb.* to stand near, Mk. 14. 47, 70; to come near, Lu. 20. 1.

AT-STEIGAN, *vb.* to descend, come down, Mat. 27. 42; Mk. 15. 32; to enter, Mat. 9. 1; dalath at-steigan, to come down, Lu. 17. 31; 19. 5.

ATTA, *wk. sb. m.* father, Ex. 20. 12; 21. 16; Mat. 5. 16, 45, 48; &c; forefather, Jo. 6. 49; Lu. 1. 72; &c.

AT-TEKAN, *vb.* to touch, Mat. 8. 3, 15; Mk. 1. 41; Lu. 5. 13; 8. 47; &c.

AT-THINSAN, *vb.* to draw towards one, Jo. 6. 44; 12. 32.

AT-TIUHAN, *vb.* to pull towards, to bring, Mk. 11. 2; 15. 22; Lu. 9. 41; Jo. 18. 16; dalath at-tiuhan, to bring down, Rom. 10 6. *Der.* inn-attiuhan.

AT-WAIRPAN, *vb.* to cast, cast down, Mat. 27. 5; Mk. 9. 22; *app. with pass. sense*, to be cast, Mk. 9. 47.

AT-WALWJAN, *vb.* to roll to, Mk. 15. 46. *Cf.* wilwan.

AT-WANDJAN, *vb. only in phr.*; at-wandjan sik aftra, to return, Lu. 19. 15.

AT-WISAN, *vb.* to be present, be at hand, Mk. 4. 29.

AT-WITAINS, *str. sb. m.* observation, Lu. 17. 20.

AT-WOPJAN, *vb.* to call, Mk. 9. 35; Jo. 9. 24.

AUD*, *sb.* good, possession, treasure; *whence the following.*

AUDAUGEI, *wk. sb. f.* happiness, blessedness, Gal. 4. 15.

AUDAGJAN, *vb.* to consider, *or* call blessed, Lu. 1. 48.

AUDAGS, *adj.* happy, blessed, Mat. 5. 8; 11. 6; Lu. 6. 20; &c.

AUDAHAFTS, *adj* happy, blessed, Lu. 1. 28.

AUFTO, *adv.* perhaps, probably, Lu. 4. 23; altogether, 1 Cor. 16. 12; ei aufto, if haply, Mk. 13; niu aufto, if perhaps, whether or no, Lu. 3. 15; ibai *and* nibai aufto, if so (Mk. 2. 22), except (2 Cor. 13. 5).

AUGA-DAURO, *wk. sb. f.* a window, 2 Cor. 11. 33. [Lit. *an eye-door.*]

AUGJAN, *vb.* to bring before the eyes, shew, Jo. 14. 8, 9. *Der.* at-augjan.

AUGJO*, *in* and-augjo, q. v.

AUGO, *wk. sb. n.* the eye, Mat. 5. 38; 9. 30; Mk. 7. 22; &c.; *in* augam skalkinon, to serve with eye-service, Col. 3. 22. [G. *auge*; D. *oog*; A. S. *edge.*]

AUHJODUS, *str. sb. m.* tumult, insurrection, Mk. 15. 7; 5. 38. *See the following.*

AUHJON, *vb.* to cry aloud, make a noise, Mat. 9. 23; Mk. 5. 39.

AUHMISTO, auhmists: *see* auhuma.

AUHNS, *str. sb. m.* an oven. Mat. 6. 30. [G. *ofen*; D. *oven.*]

AUHSA, *wk. sb. m*; *or*

AUHSUS, *str. sb. m.* an ox; 1 Tim. 5. 18; 1 Cor. 9. 9; Lu. 14. 19. [G. *ochse*; D. *os.*]

AUHUMA, *adv.* high; *hence* auhumists, auh'mists; *superl. adj.* the highest; *as in* auhumists gudja, a chief priest, Mat. 27. 62; *hence also* auhumisto, *sb.* the highest point, Lu. 4. 29.

AUK, *conj. (commonly after the first, or first closely-connected, words of the sentence; as*, batizo ist auk, ni waiht auk; *and very rarely at the beginning)*, for ($\gamma\grave{\alpha}\varrho$); also; auk—ith, *or* auk—than, *answer to Greek* $\mu\grave{\varepsilon}\nu - \delta\grave{\varepsilon}$; jah auk, for also; auk jah, but also; than auk, but; auk raihtis, for, Mk. 6. 17.

AUKAN, *vb.* (*p. t.* aiauk), to increase, *used as a neuter verb*, Skeir. 4. 11. *Der.* ga-aukan, ana-aukan, bi-aukan, bi-auknan, auknan. *Cf.* theihan. [A. S. *ékan*; E. *eke.*]

AUKNAN, *vb.* to be supplied, nourished, increased, Col. 2. 19. *Cf.* aukan.

AURAH-I(-JO?), *str. sb. f.* a grave, tomb, Mk. 5. 2.

AURALI, *str. sb. n.* a napkin, Jo. 11. 44.

AURKEIS, *str. sb. m.* a cup, Mk. 7. 8. *Cf.* balgs.

AURTI-GARDS, *str. sb. m.* an orchard, garden, Jo. 18. 1, 26. [E. *orchard*; contr. from *ort-yard*, or *wort-yard.*]

AURTJA, *wk. sb. m.* a gardener, husbandman, Lu. 20. 10, 14.

AURTS*, *str. sb. f.* a plant, wort. See waurts. *Der.* aurtigards, aurtja.

AUSO, *wk. sb. n.* the ear, Nebem. 6. 16; Mat. 10. 27; Mk. 4. 9; 14. 47; &c. See hliuma and hausjan. [G. *ohr;* D. *oor.*]

AUTHIDA, *str. sb. f.* a desert, Mk. 1. 3, 4, 12; 8. 4; Lu. 15. 4; &c.

AUTH(I)S, *adj.* desert, waste, Mk. 1. 35; Lu. 4. 42; 9. 10, 12. [G. *öde.*]

AWETHI, *str. sb. n.* a flock of sheep, Jo. 10. 16. 1 Cor. 9. 7. See awi. [D. *ooi;* E. *ewe.*]

AWI* (ὅις), *str. sb. f.* a sheep. Lat. *ovis.* *Der.* awistr, awethi.

AWILIUD, AWILIUTH, *str. sb. n.* thank. 2 Cor. 8. 16; 9. 15; giving of thanks, Eph. 5. 4. See liuth. *Der.* awiliudon.

AWILIUDON, *vb.* to thank, to give thanks, Mk. 8. 6; Lu. 17. 16; Jo. 6. 11.

AWISTR, *str. sb. n.* a sheepfold, Jo. 10. 16. *From* awi.

AWO, *wk. sb. f.* a grand-mother, 2 Tim. 1. 5. [Lat. *avia.*]

AZETABA, *adv.* easily, willingly, "gladly" (A. V.), 2 Cor. 11. 19.

AZETI, *sb. n.* pleasure, 1 Tim. 5. 6.

AZETS, *adj.* light, easy; *only in compar.* azetizo, easier, Mk. 2. 9; *spelt* azitizo, Mk. 10. 25.

AZGO, *wk. sb. f.* an ash, cinder, Lu. 10. 13; Mat. 11. 21.

AZYMUS, *sb. m.* unleavened bread; azyme = τῶν ἀζύμων, Mk. 14. 12.

B.

B, *the second letter.* As a numeral, 2. [Pronounce it as in English.]

BA: *see* Bai.

BADI, *str. sb. n.* a bed, Mk. 2. 9, 11; Lu. 5. 24; ana badjam bairan, to carry about on beds, Mk. 6. 55. [E. D. *bed;* G. *bett.*]

BAGMS, *str. sb. m.* a tree, Mat. 7. 17, 18; Mk. 8. 24; Lu. 3. 9; 6. 44. *Cf.* triu. *Der.* alewa-, baira-, peika-, smakka-bagms. [D. *boom;* G. *baum;* E. *beam.*]

BAHT*, *a root (derived from* bajan, bakan, *or* baban?), *whence* and-bahts, &c. *See* and-bahts, and-bahti, and-bahtjan.

BAI, *adj. m. (n.* ba), both; *dat.* baim; *acc.* bans, Lu. 1. 6. 7. *Cf.* twai. [A. S. *bá.*]

BAID, *pt. t. of* beidan, *vb.* q. v.

BAIDJAN, *vb.* to constrain, compel, Gal. 2. 3, 14. *Cf.* beidan.

BAIM, *dat. of* bai, both. *See* bai.

BAIRA-BAGMS, *str. sb. m.* a sycamine tree, Lu. 17. 6. [*Spelt* baina-bagms *in some editions.*]

BAIRAN, *vb. (pt. t.* bar, *pl.* berum, *pp.* baurans), *with acc.* (1), to bear, carry, bring, Mat. 5. 23; Lu. 7. 14; Jo. 12. 6; Gal. 6. 5; &c.; (2) to bear (children), 1 Tim. 5. 14; Gal. 4. 24; (3) akran bairan, to bear fruit. *See* akran. *Der.* un-bairands, un-bairandei, ga-bairan, at-bairan, inn-atbairan, us-atbairan, fra-bairan, thairh-bairan, us-bairan, ut-bairan; *also* barn, beruseis, baris, baur, aina-baur, fruma-baur; *also* ga-baurs, ga-baurjaba, ga-baurtjothus, ga-baur, baurei, baurthei, ga-baurths, ga-baurthiwaurd. [E. *bear;* D. *baren;* G. *gebären.*]

BAIRGAHEI, *wk. sb. f.* hill-country, Lu. 1. 39, 65. *From* bairgan.

BAIRGAN, *vb. (pt. t.* barg, *pl.* baurgum, *pp.* baurgans), *with dat.* to hide, preserve, keep, Jo. 12. 25; 17. 15. *Der.* ga-bairgan, bairgs (?), *and see under* bairgs. [G. D. *bergen;* A. S. *beorgan.*]

BAIRGS*, *str. sb. m.* a mountain. *Der.* bairgahei, baurgs, baurgswaddjus, baurgja, ga-baurgja, bi-baurgeins. [G. D. *berg;* A. S. *beorg.*]

BAIRHTABA, *adv.* brightly, clearly, Mk. 8. 25; Lu. 16. 19; openly, Col. 2. 15.

BAIRHTEI, *wk. sb. f.* brightness, light, manifestation, 2 Cor. 4. 2; *hence*, in bairhtein, openly, Mat. 6. 4, 6.

BAIRHTJAN, *vb.* to brighten: *hence*, to manifest, shew, Jo. 7. 4.

BAIRHTS, *adj.* bright; *hence* bairhts wairthan, to become manifest, Jo. 9. 3; to appear, Col. 3. 4; bairht thatei (δῆλον ὅτι), it is evident that. *Der.* bairhtaba, bairhtei, bairhtjan, ga-bairhtjan, ga-bairhteins, at-bairhtjan. [A. S. *beorht;* O. N. *biartr.*]

BAIT, bit *(pt. t. from* beitan), q. v.

BAITH, BAID, expected *(pt. t. from* beidan), q. v.

BAITRABA, *adv.* bitterly, Mat. 26. 75. *See* baitrs.

BAITREI, *wk. sb. f.* bitterness, Eph. 4. 31. *See* baitrs.

BAITRS, *adj.* bitter, Col. 3. 19. *Der.* baitraba, baitrei. [E. D. G. *bitter.*]

BAJOTHS, both, Lu. 5. 38. *Cf.* bai.

BALGS, *str. sb. m. (pl.* balgeis), a wine-skin, Mat. 9. 17; Mk. 2. 22; Lu. 5. 37. *Cf.* aurkeis. *Der.* mati-balgs. [E. *bag;* G. *balg.*]

BALSAGGA: *see* halsagga.

BALSAN (μύρον), balsam, balm, ointment, Mk. 14. 5; Lu. 7. 37; Jo. 12. 5.

BALTHABA, *adv.* boldly, Jo. 7. 13; openly, Col. 2. 15. *See* balths.

BALTHEI, *wk. sb. f.* boldness, 2 Cor. 3. 12; Eph. 3. 12; 6. 19; 1 Tim. 3. 13. *See* balths.

BALTHJAN, *vb.* to dare, Skeir. 2. 1.

BALTHS*, *adj.* bold. *Der.* balthaba, balthei, thrasa-balthei, us-balthei, balthjan.

BALWA-WESEI, *wk. sb. f.* wickedness, malice, 1 Cor. 5. 8. *See* balws.

BALWEINS, *str. sb. f.* torment, Mat. 25. 46; Lu. 16. 23. *See* balws.

BALWJAN, *vb.* to torment, plague, Mat. 8. 6, 29; Mk. 5. 7; Lu. 8. 28. *See* balws.

BALWS*, *adj.* evil. *Der.* balwa-wesei, balwjan, balweins. [E. *bale.*]

BAND, bound, *pt. t. of* bindan, q. v.

BANDI, *str. sb. f.* a band, Mk. 7. 35; a bond, Col. 4. 19; Lu. 8. 29; Phil. 1. 14. *From* bindan.

BANDJA, *wk. sb. m.* a prisoner, Mat. 27. 15, 16; Mk. 15. 6; Eph. 3. 1; 4. 1. *From* bindan.

BANDWA, *str. sb. f.* a sign, a sure bond, a token, 1 Cor. 14. 22. *From* bindan.

BANDWJAN, *vb.* to show a sign, betoken, Lu. 20. 37; to make signs, beckon, Lu. 1. 22; to point out, 1 Cor. 10. 28. *From* bindan.

BANDWO, *str. sb. f.* a sign, token, 2 Thess. 3. 17; a signal, Mk. 14. 44. *From* bindan.

BANJA, *str. sb. f.* bane, wound, sore, Lu. 10. 30; 16. 21. *Cf.* wundufni.

BANS, *acc. of* bai, both.

BANSTS, *str. sb. m. (pl.* bansteis), a barn, Mat. 6. 26; Lu. 3. 17. *From* bindan. [*Cf.* G. *bansen.*]

BAR, bore, *pt t. of* bairan, q. v.

BARBARUS (βάρβαρος), one who is not a Greek, Col. 3. 11.

BARIS*, *str. sb. f.* barley. *Der.* barizeins.

BARIZEINS, *adj.* of barley, Jo. 6. 9.

BARMS, *str. sb. m. (pl.* barmeis), the bosom, Lu. 6. 38; 16. 22; Jo. 13. 23. [O. E. *barm.*]

BARN, *str. sb. n.* a child, Mat. 11. 19; Mk. 7. 27; barne barna, children's children, grand-children, 1 Tim. 5. 4. *Der.* barnilo, barnisks, barniskei, barniski, unbarnahs, barnusjan(?). [E. *bairn.*]

BARNAHS*, *adj.* in un-barnahs, q. v.

BARNILO, *wk. sb. n.* a little child, son, Mat. 9. 2; Lu. 1. 76; 15. 31; Jo. 13. 33. *Cf.* barn.

BARNISKEI, *wk. sb. f.* childishness, childish things, 1 Cor. 13. 11. *Cf.* barn.

BARNISKI, *str. sb. n.* childhood, Mk. 9. 21; 2 Tim. 3. 15. *Cf.* barn.

BARNISKS, *adj.* childish, 1 Cor. 14. 20; Gal. 4. 3. *Cf.* barn.

BARNUSJAN, *possibly the right form of the following.*

BARUSNJAN, *vb.* to honour, as a child should do, to shew filial piety, 1 Tim. 5. 4. [*Perhaps we should read* barnusjan.]

BASI*, *str. sb. n.* a berry. *Der.* weina-bazi. [G. *beere;* D. *bes, bezie.*]

BATAN*, (*pt. t.* bot; *pl.* botum; *pp.* batans), to be useful, to boot. *Cf.* bats, ga-batnan, bota, bot(j)an, ga-bot(j)an. [D. *baten.*]

BATISTS, *superl. adj.* best, Lu. 1. 3. *From* bats, q. v.

BATIZA, *compar. adj.* better, Mat. 10. 31; Lu. 5. 39. *From* bats, q. v.

BATNAN*, *vb. in* ga-batnan, q. v. *Cf.* batan.

BATS*, *adj.* good, useful; *comp.* batiza; *superl.* batists. [E. *boot;* D. *baat.*]

BATWINS, *a Gothic proper name in the Gothic calendar.*

BAUAIDA (?), *pt. t. of* bauan, q. v.

BAUAINS, *str. sb. f.* a dwelling, dwelling-place, Mk. 5. 3; 2 Cor. 5. 2; Phil. 3. 20. *See* bauan.

BAUAN, *vb.* (*pt. t.* bauaida *or* baibo?), to build; *hence,* to inhabit, dwell in, 1 Tim. 6. 16; Rom. 7. 17; &c. *Der.* gabauan, bauains. [G. *bauen;* D. *bouwen;* A. S. *buian.*]

BAUD, bade, *pt. t. of* biudan, q. v.

BAUD, BAUDANA; *from* bauths, q. v. *Cf.* daubs.

BAUG, bent, *pt. t. of* biugan, q. v.

BAUGJAN*, *vb. in* us-baugjan. *Cf.* bugjan.

BAUHTA, bought, *pt. t. of* bugjan, q. v.

BAUHTS, bought, *pp. of* bugjan, q. v.

BAUHTS*, *str. sb. f.* a buying, appears *in the comp.* anda-bauhts, faura-baubts, fra-baubts.

BAULJAN*, *vb. in* uf-bauljan, q. v.

BAUR (*pl.* baureis), *str. sb. m.* (γεννητός), a child (*lit.* a thing born), Mat. 11. 11; Lu. 7. 28.

BAUR*, *appears in the comp.* gabaur, ga-baurjaba, ga-baurjothus. *Cf.* bairan.

BAURANS, GA-BAURANS, pp. of vb. bairan, to bear, q. v. Der. unbaurans.
BAURD*, str. sb. n. a board. Der. fotu-baurd. [G. bord; D. boord.]
BAUREI, the same as baurthei, q. v.
BAURGJA, wk. sb. m. a burgher, citizen, Lu. 15. 15; 19. 14. From baurgs, bairgan.
BAURGS, str. sb. f. a burgh, borough, town, city, Mat. 5. 35; 8. 33; 9. 1; &c. From bairgan. Der. baurgs-waddjus, str. sb. m. a town-wall, 2 Cor. 11. 33.
BAURTHEI, wk. sb. f. a burthen, burden, Gal. 6. 5. From bairan. [G. bürde.]
BAURTHS*, GA-BAURTHS, str. sb. f. birth. See ga-baurths. From bairan. Der. ga-baurthi-waurd.
BAUTH, bade: from biudan, q. v.
BAUTHS, adj. deaf, Mat. 11. 5; &c.; dumb, Mat. 9. 32; &c.; also insipid; bauth wairthan, to lose its savour (said of salt), Lu. 14. 34. Cf. daubs.
BEDUM, we asked. From bidjan, q. v.
BEIDAN, vb. (pt. t. baid; pl. bidum; pp. bidans), with gen. to abide, await, look for, expect, Mat. 11. 3; Lu. 1. 21; 8. 40; &c. Der. ga-beidan, us-beidan; and cf. us-beisns, us-beisnei, baidjan, ga-baidjan, bidjan, bida. [E. bide.]
BEISNS, str. sb. f. appears in comp. us-beisns, q. v.
BEIST, str. sb. n. leaven, Mk. 8. 15; 1 Cor. 5. 6; Gal. 5. 9. Der. un-beistei. Cf. beitan.
BEISTJAN*, vb. in ga-beistjan, q. v. Der. un-beistjoths. Cf. beitan.
BEIT*, appears in comp. anda-beit, q. v.

BEITAN, vb. (pt. t. bait; pl. bitum; pp. bitans), with acc., to bite, Gal. 5. 15. Der. and-beitan, andabeit, baitrs, baitraba, baitrei, beist, unbeistei, beistjan, ga-beistjan, un-beistjoths. [E. bite; G. bissen; D. bijten.]
BERUM, we bore. From bairan, q. v.
BERUSEIS, BIRUSEIS, str. sb. m. a father; pl. berusjos, parents, Lu. 2. 27; Jo. 9. 23.
BI, prep. (1) with acc. by, about, to, at, according to, concerning, towards; it represents περί, ἐπί, κατά (with acc.), ἐν, διά (with gen.), ὑπέρ (with gen.); (2) with dat. by, at, after, through, on account of, according to; representing πρός, κατά (with gen. and acc.). It occurs in very many comp. See below. [E. by; G. bei; D. bij.]
BI-ABRJAN, vb. to be exceedingly astonished, Mat. 7, 28. From abrs.
BI-ARBEIDJAN, vb. to toil for, strive, endeavour after, 1 Th. 4. 11.
BIARI, an uncertain reading in Tit. 1. 12, a beast. The reading may be un-biuri.
BI-AUKAN, vb. to increase, add to, Mk. 4. 24; Lu. 17. 5; 19. 11.
BI-AUKNAN, vb. to abound, Phil. 1. 26; 1 Thess. 4. 10.
BI-BAURGEINS, str. sb. f. the boundary of the camp, Skeir. 3. 15. Cf. bairgan.
BI-BINDAN, vb. to bind round, bind about, Jo. 11. 44.
BIDA, str. sb. f. a request, exhortation, 2 Cor. 8. 17; prayer, 1 Tim. 4. 5; Lu. 1. 13; 2. 37; &c. Der. bidagwa, bidjan, us-bidjan.

BIDAGWA, *wk. sb. m.* a beggar, Jo. 9. 8.
BIDJAN, *vb. (pt. t.* baitb; *pl.* bedum; *pp.* bidans). to pray, ask, Mat. 5. 44; 6. 5, 6, 7; 8. 5; Mk. 6. 22; Jo. 16. 24; 17. 15; &c; *often followed by* du, faur, fram, *or* bi. *Cf.* aihtron. *Der.* us-bidjan. [O. E. *bid;* D. *bidden;* G. *bitten.*]
BI-DOMJAN, *vb.* to judge, Col. 2. 16.
BIDUM, we abode, waited. *From* beidan, q. v.
BI-FAIH*, *str. sb. n.* fraud? *See* faihan. [S. *gives a reference to* 2 Cor. 12. 20.]
BI-FAIHON, *vb.* to make a gain by, defraud so as to get gain, 1 Th. 4. 6; 2 Cor. 12. 17. *See* faihan.
BI-FAIHONS, *str. sb. f.* covetousness, 2 Cor. 9. 5. *See* faihan.
BI-GAGGAN, *vb.*; *occurs in* faur-bigaggan, q. v.
BI-GAIRDAN, *vb.* to begird, gird onself up, Lu. 17. 8.
BI-GITAN, *vb.* to find, Mat. 7. 14; 8. 10; Lu. 2. 16; *with double acc.* Lu 7. 10; &c.
BI-GRABAN, *vb.* to dig a ditch *or* trench round, Lu. 19. 43.
BI-HAIT, *str. sb. n.* strife, contention, 2 Cor. 12. 20.
BI-HAITJA, *str. sb. m.* a boastful, contentious man, 2 Tim. 3. 2; Tit. 1. 7.
BI-HLAHJAN, *vb.* to laugh at, laugh to scorn, Mat. 9. 24; Mk. 5. 40.
BI-HWAIRBAN, *vb.* to throng round, press on one from all sides, Lu. 8. 45.
BIJANDZUTH-THAN, *a MS. reading in* Philem. 22: *the true reading is quite uncertain.*
BI-KUKJAN, *vb.* to kiss, Lu. 7. 45.

BI-KWIMAN, *vb.* to come upon one, 1 Thess. 5. 3.
BI-LAIBJAN, *vb.* to survive, be left alive *or* remaining, 1 Thess. 4. 15. *See* leiban.
BILAIF, *a word occurring in the fragment of a Gothic calendar.*
BI-LAIGON, *vb.* to lick, Lu. 16. 21.
BI-LAIKAN, *vb.* to mock, Mk. 10. 34; 15. 20; Gal. 6. 7; Lu. 14, 29. [O. E. *bi-lakke.*]
BI-LAISTJAN*, *vb.*; *occurs in* un-bilaistiths, q. v.
BI-LEITHAN, *vb. (pt. t.* bi-laith; *pp.* bi-litbans), to leave, forsake, Mat. 27. 46; Mk. 10. 7; 12. 19; &c.
BI-MAIT, *str. sb. n.* circumcision, Gal. 5. 6; 6. 15; Jo. 7. 22, 23. *Der.* un-bimait.
BI-MAITAN, *vb.* to circumcize, Jo. 7. 22; Lu. 1. 59; 2. 21; *also* to be circumcized, Gal. 5. 2. *Der.* un-bimaitans.
BI-MAMPJAN, *vb. (or* bi-mamjan), to deride, mock at, Lu. 16. 14.
BI-NAH, *an impers. verb, as from* bi-naban; (ἔξεστι), is lawful, 1 Cor. 10. 23; *also* (δεῖ), it behoves, 2 Cor. 12. 1.
BI-NAHAN, *vb.* to be fit *or* lawful, whence binah *and* binauht ist, q v. *See* nahan.
BI-NAUHT IST, is permitted, *answers to preceding* binah *in* 1 Cor. 10. 23. *See* nahan, bi-nahan.
BINDAN, *vb. with acc. (pt t.* band; *pl.* bundum; *pp.* bundans), to bind, to fasten, bind with fetters, Lu. 8. 29. *Der.* ga-bindan, and-bindan, bi-bindan, gabinda, ga-bindi, bandi, bandja, ga-bundi, bandwa, bandwo, bandwjan, ga-bandwjan, andbundnan. [E. *bind;* G. D. *binden.*]
BI-NIMAN, *vb.* to take away, steal, Mat. 27. 64.

BI-NIUHSJAN, *vb.* to spy out, Gal. 2. 4.

BI-RAUBON, *vb.* to rob, strip, despoil, Lu. 10. 30; 2 Cor. 11. 8.

BI-REIKEI, *wk. sb. f.* danger, peril, 2 Cor. 11. 26. *Perhaps from* rikan.

BI-REIKS, BI-REKS, endangered; bireiks wisan, *or* wairthan, to be in danger, Lu. 8. 23; 1 Cor. 15. 30. *Cf.* rikan.

BI-RINNAN, *vb.* to run about, Mk. 6. 55; to come round, surround, Jo. 10. 24.

BI-RODEINS, *str. sb. f.* murmuring, Jo. 7. 12; evil-speaking, 2 Cor. 12. 20.

BI-RODJAN, *vb.* to murmur, Lu. 15. 2; 19. 7; to murmur against, Lu. 5. 30; Jo. 6. 41; 7. 32.

BI-RUNAINS, *str. sb. f.* evil counsel, Skeir. 3. 4.

BIRUSEIS: *see* beruseis.

BI-SAIHWAN, *vb.* to look round on, Mk. 3. 34; 10. 23; to provide, have regard for, Rom. 12. 17.

BI-SATJAN, *vb.* to beset, set round any thing, Mk. 12. 1.

BI-SAULEINS, *str. sb. f.* that which sullies, defilement, 2 Cor. 7. 1.

BI-SAULJAN, *vb.* to sully, render impure, Tit. 1. 15.

BI-SAULNAN, *vb.* to be soiled *or* sullied, to be defiled, Jo. 18. 28.

BI-SITAN, *vb. only used in pres. pt.* bi-sitands, a neighbour, Lu. 1. 58; one who dwells near, Lu. 1. 65; neighbourhood, Lu. 7. 17; Mk. 1. 28.

BI-SKABAN, *vb.* to shave off the hair, 1 Cor. 11. 5.

BI-SKEINAN, *vb.* to shine on, shine round about, Lu. 2. 9.

BI-SMEITAN, *vb.* to besmear, anoint, Jo. 9. 11.

BI-SNIWAN*, *occurs in comp.* faurbisniwan, q. v.

BI-SPEIWAN, *vb.* to spit upon, Lu. 18. 32; Mk. 15. 19.

BI-STANDAN, *vb.* to stand round, surround, beseige, Lu. 19. 43; to stand round, Jo. 11. 42. [*Cf.* E. *bystander.*]

BI-STIGGKWAN, *vb.* to beat upon, Mat. 7. 25, 27; Lu. 6. 48; to stumble at, Rom. 9. 32.

BI-STUGGKWS, *or* bistuggkwo, a stumbling, Rom. 9. 32; a cause of offence, 2 Cor. 6. 3.

BI-SUNJANE, *adv.* near, round about, Mk. 3. 34; 6. 6; Lu. 9. 12; Nehem. 5. 17; 6. 16.

BI-SWAIRBAN, *vb.* to wipe, Lu. 7. 38, 44; Jo. 11. 2; 12. 3.

BI-SWARAN, *vb.* to conjure, adjure, Mk. 5. 7; 1 Thess. 5. 27.

BI-THAGGKJAN, *vb.* to think of, meditate, Lu. 5. 22.

BI-THE, *adv.* whilst, Mat. 9. 10; bithe'h-than, after that. *Cf.* the.

BI-THRAGJAN, *vb.* to run before, Lu. 19. 4.

BI-THWAHAN, *vb.* to wash oneself, Jo. 9. 11.

BI-TIUHAN, *vb.* to go about, visit, Mat. 9. 35; Mk. 6. 6; to lead about, 1 Cor. 9. 5.

BITUM, we bit. *From* beitan.

BIUDAN*, *vb.* (*pt. t.* bauth, baud; *pl.* budum; *pp.* budans), to command, bid. *Der.* ana-biudan, ana-busns, faur-biudan. [E. *bid;* D. *bieden;* G. *bieten.*]

BIUDS, *str. sb. m.* a holy table, altar; *hence* any table, Mk. 7. 28; Lu. 16. 21; 1 Cor. 10. 21. *From* biudan.

BIUGAN, *vb.* (*pt. t.* baug; *pl.* bugum; *pp.* bugans), to bow, bend, Eph. 3. 14; *neut.* to bow, bend itself, Rom. 14. 11. *Der.*

ga-biugan. [A. S. *bugan;* D. *buigen;* G. *biegen.*]
BIUHTI, *str. sb. n.* a custom, Lu. 1. 9; 2. 27; 4. 16; Jo. 18. 39; *see next word.*
BIUHTS, *adj.* accustomed, wont; biuhts wisan, to be wont, Mat. 27. 15; Mk. 10. 1 (*where was is omitted*). *Der.* biuhti.
BI-WAIBJAN, *vb.* to weave round, wind about, Mk. 14. 51; to clothe, Mk. 16. 5; to hem in, Lu. 19. 43. *See* weiban.
BI-WANDJAN, *vb.* to turn away, reject, avoid, 1 Tim. 4. 7; 5. 11; 2 Cor. 8. 20; *from* windan.
BI-WINDAN, *vb.* to wind round, enwrap, swathe, Mat. 27. 59; Mk. 15. 46; Lu. 2. 7.
BI-WISAN, *vb.* to be merry, Lu. 15. 29.
BLANDAN (*pt. t.* baibland?), *vb.* to blend; *refl.* blandan sik, to communicate with, 1 Cor. 5. 11; 2 Thess. 3. 14.
BLAUTHJAN, *vb.* to abrogate, make void, Mk. 7. 13. *Der.* ga-blauthjan.
BLEITHEI, *wk. sb. f.* mercy, Rom. 12. 1; 2. Cor. 1. 3; Gal. 5. 22.
BLEITHJAN, *vb.* to have mercy, Lu. 6. 36.
BLEITHS, *adj.* merciful, kind, Lu. 6. 36; Tit. 1. 8. *Cf.* armahairts. *Der.* bleithei, bleithjan, ga-bleithjan, ga-bleitheins. [E. *blithe; cf.* A. S. *blîpe.*]
BLESAN*, *vb.* (*pt. t.* baiblos?), to blow. *Der.* uf-blesan. [G. *blasen;* D. *blazen; cf.* E. *blare.*]
BLIGGWAN, *vb.* (*pt. t.* blaggw; *pl.* bluggwum; *pp.* bluggwans), to beat, Mk. 10. 34; Lu. 20. 11; to kill, murder, 1 Tim. 1. 9. *Cf.* slahan. *Der.* us-bliggwan.
BLINDJAN*, *vb.* to make blind, to blind; *in* ga-blindjan, q. v. *See* blinds. [A. S. *blendan.*]
BLINDNAN*, *vb.* to become blind; *in* ga-blindnan, q. v. *See* blinds.
BLINDS, *adj.* blind, Mat. 9. 27; 11. 5; Mk. 8. 23; Lu. 6. 39. *Der.* ga-blindjan, ga-blindnan. [E. G. D. *blind.*]
BLOMA, *str. sb. m.* a flower, a lily, Mat. 6. 28. [E. *bloom;* D. *bloem;* G. *blume.*]
BLOSTREIS*, *in comp.* guth-blostreis, q. v.
BLOTAN, *vb.* (*pt. t.* baiblot?), *with acc.* to reverence, worship, Mk. 7. 7; Lu. 2. 37; 1 Tim. 2. 10. *Der.* us-blotheins, blotinassus, guth-blostreis.
BLOTEINS*, *in comp.* us-bloteins, q. v.
BLOTH, *str. sb. n.* blood, Mat. 27. 4, 6, 8; Mk. 5. 25; Lu. 8. 43. [G. *blut;* D. *bloed.*]
BLOTHA-RINNANDEI, *f. adj.* a woman with an issue of blood. *lit.* blood-running, Mat. 9. 20.
BLOTINASSUS, *str. sb. m.* worship, service, Rom. 12. 1; Col. 2. 18; 2 Thess. 2. 4.
BNAUAN, *vb.* (*pt. t.* baibno?), to rub, Lu. 6. 1.
BOKA, *str. sb. f.* a letter, Rom. 7. 6; 2 Cor. 3. 6; *pl.* bokos, the writings, the scriptures, Mk. 14, 49; letters, knowledge, Jo. 7. 15; bokos af-sateinais, a bill of divorcement, Mk. 10. 4; bokos af-stassais, a writing of divorcement, Mat. 5. 31; ana-filbis bokos, letters of commendation, 2 Cor. 3. 1. *Der.* waddja-bokos, bokareis. [G. *buch;* D. *boek;* E. *book.*]
BOKAREIS, *str. sb. m.* a bookman, a scribe, Mat. 7. 29; 8. 19; &c.

BOTA, *str. sb. f.* boot, advantage, good, 1 Cor. 13. 3; 15. 32; Gal. 5. 2. *See* batan. [A. S. *bót*; D. *baat.*]

BOTJAN, *vb.* to boot, advantage, profit, Mk. 8. 36; Jo. 6. 63; 12. 19. *See* batan.

BRAHTA, brought. *From* briggan.

BRAHW, *str. sb. n. (or perhaps* brahws, *str. sb. m.),* a sudden movement, a twinkling; in brahwa *(or* brabwai) augins, in the twinkling of an eye, 1 Cor. 15. 52. [O. E. *braid.*]

BRAIDEI, *wk. sb. f.* breadth, Eph. 3. 18. *See* braids. [G. *breite.*]

BRAIDJAN*, *vb.* to broaden, *occurs in comp.* us-braidjan, q. v. *See* braids. [G. *breiten.*]

BRAIDS, *adj.* broad, wide, Mat. 7. 13. *Der.* braidei, braidjan, us-braidjan. [D. *breed;* G. *breit.*]

BRAK, brake. *From* brikan.

BRAKJA, *sb. m.* strife, contention, struggle, wrestling, Eph. 6. 12. *From* brikan.

BRANN, burnt. *From* brinnan.

BRANNJAN*, *vb. in* ga-brannjan and in-brannjan. *See* brinnan.

BREKUM, we brake. *From* brikan.

BRIGGAN, *vb. (pt. t.* brahta) *with acc.* to bring, Mk. 6. 27; Lu. 15. 23; Jo. 10. 16; to lead, Mat. 7. 13; to guide, Jo. 16. 13; to make to be, Jo. 8. 32; in aljana briggan, to bring into emulation; in thwairhein briggan, to bring into anger, make angry; *for both which see* Rom. 10. 19. [G. *bringen;* D. *brengen.*]

BRIKAN, *vb. (pt. t.* brak; *pl.* brekum; *pp.* brukans) *with acc.* to break, 1 Cor. 10. 16; to destroy, Gal. 1. 23; to contend, struggle (*cf.* brakja), 2 Tim. 2. 5. *Der.* ga-brikan, uf-brikan, uf-brikands, un-ufbrikands, us-bruknan, ga-bruka, brakja. [D. *breken;* G. *brechen.*]

BRINNAN, *vb. (pt. t.* brann; *pl.* brunnum; *pp.* brunnans), to burn, Jo. 5. 35. *Cf.* tindan. *Der.* uf-brinnan, brinno, brann-jan, ga-brannjan, in-brannjan, ala-brunsts. [A. S. *brinnan;* G. *brennen;* D. *branden.*]

BRINNO, *wk. sb. f.* a fever, Mk. 1. 30; Lu. 4. 38, 39. *See* brinnan.

BROTHAR, *str. sb. m. (dat.* brothr; *pl.* brothr-jus, -e, -um, -uns), a brother, Mat. 5. 22, 23, 24; Mk. 3. 35; &c. *Der.* galiuga-brothar, brothrabans, brothra-lubo. [G. *bruder;* D. *broeder.*]

BROTHRAHANS, *sb. m. pl.* brethren, Mk. 12. 20.

BROTHRA-LUBO, BROTHRU-LUBO, *wk. sb. f.* brotherly love, Rom. 12. 10; 1 Thess. 4. 9.

BRUHTA, used. *From* brukjan.

BRUKA*, in ga-bruka, q. v.

BRUKANS, broken. *From* brikan.

BRUKJAN, *vb. (pt. t.* bruhta) *with gen. and dat.* to make use of, 2 Cor. 1. 17; 1 Cor. 7. 21; 1 Tim. 1. 8; *hence* to partake of, 1 Cor. 10. 30. *Cf.* bruks, un-bruks. [A. S. *brúcan;* G. *brauchen.*]

BRUKS, *adj.* useful, 2 Tim. 2. 21; 4. 11; profitable, Philemon 11. *Cf.* brukjan. [D. *bruik-baar;* G. *brauch-bar.*]

BRUKUM, we broke. *From* brikan.

BRUNJO, *wk. sb. f.* a breast-plate, Eph. 6. 14; 1 Thess. 5. 8.

BRUNNA, *wk. sb. m.* a spring, well; *hence* the issue, Mk. 5. 29. [G. *brunn.*]

BRUNNANS, burnt. *From* brinnan.

BRUNNUM, we burnt. *From* brinnan.

BRUSTS, *str. sb. f., in pl.* bowels (A. V.), heart, *lit.* breasts; Philemon 20; Col. 3. 12; *also* the breast, Lu. 18. 13.

BRUTH-FATHS, *str. sb. m.* (1) bridegroom (νυμφίος), Mat. 9. 15; Mk. 2. 19. 20; *spelt* bruth-fads, Lu. 5. 34, 35; (2) *in phrase* sunjus bruth-fadis (οἱ υἱοὶ τοῦ νυμφῶνος), sons of the bridechamber. *See ref. for* (1).

BRUTHS, *str. sb. f.* a bride, Mat. 10. 35. *Der.* bruth-faths *or* bruth-fads. [G. *braut*; D. *bruid*.]

BUGJAN, *vb. (pt. t.* bauhta), to buy, sell, Mat. 10. 29; Lu 19. 45; Jo. 6. 5. *Der.* us-bugjan, fra-bugjan; bauhts *in* andabauhts, faur-bauhts, fra-bauhts.

BUGUM, we bent. *From* biugan.

BUNDANS, bound. *From* bindan.

BUNDI*, *in* ga-bundi, q. v.

BUNDNAN*, *vb. in* and-bundnan. q. v. *Cf.* bindan.

BUNDUM, we bound. *From* bindan.

BUSNS*, *in* ana-busns, q. v.

BYSSUS (βύσσος), *str. sb. m.* fine linen, Lu. 16. 19.

CH.

CH, the 23rd letter of the Gothic alphabet; as a numeral: 600. [*Answers to the Greek* χ.]

CHRISTUS (*gen.* —aus; *dat.* —au; *acc.* —u), Christ. *Der.* galiuga-Christus.

D.

D, the 4th letter; as a numeral: 4.

DABAN* *(pt. t.* dob); *in comp.* ga-duban, q. v. *Der.* ga-daban, ga-dobs, ga-dofs.

DADDJAN, *vb.* to give suck, suckle, Mk. 13. 17.

DAGAN*, *vb.* to shine; *prob. root of* dags.

DAGS, *str. sb. m.* a day, time, Lu. 4. 42; 6. 13; 9. 12; &c; nahtam jah dagam, naht jah dag, night and day, Mk. 5. 5; 4. 27; dagis hwizuh, daily, Nehem. 5. 18; daga jah daga, day by day, 2 Cor. 4. 16; daga hwammeh, daily, Mk 14. 49; Lu. 16. 19; himma daga *or* hina daga, today, Mat. 6. 11; 11. 23. *Der.* sabbato-dags, afar-dags, gistradags, fidur-dogs, ahtau-dogs. [E. *day;* G. *tag;* D. *dag.*]

DAIGS (φύραμα), *str. sb. m.* dough. a kneaded lump, Rom. 9. 21; 11. 16; 1 Cor. 5. 6; Gal. 5. 9. *See* deigan. [D. *deeg;* G. *teig.*]

DAILA, *str. sb. f.* dealing, participation, 2 Cor. 6. 14; a portion, a pound, Lu. 19. 13.

DAILJAN, *vb.* to deal, deal out, apportion, distribute, Rom. 12. 8; Eph. 4. 28; 1 Cor. 12. 11. *See* dails.

DAILS, *str. sb. f.* a deal, dole, part, portion, Lu. 15. 12; 1 Cor. 13. 10; Col. 1. 12; 2. 16. *Der.* daila, ga-daila, dailjan, gadailjan, af-dailjan, dis-dailjan. [E. *deal;* D. *deel;* G. *theil.*]

DAIMONAREIS, *str. sb. m.* a demoniac, possessed with a devil, Mat. 8. 16, 28, 33; 9. 32; Lu. 8. 36.

DAL, *sb. n.* (or dals, *m* ?), a dale, a valley, Lu. 3. 5; a ditch, Lu. 6. 39. *Der.* id-daljo, dalath, dalatha, dalathro. [E *dale;* D. *dal;* G. *thal.*]

DALATH, *adv.* down, Mat. 7. 25; und dalath, to the bottom, Mk. 15. 38; on the ground, Jo. 9. 6.

DALATHA, *adv.* below, Mk. 14. 66.

DALATHRO, *adv.* from beneath, Jo. 8. 23.

DAMAN* *(the root of* doms*?), vb.* to deem?

DAMASKS, *adj.* of Damascus, 2 Cor. 11. 32.

DAMMJAN*, *vb., in comp.* faurdammjan, q. v.

DARS, I dared. *See* daursan.

DAUBEI, *wk. sb. f.* deafness; *hence* dullness, obtuseness, blindness, Rom. 11. 25. *See* daubs.

DAUBITHA, *str. sb. f.* deafness; *hence* dulness, hardness of heart (πώρωσις), Mk. 3. 5; Eph. 4. 18. *See* daubs.

DAUBJAN*, *vb. in* ga-daubjan *and* af-daubnan, q. v.

DAUBNAN*, *vb.* in af-daubnan, q. v.

DAUBS, *adj.* deaf; *hence* hardened, dull (πεπωρωμένος), Mk. 8. 17. *Der.* daubei, daubitha, ga-daubjan, af-daubnan, af-dobnan, afdumbnan. [E. *deaf;* D. *doof;* G. *taub.*]

DAUDEI*, *in* us-daudei, q. v.

DAUDJAN*, *in* us-daudjan, q. v.

DAUDO*, *in* us-daudo, q. v.

DAUDS*, *in* us-dauds, q. v.

DAUG, is fit. *From* dugan.

DAUHTAR *(pl. acc.* dauhtruns), *str. sb. f.* a daughter, Mat. 9. 18; Mk. 5. 23; Lu. 2. 36.

DAUHTS (δοχή), *str. sb. f.* a feast, Lu. 5. 29; 14. 13.

DAUJAN*, *in* af-daujan, q. v.

DAUKA*, *in* ga-dauka, q. v.

DAUNS, *str. sb. f.* scent, odour, John 12. 3; dauns wothi, sweet savour, 2 Cor. 2. 15; Eph. 5 2; the sense of smell, 1 Cor. 12. 17. [G. *dunst.*]

DAUPEINS, *str. sb. f.* a dipping, baptism, Mk. 1. 4; 11. 30; Lu. 20. 4. *See* diupan.

DAUPJAN, *vb.* to dip, to baptize, Mk. 1. 9; 10. 38; to wash oneself, Mk. 7. 4; to be baptized, 1 Cor. 15. 29. *See* diupan.

DAUPJANDS, the Baptist, Mk. 6. 24; Lu. 7. 20, 28. *From* daupjan.

DAUR, *str. sb. n.* a door, Mat. 7. 13; Mk. 1. 33; 2. 2; Lu. 16. 20; Jo. 10. 1. *Der.* dauro, auga-dauro, faura-dauri. [E. *door;* D. *deur;* G. *thür.*]

DAURO, *wk. sb. f.* (only in pl. daurons), a door, Mat. 27. 60; Mk. 16. 3; Jo. 18. 16.

DAURSAN*, *vb. (pt. t.* dars; *pl.* daursum), to dare, *used in comp.* ga-daursan, q. v. *Cf.* nanthjan. *Der.* ga-daursan.

DAUTHEINS (νέκρωσις), *str. sb. f.* the dying, 2 Cor. 4. 10; death, peril of death, 2 Cor. 11. 23. *See* diwan.

DAUTHJAN, *vb.* to kill, mortify, Col. 3. 5. *Der.* af-dauthjan, ga-dauthjan. *See* diwan.

DAUTHNAN, *vb.* to die, Jo. 11. 25. *See* diwan, ga-dauthnan.

DAUTHS, dead, Mat 11. 5; Mk. 9. 26; 12. 27; &c. *See* diwan.

DAUTHUBL(E)IS, *adj.* destined to die, devoted to death, 1 Cor. 4. 9.

DAUTHUS, *str. sb. m.* death, Mat.

26. 66; Mk. 9. 1; Lu. 9. 27; &c. *See* diwan. [E. *death;* D. *dood;* G. *tod.*]

DEDJA*, *wk. sb. m.* a doer; *in* wai-dedja, q. v.

DEDS*, *str. sb. f.* a deed. *Cf.* missa-deds, waila-deds, ga-deds, wai-dedja. [E. *deed;* D. *daad;* G. *that.*]

DEIGAN, *also spelt* digan, Rom. 9. 20, (*pt. t.* daig; *pl.* digum; *pp.* digans), to knead, form out of plastic material, Rom. 9. 20; digans, made of earth, 2 Tim. 2. 20. *Der.* daigs, digrs, digrei, ga-dik(is).

DEIKAN*, *vb.* to form (?), *another form of* deigan (?). *See* ga-dik(is).

DEINA* *or* deino*, *in* wiga-deino, q. v.

DEIS*, *adj.* wise. *Der.* filu-deisei(ns), q. v.

DIABULA, *str. sb. f.* a female slanderer, 1 Tim. 3. 11.

DIABAULUS, DIABULUS, *str. sb. m.* a devil; Lu. 4. 3; 8. 12; Jo. 6. 70; &c.

DIAKAUNUS, *str. sb. m.* a deacon, 1 Tim. 3. 8, 12.

DIAKUN, DIAKON, a deacon, *Neap. and Arezzo documents.*

DIGAN, *perhaps another spelling of* deigan, q. v.; digandin *occurs in* Rom. 9. 20.

DIGREI, *wk. sb. f.* abundance, 2 Cor. 8. 20; *more lit.* thickness, *as* of a thing closely kneaded. *Cf.* deigan.

DIK(IS): *in* ga-dik(is), q. v.

DIS—, *an intensive prefix to verbs, meaning* in twain, to pieces; &c. *See the verbs given below. Cf.* Lat. *dis-*, Gk. διά.

DIS-DAILJAN, *vb.* to divide, Mk. 15. 24; Lu. 15. 12; 1 Cor. 1. 13.

DIS-DRIUSAN, *vb.* to befall, fall upon, Lu. 1. 12.

DIS-HABAN, *vb.* to seize upon, Lu. 5. 9; to constrain, 2 Cor. 5. 14; Phil. 1. 23.

DIS-HNIUPAN, *vb.* to tear to pieces, burst asunder, Lu. 8. 29.

DIS-HNUPNAN, *vb.* to become torn into pieces, to be broken asunder, Lu. 5. 6.

DIS-HULJAN, *vb.* to cover wholly, Lu. 8. 16.

DIS-NIMAN, *vb.* to partake in a high degree, to possess, 2 Cor. 6. 10.

DIS-SIGGKWAN, *vb.* to sink altogether, descend, Eph. 4. 26.

DIS-SITAN, *vb.* to settle upon, to seize upon, Mk. 16. 8 *(where the verb is separated)*; Lu. 5. 26; 7. 16.

DIS-SKAIDAN, *vb.* to dissever, set aside, Skeir. 8. 2.

DIS-SKREITAN, *vb.* to tear (to shreds), rend, Mk. 14. 63.

DIS-SKRITNAN, *vb.* to become torn to shreds, to be rent apart, Mk. 27. 51; Mk. 15. 38.

DIS-TAHJAN, *vb.* to scatter, Lu. 1. 51; Jo. 10. 12; 16. 32; to waste, Lu. 15. 13; 16. 1.

DIS-TAHEINS, *str. sb. f.* dispersion, Jo. 7. 35.

DIS-TAIRAN, *vb.* to tear asunder, burst, Mk. 2. 22; Lu. 5. 37; to leaven (*lit.* to corrupt), Gal. 5. 9.

DIS-TAURNAN, *vb.* to become torn asunder, to burst asunder, Mat. 9. 17.

DIS-WILWAN, *vb.* to plunder completely, Mk. 3. 27.

DIS-WINTHJAN, *vb.* to grind to powder, Lu. 20. 18.

DIS-WITHAN*, *vb. as root of the following.* [S. *gives the root* widan*, *to bind.*]

DIS-WISS (ἀνάλυσις), *str. sb. f.* releasing, dismissal, 2 Tim. 4. 6; *see preceding word.*

DIUPAN*, *vb. (pt. t.* daup; *pl.* dupum; *pp.* dupans), to dip, to be deep. *Der.* diups, diupei, diupitha, diupjan, ga-diupjan, daupjan, daupeins, uf-daupjan.

DIUPITHA (DIUPEI, Eph. 3. 18), *sb. f.* depth, deep, Rom. 8. 39; 11. 33; 2 Cor. 11. 25; Lu. 5. 4. [E. *depth;* D. *diepte;* G. *tiefe.*]

DIUPJAN*, *vb.* to deepen. *See* gadiupjan.

DIUPS, *adj.* deep, Mk. 4. 5; 2 Cor. 8. 2. [G. *tief;* D. *diep.*]

DIUS, *str. sb. n.* a beast, Mk. 1. 13; 1 Cor. 15. 32. [E. *deer;* G. *thier.*] *Cf.* biari.

DIWAN, *vb. (pt. t.* dau; *pl.* diwum; *pp.* diwans), to die; *whence* thata diwans, mortality, the mortal part, 1 Cor. 15. 53, 54; 2 Cor. 5. 4. *Der.* diwans, un-diwans, un-diwanei, daujan, af-daujan, dauths, dauthjan, dauthnan, dautheins, dauthus, dauthubls. [E. *die;* Dan. *döe.*]

DOBNAN*, *in* af-dobnan, q. v.

DOBS*, DOFS, *in* ga-dofs, ga-dobs, q. v.

DOGS: *see* dags.

DOMEINS*, *str. sb. f.* doom; *in* af-domeins *and* faur-domeins, q. v. *See* doms.

DOMJAN, *vb. with acc.* to deem, judge, 1 Cor. 10. 15; to discern, judge, 1 Cor. 11. 29; to deem right, justify, Lu. 7. 29; 10. 29; 16. 15. [E. *doom, deem.*]

DOMS, *str. sb. m.* what one deems, judgment, opinion, Skeir. 2. 16. *Der.* domjan, ga-domjan, af-domjan, bi-domjan, domeins, af-domeins, faur-domeins.

DRABAN*, *vb. (pt. t.* drof; *pl.* drobum; *pp.* drabans), to hew. *Der.* ga-draban.

DRAGAN, *vb. (pt. t.* drog; *pl.* drogum; *pp.* dragans), to drag, draw; *hence* dragan sis, draw towards themselves, choose out, 2 Tim. 4. 3. *Der.* ga-dragan. [D. *trekken;* G. *tragen.*]

DRAGGK, DRAGK, *str. sb. n.* drink. Jo. 6. 55; Rom. 14. 17; 1 Cor. 10. 4; Col. 2. 16.

DRAGGK, drank. *From* driggkan.

DRAGGKJAN, *vb.* to give to drink, Mat. 25. 42; Mk. 15. 36.

DRAIB, drove. *From* dreiban.

DRAIBJAN, *vb.* to drive, Lu. 8. 29; to trouble, vex, Lu. 8. 49; 7. 6; Mk. 5. 35. *Cf.* dreiban.

DRAKMA, *wk. sb. m.* a drachma, Lu. 15. 8.

DRAKMEI; *see* drakma, Lu. 15. 9.

DRAUHSNA, DRAUSNA, *str. sb. f.* that which falls, a crumb, fragment, Mk. 7. 28; Lu. 16. 21; Jo. 6. 12 *See* driusan.

DRAUHTI: *see Appendix.*

DRAUSJAN*, *vb. occurs in* af-drausjan, ga-drausjan. *See* driusan.

DREIBAN, *vb. (pt. t.* draib; *pl.* dribum; *pp.* dribans), to drive, drive away, expel, Jo. 10. 2. *Der.* us-dreiban, drailijan. [E. *drive;* G. *treiben;* D. *drijven.*]

DRIGGKAN, DRIGKAN *(pt. t.* draggk; *pl.* druggkum; *pp.* druggkans), *with acc.* to drink, Mk. 10. 38); Lu. 1. 15; 17. 8; &c.; druggkans *or* drugkans, drunken, 1 Cor. 11. 21. *Der.* ga-driggkan, ana-driggkan, draggk, draggkjan, ga-draggkjan, af-druggkja, wein-druggkja. [G. *trinken;* D. *drinken.*]

DRIUGAN, *vb. (pt. t.* drauh; *pl.* drugum; *pp.* drugans), serve as a soldier, to fight, 1 Tim. 1. 18. *Der.* draubti-witoth, ga-drauhts, draubtinon, drauhtinassus.

DRIUNAN, *vb.* to drone? *see* drunjus.

DRIUSAN, *vb. (pt. t.* draus; *pl.* drusum; *pp.* drusans), to fall, *followed sometimes by* ana *or* du; Mk. 5. 33; 7. 25; 9. 20; &c. *Der.* ga-driusan, at-driusan, dis-driusan, us-driusan, drausjan, ga-drausjan, af-drausjan, driuso, drus, us-drusts.

DRIUSO, *wk. sb. f.*, place where the ground falls, a steep slope, Mat. 8. 32; Mk. 5. 13; Lu. 8. 33. *From* driusan.

DROBJAN, *vb.* to cause trouble, excite to uproar, Mk. 15. 7; to trouble, vex, Gal. 1. 7; 5. 10, 12. *Der.* drobnan, ga-drobnan, in-drobnan, drobna. [G. *trüben;* D. *droef;* E. *droop?*]

DROBNA, DROBNAN: *see Appendix.*

DRUGGKANEI, *wk. sb. f.* drunkenness, Rom. 13. 13; Gal. 5. 21. *From* driggkan.

DRUGGKANS, drunken *(pp. of* driggkan), 1 Cor. 11. 21; 1 Th. 5. 7. *From* driggkan.

DRUGGKJA*, *wk. sb. m.* a drinker, *in comp.* af-drugkja, wein-drugkja.

DRUNJUS, *str. sb. m., lit.* a droning; *hence:* a sound, voice, Rom. 10. 18. [E. *drone;* G. *gedröhne.*]

DRUS, *str. sb. m.* a fall, Mat. 7. 27; Lu. 2. 34.

DRUSUM, we fell. *From* driusan.

DU, *prep. with dat. (and acc.* Col. 4. 10, 13?), to, towards (πρὸς, εἰς, ἐπι); *also with inf. mood of verbs,* to; du seina (πρὸς τὰ ἴδια), to his own, Jo. 16. 32; at-gaggan du, Lu. 8. 44; bairan du, Mk. 10. 13; lagjan du, Mat. 9. 16; duthe, duhthe, duththe *(lit.* thereto), therefore, Mk. 1. 38; 12. 24; wherefore, Mat. 27. 8; duthei ei, in order that, Mk. 4. 21; Eph. 6. 22; duhwe, wherefore. *It is prefixed to several verbs. See below.* [E. *to;* D. *toe;* G. *zu.*]

DU-ATGAGGAN, *vb.* to go to *(pt. t.* du-atiddja), Mat. 8. 5; 9. 28; 26. 69; &c.

DU-ATRINNAN, *vb.* to run to, run towards, Mk. 10. 17.

DU-ATSNIWAN, *vb.* to hasten towards, run on (shore), Mk. 6. 53.

DUBO*, *wk. sb. f.* a dove, *in comp.* hraiwa-dubo. *Cf.* abaks. [E. *dove;* D. *duif;* G. *taube.*]

DU-GAN, began. *From* du-ginnan.

DUGAN, *vb. (pt. t. as pres.* daug; *pl.* dugum; *pt. t.* duhta), to avail, to suit; ni all taug, not everything is expedient, 1 Cor. 10 23. *Cf.* 2 Tim. 2. 14.

DU-GASAIHWAN, *vb.* to behold; *occurs in* Mk. 10. 14, *if the* du *at end of verse 13 be considered to belong to it.*

DU-GAWINDAN, *vb. refl.* to entangle oneself in, 2 Tim. 2. 4.

DU-GINNAN, *vb.* to begin, undertake, Lu. 1. 1; 6. 25; 15. 14; &c.

DULGA-HAITJA, *wk. sb. m.* a creditor, Lu. 7. 41. *See* dulgs.

DULGS, *str. sb. m.* (or dulg, *n.* ?), a debt; *in phr.* dulgis skula, an ower of a debt, debtor, Lu. 7. 41. *Cf.* skulds, faihu-skula.

DULTHJAN, *vb.* to keep a feast, 1 Cor. 5. 8. *See* dulths.

DULTHS, *str. sb. f. (dat.* dulthai *and* dulth), a feast, Lu. 2. 41; Jo. 7. 2; 12. 12. *Der.* dulthjan.

DUMBNAN*, *vb. in* af-dumbnan, q. v.

DUMBS, *adj.* dumb, Lu. 1. 22; Mat. 9. 33. *Der.* af-dumbnan, *Cf.* daubs *and* bauds. [G. *dumm;* D. *dom.*]

DU-RINNAN, *vb.* to run to, Mat. 8. 2; Mk. 9. 15.

DU-STODJAN, *vb.* to begin, Lu. 14. 30; 2 Cor. 8. 6.

DU-WAKAN, *vb.* to watch, Eph. 6. 18 *(various reading)*.

DWALA-WAURDEI, *wk. sb. f.* an idle word, foolish talk, Eph. 5. 4.

DWALITHA, *str. sb. f.* folly, foolishness, simplicity, 1 Cor. 1. 18, 21, 23, 25.

DWALMON, *vb.* to be foolish, to be mad, Jo. 10. 20; 1 Cor. 14. 23.

DWALS, *adj.* foolish, Mat. 7. 26; 5. 22; 1 Cor. 1. 20; 4. 10; 2 Tim. 2. 16, 23. *Der.* dwalawaurdei, dwalitha, dwalmon. [D. dwaas; *cf.* dwalen, to err.]

E.

E, the 5th letter of the Gothic alphabet. As a numeral, it means 5. [It is convenient to pronounce it like *a* in *day;* and to pronounce *ei* like *Germ. ei* or *Engl. i.*]

EI (1), *conj.* (ὅτι, ἵνα), that, *with indic. and conj.*;

ei ni, that not;

ei hwaiwa, if haply, Phil. 3. 11;

ei hwan ni, lest, Lu. 4. 11;

ei thau (εἰ δὲ μήγε), but if not;

ei than, therefore, Jo. 9. 41; than — ei, whereas, in order that, Mat. 25. 40, 45; Lu. 5. 24;

duthe ei, for, because, Lu. 1. 13, 20;

swethauh ei, even though, 2 Cor. 12. 15;

ibai ei (μήτι), Jo. 7, 31;

in thamma ei, because;

akei, but;

und thana dag ei, till the day that, Lu. 1. 20;

thamma daga ei, on the day that, Lu. 17. 30; Col. 1. 9;

thamma haidau ei, in the same manner as, 2 Tim. 3. 8; Nehem. 5. 14

(2) *forming relatives;* as saei, he that, he who, who *(in fem.* soei, sei; *in neut.* thatei);

izei, who, which; izeei, who; ikei, I who; thuei, thou who *(dat.* thuzei; *acc.* thukei);

juzei, ye who; izwizei (οἷς), you to whom, Gal. 3. 1;

theei *or* th'ei, that;

thadei (ὅπου, ὅπου ἐὰν, οὗ), where;

thatainei, only;

tharei, where; thathroei (ἐξ οὗ), whence; thanei, that; *also* thizei, of whom; in thizei, wherefore; faur thizei, before;

thizeei, thaimei, thanei *(compounded of* thize, thaim, than and ei), *used as relatives;* also mithbanei, whilst that; swaei, as; sunsei, as soon as. *It is also used to begin dependent clauses, in the sense of* if, whether, *as in* Mk. 11. 13; 15. 44; Rom. 11. 14; 1 Cor. 1. 16; 7. 16; Phil. 3. 12.

EIS, they. *See* is.

EISARN, *str. sb. n.* iron; ei.ana fotum (πέδη), a fetter, Mk. 5. 4. *Der.* eisarna-bandi, eisarneins. [D. *ijzer;* G. *eisen.*]

EISARNA-BANDI, *str. sb. f.* an iron bond, Lu. 8. 29.
EISARNEINS, *adj.* iron, Mk. 5. 3.
EITHAN, therefore, *comp. of* ei *and* than; Jo. 9. 41; 1 Cor. 11. 27.

EIZEI, they that, they who, who, which; *comp. of* eis, they; *and* ei, that.
ETA*, *in* uz-eta, q. v.
ETJA*, *in* af-etja, q. v.
ETUM, we ate. *From* itan.

F.

F, the 22nd letter in the Gothic alphabet. As a numeral, it means 500. [Pronounce it as in English.]
FADAR, *str. sb. m. (gen.* fadrs: *dat.* fadr) a father, Gal. 4. 6. *Der.* fadreins, fadreina, fadrein.
FADREIN, *str. sb. n.* a family, Eph. 3. 15; *pl.* fadreina, parents, 2 Cor. 12. 14; Col. 3. 20.
FADREIN, *pl. sb.* parents, Lu. 8. 56; 18. 29; Jo. 9. 2, 3; &c. [*Strictly, it is the neut. sing. of* fadreins.]
FADREINS, *adj.* fatherly; *the neut.* fadrein *is used as a sb. See* fadrein.
FADREINS, *sb. f.* a family, Lu. 2. 4.
FAGINON, *vb. (with dat. or followed by* fram, ana, in), to rejoice; [*in imp.* fagino (χαῖρε), rejoice thou, hail! Lu. 1. 28;] Lu. 1. 14; 10. 20; 15. 5; &c. *Der.* mith-faginon, faheths. *Cf.* faihan. [E. *to be fain.*]
FAGRS, *adj.* fair, suitable, Lu. 14. 35. *Der.* un-fagrs, ga-fahrjan. *See* fahjan *and* faihan.
FAH*, *in* ga-fah, q. v.
FAHAN, *vb. (pt. t.* faifah; *pl.* faifahum; *pp.* fahans), *with acc.* to catch, take, apprehend as a criminal, Jo. 8. 20; 7. 44.

Der. gafahan, gafah(s). [G. *fahen;* A. S. *fôn.*]
FAHETHS, FAHEDS, *str. sb. f.* joy, Lu. 1. 14; 15. 7; Jo. 15. 11; 16. 24; &c. *Cf.* faginon.
FAHJAN*, *vb. in* fulla-fahjan, q. v.
FAHRJAN*, *in* ga-fahrjan, q. v.
FAIAN, *vb.* to treat as an enemy, to find fault with; hwa nauh faianda, why then are we blamed? Rom. 9. 19. *See* fijan.
FAIFAH, took. *From* fahan.
FAIFALTH, folded. *From* faltban.
FAIFLOKUM, we mourned. *From* flekan.
FAIH*, *in* bi-faih, q. v.
FAIHAN*, *vb. (pt. t.* fah; *pl.* febum; *pp.* faihans?), to suit (?). *Der.* bi-faih, bi-faihon, bi-faihons, ga-faihon; *and perhaps* fagrs, faheths, faginon. [G. *fügen.*]
FAIHON*, FAIHONS*; *in* bi-faihon, bi-faihons, ga-faihon, q. v.
FAIHU, *str. sb. n.* cattle, property; hence possessions, Mk. 10. 22, 23, 24; Lu. 18, 24; a fee, money, Mk. 14, 11. *Der.* faihu-gawaurki, faihu-thraihns, faihu-friks, faihu-gairns, faihu-geironjan, faihu-skula. [E. *fee;* G. *vieh;* D. *fooi.*]
FAIHU: *see Appendix.*
FAIHUS*, *adj.; in* filu-faibus, q. v.

FAIR —, *a verbal prefix, answering to the German* ver-, ent-; *cf.* fairra *and* fairnis. *See below.*

FAIR-AIHAN, *vb. with gen.* to partake of, 1 Cor. 10. 21.

FAIRAN*, *vb. (pt. t.* far; *pl.* ferum; *pp.* faurans), to accuse. *Cf.* fairins, fairina.

FAIR-GREIPAN, *vb.* to grip, catch hold of, Mk. 5. 41; 8. 23; Lu. 8. 54; 9. 47.

FAIRGUNI, *str. sb. n.* a mountain, Lu. 4. 29; Mat. 8. 1; Jo. 6. 3. *Cf.* bairgahei.

FAIR-HAITAN, *vb. refl.* to give thanks to, to thank; fairhaitis thu(s) thaggk, dost thou give thanks to, Lu. 17. 9; *where the 2nd person is used for the 3rd.*

FAIRHWJAN*, *in* wai-fairhwjan, q. v.

FAIRHWUS, *str. sb. m.* the world, Mk. 8. 36; Jo. 8. 23; 9. 5. [A. S. *feorh.*]

FAIRINA, *str. sb. f.* charge, accusation, Mat. 5. 32; Mk. 15. 26; Jo. 19. 6; a complaint, charge, Col. 3. 13. *Cf.* fairins. *Der.* fairinon.

FAIRINON, *vb.* to blame, accuse falsely, 2 Cor. 8. 20; Gal. 5. 15; 2 Tim. 3. 3. *Der.* ungafairinonds, un-gafairinoths, unfairinodaba.

FAIRINS*, *adj.* blameable; *only in comp.* un-fairins, us-fairins.

FAIR-LAISTJAN*, *vb., occurs in* unfairlaistiths, q. v.

FAIRNITHA, *str. sb. f.* oldness, antiquity, Rom. 7. 6.

FAIRNIS, *adj.* old, Mat. 9. 16; Mk. 2. 21; Lu. 5. 36; &c. *Der.* fairnitha. [A. S. *fyrn.*]

FAIRRA, *adv.* far; fairra wisan, *followed by dat.* to be far from, Lu. 14. 32; Mat. 8. 30; *also as a prep.* far from, from, Lu. 2. 37. *Der.* fairrathro.

FAIR-RINNAN, *vb.* to belong to, pertain to, befit, Eph. 5. 4; to reach towards, attain, 2 Cor. 10. 13, 14.

FAIR-WAURKJAN, *vb.* to work out for oneself, to obtain, acquire, 1 Tim. 3. 13.

FAIR-WEITJAN, *vb.* to be inquisitive *or* over-curious, 1 Tim. 5. 13; 2 Thess. 3. 11; to look upon intently, Lu. 4. 20.

FAIR-WEITL, *str. sb. n.* a spectacle, a show, 1 Cor. 4. 9. *See* weitan.

FAIRZNA, *str. sb. f.* the heel. Jo. 13. 18. [G. *ferse.*]

FALH, *pt. t.* of filhan, q. v.

FALTHABA*, *in* ain-falthaba, q. v. *Cf.* falthan.

FALTHAN, *vb. (pt. t.* faifalth; *pl.* faifaltbum; *pp.* falthans), to fold, fold *or* roll up, Lu. 4. 20. *Der.* ain-falths, ain-falthaba, ain-faltbei, fidur-falths, manag-falths, taihun-taihundfalths. [G. *falten;* E. *fold.*]

FALTHS*, *in* ain-falths; &c. *See* falthan.

FANA, *wk. sb. m.* a bit of cloth, a napkin, Lu. 19. 20; a patch, Mk. 2. 21. *Cf.* plat-fana, a patch, Mat. 9. 16.

FANI, *str. sb. n.* clay, mud, Jo. 9. 6, 11, 14. [O. E. *fen.*]

FANTH, found. *From* finthan.

FARAN, *vb. (p. t.* for; *pl.* forum; *pp.* farans), to fare, go, Lu. 10. 7. *Der.* farjan, at-farjan, usfartho.

FAREISAIUS, *str. sb. m.* a Pharisee, Lu. 18. 10; &c.

FARJAN, *vb.* to travel by ship, to sail, to row, Lu. 8. 23; Jo. 6. 19.

FARTHO*, *in* us-fartho, q. v.

FASKJA, *str. sb. m.* a bandage, Jo. 11. 44. [Lat. *fascia.*]

FASTAN, *vb. with acc.* to hold fast, observe, keep, Mk. 7. 9; Jo.

8. 51; to keep, reserve, Jo. 12. 7; to keep, preserve, Phil. 4. 7. *Der.* ga-fastan, witodafasteis, fastubni.

FASTAN, *vb.* to fast, Mat. 6. 16; Mk. 2. 18; Lu. 5. 33.

FASTUBNI, *sb. n.*, or FASTUBNJA, *f.* (ἐθελοθρησκεία), *sb. f.* observance, "will-worship" (A. V.), Col. 2. 23; observance, right keeping, 1 Cor. 7. 19; (2) fasting, Mat 9. 29; Lu. 2. 37.

FATHA, *str. sb. f.* a hedge, Mk. 12. 1; Lu. 14. 23; Eph. 2. 14.

FATHS*, *str. sb. m.* (*gen.* fadis; *pl.* fadeis), a leader, chief. *See the derived words. Der.* bundafaths, thusundi-faths, bruthfaths, synagoga-faths.

FAUHO, *wk. sb. f.* a fox, Mat. 8. 20; Lu. 9. 58.

FAUR, *prep. with acc.* for, before, to, along (παρά, *with acc.*); (πρό, ὑπέρ, *with gen.*); *also as an adv.* forward, forth, Mk. 8. 6; Lu. 19. 4; faurthis, faurthizei, before, before that, first. *Prefixed to many verbs, as seen below.*

FAURA, *prep. with dat.* (ἔμπροσθεν, ἐνώπιον, ἐναντίον), before, for, because of; (κατὰ *with acc.*), (παρὰ, ἀπὸ, διὰ *with acc.*), Mat. 6. 2; Col. 1. 17; Mk. 2. 4; *also as an adv.* (ἔμπροσθεν, πρότερον), before, Phil. 3. 14; Lu. 14. 24. *Prefixed to many subs. and verbs, as seen below.*

FAURA-DAURI, *str. sb. n.* the part of a street before the towngate, Lu. 10. 10.

FAURA-DUSTODJAN, *vb.* to begin beforehand, 2 Cor. 8. 6.

FAURA-FAURSNIWAN, *vb.* to go before, to be current beforehand, 1 Tim. 1. 18.

FAURA-FILLI, *str. sb. n.* uncircumcision, Gal. 5. 6; 6. 15; Col. 3. 11; 1 Cor. 7. 18. *See* fill.

FAURA-FRAWAUREJAN, *vb.* to sin formerly, 2 Cor. 12. 21; 13. 2.

FAURA-GAGGA, *wk. sb. m.* a steward (*lit.* a fore-goer), Gal. 4. 2. *See* faura-gaggja.

FAURA-GAGGAN, *vb.* to go before, Mk. 11. 9; Lu. 1. 76; 18. 39; to rule over, 1 Tim. 3. 5.

FAURA-GAGGI, *str. sb. n.* stewardship, Lu. 16. 2, 3, 4; dispensation, Eph. 1. 10; 3. 9.

FAURA-GAGGJA, *wk. sb. m.* a steward, Lu. 16. 2; 8. 3; Rom. 16. 23; Tit. 1. 7.

FAURA-GAHAITAN, *vb.* to announce beforehand, promise before, 2 Cor. 9. 5.

FAURA-GAHUGJAN, *vb.* to think beforehand, fore-determine, purpose, 2 Cor. 9. 7.

FAURA-GALEIKAN, *vb.* to please beforehand, Eph. 1. 9. [*The reading of the MS. See M.'s note.*]

FAURA-GAMANWJAN, *vb.* to prepare beforehand, Rom. 9. 23; Eph. 2. 10; 2 Cor. 9. 5.

FAURA-GAMELJAN, *vb.* to write beforehand, Rom. 15. 4; Eph. 3. 3.

FAURA-GAREDAN, *vb.* to predestine, Eph. 1. 5, 11.

FAURA-GASANDJAN, *vb.* to send beforehand, 2 Cor. 9. 3.

FAURA-GASATJAN, *vb.* to present, 2 Cor. 4. 14.

FAURA-GATEIHAN, *vb.* to inform beforehand, Mk. 13. 23; 2 Cor. 13. 2.

FAURA-HAH, *str. sb. n.* that which hangs before, a curtain, veil, Mk. 15. 38. *Cf.* faur-hah.

FAURA-HAITANS, *p. pt.* invited, Lu. 14. 24.

FAURA-KWIMAN, *vb.* to come or go before, Lu. 1. 17.

FAURA-KWITHAN, *vb.* to prophesy, Mat. 11. 13; to tell beforehand, Rom. 9. 29; 2 Cor. 13. 2; 1 Thess. 3. 4; 4. 6.
FAURA-MANWJAN, *vb. act.* to prepare beforehand, Skeir. 4. 8.
FAURA-MATHLEIS, *str. sb. m.* a chief speaker; *hence* a ruler, prince, Mat. 9. 34; Lu. 8. 41, 49; 19. 2.
FAURA-MATHLI, *str. sb. n.* chief office; blaif faura-mathli, the allowance of food proper to the office of a governor, Nehem. 5. 14, 18.
FAURA-MELJAN, *vb.* to write beforehand, describe, Gal. 3. 1.
FAURA-RAHNJAN, *vb.* to prefer, set another before oneself, Rom. 12. 10.
FAURA-STANDAN, *vb.* to stand before; *hence*, to rule, govern, Rom. 12. 8; to stand near, Mk. 14. 69; Lu. 19. 24.
FAURA-TANI, *str. sb. n.* a sign, wonder, Mk. 13. 22; Jo. 6. 26; 2 Cor. 12. 12.
FAURA-WENJAN, *vb.* to put one's hope in beforehand, Eph. 1. 12.
FAURA-WISAN, *vb.* to be forward, ready, 2 Cor. 8. 11.
FAUR-BAUHTS, *str. sb. f.* redemption, Eph. 1. 7, 14; Col. 1. 14. *From* bugjan.
FAUR-BIGAGGAN, *vb.* to go before, precede, Mk. 10. 32; 16. 7.
FAUR-BISNIWAN, *vb.* to hasten on before, go before, 1 Tim. 5. 24.
FAUR-BITHRAGJAN, *vb.* to run on before, Lu. 19. 4.
FAUR-BIUDAN, *vb.* to command, Lu. 8. 25; to forbid, command not to do, Mk. 6. 8; 8. 30; Lu. 5. 14; 8. 56; 9. 21.
FAUR-DAMMJAN, *vb.* to shut off as with a dam, to stop up, 2 Cor. 11. 10.
FAURDS*, *in* ga-faurds, q. v.
FAUR-GAGGAN, *vb.* to go by, pass by, Mk. 11. 20; 15. 29; Lu. 18. 36.
FAUR-HAH, *str. sb. n.*, the same as faura-hah, q. v. Mat. 27. 51.
FAUHRTEI, *wk. sb. f.* fright, fear, astonishment, Mk. 5. 42; 2 Tim. 1. 7.
FAUHRTJAN, *vb.* to be frightened, to fear, Mk. 5. 36; Lu. 8. 50; 9. 34; Jo. 14. 27.
FAURHTS, *adj.* fearful, Mk. 4. 40; faurhts wairthan, to be afraid, Mk. 10. 32, *Der.* guda-fauhrts, fauhrtei, faurhtjan.
FAUR-KWITHAN, *vb.* to gainsay, frustrate, Gal. 2. 21; to make excuse, Lu. 14. 18.
FAUR-LAGEINS, *str. sb. f.* a setting or laying forth; *hence* hlaibos faur-lageins, shew-bread, Mk. 2. 26; Lu. 6. 4.
FAUR-LAGJAN, *vb.* to lay *or* set before, Lu. 9. 16; 10. 8; 1 Cor. 10. 27.
FAUR-MULJAN, *vb.* to bind up one's mouth, muzzle, 1 Cor. 9. 9. *See* mul.
FAUR-RINNAN, *vb.* to run before; faurrinnand, a fore-runner, Skeir. 3. 11.
FAURS*, *in* ga-faurs *and* un-faurs, q. v.
FAUR-SIGLJAN, *vb.* to set a seal upon, to seal, Mat. 27. 66.
FAUR-SNIWAN, *vb.* to hasten before, anticipate, 1 Cor. 11. 21; Mk. 14. 8; *with prep.* faura, to go before, 1 Tim. 1. 18.
FAUR-STASSEIS, *str. sb. m.* one that stands before, a ruler, 1 Thess. 5. 12.
FAUR-THIS, *adv.* first of all, be-

foreband, before, Mk. 3. 27; 9. 11.

FAUR-THIZEI, FAURTHIZE, *adv.* before that, before, Mat. 6. 8; Mk. 14. 72.

FAUR-WAIPJAN, *vb.* to bind up; faur-waipjan munth, to muzzle, 1 Tim. 5. 18.

FAUR-WALWJAN, *vb.* to roll before, Mat. 27. 60.

FAUR-WEIS*, *in* un-faurweis, q. v.

FAUS, FAWS, *adj.* few (*gen. with pl. nouns*), Mat. 7. 14; 9. 37; Mk. 6. 5; 8. 7; du fawamma, a little, 1 Tim. 4. 8; *comp.* fawiza; *in phrase* fawizo (haban), (ἐλαττονεῖν), to have lack, to lack, come short in, 2 Cor. 8. 15.

FEHABA*, *in* ga-fehaba, q. v.

FEHS*, *in* ga-fehs, q. v.

FEIAN*, *vb.* (*pt. t.* fai; *pl.* fijum; *pp.* fijans?) to hate? *Cf.* faian, fijan, *and* feinan.

FEINAN*, *vb. in* in-feinan, q. v.

FERA, *str. sb. f.* a country, region, coast, Mk. 8. 10; Mat. 25. 41; Gal. 1. 21; Eph. 4. 16.

FERJA, *wk. sb. m.* a spy, Lu. 20. 20. *Cf.* fairinon.

FETEINS*, *str. sb. f. in* ga-feteins, q. v.

FETJAN, *vb.* to adorn, deck; fetjan sik, to adorn oneself, 1 Tim. 2. 9. *Der.* ga-feteins. *Cf.* fitan.

FIAN, *vb.*, *another form of* fijan, *vb.* to hate, Jo. 12. 25. *See* fijan.

FIANDS, *the same as* fijands, q. v.

FIATHWA, *the same as* fijathwa, q. v.

FIDUR-DOGS, *adj.* on the fourth day; *hence* four days dead, Jo. 11. 39.

FIDUR-FALTHS, *adj.* four-fold, Lu. 19. 8.

FIDUR-RAGINEIS, *str. sb. m.* a tetrarch, Lu. 3. 1. *From* fidur *and* ragineis.

FIDWOR (*dat.* fidworim), four, Mk. 2. 3, 13. 27; Lu. 2. 37; Jo. 11. 17; *in comp.* fidur-dogs, fidur-falths, fidur-ragineis; fidwor-tigjus, fidwor-taihun.

FIDWOR-TAIHUN, fourteen, Gal. 2. 1.

FIDWOR-TIGJUS, forty, Mk. 1. 13; Lu. 4. 2; 2 Cor. 11. 24.

FIF, five, 1 Cor. 15. 6. *Another spelling of* fimf, q. v.

FIGGRA-GULTH, *str. sb. n.* a finger-ring, Lu. 15. 22. *From* figgrs *and* gulth.

FIGGRS, *str. sb. m.* a finger, Mk. 7. 33.

FIJAN, *vb.* (*also* FIAN, Jo. 12. 25); *with acc.* to hate, Mat. 6. 24; Lu. 14. 26; 16. 13; &c. *Der.* fijands, fijathwa.

FIJANDS, FIANDS, *sb. m.* (*pres. p. t. of* fijan), an enemy, Mat. 5. 43; 6. 24; &c. [G. *feind;* E. *fiend.*]

FIJATHWA, FIATHWA, *str. sb. f.* hatred, Eph. 2. 15, 16; Gal. 5. 20.

FILAU, FILAUS, *adv.* much. *See* filu.

FILEGRI. *See* filigri.

FILH*, *str. sb. n.*, *in* ga-filh, ana-filh, us-filh.

FILHAN, *vb.* (*pt. t.* falh; *pl.* fulhum; *pp.* fulhans), *with acc.* to hide, conceal, 1 Tim. 5. 25; to bury, Mat. 8. 22. *Der.* ga-filhan, af-filhan, ana-filhan, us-filhan; ana-filh, ga-filh, us-filh; filigri, ga-fulgins, fulhsni.

FILIGRI, *str. sb. n.* (*also* filegri), a hidden place, a cave, den, Mk. 11. 17; Lu. 19. 46. *From* filhan.

FILL*, *str. sb. n.* a skin, a hide. [O. E. *fell;* G. *fell.*] *Der.* thruts-fill, thruts-fills, faura-filli, filleins.

3*

FILLEINS, *adj.* made of skin, leathern, Mk. 1. 6.

FILM(s)*, *sb.* fear? [O. N. *felmr?*] *Der.* us-filma, us-filmei.

FILU(s), *adj.* much; *also* filu, *adv.* much; *in phrases* afar ni filu, not long after; *and* ufar filu, overmuch, 2 Cor. 1. 5; 12. 11. *It is generally used in the neuter* filu, *and often followed by gen. case of sb.* See Lu. 9. 37; Jo. 6. 2, *where the vb. is in sing.*; *and* Mk. 3. 7; 5. 21; *where the vb. is in pl.* Mais filu, *or* filu mais, much more, Lu. 18. 39; 2 Cor. 3. 9. *Der.* filu-deisei, filu-waurdei, filu-waurdjan, filu-faihus, filu-galaubs, filusna, filaus.

FILU-DEISEI, *wk. sb. f.* subtlety, 2 Cor. 11. 3; Eph. 4. 14.

FILU-FAIHUS, *adj.* manifold, Eph. 3. 10.

FILU-GALAUBS, *adj.* very precious, Jo. 12. 3. *From* liubs.

FILUSNA, *str. sb. f.* excess, magnitude, 2 Cor 12. 7; du filusnai, to excess, still further, 2 Tim. 3. 9; multitude, Neh. 5. 18.

FILU-WAURDEI, *wk. sb. f.* much speaking, Mat. 6. 7.

FILU-WAURDJAN, *vb.* to use many words, Mat. 6. 7.

FIM (*for* fimf), five, Lu. 16. 6. *See* fimf.

FIMF, five (*we find* fim *in* Lu. 16. 6; *and* fif *in* 1 Cor. 15. 6), Mk. 8. 19; Lu. 1. 24; 9. 13; &c. *Der.* fimf-tigjus, fimf-hunda, fimf-taihun.

FIMF-HUNDA, five hundred, 1 Cor. 15. 6.

FIMF-TAIHUN, fifteen, Jo. 11. 18.

FIMF-TIGJUS, fifty, Lu. 7. 41; 9. 14; Jo. 8. 57.

FINTHAN, *vb. with acc. (pt. t.* fanth; *pl.* funthum; *pp.* funthans), to find out, know, Mk. 5. 43; 15. 45; Lu. 9. 11; Jo. 12. 9.

FISKON, *vb.* to fish, Lu. 5. 4; *from* fisks.

FISKJA, *wk. sb. m.* a fisher, Mk. 1. 16; Lu. 5. 2. *From* fisks.

FISKS, *str. sb. m.* a fish, Mk. 8. 7; Lu. 5. 6; 9. 13. *Der.* fiskja, fiskon.

FITAN, *vb. (pt. t.* fat; *pl.* fetum; *pp.* fitans), to travail in birth with, Gal. 4. 19; *intr.* to travail, Gal. 4. 27.

FLAHTA, *or* FLAHTO, *sb. f.* a plaiting of the hair, 1 Tim. 2. 9. [G. *flechte.*]

FLAIHTAN*, *vb. (pt. t.* flaht; *pl.* flauhtum; *pp.* flauhtans), to weave. *Der.* flahta. [Gk. πλέκειν; Lat. *flectere*; G. *flechten*; Engl. *plait*]

FLAUTAN, *vb. (pt. t.* fai-flaut?), to boast; *hence pres. pt.* flautands, vain-glorious, boasting arrogantly, desirous of vainglory, Gal. 5. 26. *Der.* flautjan.

FLAUTJAN, *vb.* to vaunt oneself, 1 Cor. 13. 4. *Cf.* flautan. [Engl. *flout* (?)]

FLEKAN, *vb. with acc. (pt. t.* fai-flok; *pl.* faiflokum; *pp.* flekans), to lament, Lu. 8. 52.

FLODUS, *str. sb. f.* a flood, river, stream, Lu 6. 49. *Cf.* ahwa, garunjo, midjasweipains.

FODEINS, *str. sb. f.* food, Mat. 6. 25; luxurious feeding, Lu. 7. 25.

FODJAN, *vb. with acc.* to feed, Mat. 6. 26; Lu. 4. 16; 1 Tim. 5. 10. *Der.* fodeins, us-fodeins.

FODR, *str. sb. n.* a sheath, Jo. 18. 11. [G. *futter.*]

FON, *str. sb. n. (gen.* funins; *dat.* funin), fire, Mk. 9. 22; Lu. 3. 9; 9. 54; &c. *Der.* funisks.

FOR, fared (*pt. t. of* faran), q. v.

FOTUS, *str. sb. m.* the foot, Mat. 5. 35; Mk. 5. 4; &c. *Der.* fotu-bandi, fotu-baurd.

FOTU-BANDI, *str. sb. f.* a fetter, Lu. 8. 29.

FOTU-BAURD, *str. sb. n.* a footboard, footstool, Mat. 5. 35; Mk. 12. 36; Lu. 20. 43.

FRA —, *a prefix of verbs, equiv. to* Germ. *ver-*, Engl. *for-*, *giving the verbs an intensive and often a destructive force. See below. Prefixed also to nouns.*

FRA-AT; *from* fra-itan, q. v.

FRA-ATJAN, *vb.* to give away in food, 1 Cor. 13. 3. *From* fraitan.

FRA-BAIRAN, *vb.* to bear, endure, Jo. 16. 12.

FRA-BUGJAN, *vb.* to sell, Mk. 14. 5; Jo. 12. 5; &c.

FRA-DAILJAN, *vb.* to deal away, to give away, Jo. 12. 5.

FRAGAN (?), *vb.* to ask, examine, 2 Cor. 13. 5: (fraisith, fragith, *are MS. readings; we should expect* fraihnith, *from* fraihnan).

FRA-GIBAN, *vb.* to give, grant, Mk. 10. 37; Jo. 10. 29; &c.

FRA-GIBTS, FRA-GIFTS, *str. sb. f.* promise, gift, Skeir. 3. 19; espousal, Lu. 1. 27; 2. 5.

FRA-GILDAN, *vb.* to restore, pay back, Lu. 19. 8; Rom. 11. 35; 12. 19.

FRAH, asked. *From* fraihnan.

FRA-HINTHAN, *vb.* to take captive, Rom. 7. 23; 2 Cor. 10. 5; 2 Tim. 3. 6; *hence pp.* frabunthans, a captive, Lu. 4. 19.

FRAIHANS, *pp. of* fraihnan.

FRAIHNAN, *vb.* (*pt. t.* frah; *pl.* frebum; *pp.* fraihans), *with an acc.* to ask, Mk. 5. 9; 8. 23; 12. 28; &c. *Der.* ga-fraihnan. [G. *fragen*; D. *vragen.*]

FRAISAN, *vb. with acc.* (*pt. t.* faifrais; *pl.* faifraisum; *pp.* fraisans), to tempt, Mk. 12. 15; Lu. 4. 2; 20. 23; &c. *Der.* usfraisan, fraistubni.

FRAISTUBNI, *str. sb. f.* temptation, Lu. 4. 13; briggan in fraistubni, to lead into temptation, Mat. 6. 13.

FRA-ITAN, *vb.*, to eat up, devour, Mk. 4. 4; Lu. 8. 5; 15. 30.

FRAIW, *str. sb. n.* seed, Mk. 4. 3, 26, 27; Lu. 8. 5; &c. *Cf.* kuni.

FRA-KUNNAN, *vb.* to despise, Mat. 6. 24; Lu. 16. 13; 18. 9; &c.

FRA-KWIMAN, *vb.* to expend, spend, Mk. 5. 26; Lu. 8. 43; 9. 54.

FRA-KWISTEINS, *str. sb. f.* waste, Mk. 14. 4.

FRA-KWISTJAN, *vb.* to destroy, Mat. 10. 39; Mk. 8. 35; &c.

FRA-KWISTNAN, *vb.* to be destroyed, to perish, Lu. 15. 17; Jo. 10. 28; &c.

FRA-KWITHAN, *vb.* to declare against, despise, Lu. 7. 30; to curse, Lu. 6. 28; Jo. 7. 49.

FRA-LETAN, *vb.* to let go, release, Mat. 27. 15; Mk. 8. 9; 15. 6; &c.; to remit, forgive, Lu. 7. 47; to let down, Mk. 2. 4.

FRA-LETS, *str. sb. m.* (1) remission, forgiveness, Mk. 3. 29; Lu. 3. 3; 4. 19; (2) a freed man, 1 Cor. 7. 22.

FRA-LIUSAN, *vb.* to loose, Lu. 15. 8; 19. 10; Jo. 6. 27. [G. *verlieren*; D. *verliezen.*]

FRA-LUSNAN, *vb.* to be lost, to perish, 1 Cor. 1. 18; 2 Cor. 4. 3.

FRA-LUSTS, *str. sb. m.* destruction, Rom. 9. 22; 1 Thess. 5. 3; 2 Thess. 1. 9; Jo. 17. 12. [G. *verlust.*]

FRAM, *prep. with dat.* from (ἀπό); since, by (ὑπό). *The compound words are few, viz.* fram-aldrs, fram-gahts, fram-wairthis, fram-wigis. *Der.* framis, framath(e)is, framathjan.

FRAM-ALDRS, *adj.* very old, Lu. 1. 8, 18; 2. 36.

FRAMATHEIS, *adj.* foreign, strange, Jo. 10. 5; alien, Eph. 4. 18; not one's own, Lu. 16. 12; Rom. 14. 4; 2 Cor. 10. 15; 1 Tim. 5. 22. [G. *fremde*; D. *vreemd.*]

FRAMATHJAN, *vb.* to alienate, estrange, Col. 1. 21.

FRAM-GAHTS, *str. sb. f.* progress, advancement, furtherance, Ph. 1. 25.

FRAMIS, *adv.* further, onward, Mk. 1. 19; Rom. 13. 12.

FRAM-WAIRTHIS, *adv.* further on; *only in phrase* thu fr. wisais, continue thou, 2 Tim. 3. 14.

FRAM-WIGIS, *adv.* continually, evermore, Jo. 6. 34; 1 Thess. 4. 17.

FRA-NIMAN, *vb.* to take, receive, Lu. 19. 12; Jo. 14. 3.

FRA-RINNAN, *vb.* to run among, fall among, Lu. 10. 30.

FRA-SLINDAN, *vb.* to swallow up, 2 Cor. 5. 4. [G. *verschlingen.*]

FRASTI-SIBJA (υἰοθεσία), *str. sb. f.* adoption as sons, Rom. 9. 4. *From* frasts *and* sibis.

FRASTS (*pl.* frasteis), *str. sb. m.* a child, 2 Cor. 6. 13. *Der.* frastisibja. *Cf.* barn.

FRAT, ate. *From* fra-itan, q. v.

FRATHI, *wk. sb. n.* understanding, mind, Mk. 12, 33; Rom. 11. 34; 12. 2; &c. *Cf.* frathjan.

FRATHJA-MARZEINS, *str. sb. f.* a deceiving, a deceit, Gal. 6. 3.

FRATHJAN, *vb.* (*pt. t.* froth; *pl.* frothum; *pp.* frathans), to perceive, know, think, understand, Mk. 7. 18; 12. 12; Lu. 2. 50; 8. 10; &c.;
    mais frathjan (ὑπερφρονεῖν), to think more highly, Rom. 12. 3; waila frathjan, to think well *or* soberly, Rom. 12. 3. *Der.* un-frathjands, fulla-frathjan, frathi, frathja-marzeins, frath-(j)is, grinda-frathjis, sama-frathjis, ga-frathjei, froths, un-froths, frodaba, frodei, un-frodei.

FRATH(J)IS*, *adj.* thinking; *only in comp.* grinda-frathis, sama-frathis.

FRAT(H)WJAN*, *vb. in comp.* usfratwjan, q. v.

FRAUJA, *wk. sb. m.* lord, master, Lu. 1. 25; 14. 23; 16. 3; &c. *Der.* heiwa-frauja, leika-frauja, fraujinon, ga-fraujinon, fraujinassus. [A. S. *freá.*]

FRAUJINASSUS, *str. sb. m.* lordship, Col. 1. 16; Eph. 1. 21.

FRAUJINON, *vb.* to rule over, Rom. 7. 1; 14. 9.

FRA-WAIRPAN, *vb.* to cast away, Mat. 9. 36; Mk. 9. 42. [G. *verwerfen.*]

FRA-WAIRTHAN, *vb.* to destroy, corrupt, 2 Tim. 3. 8.

FRA-WARDEINS, *str. sb. f.* destruction, 1 Tim. 6. 9.

FRA-WARDJAN, *vb.* to corrupt, 2 Cor. 4. 16; 1 Tim. 6. 5; to disfigure, Mat. 6. 16.

FRA-WAURHTS, *str. sb. m. or adj.* a sinner, sinful man, Mat. 9. 10; Mk. 2. 17; 14. 41; &c.

FRA-WAURHTS, *str. sb. f.* evil working, evil-doing, sin, Mk. 3. 28; 4. 12; Lu. 5. 20, 23; &c.

FRA-WAURKJAN, *vb.* to work ill, to sin, Lu. 15. 21; 17. 4; *refl.* to sin, Mat. 27. 4; Lu. 15. 18; &c.

FRA-WEIT, *str. sb. n.* revenge, vengeance, 2 Cor. 7. 11; 2 Thess. 1. 8, 9; Rom. 12. 19.

FRA-WEITAN, *vb.* to avenge, Lu. 18. 3, 5; Rom. 13. 4; 2 Cor. 10. 6; 1 Thess. 4. 6.

FRA-WILWAN, *vb.* to seize, catch, Lu. 8. 29; Jo. 10. 12; to snatch away, Jo. 10. 28, 29; to catch, snatch, 2 Cor. 12. 2, 4.

FRA-WISAN, *vb. with dat.* to spend, consume, Lu. 15. 14.

FRA-WRIKAN, *vb.* to persecute, 1 Thess. 2. 15.

FRA-WROHJAN, *vb.* to accuse, Lu. 16. 1.

FREHUM, we asked. *From* fraihnan.

FREIDEINS*, *str. sb. f., only in comp.* ga-freideins, un-freideins, q. v.

FREIDJAN, *vb.* to spare, Rom. 11. 21; 1 Cor. 7. 28; 2 Cor. 1. 23; 12. 6; 13. 2. *Der.* ga-freideins, un-freideins.

FREIHALS, FREIJHALS, *str. sb. m.*, freedom (*lit.* a free neck), Gal. 2. 4; 5. 1, 13; Eph. 3. 12. *From* freis *and* hals.

FREIS, *adj.* (*fem.* freija; *neut.* freijata), *sometimes followed by a gen.*, free, Jo. 8. 32; Gal. 4. 22; 5. 1; &c.; freijana briggan, to set free, make free, Jo. 8. 32. *Der.* frei(j)hals, frijei, frijon. [G. *frei*; E. *free*; D. *vrij*.]

FRETUM, we ate. *From* fra-itan, q. v.

FRI—, *a prefix. Cf.* fra-. *It occurs in* fri-sahts, gafri-sahtjan, gafri-sahtnan.

FRIATHWA: *see* frijathwa.

FRIATHWA-MILDS, *adj.* kindly affectioned, Rom. 12. 10. *From* frijon.

FRIJATHWA, *str. sb. f.* love, Jo. 13. 35; 15. 9; 17. 26.

FRIJEI, *wk. sb. f.* freedom, 1 Cor. 10. 29. *From* freis.

FRIJON, *vb. with acc.* to love, Mat. 6. 24; 10. 37; Mk. 12. 30; &c. *Der.* frijonds, frijondi, frijons, ga-frijons, frijathwa, friathwa-milds.

FRIJONDI, *str. sb. f.* a female friend, Lu. 15. 9.

FRIJONDS, *str. sb. m.* a friend (*pl.* frijonds), Mat. 5. 47; 11. 19; Lu. 7. 6; &c. [G. *freund*; D. *vriend*.]

FRIJONS, *str. sb. f.* a token of love, a kiss, 1 Cor. 16. 20; 2 Cor. 13. 12.

FRIKEI*, *in* faihu-frikei, q. v.

FRIKS*, *adj.* greedy, *only in* faihufriks. [G. *frech*; D. *vrek*.]

FRI-SAHTJAN*, *vb. in comp.* ga-frisahtjan, q. v.

FRI-SAHTS, *str. sb. f.* a likeness, image, 1 Cor. 15. 49; 2 Cor. 3. 18; an example, Jo. 13. 15; 1 Tim. 1. 16; in frisahtai, enigmatically, 1 Cor. 13. 12.

FRITHA-REIKS (Frederick), a proper name in the Gothic calendar.

FRITHON*, *vb. in comp.* ga-frithon, q. v.

FRITHONS*, *str. sb. f., in* ga-frithons, q. v.

FRITHUS(?)*, *str. sb. m.* peace. *Der.* sunjai-frithas, fritha-reiks, ga-frithon, ga-frithons. [*Cf.* G. *friede*.]

FRIUS, *str. sb. n.* frost, cold, 2 Cor. 11. 27.

FRODABA, *adv.* wisely, Mk. 12. 34; Lu. 16. 8. *From* frods.

FRODEI, *wk. sb. f.* wisdom, understanding, Lu. 1. 17; 2. 52; 1 Cor. 1. 19; &c.

FRODOZA, *comp. of* froths; *adj.* wiser, Lu. 16. 8.

FRODS, FROTHS, *adj.* wise, Mat. 7. 24; Lu. 10. 21; 16. 8; &c.

FRUMA, *adj.* the first, first (*fem.* frumei), Mk. 15. 42; Lu. 6. 1; Jo. 15. 18; anthar fruma ($δευτερόπρωτος$), Lu. 6. 1; fruma sabbato, first day of the week, Mk. 16. 9; fruma giban, to give first to one, Rom. 11. 35. *Der.* frumists, frumist, frumisto, frumisti, frumadei, frums.

FRUMA-BAUR, *str. sb. m.* a firstborn, Lu. 2. 7; Col. 1. 15.

FRUMADEI, *wk. sb. f.* pre-eminence, Col. 1. 18.
FRUMIST, *adv.* first, Mat. 8. 21; Mk. 4. 28; 16. 9; &c.
FRUMISTI, *str. sb. n.* beginning, Jo. 6. 24; 8. 44; 1 Cor. 15. 3.
FRUMISTO, *wk. sb. n.* beginning, Lu. 1. 2.
FRUMISTS, *superl. of* fruma, *adj.* first, Mk. 9. 35; 10. 44; 12. 28.
FRUMS, *str. sb. m.* beginning, Jo. 15. 27; 16. 4.
FUGLS, *str. sb. m.* a fowl, a bird, Mat. 6. 26; 8. 20; Mk. 4. 4, 32; Lu. 8. 5; 9. 58. [G. *vogel.*]
FULA, *wk. sb. m.* a foal, Mk. 11. 2; Lu. 19. 30; Jo. 12. 15.
FULGINS*, *in* ga-fulgins, q. v.
FULHANS, hidden; *pp. of* filhan, q.v.
FULHSNI, *str. sb. n.* that which is hidden, secrecy, Mat. 6. 4, 6, 18.
FULLA-FAHJAN, *vb.* to satisfy, Mk. 15. 15; to serve, Lu. 4. 8.
FULLA-FRATHJAN, *vb.* to be sober, 2 Cor. 5. 13.
FULLA-TOJIS, *adj.* perfect, Mat. 5. 48. *From* taujan.
FULLA-WEIS, *adj.* arrived at the full wisdom of manhood, 1 Cor. 14. 20.
FULLA-WEISJAN, *vb.* to inform fully, to persuade, 2 Cor. 5. 11.
FULLA-WITS, *adj.* perfect, Phil. 3. 15; Col. 1. 28; 4. 12.
FULLEI*, *wk. sb. f.* fulness; *in* ufar-fullei, q. v.

FULLEINS*, *str. sb. f.* fulness, *in* us-fulleins, q. v.
FULLEITHS, *sb. f.* fulness, Mk. 4. 28.
FULLITH (?), *sb. n.*; *only in gen. pl.* fullithe (νουμηνίας), Col. 2. 16; *where* fullith = *full* moon rather than *new* moon.
FULLJAN, *vb.* to fill, Mat. 27. 48; Rom. 15. 13; 2 Thess. 1. 11. *See* fulls.
FULLNAN, *vb.* to be full, Lu. 2. 40; Eph. 3. 19; 5. 18; Col. 1. 9.
FULLO, *wk. sb. f.* fulness, Mat. 9. 16; Mk. 2. 21; Rom. 11. 12, 25.
FULLS, *adj.* full; *often followed by gen.* Lu. 4. 28; 5. 26; perfect, Eph. 4. 13. *Der.* ufar-fulls, ufar-fullei, fullo, fulleiths, fullith, fulla-tojis, fulla-weis, fulla-weisjan, fulla-wits, fulla-fahjan, fulla-frathjan, fulljan, ga-fulljan, us-fulljan, ufar-fulljan, fullnan, ga-fullnan, us-fullnan, us-fulleins. [Germ. *voll*; D. *vol*; E. *full.*]
FULS, *adj.* foul; fuls ist, be stinketh, Jo. 11. 39. [G. *faul*; D. *vuil*; E. *foul.*]
FUNA, FUNINS, FUNIN. *See* fon.
FUNISKS, *adj.* fiery, Eph. 6. 16.
FUNTHANS, found; *pp. of* finthan.
FUNTHUM, we found; *see* finthan.
FYNIKISKA (φοινίσσα), *adj.* Phœnician, Mk. 7. 26.

G.

G, the third letter in the Gothic alphabet. As a numeral: 3; *pronounced hard*. [For words, as *ga-bairan*, beginning with *ga-*, see under the simple forms *bairan*, &c., for further information.]
GA—, a prefix to verbs, substantives, and adjectives, of very common occurrence; it is found

doubled, as in *ga-ga-wairth-jan*, &c., and sometimes separated from the word to which it belongs by a particle, as in *ga-u-hwasehwi*. [*Cf.* A. S. *and* G. *ge-;* Lat. *con-*.]

GA-AGGWEI(NS), *sb. f.* constraint, restraint, Skeir. 1. 18, 27. *From* aggwus.

GA-AGGWJAN, *vb.* to constrain, distress greatly, 2 Cor. 4. 8. *From* aggwus.

GA-AGGWO, *adv.* assuredly(?), 1 Thess. 5. 2. [*So in* MS., *but the reading* glaggwo *has been proposed.*]

GA-AIGINON, *vb.* to make a gain of, get an advantage over, 2 Cor. 2. 11.

GA-AINANAN, *vb.* to leave alone, desert, 1 Thess. 2. 17. [*Perhaps* ga-ainanadai *should be* ga-ainadai, *and the verb* ga-ainan.]

GA-AISTAN, *vb.* to reverence, respect, Mk. 12. 6.

GA-AIWISKON, *vb.* to make ashamed, to shame, 1 Cor. 11. 22; 2 Cor. 7. 14: 9. 4; to maltreat, Mk. 12. 4.

GA-ANDIDA: *see* ga-nanthjan.

GA-ARBJA, *wk. sb. m.* a fellow-heir, Eph. 3. 6.

GA-ARMAN, *vb. with acc.* to have pity on, pity, Mk. 5. 19; Rom. 11. 30; 1 Cor. 7. 25; 2 Cor. 4. 1.

GA-AUKAN, *vb.* to increase, abound, 1 Thess. 4. 1.

GA-BAIDJAN, *vb.* to compel, 2 Cor. 12. 11.

GA-BAIRAN, *vb.* to bear (children), Lu. 1. 31, 57; *pass.* to be born, Jo. 9. 2; Lu. 2. 11; to engender, 2 Tim. 2. 23; to compare, Mk. 4. 30.

GA-BAIRGAN, *vb.* to keep, preserve, Mat. 9. 17.

GA-BAIRHTEI, *wk. sb. f.* a making bright, a manifestation, 2 Tim. 1. 10.

GA-BAIRHTJAN, *vb.* to make bright *or* clear, to manifest, Mk. 4. 22; to give light to, Lu. 1. 79; *pass.* to be made manifest, 1 Tim. 3. 16; Gal. 4. 19; 2 Cor. 11. 6.

GA-BANDWJAN, *vb.* to make signs, Lu. 1. 62; to point out, signify, shew, Skeir. 6. 16.

GA-BATNAN, *vb.* to profit, boot, benefit, Mk. 7. 11.

GA-BAUAN, *vb.* to make *or* to build nests, to dwell, Mk. 4. 32.

GA-BAUR, *str. sb. n.* tribute, Rom. 13. 7; collection of money, 1 Cor. 16. 1, 2. *From* bairan.

GA-BAURGJA, *wk. sb. m.* a fellow-citizen, Eph. 2. 19.

GA-BAURJABA, *adv.* with pleasure, willingly, gladly, Mk. 6. 20; 12. 37; 2 Cor. 12. 9, 15; heartily, gladly, Mk. 14. 65; *not expressed in the Greek.*

GA-BAURJOTHUS, *str. sb. m.* pleasure, Lu. 8. 14.

GA-BAURS (κῶμος), *str. sb. m.* feasting, Gal. 5. 21; Rom. 13. 13.

GA-BAURTHI-WAURD, *str. sb. n.* a genealogy, 1 Tim. 1. 4.

GA-BAURTHS, *str. sb. f.* birth, Mk. 7. 26; Lu. 1. 14; Jo. 9. 1; mel ga-baurthais, birthday, Mk. 6. 21; native country, Mk. 6. 4; Lu. 4. 23; generation, Mk. 8. 38; nature, Rom. 11. 21.

GABEI, *wk. sb. f.* riches, Mk. 4. 19; Lu. 8. 14; gain, reconciliation, Rom. 11. 15. *From* giban.

GA-BEIDAN, *vb.* to abide, endure, 1 Cor. 13. 7.

GABEIGS, *adj.* rich, Mat. 27. 57; Mk. 10. 25; Lu. 16. 1, 19. *From* giban.

GA-BEISTJAN, *vb.* to embitter; *hence:* to leaven, 1 Cor. 5. 6.

GABIGABA, *adv.* richly, Col. 3. 16.

GABIGS, *same as* gabeigs, q. v.

GA-BINDA, *str. sb. f.* a band, bond, Col. 2. 19.

GA-BINDAN, *vb.* to bind, Mk. 3. 27; 5. 3; 11. 4; 15. 7.

GA-BINDI, *str. sb. f.* a band, Col. 3. 14. *Cf.* ga-binda.

GA-BIUGAN, *vb.* to bow, bend; eisarnam gabuganaim, with bent irons, Mk. 5. 4.

GA-BLAUTHJAN, *vb.* to nullify, make of none effect, triumph over, Col. 2. 15. *Cf.* Mk. 7. 13.

GA-BLEITHEI(NS), *sb. f.* pity, Phil. 2. 1.

GA-BLEITHJAN, *vb.* to pity, Mk. 9. 22; Rom. 9. 15.

GA-BLINDJAN, *vb.* to blind, make blind, Jo. 12. 40; 2 Cor. 4. 4.

GA-BLINDNAN, *vb.* to become blind; ga-blindnodedum, *marg. gloss on* afdaubnodedum, 2 Cor. 3. 14.

GA-BOTJAN, *vb.* to make useful; aftra ga-botjan, to restore, Mk. 9. 12. *From* batan.

GA-BRANNJAN, *vb.* to burn, 1 Cor. 13. 3; Skeir. 3. 14.

GA-BRIKAN, *vb.* to break, Mk. 5. 4; 8. 6, Lu. 9. 16, 39.

GA-BRUKA, *str. sb. f.* a broken bit, a fragment, Mk. 8. 8; Lu. 9. 17; Jo. 6. 13.

GA-BUNDI, *str. sb. f.* a bond, Eph. 4. 3. *Cf.* gabindi.

GA-DABAN, *vb.* to happen, befall, Mk. 10. 32; to be fit, Skeir. 3. 16.

GA-DAILA, *wk. sb. m.* a partaker, 1 Cor. 10. 20; 2 Cor. 1. 7; Eph. 3. 6; a partner, Lu. 5. 10. *From* dails.

GA-DAILJAN, *vb.* to deal, distribute, Rom. 12. 3; to impart, 1 Cor. 7. 17; to give, Lu. 18. 22; 19. 8; to divide, Mk. 3. 26.

GA-DAUBJAN, *vb.* to deafen; *hence* to harden, Jo. 12. 40; 16. 6.

GA-DAUKA, *sb.* household, 1 Cor. 1. 16. [M. *proposes to read* ga-daurans.]

GA-DAURSAN, *vb.* to dare, Mk. 12. 34; Lu. 20. 40; to speak boldly, Eph. 6. 20.

GA-DAUTHJAN, *vb.* to do to death, to kill, Rom. 8. 36.

GA-DAUTHNAN, *vb.* to die, Mat. 8. 32; Mk. 9. 48; 12. 19; Lu. 8. 49; 20. 29. *Der.* mith-gadauthnan.

GA-DEDS, *str. sb. f.* a doing; suniwe ga-deds, adoption of sons, Eph. 1. 5.

GA-DIK(IS), *str. sb. n.* a thing formed, a creature, thing made, Rom. 9. 20. *From* deigan.*

GADILIGGS, *str. sb. m.* a sister's son, nephew, Col. 4. 10.

GA-DIUPJAN, *vb.* to deepen, dig deeply, Lu. 6. 48.

GA-DOBS, GA-DOFS, *adj.* fitting; *hence* ga-dobs wisan, to be fit, Eph. 5. 3; .1 Tim. 2. 10; Tit. 2. 1. [*Cf.* E. *dab.*]

GA-DOMJAN, *vb.* to doom, judge, condemn, Mk. 14. 64; to deem, Phil. 3. 12; 1 Tim. 3. 16; to justify, Mat. 11. 19; to judge of, 2 Cor. 10. 12.

GA-DRABAN, *vb.* to hew out, Mk. 15. 46.

GA-DRAGAN, *vb.* to drag, draw; A. V. heap, 2 Tim. 4. 3. [*Another reading is* dragand.]

GA-DRAGGKJAN, *or* GA-DRAGKJAN,

vb. to give to drink, Mat. 10. 42; Mk. 9. 41.

GA-DRAUHTS, *str. sb. m.* a soldier, Mat. 8. 9; Mk. 15. 16; Lu. 7. 8; Jo. 19. 2; 2 Tim. 2. 3. *From* driugan.

GA-DRAUSJAN, *vb.* to thrust down, Lu. 1. 52; 10. 15; 2 Cor. 4. 9. *Cf.* driusan.

GA-DRIGGKAN, *or* GA-DRIGKAN, *vb.* to drink, Lu. 17. 8.

GA-DRIUSAN, *vb.* to fall, Mat. 10. 29; Mk. 4. 4, 7, 8; Lu. 8. 6; &c.; to be cast *or* thrust, Mat. 5. 29.

GA-DROBNAN, *vb.* to be troubled, Lu. 1. 12; Jo. 12. 27.

GAF, gave. *From* giban.

GA-FAH, *sb.* (*n.?*), a catch, taking, catching, Lu. 5. 9. *Cf.* fahan.

GA-FAHAN. *vb.* to catch, Lu. 20. 20, 26; Jo. 7. 30; 12. 35.

GA-FAHRJAN, *vb.* to prepare, Lu. 1. 17.

GA-FAIHON, *vb.* to make a gain of; *marg. gloss to* ga-aiginondau, 2 Cor. 2. 11.

GA-FAIRINON*, *vb.* to accuse. *Cf.* fairan, fairinon. *Der.* un-gafairinonds.

GA-FASTAN, *vb.* to hold fast, keep, Lu. 2. 19; 18. 21; Jo. 17. 6; &c.

GA-FAURDS, *str. sb. m.* chief council, Sanhedrim, Mk. 14. 55; 15. 1.

GA-FAURS, *adj.* sober, well behaved, 1 Tim. 3. 2, 11.

GA-FEHABA. *adv.* honestly, 1 Th. 4. 12.

GA-FETEINS, *str. sb. f.* adornment, apparel, 1 Tim. 2. 9. *Cf.* fetjan.

GA-FILH, *str. sb. n.* burial, Jo. 12. 7.

GA-FILHAN, *vb.* to hide, bury, Mat. 8. 21; Lu. 16. 22; gafilhan sik, to hide oneself, Jo. 8. 59; 12. 36.

GA-FRAIHNAN, *vb.* to ask, seek, Rom. 10. 20; gafrehun, they found out by inquiry, they heard, Mk. 2. 1.

GA-FRATHJEI, *wk. sb. f.* understanding, sobriety, 1 Tim. 2. 15.

GA-FRAUJINON, to exercise lordship, *vb.* Mk. 10. 42.

GA-FREIDEINS, *str. sb. f.* possession, Eph. 1. 14; possession, attainment of, 1 Thess. 5. 9.

GA-FRIJONS, *str. sb. f.* a kiss, 1 Thess. 5. 26.

GA-FRISAHTJAN, *vb.* to make a resemblance *or* image; *hence,* to engrave (A. V.), 2 Cor. 3. 7.

GA-FRISAHTNAN, *vb.* to resemble; *hence* to be formed (in resemblance), Gal. 4. 19.

GA-FRITHON, *vb.* to reconcile, 2 Cor. 5. 18, 19; Eph. 2. 16; Col. 1. 20, 21.

GA-FRITHONS, *str. sb. f.* reconciliation, 2 Cor. 5. 18, 19.

GA-FULGINS, hidden, Lu. 18. 34; 19. 42; Col. 1. 26; 3. 3. *Cf.* filhan.

GA-FULLAWEISJAN, *vb.* to make known fully, Lu. 1. 1. *From* weis.

GA-FULLJAN, *vb.* to fill, Lu. 1. 15; 5. 7; Mk. 15. 36; Jo. 6. 13.

GA-FULLNAN, *vb.* to become full, be filled, Mk. 4. 37; Lu. 1. 41, 67; 8. 23.

GA-GAGGAN, *vb.* (*pt. t.* ga-iddja), to come together, resort, Mk. 6. 30; Lu. 8. 4; Jo. 18. 2; *refl.* Mk. 3. 20; to come to pass, Mk. 11. 23; to conduce, Phil. 1. 19. *Der.* samath-gagaggan.

GA-GAHAFTJAN, *vb.* to fit together

closely, to compact, Eph. 4. 16. *From* haban.

GA-GALEIKON SIK, *vb. refl.* to liken oneself, make oneself resemble, 2 Cor. 11. 13, 14.

GA-GAMAINJAN, *vb.* to make common, defile, Mk. 7. 23. *Cf.* gamains.

GA-GATILON, *vb.* to join together closely and well, Eph. 2. 21; 4. 16.

GA-GAWAIRTHJAN, *vb.* to reconcile; *but in* 1 Cor. 7. 11 *it rather means* to reconcile oneself. *See next word.*

GA-GAWAIRTHNAN, *vb.* to be reconciled, 2 Cor. 5. 20.

GA-GEIGAN, *vb.* to win, gain, Mk. 8. 36; Lu. 9. 25; 1 Cor. 9. 19—22.

GAGGA*, *in comp.* faura-gagga, q. v.

GAGGAN, *vb.* (*pt. t.* iddja, *and once* gaggida, Lu. 19. 12; *pl.* iddjedum; *pt. p.* gaggans), to gang, go, go one's way, Mk. 3. 6; 7. 29; 10. 21; 16. 7; &c.; *used to translate very many different words, as:* ὑπάγειν, στοιχεῖν, πορεύεσθαι, κ. τ. λ.; gaggan afar, to go after, to follow, Mk. 2. 14; 5. 24; 14. 13. *Der.* gaguggan, af-gaggan, afar-gaggan, mith-afargaggan, ana-guggan, at-gaggan, du-at-gaggan, inn-at-gaggan, faur-gaggan, faur-bigaggan, faura-gaggan, inn-gaggan, mith-gaggan, thairh-gaggan, ufar-gaggan, us-gaggan, ut-gaggan, withra-gaggan, gagga, faura-gagga, fauragaggi, gaggs, at-gaggs, framgahts, inn-at-gahts, un-at-gahts. *Cf.* leithan, sniwan. [G. *gehen;* D. *gaan;* Scot. *gang.*]

GAGGI*, *in comp.* faura-gaggi, q. v.

GAGGJA*, *see* faura-gaggja.

GAGGS, *str. sb. m.* a way, a street, Mk. 6. 56; 11. 4. *Der.* at-gaggs. [Germ. *gang.*]

GA-GREFTS, *str. sb. f.* a decree, Lu. 2. 1; in ga-greiftai ist (πρόκειται), is set forth, is present, 2 Cor. 8. 12.

GA-GUDABA, *adv.* godly, piously, 2 Tim. 3. 12. *From* guth.

GA-GUDEI, *wk. sb. f.* godliness, piety, holiness, 1 Tim. 3. 16; 4. 8; 6. 6, 11. *From* guth.

GA-GUDS, *adj.* godly, pious, Mk. 15. 43. *From* guth.

GA-HABAN, *vb.* to have, hold, possess, Mk. 10. 23; hold fast, retain, detain, Lu. 4. 42; 8. 15; to lay hold on, Mk. 3. 21; 6. 17. *Der.* un-gahabands.

GA-HAFTJAN SIK, *vb. refl.* to cleave to, join oneself to, Lu. 15. 15.. *Cf.* gaga-haftjan.

GA-HAFTNAN, *vb. neut.* to cleave to, adhere, Lu. 10. 11.

GA-HAHJO, *adv.* in order, connectedly, Lu. 1. 3. *From* hahan.

GA-HAILJAN, *vb.* to heal, Mk. 1. 34; 3. 10; 6. 13; &c.

GA-HAILNAN, *vb.* to become whole, to be healed, Mat. 8. 8; Mk. 5. 29; Lu. 7. 7; 8. 47.

GA-HAILS (ὁλόκληρος), *adj.* whole, 1 Thess. 5. 23.

GA-HAIT, *str. sb. n.* a promise, Rom. 9. 8; Eph. 1. 13; 3. 6; Gal. 3. 29; &c.

GA-HAITAN, *vb.* to call together, Mk. 15. 16; Lu. 9. 1; 15. 9; to promise, Mk. 14. 11; Tit. 1. 2; to profess, 1 Tim. 2. 10. *Der.* faura-gahaitan.

GA-HAMON, *vb.* to clothe oneself with, put on, Rom. 13. 14; 1 Cor. 15. 53; Eph. 4. 24; Col. 3. 10, &c.

GA-HARDJAN, *vb.* to harden, Rom. 9. 18.
GA-HAUNJAN, *vb.* to humble, 2 Cor. 12. 21; Phil. 2. 8. [*Cf.* G. *höhnen.*]
GA-HAUSEINS, *str. sb. f.* bearing, Rom. 10. 17; Gal. 3. 2.
GA-HAUSJAN, *vb.* to hear, Mk. 5. 27; 7. 25; Lu. 7. 3; &c.
GA-HILPAN, *vb.* to help, 2 Cor. 6. 2.
GA-HLAIBA, *wk. sb. m.* a partaker of one's loaf, messmate; *hence* a fellow-disciple, Jo. 11. 16; a fellow-soldier, Phil. 2. 25.
GA-HNAIWJAN, *vb.* to humble, Lu. 1. 52; 3. 5; 14. 11; 18. 14.
GA-HOBAINS, *str. sb. f.* temperance, self-restraint, Gal. 5. 23. *From* haban. *Der.* un-gahobains.
GA-HORINON, *vb.* to whore, commit whoredom, Mat. 5. 28.
GA-HRAINEINS, *str. sb. f.* cleansing, Mk. 1. 44; Lu. 5. 14.
GA-HRAINJAN, *vb.* to cleanse, Mat. 8. 2; Mk. 1. 40; 7. 19, &c. *Der.* faura-gahrainjan.
GAHTS*, *sb.* a going; *from* gaggan. *See* inna-gahts, unat-gahts, fram-gahts.
GA-HUGJAN, *vb.* to think, deem, consider, 1 Tim. 1. 12. *Der.* faura-gahugjan.
GA-HUGDS, *str. sb. f.* a thought, Lu. 1. 51; the thought, *i. e.* the mind, Mk. 12. 30; Lu. 10. 27; conscience, 1 Tim. 3. 9. *Cf.* hugs.
GA-HULJAN, *vb.* to conceal, hide, Mat. 8. 24; 10. 26; Lu. 9. 45; &c.
GA-HWAIRBS, *adj.* pliant; *hence* obedient, Skeir. 6. 25. *Der.* un-gahwairbs; *see* hwairban.
GA-HWEILAINS, *str. sb. f.* respite for a while, rest, 2 Cor. 2. 13; 7. 5.

GA-HWEILAN, *vb.* to remain a while, to rest, Lu. 10. 6; to cease, 1 Cor. 13. 8.
GA-HWEITJAN, *vb.* to whiten, Mk. 9. 3.
GA-HWOTJAN, *vb.* to rebuke, Mk. 1. 43; 9. 25; Lu. 4. 35; 9. 21, 32. *Cf.* hwatan.
GAIAINNA, *sb.* Gehenna, Mat. 5. 22; &c.; Mk. 9. 43, 45, 47.
GA-IBNJAN, *vb.* to make even, Lu. 19. 44.
GA-IDREIGON, *vb.* to repent, Lu. 10. 13.
GAIDW, *str. sb. n.* that which is lacking, want, defect, 2 Cor. 9. 12; Phil. 2. 30; Col. 1. 24.
GAI-GROT, wept. *From* gretan.
GAILJAN, *vb. with acc.* to make glad, 2 Cor. 2. 2.
GAIRDA, *str. sb. f.* a girdle, Mk. 1. 6; 6. 8.
GAIRDAN*, *vb.* (*perf.* gard; *pl.* gaurdum: *pp.* gaurdans), to gird. *Der.* bi-gairdan, uf-gairdan, gairda, gards, garda-waldands, aurti-gards, weina-gards, midjun-gards, in-gardeis, in-gardja, thiudan-gardi, garda, mith-garda-waddjus. [G. *gürten;* E. *gird;* D. *gorden.*]
GAIRNEI, *wk. sb. f.* yearning, longing, desire, 2 Cor. 7. 7, 11; 8. 19; 9. 2. *From* geiran. *Der.* faihu-gairnei. [E. *yearning.*]
GAIRNJAN, *vb. with gen.* to yearn for, long for, desire, wish, Mk. 11. 3; Lu. 15. 16; 17. 22; &c. *See* geiran. [E. *yearn.*]
GAIRNS*, *adj.* yearning for. *From* geiran. *Der.* faihu-gairns, faihu-gairnei, seinai-gairns.
GAIRU, *str. sb. n.* a thorn; *as gloss to* houto, 2 Cor. 12. 7.
GAIRUNI, *str. sb. n.* an (evil) yearning, lust, 1 Thess. 4. 5. *From* geiran.

GAISJAN*, vb. in un-gaisjan, q. v. Cf. geisan.

GAITEIN, str. sb. n. a little goat, a kid, La. 15. 29.

GAITEINS, adj. belonging to a goat, the neuter of which is used to mean a kid. See gaitein.

GAITSA, str. sb. f. a goat, Nehem. 5. 18. Der. gaitein, gaiteins. [G. geiss; E. goat; D. geit.]

GA-JIUKAN, vb. to overcome, conquer, Jo. 16. 33; Rom. 12. 21; to beguile, Col. 2. 18.

GA-JUK, str. sb. n. (lit. a yoke), a pair, Lu. 2. 24.

GA-JUKA, wk. sb. m. one who is yoked with one, a yoke-fellow, comrade, 2 Cor. 6. 14; Phil. 4. 3; 2 Tim. 2. 1.

GA-JUKO, wk. sb. f. that which yoked or paired; hence a comparison, parable, Mk. 3. 23; 4. 2; 12. 1; &c.

GA-JUKO, wk. sb. n. a yoke-fellow; put for ga-juka in Phil. 4. 3.

GA-KANNJAN, vb. to make known, Lu. 2. 17; Jo. 15. 15; Col. 1. 8; to praise; but used as equal to be praised, 2 Cor. 12. 11.

GA-KARAN, vb. to take care of, 1 Tim. 3. 5.

GA-KAUSJAN, vb. to prove, try, test, prove by testing, 2 Cor. 8. 22. From kiusan.

GA-KIUSAN, vb. to prove by testing, try, approve, Rom. 12. 2; 2 Cor. 13. 7; Eph. 5. 10; 1 Tim. 3. 10. Der. un-gakusans.

GA-KROTON, vb. to maim, to break (the limbs of any one), Lu. 20. 18.

GA-KUNDS, str. sb. f. persuasion, Gal. 5. 8. From kunnan.

GA-KUNNAN, vb. to know, Lu. 8. 17; 19. 15; to consider, Mat. 6. 28; to read, Mk. 12. 26; to subject oneself, Gal. 2. 5; 1 Cor. 15. 28; ga-kunnands, by permission, 1 Cor. 7. 6.

GA-KUNTHS, str. sb. f. only in phrase: uf ga-kunthai, in becoming known, in appearance (?) (ἀρχομένος), Lu. 3. 23.

GA-KUSTS, str. sb. f. proof, trial, test, 2 Cor. 9. 13. From kiusan.

GA-KWIMAN, vb. to come together, Mat. 27. 17; Mk. 2. 2; 7. 1; followed by in with dat., to arrive at, attain to, Phil. 3. 11; gakwimith (Lat. convenit), it is fit, Col. 3. 18.

GA-KWISS, str. sb. f. consent, 1 Cor. 7. 5. From kwithan.

GA-KWISS, adj. (used with wisan), consenting; ga-kwiss im, I consent, admit, Rom. 7. 16. From kwithan.

GA-KWITHAN, vb. refl. to agree among themselves, Jo. 9. 22. Cf. ga-kwiss.

GA-KWIUJAN, vb. to quicken, make alive, 2 Cor. 3. 6; 1 Tim. 6. 13. Der. mith-gakwiujan.

GA-KWIUNAN, vb. to be quickened, be made alive again, Lu. 15. 24, 32; Rom. 7. 9; 1 Cor. 15. 22. From kwius.

GA-KWUMTHS, str. sb. f. the council, sanhedrim, assembly, Mat. 5. 22; 6. 2; 9. 35; us ga-kwumths dreiban, to put out of the synagogue, Jo. 16. 2; From kwiman. Der. mith-ga-kwumths.

GA-LAGJAN, vb. to lay, lay down, set, place, make (with double acc.), Mk. 12. 36; Lu. 20. 43. See also Lu. 2. 7; 5. 18; Mk. 11. 7; &c.; to lay up, 1 Tim. 4. 8. From ligan.

GA-LAISJAN, vb. to teach, 1 Tim. 2. 12; to instruct, Lu. 1. 4; refl. to learn, 1 Tim. 2.

11; 2 Tim. 3. 14. *From* leisan.

GA-LAISTA, *wk. sb. m.* a follower, ga-laista wairthan, to follow, Mk. 1. 36; ga-laista wisan, to follow, Gal. 6. 16. *Cf.* laists.

GA-LAISTJAN, *vb. with acc.* to follow, Rom. 12. 13; 1 Tim. 4. 6. *From* laists.

GA-LATJAN, *vb.* to let, hinder, Gal. 5. 7. [*So* S.; *but* M. *has* latida; *from* latjan.]

GA-LATHON, *vb.* to invite, Lu. 15. 6; to take to one's home, take in, Mat. 25. 38; to call, 1 Cor. 1. 24; 7. 21.

GA-LAUBEINS, *str. sb. f.* belief, faith, Mat. 9. 22; Mk. 5. 34; 10. 52; Lu. 7. 50; &c. *From* liubs. *Der.* un-galaubeins. [G. *glaube; cf.* E. *be-lief.*]

GA-LAUBEINS, *adj.* believing, Tit.1.6.

GA-LAUBJAN, *vb* to believe, Mat. 27. 42; Mk. 11. 31; &c. *From* liubs. *Der.* un-galaubjands. [G. *glauben*]

GA-LAUBS, *adj.* valuable, costly, precious, 1 Cor. 7. 23; Rom. 9. 21. *From* liubs. *Der.* un-ga-laubs, filu-galaubs.

GA-LAUGNJAN, *vb.* to lie hid, be hid, Mk. 7. 24; Lu. 8. 47; *refl.* to hide oneself, Lu. 1. 24. *From* liugan.

GA-LAUSJAN, *vb.* to loose, loosen, Mk. 5. 4; to deliver, set free, Lu. 1. 74; to get again, receive again, Lu. 19. 23; to guard, 2 Thess. 3. 3. *From* liusan.

GA-LEIKA, *wk. sb. m.* one of the same body with, Eph. 3. 6.

GA-LEIKAN, *vb.* to please, Mk. 6. 22; Rom. 8. 8; galeikaith mis, it seems good to me, Lu. 1. 3; 1 Cor. 1. 21; to take pleasure in, Mk. 1. 11; Lu. 3. 22. *Der.* faura-galeikan.

GA-LEIKI, *str. sb. n.* likeness, Rom. 8. 3; Phil. 2. 7. *From* leiks.

GA-LEIKINON, *vb.* to heal, Lu. 8. 43; (*with gen.* of the disease), Lu. 8. 2.

GA-LEIKO, *adv.* like, on an equality with; *in phrase* wisan galeiko gutha, to be equal to God; *but* M. *reads:* wisan, sik galeiko(n) gutha, *which seems better*, Phil. 2. 6.

GA-LEIKON, *vb.* to liken, Mat. 7. 24; Mk. 4. 30; Lu. 7. 31; *with* or *without* sik, to be like, resembled, be conformed to, Rom. 12. 2; Mat. 6. 8; to imitate, Skeir. 1. 25. *From* leikan *See* ga-leiko. *Der.* in-galeikon, mith-galeikon, thairh-galeikon.

GA-LEIKS, *adj.* like, Mk. 7. 8; 14. 70; Lu. 6. 47; &c. *See* leiks. [G. *gleich.*]

GA-LEITHAN, *vb.* to go, come (*answering to many Greek verbs*), Mk. 5. 38; 11. 11; 12. 12; 14. 10; &c., &c. *Der.* inn-galeithan, mith-inn-galeithan.

GA-LEWJAN ($\pi\alpha\rho\acute{\epsilon}\chi\epsilon\iota\nu$), *vb.* to present, Lu. 6. 29; to betray, Mk. 14. 10; Jo. 18. 36; 19. 11; &c.

GALGA, *wk. sb. m.* a cross, Mk. 8. 34; 10. 38; 15. 21. *Cf.* hramjan. [G. *galgen;* E. *gallows.*]

GA-LIGINON, *vb.* to make a gain of, take advantage of, *a* MS. *reading in* 2 Cor. 2. 11: gali-ginondau, *for which* ga-aigi-nondau *is proposed. See* ga-aiginon.

GA-LIGRI, *str. sb. n.*, consummation of marriage, Rom. 9. 10. *From* ligan.

GA-LISAN, *vb.* to collect, gather together, Mk. 4. 1; 13. 27; Lu. 17. 37; Jo. 6. 13.

GA-LIUGA or GA-LIUG, *str. sb. n.* a a lie; ga-liug taujan, to falsify, 2 Cor. 4. 2; ga-liug weitwodjan, to bear false witness, Mk. 14. 56; an idol, 1 Cor. 5. 10; 8. 10; 10. 19.

GA-LIUGA-APAUSTAULUS, *str. sb. m.* a false apostle, 2 Cor. 11. 13.

GA-LIUGA-BROTHAR, *str. sb. m.* a false brother, Gal. 2. 4; 2 Cor. 11. 26.

GA-LIUGA-CHRISTUS, *str. sb. m.* a false Christ, Mk. 13. 22.

GA-LIUGA-PRAUFETUS, *str. sb. m.* a false prophet, Mk. 13. 22; Lu. 6. 26.

GA-LIUGAN, *vb.* to marry, Mk. 6. 17.

GA-LIUGS, *adj.* lying, false. See 2 Cor. 4. 2, *where it is doubtful, whether guliug is a sb. or an adj.*

GA-LIUHTJAN, *vb.* to enlighten, bring to light, 1 Cor. 4. 5; 2 Tim. 1. 10.

GA-LUBS, *adj.* costly, 1 Tim. 2. 9. *From* liubs. *Cf.* ga-laubs.

GA-LUKAN, *vb.* to lock; *hence to* shut, close, Mat. 6. 6; 27. 66; to shut up, Lu. 3. 20; to enclose, Rom. 11. 32; Lu. 5. 6.

GA-LUKNAN, *vb.* to be locked *or* closed, Lu. 4. 25.

GA-MAGAN, *vb.* to have might *or* force, to avail, Gal. 5. 6.

GA-MAIDS, *adj.* bruised, Lu. 4. 19; maimed, Lu. 14. 13, 21.

GA-MAINDUTHS, *str. sb. f.* communion, fellowship, 1 Cor. 10. 16; 2 Cor. 6. 14; 9. 13; Phil. 2. 1; 3. 10.

GA-MAINEI, *wk. sb. f.* communion, Gal. 2. 9; fellowship, participation in, 2 Cor. 8. 4.

GA-MAINJA, *wk. sb. m.* a partaker, 1 Tim. 5. 22.

GA-MAINJAN, *vb.* to make common, defile, Mk. 7. 15; 18. 20; to communicate, Gal. 6. 6; Phil. 4. 15; to distribute, Rom. 12. 13; to partake of, 1 Cor. 10. 18.

GA-MAINS, *adj.* common, Tit. 1. 4; unclean, Mk. 7. 2; Rom. 14. 14; partaking of, Rom. 11. 17; gamains bringan, *the same as* gamainjan, Phil. 4. 14. [G. *gemein;* A. S. *gemæne.*]

GA-MAINTHS, *str. sb. f.* assembly, multitude, Nehem. 5. 13. [G. *gemeinde.*]

GA-MAITANO (κατατομή), *sb. f.* concision, Phil. 3. 2.

GA-MALTEINS, *str. sb. f.* release, departure, 2 Tim. 4. 6. [*A gloss to* diswissais *is* gamalteinais.]

GA-MALWJAN, *vb.* to grind like wheat, bruise, crush; gamalwidans hairtin, brokenhearted, Lu. 4. 18.

GA-MAN, *str. sb. n.* a fellow-man, comrade, companion, Lu. 5. 7; 2 Cor. 8. 23; 13. 13.

GA-MANWJAN, *vb.* to prepare, make ready, Mat. 11. 10; Mk. 1. 2; Lu. 6. 40; 7. 27. *Der.* fauragamanwjan.

GA-MARKO, *sb. f.* a neighbour to, on the confines of (*lit.* on the same marches with); *hence* neighbouring to, answering to, Gal. 4. 25.

GA-MARZEINS, *str. sb. f.* a stumbling block, Rom. 9. 33; 14. 13; 1 Cor. 1. 23.

GA-MARZJAN, *vb.* to offend; *pass.* to be offended, Mat. 11. 6; Lu. 7. 23; Jo. 6. 61.

GA-MATJAN, *vb.* to eat, Mk. 8. 8; Lu. 17. 8.

GA-MAUDEINS, *str. sb. f.* remembrance, 2 Tim. 1. 5.

GA-MAUDJAN, *vb.* to cause to remember, to remind, Jo. 14.

26; 2 Tim. 1. 6; 2. 14; Skeir. 7. 21.

GA-MAURGJAN, *vb.* to curtail, cut short, Mk. 13. 20; Rom. 9. 28.

GA-MELEINS, *str. sb. f.* a writing; *esp.* the scripture, Jo. 7. 38, 42; 2 Cor. 3. 7; 1 Tim. 5. 18.

GA-MELJAN, *vb.* to write, Mk. 1. 2; 7. 6; 12. 10; &c. *Der.* faura-gameljan, inna-gameljan.

GA-MIKILJAN, *vb.* to make much (*or* mickle) of, to magnify, enlarge, Lu. 1. 58.

GA-MINTHI, *str. sb. n.* a minding, remembrance, 2 Tim. 1. 3; 1 Th. 3. 6. *From* minan.

GA-MITAN, *vb.* to mete, measure out, 2 Cor. 10. 13. [G. *messen;* E. *mete.*]

GA-MITONS, *str. sb. f.* an intention, Eph. 2. 3. *From* mitan. (S.)

GA-MOTAN, *vb.* to have room, find room, have place, Mk. 2. 2; Jo. 8. 37; 2 Cor. 7. 2.

GA-MOTJAN, *vb.* to meet, Mk. 5. 2; 14. 13; Lu. 14. 31; 17. 12. *Der.* witbra-gamotjan.

GA-MUNAN, *vb.* to mind, to remember, Mk. 8. 18; Lu. 17. 32; Jo. 15. 20; &c. *From* minan.

GA-MUNDS, *str. sb. f.* remembrance, Mk. 14. 9; 1 Cor. 11. 24; Eph. 1. 16. *From* minan.

GA-NAGLJAN, *vb.* to nail, Col. 2. 14. [G. *nageln;* E. *nail.*]

GA-NAH, *impers. vb.* 'tis enough, it suffices, Mat. 10. 25; Jo. 14. 8; 2 Cor. 2. 6; 12. 9. *From* ga-naban.

GA-NAHAN, *vb.* to be enough, to suffice. *See* ga-nah.

GA-NAITJAN, *vb.* to maltreat, handle shamefully, Mk. 12. 4.

GA-NAMJAN, *vb.* to name, Skeir. 2. 24.

GA-NANTHJAN, *vb. In* Lu. 5. 4 *the MS. has* ga-nanthida (*i. e.*

dared; *see* nanthjan), *evidently by error for a word meaning* ended, *perhaps* ga-andida.

GA-NASJAN, *vb.* to save, Mk. 8. 35; 10. 52; to heal, Lu. 4. 18; 6. 19. *From* nisan. [*Cf.* G. *genesen.*]

GA-NATJAN, *vb.* to make wet, to wet, Lu. 7. 44. [G. *benetzen.*]

GA-NAUHA, *wk. sb. f.* sufficiency, contentment, 2 Cor. 9. 8; 1 Tim. 6. 6. *From* naban.

GA-NAWISTRON, *vb.* to bury, 1 Cor. 15. 4. *From* naus. *Der.* mith-ganawistron.

GA-NIMAN, *vb.* to take, take with one, Mk. 5. 40; 9. 2; Lu. 9. 28; to receive, possess, 1 Cor. 15. 50; to conceive, Lu. 1. 31; 2. 21; to learn, Mat. 9. 13; Jo. 6. 45.

GA-NIPNAN, *vb.* to mourn, be sorrowful, Mk. 10. 22.

GA-NISAN, *vb.* to become whole, Mat. 9. 21; Mk. 5. 28; to be saved, Jo. 10. 9; Rom. 9. 27. [*Cf.* G. *genesen.*]

GA-NISTS, *str. sb. m.* health, salvation, Rom. 10. 10; 11. 11; Phil. 1. 19, 28.

GA-NITHJIS, *str. sb. m.* a kinsman, Lu. 1. 58; 2. 44; Mk. 6. 4.

GA-NIUTAN, *vb.* to net, catch with nets, Lu. 5. 9; to catch, Mk. 12. 13.

GANN, began; *from* ginnan.

GA-NOHJAN, *vb.* to be contented (*gloss to* waldaith), Lu. 3. 14; Phil. 4. 11; ufarassau g., to abound, Eph. 1. 8. *From* naban. [G. *genügen.*]

GA-NOHNAN, *vb.* to be very well provided with, to abound, 1 Th. 3. 12.

GA-NOHS, *adj.* sufficient, numerous, Lu. 7. 11; 20. 9; Jo. 6. 7; 1 Cor. 11. 30. [G. *genug.*]

GANSJAN, *vb.* to trouble, molest, Gal. 6. 17.

GA-PAIDON, *vb.* to clothe oneself with, put on, Eph. 6. 14.

GA-RAGINON, *vb.* to counsel, give counsel to, Jo. 18. 14.

GA-RAHNJAN, *vb.* to value, estimate the price of, Mat. 27. 9.

GA-RAIDEINS, *str. sb. f.* an ordinance, rule, authority, Rom. 13. 2; 9. 4; 2 Cor. 10. 13; Gal. 6. 16.

GA-RAIDJAN, *vb.* to enjoin, command, 1 Cor. 16. 1; Tit. 1. 5.

GA-RAIDS, *adj.* enjoined, commanded, Lu. 3. 13. [*Cf.* G. *bereit.*]

GA-RAIHTABA, *adv.* righteously, rightly, 1 Cor. 15. 34; 1 Th. 2. 10. *From* raihts.

GA-RAIHTEI, *wk. sb. f.* righteousness, Mat. 5. 20; Lu. 1. 6; Rom. 8. 4; 10. 6; &c. *Der.* un-garaihtei.

GA-RAIHTEINS, *str. sb. f.* the same as ga-raihtei.

GA-RAIHTITHA, *str. sb. f.* righteousness, Jo. 16. 8, 10; Rom. 10. 10.

GA-RAIHTJAN, *vb.* to make right, prepare, direct, Lu. 1. 79; 1 Th. 3. 11; 2 Th. 3. 5; to justify, 1 Cor. 4. 4. *Der.* at-garaihtjan. [G. *richten.*]

GA-RAIHTS, *adj.* right, just, righteous, Lu. 1. 17; 2. 25; 7. 29; &c. [G. *gerecht*; E. *right.*]

GA-RATHJAN, *vb.* to reckon, number, Mat. 10. 30.

GA-RAZNA, *wk. sb. m.* a neighbour, Lu. 14. 12; 15. 6; Jo. 9. 8. *From* razn.

GA-RAZNO, *wk. sb. f.* a female neighbour, Lu. 15. 9.

GARDA, *wk. sb. m.* a yard, fold, Jo. 10. 1.

GARDA-WALDANDS, *str. sb. m.* the master of a house, a householder, Mat. 10. 25; Lu. 14. 21. *From* gairdan *and* waldan.

GARD(E)IS*; *in comp.* in-gard(e)is, q. v.

GARDI*; *in comp.* thiudan-gardi, q. v.

GARDS, *str. sb. m.* a house, Lu. 8. 39; 14. 23; 19. 46; &c. [E. *yard.*]

GA-REDABA, *adv.* honestly, in a well conducted manner, Rom. 13. 13.

GA-REDAN, *vb.* to provide for oneself, provide, 2 Cor. 8. 21. *Der.* faura-garedan.

GA-REHSNS, *str. sb. f.* a set time, Gal. 4. 2; counsel, instruction, Skeir. 1. 7, 19; 2. 20; 3. 3.

GA-RINNAN, *vb.* to run together, come together, Mk. 1. 33; 14. 53; Lu. 5. 15; to go, Jo. 12. 11; to meet together, Eph. 4. 13.

GA-RIUDI, *str. sb. n.* honesty, decent behaviour, 1 Tim. 2. 2.

GA-RIUDJO, *wk. sb. f.* bashfulness, shamefastness, 1 Tim. 2. 9.

GA-RIUDS, *adj.* modest, honest, well behaved, 1 Tim. 3. 2, 8, 11; Phil. 4. 8.

GA-RUNI, *str sb. n.* counsel, Mat. 27. 1, 7; Mk. 3. 6; 15. 1.

GA-RUNJO, *wk. sb. f.* a flood, inundation, Lu. 6. 48. *From* rinnan. *Cf.* flodus. [E. *run.*]

GA-RUNS, *str. sb. f.* the place where people run together or congregate, market-place, Lu. 7. 32; a street, Mat. 6. 2. *From* rinnan.

GA-SAHTS, *str. sb. f.* reproof, 2 Tim. 3. 16; Skeir. 8. 7. *From* sakan.

GA-SAIHWAN, *vb.* to see, behold, Mat. 11. 4; Mk. 3. 11; 5. 15; Lu. 5. 27; &c. *Der.* du-gasaihwan, un-gasaihwans, us-gasaihwan.

GA-SAKAN, *vb.* to reprove, rebuke, Mat. 8. 26; Mk. 4. 39; Lu. 4. 39; &c.

GA-SALBON, *vb.* to salve, anoint, Mk. 6. 13; 16. 1; Lu. 4. 18; 7. 38; Jo. 12. 3. [G. *salben;* E. *salve.*]

GA-SALJAN, *vb.* to sacrifice, offer up as sacrifice, 1 Cor. 8. 10; 10. 28; Skeir. 1. 5.

GA-SANDJAN, *vb.* to unite in sending; *hence*, to accompany, 1 Cor. 16. 6; 2 Cor. 1. 16. *From* sinthan. *Der.* faura-gasandjan.

GA-SATEINS, *str. sb. f.* foundation, Eph. 1. 4. *From* sitan.

GA-SATJAN, *vb.* to set, place, Lu. 7. 8; 8. 16; to lay, found, Lu. 6. 48; 14. 29; to let down, Lu. 5. 19. *From* sitan. *Der.* faura-gasatjan, mith-gasatjan. [G. *setzen;* E. *set.*]

GA-SIBJON, *vb.* to reconcile oneself to, be reconciled to, Mat. 5. 24. *Cf.* sibis, sibja.

GA-SIGGKWAN, *vb.* to sink, Mk. 1. 32; to sink under, be swallowed up by, 2 Cor. 2. 7.

GA-SIGLJAN, *vb.* to seal, confirm by sealing, Jo. 6. 27; Eph. 1. 13; 4. 30.

GA-SINTH(J)A, *wk. sb. m.* one who is sent with another, travelling companion, Lu. 2. 44; 2 Cor. 8. 19. *From* sinthan. *Der.* mith-gasintha.

GA-SITAN, *vb.* to set oneself down, to sit down, sit, Mk. 4. 1; 11. 7; Lu. 4. 20; Jo. 12. 14.

GA-SKADWEINS, *str. sb. f.* that which shades, clothing, 1 Tim. 6. 8. *From* skadus.

GA-SKAFTS, *str. sb. f.* shaping, formation, creation, things created, Mk. 10. 6; Jo.

17. 24; Rom. 8. 39. *From* skapan.

GA-SKAIDAN, *vb.* to part, separate, 2 Th. 3. 6. [G. *scheiden.*]

GA-SKAIDEI(NS), *sb. f.* parting, separation, difference, Rom. 10. 12.

GA-SKAIDNAN, *vb.* to become parted, separated, *or* divorced, 1 Cor. 7. 11.

GA-SKALKI, *str. sb. n.* fellow-servant, Col. 1. 7; 4. 7. [G. *schalk.*]

GA-SKAMAN SIK, *vb. refl.* to be ashamed, 2 Th. 3. 14.

GA-SKAPJAN, *vb.* to shape, create, make, Mk. 13. 19; Col. 3. 10; 1 Tim. 4. 3; *pass.* to be made, Mk. 2. 27.

GA-SKATHJAN, *vb.* to scathe, injure, Lu. 4. 35; 10. 19; 2 Cor. 7. 2; Gal. 4. 12.

GA-SKEIRJAN, *vb.* to make sheer or clear, to interpret, Mk. 5. 41; 15. 22; Jo. 9. 7.

GA-SKOHI, *str. sb. n.* a pair of shoes, sandals, Lu. 10. 4; 15. 22. [S. *has the form* gaskoh.]

GA-SKOHS, *adj.* shod, Mk. 6. 9; Eph. 6. 15.

GA-SLAWAN, *vb.* to be silent, Mk. 4. 39.

GA-SLEITHJAN, *vb.* to slight, injure; *with* sik, to be injured in, suffer the loss of, Mk. 8. 36; Lu. 9. 25; *pass.* to receive damage, 2 Cor. 7. 9; Phil. 3. 8.

GA-SLEPAN, *vb.* to sleep, to fall asleep, Jo. 11. 11; 1 Cor. 11. 30; 15. 6, 18, 20.

GA-SMEITAN, *vb.* to besmut, besmear, anoint, Jo. 9. 6.

GA-SMITHON, *vb.* (to do *smith's* work), to work, 2 Cor. 7. 10.

GA-SNIUMJAN, *vb.* to reach (*Greek* φθάνειν), 2 Cor. 10. 14.

GA-SNIWAN, *vb.* to reach, attain

to (*Greek* φθάνειν), Rom. 9. 31; Phil. 3. 16.

GA-SOKJAN, *vb.* to seek, Rom. 10. 20; Phil. 4. 17. *Cf.* sakan.

GA-SOTHJAN, *vb.* to fill, satisfy, Mk. 8. 4; Lu. 1. 53. *From* saths.

GA-SPEIWAN, *vb.* (*lit.* to spew) to spit, Jo. 9. 6.

GA-SPILLON, *vb.* to preach, Lu. 9. 60.

GA-STAGGKWAN, *vb.* to strike (one's foot against), Lu. 4. 11. *See* ga-stiggkwan. *From* stiggkwan.

GA-STALDAN, *vb.* to win, gain, possess, Lu. 18. 12; 1 Cor. 7. 28; 9. 20; 1 Th. 4. 4.

GA-STALDS*, *adj.* in comp. aglait-gastalds, q. v.

GA-STANDAN, *vb.* to stand still, Mk. 10. 49; Lu. 6. 8; 7. 14; 8. 44. *Der.* aftra-gastandan.

GA-STAURKNAN, *vb.* to dry up, pine away, Mk. 9. 18.

GA-STEIGAN, *vb.* to ascend, embark, Jo. 6. 24; to descend, Rom. 10. 7.

GA-STIGGKWAN, *vb.* to stumble, Jo. 11. 9, 10.

GASTI GODEI, *wk. sb. f.* hospitality, Rom. 12. 13.

GASTI-GODS, *adj.* hospitable (*lit.* good to guests), 1 Tim. 3. 2; Tit. 1. 8.

GA-STOJAN, *vb.* to judge, 1 Cor. 5. 3; 2 Cor. 2. 1; *see also* G. & L. *upon* 2 Th. 3. 2. *From* staua.

GA-STOTHANAN (GA-STOTHAN?), *vb.* to make to stand, Rom. 14. 4. *From* standan. *Der.* unga-stothans, af-gastothans.

GA-STRAUJAN, *vb.* to strew, straw, furnish, Mk. 14. 15.

GASTS, *pl.* gasteis, *str. sb. m.* a stranger, Mat. 25. 38, 43; 27. 7; Eph. 2. 12, 19; 1 Tim. 5. 10.

Der. gasti-gods, gasti-godei. [G. D. *gast*; E. *guest*.]

GA-SUKWON, *vb.* to season (as with salt), Col. 4. 6. *Cf.* ga-supon.

GA-SULJAN, *vb.* to found, lay a foundation for, Mat. 7. 25; Lu. 6. 48; Eph. 3. 18.

GA-SUNJON, *vb.* to justify, Lu. 7. 35.

GA-SUPON, *vb.* to season (as with salt), Lu. 14. 34. *Cf.* ga-sukwon.

GA-SWERAN, *vb.* to glorify, Jo. 12. 16; 13. 31. *From* swers.

GA-SWIKUNTHJAN, *vb.* to manifest, make known, Mk. 3. 12; 2 Cor. 10. 18; Col. 1. 26; *pass.* to appear, Lu. 19. 11.

GA-SWILTAN, *vb.* to die, Mat. 9. 24; Mk. 5. 35; 9. 26; 12. 20; &c. *Der.* mith-gaswiltan.

GA-SWINTHJAN, *vb.* to strengthen, Col. 1. 11.

GA-SWINTHNAN, *vb.* to become strong, Eph. 3. 16.

GA-SWOGJAN, *vb.* to sigh, Mk. 7. 34.

GAT, gat; *from* gitan.

GA-TAIKNJAN, *vb.* to give a token, warn, Lu. 3. 7.

GA-TAIRAN, *vb.* (*lit.* to tear), to break, destroy, Mat. 5. 17, 19; Mk. 14. 58; 15. 29; Jo. 7. 23; 10. 35.

GA-TALZJAN, *vb.* to teach, instruct, 1 Tim. 1. 20. *From* tilan.

GA-TAMJAN, *vb.* to tame, Mk. 5. 4. *From* timan.

GA-TANDJAN, *vb.* to cauterize, sear, 1 Tim. 4. 2. *From* tindan.

GA-TARHITHS, *adj.* (*pp. of* ga-tarhjan), worthy of blame, Gal. 2. 11; notable, Mat. 27. 16; manifest, 2 Tim. 3. 9.

GA-TAHRJAN, *vb.* to make a shew of, Col. 2. 15; to mark, 2 Th.

3. 14; to mark with blame, Skeir. 4. 25.

GA-TARNJAN, *vb.* to conceal; at thaimei ga-tarnith ist dunja, they are destitute of the truth, 1 Tim. 6. 5.

GA-TASS*, *in* un-gatass, q. v.

GA-TAUJAN, *vb.* to do, make, Mk. 2. 25; 5. 19; 6. 20; 9. 13; &c. *Gk* ποιεῖν, πράττειν, κατεργάζεσθαι. *From* tiwan.

GA-TAURA, *wk. sb. f.* a tear, rent, Mat. 9. 16; Mk. 2. 21. *From* tairan.

GA-TAURNAN, *vb.* to become torn; *hence*, to come to naught, be done away, 1 Cor. 13. 8; 2 Cor. 3. 7, 11, 13. *From* tairan.

GA-TEIHAN, *vb.* to teach, tell, announce to, make known to, Mat. 8. 33; 11. 4; Mk. 6. 30; 16. 10; to bring good tidings, 1 Th. 3. 6 *Der.* faura-gateihan.

GA-TEMIBA, *adv.* fitly, Skeir. 2. 23. *From* timan.

GA-TEWJAN, *vb.* to appoint, 2 Cor. 8. 19. *From* tiwan. *Der.* un-gatewiths.

GA-THAGKI, *str. sb. n.* thought; *hence*, us gathagkja, sparingly, 2 Cor. 9. 6.

GA-THAHAN, *vb.* to be silent, Mk. 10. 48; Lu. 20. 26.

GA-THAIRSAN, *vb.* to wither, Mk. 3. 1, 3.

GA-THARBAN, *vb.* to abstain from, 1 Tim. 4. 3. *From* thaurban.

GA-THARBJAN SIK, *vb. refl. with gen.* to be abstemious *or* temperate with regard to, 1 Cor. 9. 25.

GA-THAURBS, *adj.* temperate, Tit. 1. 8. *From* thaurban.

GA-THAURSNAN, *vb.* to become dry, to wither away, Mk. 4. 6; 5. 29; 11. 21; Lu. 8. 6; Jo. 15. 6. *From* thairsan.

GA-THEIHAN, *vb.* to thrive, increase, flourish, Phil. 4. 10; Skeir. 4. 10. [G. *gedeihen.*]

GA-THIUTHJAN, *vb.* to bless, Mk. 8. 7; Lu. 9. 16; Eph. 1. 3; Skeir. 7. 12.

GA-THIWAN, *vb.* to enslave, put in bondage, 1 Cor. 7. 15; 2 Cor. 11. 20; Gal. 2. 4; to pierce through, 1 Tim. 6. 10; mannans g., to steal men, kidnap, 1 Tim. 1. 10.

GA-THLAHSNAN, *vb.* to be astonished, to be troubled in mind, Lu. 1. 29.

GA-THLAIHAN, *vb.* to take in the arms, caress, Mk. 10. 16; to comfort, console, 2 Cor. 2. 7; to exhort, 2 Cor. 5. 20; 1 Tim 5. 1; to provide for, 1 Tim. 5. 8.

GA-THLAIHTS, *str. sb. f.* comfort, consolation, Lu. 6. 24.

GA-THLIUHAN, *vb.* to flee, Mat. 8. 33; Mk. 5. 14; 14. 50; 16. 8; Lu. 8. 34.

GA-THRAFSTEINS, *str. sb. f.* comfort, Rom. 15. 4; 2 Cor. 1. 5; 7. 13; *it should have the same sense in* Lu. 4. 19.

GA-THRAFSTJAN, *vb.* to comfort, Jo. 11. 19; 2 Cor. 1. 4; 7. 6; to refresh, 1 Cor. 16. 18.

GA-THRASK, *str. sb. n.* a threshing-floor, Lu. 3. 17. *From* thriskan.

GA-THREIHAN, *vb.* to throng; *hence*, to oppress, 2 Th. 1. 6, 7.

GA-THULAN, *vb.* to suffer, endure, Mk. 5. 26; Lu. 17. 25; 2 Tim. 2. 10, 12; 1 Cor. 13. 7. [O. E. *thole.*]

GA-THWASTJAN, *vb.* to stablish, confirm, 2 Cor. 1. 21; Col. 1. 23; *pp.* established, strong, 1 Cor. 16. 13.

GA-TILABA, *adv.* conveniently, Mk. 14. 11. *From* tilan.

GA-TILON, *vb.* to obtain, 2 Tim. 2. 10.

GA-TILS, *adj.* convenient, Mk. 6. 21; fit, Lu. 9. 62. *From* tilan.

GA-TIMAN, *vb.* to suit, agree with, Lu. 5. 36.

GA-TIMREINS, *str. sb. f.* a building up, edifying, 2 Cor. 12. 19; 13. 10.

GA-TIMRJAN, *vb.* to build, Mat. 7. 24; Mk. 12. 1; 14. 58; 15. 29; Lu. 4. 29. *Der.* mith-gatimrjan. [A. S. *timbrian; cf.* E. *timber.*]

GA-TIMRJO, *wk. sb. f.* a building, 2 Cor. 5. 1; Eph. 2. 21.

GA-TIUHAN, *vb.* to lead, bring (*lit.* to tow), Mat. 27. 2; Mk. 14. 53; 15. 16; Lu. 4. 9. *Der.* mith-gatiuban.

GA-TRAUAN, *vb.* to trust, 2 Cor. 2. 3; 10. 7; Gal. 5. 10; to be confident, 2 Cor. 5. 6, 8. [G. *trauen;* E. *trow.*]

GA-TRUDAN, *vb.* to tread down, Lu. 8. 5.

GA-TULGJAN, *vb.* to set, confirm, Lu. 9. 51; Rom. 15. 8; *with* sik, to abide, Rom. 11. 23; *pp.* steadfast, 2 Cor. 1. 6; Col. 1. 23.

GATWO, *wk. sb. f.* a street, Lu. 14. 21. [O. E. & Sc. *gate.*]

GA-U-HWA-SEHWI, whether he saw ought, Mk. 8. 23; *comp. of* ga, u, *and* saihwan.

GA-U-LAUBJATS, do ye believe, Mat. 9. 28; *comp. of* ga, u, *and* laubjan.

GAUJA, *wk. sb. m.* the surrounding country, Lu. 3. 3; 8. 37. *From* gawi.

GAUMJAN, *vb. with dat.* to see, perceive, behold, observe, Mat. 9. 11; Mk. 4. 12; to attend to, 1 Tim. 4. 13; *pass.* to be seen, Mat. 6. 5. *Cf.* saihwan.

GA-UNLEDJAN, *vb.* to make poor; *refl.* to become poor, 2 Cor. 8. 9. *From* leds.

GAUNON, *vb.* to mourn, lament, Lu. 6. 25; 7. 32; Jo. 16. 20. [*Cf.* A. S. *geong,* sighs.]

GAUNOTHS, *or* GAUNOTHA, *sb. only in acc.* gaunotha, mourning, sorrow, 2 Cor. 7. 7.

GAUREI, *wk. sb. f.* mourning, sorrow, Phil. 2. 27. *From* gaurs.

GAURITHA, *str. sb. f.* grief, sorrow, Jo. 16. 6. *From* gaurs.

GAURJAN, *vb.* to grieve, make to grieve, Rom. 14. 15; 2 Cor. 2. 2; 7. 8; Eph. 4. 30.

GAURS, *adj.* sorrowful, sad, grieved, Mk. 6. 26; 10. 22; Lu. 18. 23; of a sad countenance, Mat. 6. 16. *Der.* gaurei, gauritha, gaurjan.

GAUT, poured; *from* giutan.

GA-WADJON, *vb.* to pledge, betroth, 2 Cor. 11. 2. *From* widan.

GA-WAGJAN, *vb.* to make to wag, stir, shake, Mk. 13. 25; Lu. 6. 48; to stir to emulation, 2 Cor. 9. 2. *Der.* un-gawagiths.

GA-WAIRPAN, *vb.* to cast, cast down, throw down; Mk. 9. 45; Lu. 4. 35; to dash, Mk. 9. 18.

GA-WAIRTHEIGS, *adj.* at peace, peaceably disposed, Mk. 9. 50.

GA-WAIRTHI, *str. sb. n.* peace, Mat. 10. 34; Mk. 5. 34; Lu. 1. 79; 2. 14; &c.

GA-WAKNAN, *vb.* to be awake, Lu. 9. 32.

GA-WALDAN, *vb.* to rule, bear rule, Mk. 10. 42.

GA-WALEINS, *str. sb. f.* choice, Rom. 9. 11; 11. 28.

GA-WALIS, *adj.* elect, Col. 3. 12.

GA-WALITHS, *adj.* chosen, elect, Mk. 13. 20; Lu. 18. 7; 1 Tim. 5. 21. [G. *wählen;* O. E. & Sc. *wale.*]

GA-WAMMS, *adj.* spotted, tainted;

hence, unclean, Rom. 14. 14. [A. S. *wem*, a spot.]

GA-WANDEINS, *str. sb. f.* a turning, Skeir. 1. 27.

GA-WANDJAN, *vb.* to turn, Lu. 1. 17; to return, Lu. 8. 55; *refl.* to turn oneself, Lu. 7. 44; to be converted, Mk. 4. 12; &c. [G. *wenden*; E. *wend.*]

GA-WARGEINS, *str. sb. f.* condemnation, 2 Cor. 7. 3.

GA-WARGJAN, *vb.* to condemn, Mk. 10. 33; Rom. 8. 3.

GA-WASEINS, *str. sb. f.* clothing, Lu. 9. 29.

GA-WASJAN, *vb.* to clothe, Mat. 11. 8; Mk. 1. 6; 5. 15; Lu. 8. 35; &c.

GA-WAURDI, *str. sb. n.* a word, conversation, communication, 1 Cor. 15. 33.

GA-WAURKI, *str. sb. n.* work, business, 2 Tim. 2. 4; gain, Phil. 1. 21; 3. 7; 1 Tim. 6. 6.

GA-WAURKJAN, *vb.* to work, make, Mk. 9. 5; Lu. 1. 68; to do, Lu. 3. 19; to appoint, Mk. 3. 14.

GA-WAURSTWA, *wk. sb. m.* a fellow-worker, 2 Cor. 1. 24; 8. 23; Phil. 2. 25; 4. 3.

GA-WAURTS, *adj.* rooted, Eph. 3. 18.

GA-WEIHAN, *vb.* to consecrate, sanctify, make holy, Jo. 10. 36; 1 Cor. 7. 14; Eph. 5. 26. [G. *weihen.*]

GA-WEISON, *vb.* to visit, Mat. 25. 43; Lu. 1. 68; 7. 16; to seek out, Nehem. 7. 1.

GA-WENJAN, *vb.* to ween, suppose, Lu. 7. 43. *From* wens.

GAWI, *str. sb. n.* a province, country, region, Mat. 8. 28; Mk. 6. 55; Lu. 4. 14; 8. 26; 15. 14. *Der.* gauja. [G. *gau.*]

GA-WIDAN, *vb.* to join together, Mk. 10. 9. [G. *wetten*; D. *wedden*; E. *wed.*]

GA-WIGAN, *vb.* to make wag about, to shake up, Lu. 6. 38. [G. D. *bewegen*; E. *wag.*]

·GAWILEIS, GAWILJA, *adj.* willing, 1 Cor. 7. 12, 13; unanimous, Rom. 15. 6.

GA-WINDAN*, *in* du-gawindan, q. v.

GA-WINNAN, *vb.* to suffer, Gal. 3. 4.

GA-WISAN, *vb.* to remain, stay, abide, Lu. 8. 27. *Der.* mithgawisan.

GA-WISS, *str. sb. f.* a joint, Eph. 4. 16; Col. 2. 9. *From* widan.

GA-WIZNEIGS, *adj.* joyful, glad, Rom. 7. 22. *From* wizon.

GA-WRIKAN, *vb.* to wreak, avenge, Lu. 18. 7, 8; Rom. 12. 19.

GA-WRISKWAN, *vb.* to bear fruit well, bring fruit to perfection, Lu. 8. 14.

GA-WUNDON, *vb.* to wound, Lu. 20. 12.

GAZAUFYLAKIAUN (*Greek* γαζοφυλάκιον), the treasury, Jo. 8. 20.

GAZDS, *str. sb. m.* a goad, prick, sting, 1 Cor. 15. 55, 56.

GEIGAN*, GEIGGAN*, *vb. with acc.* to make use of (?). *Der.* ga-geigan, ga-geiggan. [*Cf.* O. E. *gain*, to profit.]

GEIRAN*, *vb.* (*perf.* gair, *pl.* gairum, *pp.* gairans), to yearn for, desire. *Der.* faihu-geiro, faihu-geironjan, gairuni, gairns, faihu-gairnei, seina-gairns, gairnjan. [G. *begehren*; D. *begeeren*; *cf.* E. *yearn.*]

GEISAN*, *vb.* (*perf.* gais, *pl.* gisum, *pp.* gisans), to make aghast, terrify. *Der.* us-geisnan, us-gaisjan. [*Cf.* E. *aghast.*]

GETUM, we gat; *from* gitan.

GIBA, *str. sb. f.* a gift, Mat. 5. 24.

Rom. 11. 29; 1 Cor. 7. 7; 2 Cor. 1. 11.

GIBAN, *vb.* (*perf.* gaf, *pl.* gebum, *pp.* gibans), to give, Mat. 5. 31; 6. 11; 9. 8; 25. 42; &c.; gibands, the giver, 2 Cor. 9. 7. *Der.* af-giban, at-giban, fra-giban, us-giban, giba, fra-gifts, gabei, gabigs, gabigaba, gabigjan, gabignan. [G. *geben;* D. *geven;* E. *give.*]

GIBLA, *sb. m.* a gable, pinnacle, Lu. 4. 9. [G. *giebel;* D. *gevel.*]

GIBTS*, *in* fra-gibts, Lu. 1. 27.

GIF, give thou; *from* giban.

GIFTS*, *in* fra-gifts, q. v.

GILD, *str. sb. n.* pay, tribute-money, tribute, Lu. 20. 22.

GILDAN*, *vb.* to yield, pay. *Der.* fra-gildan, us-gildan, gild, kaisara-gild, gilstr, gilstra-meleins. [G. *gelten;* D. *gelden;* E. *yield.*]

GILSTR, *str. sb. n.* tribute, Rom. 13. 6. *From* gildan.

GILTHA, *str. sb. f.* a sickle, Mk. 4. 29. [*Cf.* E. *geld, vb.*]

GINNAN*, *vb.* (*perf.* gann, *pl.* gunnum, *pp.* gunnans), to begin. *Der.* du-ginnan. *Cf.* ana-stodjan. [O. E. *gin.*]

GISTRA-DAGIS, *sb.* yesterday; MS. *reading in* Mat. 6. 30; *by error for* afar-daga, the morrow (*Gk.* αὔριον); see Lu. 7. 11.

GITAN*, *vb.* (*perf.* gat, *pl.* getum, *pp.* gitans), to get. *Der.* bi-gitan. [E. *get.*]

GIUTAN, *vb.* (*perf.* gaut, *pl.* gutum, *pp.* gutans), *with acc.* to pour, Mat. 9. 17; Mk. 2. 22; Lu. 5. 37, 38. *Der.* ufar-giutan, us-gutnan. [G. *giessen;* D. *gieten; cf.* E. *gush.*]

GLAGGWABA, *adv.* diligently, Ln.15.8.

GLAGGWO, *adv.* assuredly; *a conjectural word in* 1 Th. 5. 2. [*The* MS. *has* gaaggwo.]

GLAGGWUBA, *adv. as* GLAGGWABA, accurately, Lu. 1. 3.

GLAGGWUS*, *adj.* diligent. *Der.* glaggwaba. [G. *glau;* A. S. *gleáw.*]

GLITMUNJAN, *vb.* to shine, glitter, glister, Mk. 9. 3. [G. *gleissen;* D. *glinsteren;* E. *glitter.*]

GODA-KUNDS, *adj.* of good kin, of noble birth, Lu. 19. 12. *From* goths *and* kuni.

GODEI, *wk. sb. f.* goodness, virtue, Phil. 4. 8.

GODS, *see* GOTHS.

GOLEINS, *str. sb. f.* greeting, Lu. 1. 29, 41, 44; 1 Cor. 16. 21; Col. 4. 18; 2 Th. 3. 17.

GOLJAN, *vb. with acc.* to salute, greet, Mat. 5. 47; Lu. 1. 40; 10. 4; &c. *Der.* goleins.

GOTHS, GODS. *adj.* good, Mat. 5. 45; 7. 17; Lu. 8. 8; &c. *Der.* gasti-gods, gasti-godei, godei, goda-kunds. [G. *gut;* D. *goed;* E. *good.*]

GRABA, *str. sb. f.* a ditch (*lit.* a grave), Lu. 19. 43.

GRABAN, *vb.* (*perf.* grof, *pl.* grobum, *pp.* grabans), to grave, dig, Lu. 6. 48; 16. 3. *Der.* bi-graban, uf-graban, us-graban, graba, groba. [G. *graben;* D. *graven;* E. *grave.*]

GRAIF, gripped; *from* greipan.

GRAMJAN, *vb. with acc.* to make angry, provoke to wrath, Col. 3. 21. *Der.* in-gramjan. [*Cf.* G. *gram,* grief. D. *gram,* angry. O. E. *grame,* anger.]

GRAMSTS, *str. sb. m.* a mote, Lu. 6. 41; *lit.* any thing that irritates. *From* gramjan. *Cf.* gairu.

GRAS, *str. sb. n.* grass, a blade of grass, a herb, Mk. 4. 28, 32; Rom. 14. 2. [G. D. *gras;* E. *grass.*]

GREDAGS, *adj.* greedy, hungry; gr. wisan, to hunger, Mat. 25. 42; Mk. 2. 25; 11. 12. *From* gredus.

GREDON, *vb.* to be greedy, to hunger, Rom. 12. 20.

GREDUS, *str. sb. m.* greed, hunger, 2 Cor. 11. 27. *Der.* gredags, gredon. [E. *greed; cf.* D. *gretig.* greedy.]

GREFTS*, *in* ga-grefts, q. v.

GREIPAN, *vb.* (*perf.* graip, *pl.* gripum, *pp.* gripans), to gripe, grip, seize, lay hold of, take (prisoner), Mk. 14. 44, 48, 49, 51. *Der.* fair-greipan, und-greipan. [G. *greifen;* D. *grijpen;* E. *gripe.*]

GRETAN, GREITAN, *vb.* (*perf.* gaigrot, *pp.* gretans), to weep, lament, Mat. 26. 75; Mk. 5. 38; 14. 72. *Der.* grets. [O. E. *greet;* Sc. *greit.*]

GRETS, *str. sb. m.* weeping, Mat. 8. 12.

GRIDS, *str. sb. f.* a grade, degree, 1 Tim. 3. 13. [*So in MS.* M. *suggests* trid *or* trud; *but why?*]

GRIND*, *adj.* ground small, little; whence

GRINDA-FRATHJIS, feebleminded, 1 Th. 5. 14. *From* frathjan.

GROB, dug; *from* graban.

GROBA, *str. sb. f.* a hole, fox-hole, Mat. 8. 20; Lu. 9. 58. *From* graban. [G. *grube.*]

GRUDS*, *adj.* tired, sluggish (?). *Der.* us-gruds. [*Cf* E. *grudge* (?).]

GRUNDUS*, *str. sb. m.* the ground. *Der.* grundu-waddjus, af-grunditha. [G. *grund;* D. *grond;* E. *ground.*]

GRUNDU-WADDJUS, *str. sb. m.* a ground-wall, foundation, Lu. 6. 48, 49; 14. 29; Eph. 2. 20; 2 Tim. 2. 19.

GUDA, *str. sb. pl.* gods, Jo. 10. 34. *See* gutha *and* guth.

GUDA-FAURHTS, *adj.* God-fearing, devout, Lu. 2. 25.

GUDA-LAUS, *adj.* godless, without God, Eph. 2. 12.

GUD-HUS, *str. sb. n.* the house of God, the temple, Jo. 18. 20.

GUDI-LUB, *a proper name in Arezzo document.* [G. *Gottlieb.*]

GUDISKS, *adj.* godly, spiritual, divine, 2 Tim. 3. 16.

GUDJA, *wk. sb. m.* a priest, Mat. 8. 4; Mk. 1. 44; Lu. 1. 5; &c.; auhumists g., maists g., reikists g., a chief priest, high priest.

GUDJINASSUS, *str. sb. m.* the priestly office, ministry, Lu. 1. 9; 2 Cor. 9. 12.

GUDJINON, *vb.* to execute a priest's office, Lu. 1. 8.

GULTH, *str. sb. n.* gold, 1 Tim. 2. 9. *Der.* gultheins, figgra-gulth.

GULTHEINS, *adj.* golden, 2 Tim. 2. 20. [G. & E. *golden;* D. *gouden.*]

GUMA, *wk. sb. m.* a man, Lu. 19. 2; Nehem. 5. 17. *Der.* gumakunds, gumeins. [A. S. *guma;* E. *bride-g(r)oom*]

GUMA-KUNDS, *adj.* of manly kind, male, Lu. 2. 23; Gal. 3. 28.

GUMEINS, *adj.* manlike, male, Mk. 10. 6.

GUND, *str. sb. n.* a cancer, a canker, 2 Tim. 2. 17. [*The MS. has* gun-, *for which* S. *proposes* gunds, *and* G. & L. gund; *cf.* A. S. *gund.*]

GUTA*, *wk. sb. m.* a Goth. *Der.* gut-thiuda.

GUTANS, poured out; *from* giutan.

GUTH, *str. sb. m.* God, Mat. 5. 8; 8. 29; 27. 46; &c. *Der.* guth-blostreis, gutba, galiuga-guth, gutba-skaunei, guda-faurhts, guda-laus, gud-hus, Gudi-lub, gudisks, ga-guds, ga-gudaba, ga-gudei, af-guds, af-gudei, gudja, ufar-gudja, gudjinon, gudjinassus.

GUTHA, *str. sb. pl.* gods, Gal. 4. 8. See guda.

GUTHA-SKAUNEI, *wk. sb. f.* the form of God, Phil. 2. 6.

GUT-THIUDA, *str. sb. f.* the Gothic people, *in Gothic calendar.* From guta.

GUTUM, we poured out. *From* giutan.

GUTNAN*, *vb.* to gush, *only in comp.* us-gutnan. *From* giutan. [E. *gush*.]

H.

H, the eighth letter of the Gothic alphabet. As a numeral, it means 8. [Aspirate it as in English.]

ʜ, *a short form of* uh, q. v.

HABAN, *vb.* (*perf.* habaida), to have, Mat. 5. 23; 6. 1; 7. 29; &c.; (fimf tiguns jere h., to be fifty years old, Jo. 8. 57; ubil h., to be ill, Mat. 8. 16); to take hold of, Mat. 9. 25; to hold, esteem, Mk. 11. 32; to be able to do, Mk. 14. 8; to be about to, Mk. 10. 32. *Der.* un-habands, ga-baban, af-baban, ana-haban, at-haban, dis-haban, uf-haban, hafts, auda-hafts, kwithu-hafts, haftjan, ga-haftjan, ga-haftnan, ga-gabaftjan, hoban, ga-hobains, un-gahobains. [G. *haben*; D. *haven*; E. *have*.]

HAFJAN, *vb.* (*perf.* hof, *pl.* hofum, *pp.* hafans), to heave, heave up, carry, bear, Mk. 2. 3. *Der.* and-hafjan, anda-hafts, at-hafjan, us-hafjan, ufar-hafjan, ufar-hafnan. [G. *heben*; D. *heffen*; E. *heave*.]

HAFTJAN, *vb.* to cleave to, apply oneself to continually, Rom. 12. 9, 12; 1 Tim. 3. 8; (*refl.*) Col. 4. 2. *From* haban. *Der.* ga-, gaga-; ga-haftnan. [G. *heften*.]

HAFTNAN*, *vb. in comp.* ga-haftnan, q. v.

HAFTS, *adj.* joined; *in phr.* liugom hafts, joined in matrimony, married, 1 Cor. 7. 10. See haftjan.

HAFTS*, *str. sb. f. in comp.* anda-hafts, q. v.

HAH*, *in* faura-hah *and* faur-hah, q. v.

HAHAN, *vb.* (*perf.* baihah, *pl.* baibahum, *pp.* baihans), *with acc.* to let hang, leave in suspense, Jo. 10. 24; (2) *vb. neut.* (*perf.* hahaida), to hang, be in suspense, be very anxious about, Lu. 19. 48. *Der.* at-hahan, us-hahan, faura-hah, ga-hahjo.

HAIBRAIUS, *str. sb. m.* a Hebrew, 2 Cor. 11. 12; Phil. 3. 5, 11.

HAIDUS, *str. sb. m.* manner, way, Phil. 1. 18; 2 Th. 2. 3; 2 Tim. 3. 8. [G. -*heit*; E. -*hood*.]

HAIFSTJAN, *vb.* to strive, struggle, contend, 1 Cor. 9. 25; 1 Tim. 6. 12; 2 Tim. 2. 5; 4. 7. *From* haifsts.

HAIFSTS, *str. sb. f.* strife, contest, Rom. 13. 13; Gal. 5. 20; Phil. 1. 15, 16; 2. 3; whispering, slander, 2 Cor. 12. 20. *Der.* haifstjan.

HAIHAH, hung; *from* hahan.

HAIHAIT, promised; *from* haitan.
HAIHALD, *held; from* haldan.
HAIHS, *adj.* half-blind, with one eye, Mk. 9. 47. [*Cf.* Lat. *cæcus.*]
HAILI, *str. sb. n.* haleness; *in comp.* un-haili, q. v.
HAILJAN, *vb.* to heal, Mat. 9. 35; Mk. 3. 2, 15; Lu. 4. 23; (*refl.*) to be healed, Lu. 6. 17.
HAILNAN*, *vb.* to become whole, *in comp.* ga-hailnan, q. v.
HAILS, *adj.* hale, whole, Mk. 5. 34; Jo. 7. 23; Lu. 5. 31; Mat. 9. 12; hails wisan, to be sound, Tit. 1. 13; hails wairthan, to fare well, Jo. 11. 12; *cf.* Mk. 15. 18. *Der.* un-hails, ga-hails, haili, un-haili, hailjan, ga-hailjan, ga-hailnan. *Cf.* ga-nisan. [G. & D. *heil.*]
HAIMIS*, *or* HAIMS*, *adj. in comp.* ana-haims (*or* ana-haimis), *and* af-haims (*or* af-haimis). *Cf.* haims.
HAIMOTHLI, *str. sb. n.* a homestead, landed possession, Mk. 10. 29, 30. *From* haims.
HAIMS, *str. sb. f. (pl.* haimos), a village, country place, Mat. 9. 35; Mk. 6. 56; Lu. 5. 17; h. jah baurgs (κωμοπόλεις), Mk. 1. 38. *Der.* ana-haims, af-haims, haimothli. [G. *heim;* E. *home, -ham.*]
HAIRAISIS, *str. sb. f. (pl.* hairaiseis), a heresy, Gal. 5. 20.
HAIRDA, *str. sb. f.* a herd, flock, Mat. 8. 30; Mk. 5. 11; Lu. 2. 8; 8. 32. *Der.* hairdeis. *Cf.* writhus, awethi. [G. *heerde;* E. *herd.*]
HAIRDEIS, *str. sb. f.* a herd, shepherd, Mat. 9. 36; Lu. 2. 8; Jo. 10. ?. *From* bairda. [G. *hirte;* D. *herder;* E. *herd.*]
HAIRTEI*, *in* arma-hairtei, hauh-hairtei, hardu-hairtei. *Cf* hairto.

HAIRTHRA, *sb. n. pl.* bowels, 2 Cor. 6. 12.
HAIRTITHA*, *in* arma-hairtitha. *Cf.* hairto.
HAIRTO, *wk. sb. n.* the heart, Mat. 5. 28; 6. 21; 9. 4; Lu. 1. 17; 2. 19; 3. 15; &c. *Der.* arma-hairts, arma-hairtei, arma-hairtitha, hauh-hairts, hauh-hairtei, brainja-hairts, hardu-hairtei. [G. *herz;* D. *hart;* E. *heart.*]
HAIRTS*, *in* arma-hairts, &c. *Cf.* hairto.
HAIRUS, *str. sb. m.* a sword, Mat. 10. 34; Mk. 14. 43; Jo. 18. 10; Lu. 2. 35. [A. S. *heor.*]
HAIS, *str. sb. n.* a torch, Jo. 18. 3.
HAISTS*, *in* us-haists, q. v.
HAIT*, *in* anda-hait, bi-hait, ga-hait. *From* haitan.
HAITAN, *vb.* (*perf.* baihait, *pl.* haibaitum, *pp.* haitans), to name, call, Mat. 5. 19; 10. 25; 27. 8; Mk. 11. 17; Lu. 1. 13, 31; *pass.* to be hight, be called, Jo. 11. 16; Rom. 7. 3; *also* to call to one, bid to come, Mk. 1. 20; Lu. 7. 39; to command, Mat. 8. 18. *Der.* ga-haitan, faura-gahaitan, ana-haitan, and-haitan, at-haitan, fair-haitan, us-haitan, hait, ga-hait, anda-hait, bi-hait, haiti, haitja, bi-haitja, dulga-haitja, us-haista. [G. *heissen.*]
HAITHI, *str. sb. f.* heath, uncultivated field, Mat. 6. 28; Lu. 15. 15; 17. 7. *Der.* haithi-wisks. [G. *heide;* E. *heath;* D. *heyde.*]
HAITHI-WISKS, *adj.* of *or* belonging to a heath; wild, Mk. 1. 6.
HAITHNO, *wk. sb. f.* a heathen woman, a Gentile woman, Mk. 7. 26. G. *heidinn;* E. *heathen.*]
HAITI, *str. sb. f.* a hest, command, 1 Th. 4. 16; 1 Cor. 7. 6. *From* haitan.]

HAITJA*, in bi-haitja, dulga-haitja, q. v.

HAKUL, sb. n. a cloak, 2 Tim. 4. 13. Cf. snaga. [A. S. hacele.]

HALBA, str. sb. f. the half, a part, 2 Cor. 3. 10; 9. 3; only in phr. in thizai balbai. [G. hälfte; E. half.]

HALBS, adj. half, Mk. 6. 23; Lu. 19. 8. Der. halba. [G. halb; D. & E. half.]

HALDAN, vb. (perf. haibald, pl. haibaldum, pp. baldans), to hold, keep; hence, to feed, keep sheep, Mat. 8. 30; Mk. 5. 11; Lu. 8. 32; 17. 7. [G. halten; D. houden; E. hold.]

HALDIS, adv. in compar. degree, rather, more, Skeir. 4. 22. From biltban.

HALIS-AIW, adj. scarcely, Lu. 9. 39. From aiws.

HALJA, str. sb. f. hell, Hades, Mat. 11. 23; Lu. 10. 15; 1 Cor. 15. 55. [G. hölle; E. hell; D. helle.]

HALKS, adj. needy, poor, 1 Cor. 15. 10; Gal. 4. 9. Cf. arms.

HALLUS, str. sb. m. a rock, stone, Rom. 9. 33.

HALP, helped; from hilpan.

HALS, str. sb. m. a neck, Lu. 15. 20. Der. sla-hals, frei-hals, hals-agga. [G. & D. hals; A. S. hals.]

HALS-AGGA (?), wk. sb. m. the neck, a proposed reading in Mk. 9. 42. Cf. hals. [The MS. has hals-agga.]

HALTHEI*, in wilja-balthei, q. v.

HALTS, adj. halt, lame, Mat. 11. 5; Mk. 9. 45; Lu. 7. 22; 14. 13, 21. [E. halt.]

HAMA*, HAM*, sb. skin of the body (whence A. S. lic-hama); this seems to be the root of hamon, ga-hamon, af-hamon, ana-hamon, and-hamon, ufar-hamon.

HAMFS; see HANFS.

HAMON*, vb. to clothe, in ana-hamon, and-, af-, ga-, ufar-hamon. See hama.

HANA, wk. sb. m. a cock, Mat. 26. 74; Mk. 14. 68; Jo. 13. 38; 18. 27. [G. hahn; E. hen; D. haen.]

HANDUGEI, wk. sb. f. handiness, cleverness, wisdom, Mat. 11. 19; Mk. 6. 2; Lu. 2. 40; &c.

HANDUGS, adj. handy, clever, wise, 1 Cor. 1. 20; comp. handugoza, wiser, 1 Cor. 1. 25. [O. N. höndugr; E. handy; cf. O. E. hende.]

HANDUS, str. sb. f. the hand, Mat. 5. 30; 8. 3; Mk. 1. 31; Lu. 1. 66; &c. Der. handu-waurhts, un-banduwaurhts, laus-handus, handugei, handugs. [G. D. E. hand.]

HANDU-WAURHTS, adj. wrought by hand, Mk. 14. 58; Eph. 2. 11.

HANFS, HAMFS, adj. one-handed, maimed, Mk. 9. 43.

HANSA, str. sb. f. a company, a band of men, Lu. 6. 17; Mk. 15. 16; Jo. 18. 3. [O. E. hans.]

HANTH, caught; from hinthan.

HARDABA, HARDUBA, adv. hard, grievously, severely, Mat. 8. 6; 2 Cor. 13. 10.

HARDU-HAIRTEI, wk. sb. f. hard-heartedness, hardness of heart, Mk. 10. 5.

HARDUS, adj. hard, severe, austere, Lu. 19. 21; Jo. 6. 60; comp. hardiza, harder, Skeir. 6. 21. Der. harduba, hardu-hairtei, ga-hardjan. [G. hart; D. E. hard.]

HARJIS, str. sb. m. an army, legion, Lu. 2. 13; 8. 30. Cf.

hansa, hiuhma, iumjo, managei. [G. D. *heer;* A. S. *here.*]

HATAN, HATJAN, *vb.* to hate, *with acc.* Mat. 5. 44; Lu. 1. 71; Rom. 7. 15; hatands, one who hates, an enemy, Lu. 6. 27. *Der.* hatis, hatizon. [G. *hassen;* D. *haten;* E. *hate.*]

HATIS, *str. sb. n.* hate, wrath, anger, Lu. 3. 7; Eph. 2. 3; Col. 3. 6; Gal. 5. 20. *From* hatan. [G. *hass;* D. *haat;* E. *hate.*]

HATIZON, *vb.* to feel hate, be angry, Jo. 7. 23. *From* hatan.

HATJAN; *see* HATAN.

HAUBITH (*gen.* haubidis), *str. sb. n.* the head, Mat. 5. 36; 6. 17; Mk. 6. 24; Lu. 7. 38; Jo. 19. 2.; &c.; h. afmaitan, to behead, Mk. 6. 27; Lu. 9. 9; h. waihstins, corner-stone, Mk. 12. 10; Lu. 20. 17. [G. *haupt;* D. *hoofd;* A. S. *heafod.*]

HAUF, lamented; *from* hiufan.

HAUHABA, *adv.* high; *in phr.* h. hugjan, to think highly, Rom. 11. 20.

HAUHEI, *wk. sb. f.* height, Eph. 3. 18. [G. *höhe;* D. *hoogte;* E. *height.*]

HAUHEINS, *str. sb. f.* a raising on high; *hence,* glory, Jo. 8. 50, 54.

HAUH-HAIRTEI, *wk. sb. f.* high-heartedness, pride, Mk. 7. 22. *From* hauhs *and* hairto.

HAUH-HAIRTS, *adj.* high-hearted, proud, Tit. 1. 7; 2 Tim. 3. 2. *From* hauhs *and* hairto.

HAUHIS, *adv.* higher, Lu. 14. 10. *From* hauhs.

HAUHISTA, *adj. superl.* the highest, Mk. 5. 7; Lu. 1. 32. *From* hauhs.

HAUHISTI, *str. sb. m.* that which is highest, Mk. 11. 10; Lu. 2. 14; 19. 38. *From* hauhs.

HAUHITHA, *str. sb. f.* the height, that which is lofty *or* above, Lu. 1. 78; Eph. 4. 8; *see* Rom. 12. 16; loftiness, Rom. 8. 39; 2 Cor. 10. 5; exaltation, honour, Lu. 14. 10; Jo. 7. 18. [G. *höhe;* D. *hoogte.*]

HAUHIZA, *adj. comp.* higher. *See* hauhs.

HAUHJAN, *vb.* to exalt, lift on high, Lu. 14. 11; 18. 14; Jo. 12. 32; to glorify, magnify, Mat. 5. 16; 6. 2; Lu. 17. 15; &c. *From* hauhs.

HAUHNAN*, *vb.* to be lifted on high, exalted, *in* us-hauhnan, q. v.

HAUHS, *adj. (comp.* hauhiza, *sup.* hauhista), high, Mk. 9. 2; Lu. 4. 5; 16. 15; *superl.* Mk. 5. 7; Lu. 1. 32, 35, 76. *Der.* hauhis, hauhisti, hauhaba, hauhhairts, huoh-hairtei, hauh-thuhts, hauhei, hauhitha, hauhjan, us-hauhjan, us-hauhnan, ufar-hauhjan, hauheins. [G. *hoch;* D. *hoog;* E. *high.*]

HAUH-THUHTS, *adj.* having high thoughts, puffed up, 1 Tim. 6. 4.

HAUITHA; *a disputed reading in* 1 Tim. 2. 11.

HAUNEINS, *str. sb. f.* humility, Phil. 3. 21; Eph. 4. 2; Col. 2. 18; 3. 12; h. gahugdais, lowliness of mind, Phil. 2. 3. *From* hauns.

HAUNJAN, *vb.* to humiliate, 2 Cor. 11. 7; Phil. 4. 12. *From* hauns. [A. S. *hynan.*]

HAUNS, *adj.* humble, base, contemptible, 2 Cor. 10. 1. *Der.* hauneins, haunjan, ga-haunjan. *Cf.* hnaiws. [*Cf.* G. *hohn;* D. *hoon,* a scoff, taunt; O. Fr. *honnir,* to disgrace.]

HAURDS, *str. sb. f.* a door, Mat.

6. 6; 1 Cor. 16. 9; 2 Cor. 2. 12; Col. 4. 3; Nehem. 7. 1. *Cf.* daur. [E. *hurd-le.*]

HAURI, *str. sb. n.*, *only in pl.* haurja, coals, burning coals, Rom. 12. 20; a fire of coals, Jo. 18. 18. [E. *hear-th.*]

HAURN, *str. sb. n.* a horn, Lu. 1. 69; a busk, Lu. 15. 16. *Der.* thut-haurn, haurnja, haurnjan, thut-haurnjan. [G. E. *horn;* D. *horen.*]

HAURNJA, *wk. sb. m.* a horn-blower, trumpeter, Mat. 9. 23.

HAURNJAN, *vb.* to blow a horn, Mat. 6. 2; 9. 23. *From* haurn.

HAUSEINS, *str. sb. f.* the hearing, 2 Tim. 4. 3; a report, preaching, Jo. 12. 38; Rom. 10. 16; 1 Th. 2. 13. *Der.* ga-, uf-, ufar-. *From* hausjan.

HAUSJAN, HAUSJON, *vb. with acc.* to hear, Mat. 7. 24; Mk. 4. 16; *with dat.* to listen to, Mk. 6. 11; 7. 14; 9. 7; *even with gen.* to listen to, Lu. 2. 47; Jo. 6. 60; *with prep.* fram, at, *or* bi, Jo. 7. 51; 15. 15; Lu. 9. 9. *Der.* ga-, and-, uf-; hauseins, ga-, uf-, ufar-. [G. *hören;* D. *hooren;* E. *hear.*]

HAWI, *sb. m.* grass, Mat. 6. 30; Jo. 6. 10; Skeir. 7. 8. [G. *heu;* D. *hooi;* E. *hay.*]

HAZEINS, *str. sb. f.* praise, Lu. 18. 43; Rom. 13. 3; a song of praise, hymn, Eph. 5. 19; Col. 3. 16.

HAZJAN, *vb.* to praise, Lu. 2. 13; 19. 37; 16. 8. [A. S. *herian;* O. E. *hery.*]

HEITO, *wk. sb. f.* a heat, a fever, Mat. 8. 14. *Cf.* brinno. [G. *hitze;* D. *hitte;* E. *heat.*]

HEIW*, *sb.* a household, *in* heiwa-frauja, q. v. [E. *hive.*]

HEIWA-FRAUJA, *wk. sb. m.* a master of a house, Mk. 14. 14. *Cf.* garda-waldands.

HER, *adv.* here, hither, Mat. 8. 29; Mk. 6. 3; Lu. 4. 23; Jo. 6. 9. [G. *her, hier;* D. *hier;* E. *here.*]

HETHJO, *wk. sb. f.* a chamber, *lit.* a place of shelter, Mat. 6. 6. [G. *hütte;* D. E. *hut.*]

HIDRE, *adv.* hither, Mk. 11. 3; Lu. 9. 41; 14. 21. [O. E. *hider.*]

HIJA*, *fem. of* his, q. v.

HILMS, *str. sb. m.* helmet, Eph. 6. 17; 1 Th. 5. 8. [G. D. E. *helm.*]

HILPAN, *vb. with gen.* (*perf.* halp, *pl.* hulpum, *pp.* hulpans), to help, Mk. 9. 22; Lu. 5. 7; 2 Cor. 1. 11. *Der.* ga-hilpan. [G. *helfen;* D. *helpen;* E. *help.*]

HILTHAN*, *vb.* (*perf.* halth, *pl.* hulthum, *pp.* hulthans), to be gracious to, to favour. *Der.* haldis, wilja-halthei, hulths, un-hultha, un-hultho. [*Cf.* G. *hold;* D. *hulde;* O. E. *hold.*]

HIMINA-KUNDS, *adv.* heavenly, Lu. 2. 13; 1 Cor. 15. 49; Eph. 1. 3; 2. 6. *From* himins *and* kunds.

HIMINS, *str. sb. m.* heaven, Mat. 5. 16; 6. 1; 8. 11; 11. 11; &c. *Der.* himina-kunds, ufar-himina-kunds. [G. *himmel;* D. *hemel.*]

HIMMA-DAGA, *adv.* this day, to-day, Mat. 6. 11; Lu. 2. 11; 4. 21. *From* himma *and* dags. *See under* his.

HINA-DAG, *adv. same as* himma-daga, to-day; *only* hina-dag *is the acc., used after prep.* und, Mat. 11. 23; 27. 8.

HINDA*, HIND*, *prep. or adv.* behind; *whence,* hindana, hindar, hindumists.

HINDANA, *prep. with gen.* behind, on that side of, beyond, Mk 3. 8.

HINDAR, *prep. with dat. and acc.* on that side of, beyond, behind, Mk. 8. 33; Mat. 8. 18; Lu. 8. 22; Jo. 3. 26. *Der.* hindar-leithan, -weisei, -weis, un-bindar-weis. [G. *hinter*; E. *behind*.]

HINDAR-LEITHAN, *vb.* to pass away, Lu. 16. 17; to go, Lu. 17. 7.

HINDAR-WEIS, *adj.* deceitful, 2 Cor. 11. 13.

HINDAR-WEISEI, *wk. sb. f.* guile, 2 Cor. 12. 16.

HINDUMISTS, *superl. adj.* hindmost, uttermost, Mat. 8. 12.

HINTHAN*, *vb.* (*perf.* hanth, *pl.* hunthum, *pp.* hunthans), to catch with the hand. *Der.* fra-hinthan, us-binthan, fra-hunthans, mith-fra-hunthans, hunths. [O. E. *hent;* E. *hunt*.]

HIRI, *interj.* come here; Mk. 10. 21; Lu. 18. 22; hiri ut, come out, come forth, Jo. 11. 43.

HIRJATS, *interj.* come here, you two! Mk. 1. 17; *dual form of* hiri.

HIRJITH, *interj.* come ye here! Mk. 12. 7; *a plural form of* hiri.

HIS*, *pron. of which the fem. is* hija*, *neut.* bita, this; — und hita, till this time, till now, Mk. 13. 19; Mat. 11. 12; — und hita nu, till now, Skeir. 4. 10. *The dative is* himma, *acc.* hina, *whence* himma daga, to-day; *see* himma-daga; — hina dag, to-day; *see* hina-dag. *Der.* hidre, hiri, hirjats, hirjith, her, hindar. [*Cf.* E. *he, him, it.*]

HITA, *neut. of* his, q. v.

HIUFAN, *vb.* (*perf.* hauf, *pl.* bufum, *pp.* hufans), to sing dirges, mourn, lament, Mat. 11. 17; Lu. 7. 32. *Cf.* gaunon, hwopjan. [A. S. *heofian*.]

HIUHMA, HIUMA, *str. sb. m.* a crowd, number of people, Mat. 8. 18; Lu. 5. 15; 6. 17. *Cf.* iumjo, managei, bansa, harjis.

HIWI, *str. sb. n.* form, show, appearance, 2 Tim. 3. 5. [E. *hue*.]

HLAHJAN, *vb.* (*perf.* hloh, *pl.* blohum, *pp.* blahans), to laugh, Lu. 6. 25. *Cf.* hlas. *Der.* bi-hlahjan, uf-blohjan. [G. *lachen;* D. *lagchen;* E. *laugh*.]

HLAIFS, HLAIBS, *str. sb. m.* a loaf, bread, Mat. 6. 11; Mk. 2. 26. *Der.* ga-blaiba. [G. *laib;* E. *loaf*.]

HLAINS, *str. sb. m.* a hill, Lu. 3. 5.

HLAIW, *str. sb. n.* a grave, tomb, Mat. 27. 60; Mk. 6. 20; 15. 46; 16. 2. [A. S. *hlǽw;* E. *-low, -law*.]

HLAIWASNA, *wk. sb. f.* only in *pl.* hlaiwasnos, graves, sepulchres, Mat. 8. 28; 27. 52; Lu. 8. 27.

HLAMM, HLAMMA, *sb. n. or f.* a snare, 1 Tim. 3. 7; 6. 9. [O. E. *gleym*.]

HLAS, *adj.* laughing, joyful, glad, 2 Cor. 9. 7; Phil. 2. 28. *Cf.* hlahjan. [E. *glad*.]

HLASEI, *wk. sb. f.* joy, gladness, Rom. 12. 8. *From* hlas.

HLATHAN*, *vb.* (*perf.* hloth, *pl.* blothum, *pp.* hlathans), to load. *Der.* af-hlathan. [G. D. *laden;* E. *load*.]

HLAUPAN*, *vb.* (*perf.* hlaiblaup), to leap. *Der.* us-hlaupan. [G. *laufen;* D. *loopen;* E. *leap*.]

HLAUTS, *str. sb. m.* a lot, Mk. 15. 24; Col. 1. 12; hl. gasatiths wisan, to be called by lot, Eph. 1. 11. *See also* Lu. 1. 9. [G. *looss;* D. E. *lot*.]

HLEIBJAN, *vb. with dat.* to help, Lu. 1. 54.

HLEIDUMA, *adj.* left, on the left hand, Mat. 6. 3; 2 Cor. 6. 7; hl. fera, the left side, Mat. 25, 41.

HLEITHRA, *str. sb. f.* a hut, a tent, tabernacle, Lu. 9. 33; 16. 9; 2 Cor. 5. 1, 4. *Der.* hletbrastakeins, ufar-bleitbrjan. *See* hlija.

HLETHRA-STAKEINS, *str. sb. f.* feast of tabernacles, Jo. 7. 2. *From* hleithra *and* stikan.

HLIFAN, *vb.* to steal, Mat. 6. 19; Mk. 10. 19; Lu. 18. 20. *Der.* hliftus. [Lat. *clepere.*]

HLIFTUS, *str. sb. m.* a thief, Jo. 10. 1.

HLIJA, *wk. sb. m.* a tent, tabernacle, Mk. 9. 5. *Cf.* hleithra.

HLIUMA, *str. sb. m.* hearing, Mk. 7. 35; Lu. 7. 1; 1 Cor. 12. 16.

HLIUTH, *sb. n.* quietness, silence, *a conjectural reading in* 1 Tim. 2. 11. [*Cf.* O. N. *hlioth.*]

HLOHJAN*, *vb.* to rejoice; *in* uf-hlohjan, q. v. *See* hlahjan.

HLUTREI, *wk. sb. f.* purity, sincerity, 2 Cor. 1. 12. *From* hlutrs.

HLUTRITHA, *str. sb. f.* (the same as hlutrei), purity, sincerity, 2 Cor. 2. 17.

HLUTRS, *adj.* pure, 2 Cor. 7. 11. *Der.* hlutrei, hlutritha. [G. *lauter*; A. S. *hlutor.*]

HNAIWEINS, *str. sb. f.* lowliness, humility, Lu. 1. 48. *From* hneiwan. *Der.* uf-hnaiweins.

HNAIWS, *adj.* lowly, humble, Rom. 12. 16. *From* hneiwan.

HNAIWJAN, *vb.* to abase; *pp.* hnaiwiths, cast down, 2 Cor. 7. 6. *See* hneiwan.

HNASKWUS, *adj.* soft, tender, delicate, Mat. 11. 8; Lu. 7. 25. [O. E. *nesh.*]

HNEIWAN, *vb.* (*perf.* hnaiw, *pl.* hniwum, *pp.* hniwans), to bend downwards, decline, Lu. 9. 12. *Der.* ana-hneiwan; hnaiws, hnaiwjan, ga-hnaiwjan, ana-hnaiwjan, uf-hnaiwjan, hnaiweins. [G. *neigen*; A. S. *hnigan.*]

HNIUPAN*, *vb.* (*perf.* hnaup, *pl.* hnupum, *pp.* hnupans), to knap, break. *Der.* dis-hniupan, dis-hnupnan. [G. & D. *knappen*; E. *knap.*]

HNUTHO, HNUTO, *wk. sb. f.* a thorn, prick, sting, 2 Cor. 12. 7.

HOBAINS*, *in* ga-hobains, q. v.

HOHA, *wk. sb. m.* a plough, Lu. 9. 62. [G. *haue*; E. *hoe.*]

HOLON, *vb. with acc.* to treat with violence, Lu. 3. 14. *Der.* af-.

HORINASSUS, *str. sb. m.* whoredom, adultery, Mk. 9. 21; Jo. 8. 41; 2 Cor. 12. 21.

HORINON, *vb.* to commit adultery, Mat. 5. 27; Mk. 10. 11; Lu. 16. 18. *Der.* ga-.

HORINONDEI, *pt. pres. fem. from vb.* horinon, an adulteress, Mk. 8. 38; Rom. 7. 3.

HORS, *str. sb. m.* a whoremonger, Lu. 18. 11; 1 Cor. 5. 9; Eph. 5. 5. *Der.* horinon, horinondei, ga-horinon, horinassus. [G. *hure*; D. *hoer*; E. *whore.*]

HRAINEI, *wk. sb. f.* purification, purity, Skeir. 3. 9. *From* hrains.

HRAINEINS, *str. sb. f.* purification, Lu. 2. 22, Skeir. 3. 8, 22. *From* hrains.

HRAINITHA*, *in* un-brainitha, q. v.

HRAINJA-HAIRTS, *adj.* pure in heart, pure-hearted, Mat. 5. 8.

HRAINJAN, *vb.* to cleanse, purify, 2 Cor. 7. 1. *From* hrains.

HRAINS, *or* HRAINIS, *adj.* pure, clean, Mat. 27. 59; Mk. 1. 41; Lu. 5. 13. *Der.* un-hrains, hrainja-hairts, hrainei, un-hrainei, un-hrainitha; hrainjan, af-, ga-, us-; hraineins, ga-. [G. *rein*; D. *rein*; *cf.* E. *rinse.*]

HRAIW*, *sb. n.* a carcase (?), *in* hraiwa-dubo. [A. S. *hréaw.*]

HRAIWA-DUBO, *wk. sb. f.* a turtle-dove, Lu. 2. 24.

HRAMJAN, *vb.* to crucify, Jo. 19. 6. *Der.* us-, mith-us. *Cf.* galga.

HRISJAN*, *vb.* to shake. *Der.* af-, us-. [A. S. *hrysian.*]

HROPRI, HROPI, *wk. sb. f.* a crying out, clamour, Eph. 4. 31. [O. E. *roupe.*]

HROPJAN, *vb.* to call out, cry out, Mat. 8. 29; 9. 27; Mk. 1. 26; 3. 11. *Der.* uf-. [G. *rufen;* D.ʹ*roepen.*]

HROT, *str. sb. n.* a roof, Mat. 8. 8. Mk. 2. 4; Lu. 7. 6. [D. *roef;* E. *roof.*]

HROTHS*, or HROTH(?) *sb.* praise, victory, triumph. *Der.* hrotheigs. [O. E. *roose.*]

HROTHEIGS, *adj.* victorious, triumphant, 2 Cor. 2. 14. *See* broths.

HRUGGA, *str. sb. f.* a staff, Mk. 6. 8. [E. *rung; Cf.* G. *runge;* D. *rong.*]

HRUKJAN, *vb.* to crow (as a cock), Mat. 26. 74; Mk. 14. 72; Jo. 13. 38. [*Cf.* E. *rook,* a hoarse-voiced bird. Lat. *raucus.*]

HRUKS, *sb. (m.?)* the crowing of a cock, Mat. 26. 75. *Der.* hrukjan.

HRUSKAN*, *vb. in* and-hruskan, q. v.

HUGGRJAN, *vb.* to hunger, 1 Cor. 4. 11; *used impers. in phr.* huggreith mik, I am hungry, Jo. 6. 35. *Der.* huhrus. [G. *hungern;* D. *hongeren;* E. *hunger.*]

HUGJAN, *vb.* to think, imagine, believe, Mat. 5. 17; Lu. 2. 44; — hugjan hauhaba, to think highly, be proud, Rom. 11. 20; — waila h., to think well towards, agree with, Mat. 5. 25. *Der.* ga-, faura-ga-, af-, afar-, and-, ufar-, gahugds. [A. S. *hogian.*] *See* hugs.

HUGS, *str. sb. m.* intelligence, thought, understanding, Eph. 4. 17.

HUGS, *sb. n.(?), gen.* hugsis, a field, estate; *occurs in the Arezzo document.*

HUHJAN, *vb.; see* huzdjan.

HUHRUS, *str. sb. m.* hunger, Lu. 4. 25; 15. 14; Rom. 8. 35. *From* huggrjan.

HULISTR, *str. sb. n.* a veil, 2 Cor. 3. 13, 14. *From* huljan.

HULJAN, *vb. with acc.* to hide, cover, Mk. 14. 65; 1 Cor. 11. 6. *Der.* ga-, and-, dis-, un-; andhuliths, and-huleine, hulistr. [G. *hüllen;* D. *hullen;* O. E. *hele, hull.*]

HULON*, *vb.* to make hollow. *From* huls. *Der.* us-.

HULPUM, we helped; *from* hilpan.

HULS*, *adj.* hollow; *in* hulon, ushulon, hulundi. [G. *hohl;* D. *hol;* E. *hollow.*]

HULTHS, *adj.* gracious, merciful, Lu. 18. 13. *From* hilthan. [G. *hold;* O. E. *holde.*]

HULUNDI, *str. sb. f.* a hollow, cleft, cave, Jo. 11. 38. *From* huls.

HUN, *a suffix rendering a word indefinite, as in* ainshun, any one; hwashun, any one; hwanhun, at any time; hweilohun, any while; manna-hun, any man; *also in* thishun.

HUND, *sb. n. (pl.* hunda), a hundred, *only used in pl. preceded by* twa, &c.; — twa h., 200; — thrija h., 300; — fimf hunda, 500; — niun hunda, 900. *Der.* hunda-faths. *Cf.* taihuntehund. [G. *hundert;* D. *honderd;* E. *hundred.*]

HUNDA-FATHS, *str. sb. m.* a centurion, Mat. 8. 5; Lu. 7. 2; Mk. 15. 39.

HUNDS, *str. sb. m.* a dog, hound, Mk. 7. 27; Lu. 16. 21; Phil. 3. 2. [G. *hund;* D. *hond;* E. *hound.*]

HUNJAN, *vb.* to strive for (?). *In* Mk. 10. 24 *the MS. has* hunjandam, *for which Uppström proposed* huzjandam *or* huzdjandam; *M. suggests* hngjandam.

HUNSL, *str. sb. n.* a sacrifice, Mat. 9. 13; Mk. 9. 49; Lu. 2. 24; service, Jo. 16. 2. *Der.* hnnsla-staths, nn-hnnslags, hunsljan. [A. S. *husel*; O. E. *housel*.]

HUNSLA-STATHS, *str. sb. m.* an altar, Mat. 5. 23; Ln. 1. 11; 1 Cor. 10. 18.

HUNSLJAN, *vb.* to offer, 2 Tim. 4. 6.

HUNTHS, *sb.* captivity, Eph. 4. 8.

HUPS, *str. sb. m.* the hip, loins, Mk. 1. 6. Eph. 6. 14. [G. *hüfte*; D. *heup*; E. *hip*.]

HUS*, *str. sb. m.* a house. *Der.* gud-hus. *Cf.* gards, razn. [G. *haus*; D. *huis*; E. *house*.]

HUZD, *str. sb. n.* a treasure, Mat. 6. 19; Mk. 10. 21; Lu. 6. 45; 2 Cor. 4. 7. *Der.* huzdjan.

HUZDJAN, *vb.* to heap up treasure, Mat. 6. 19; 2 Cor. 12. 14. *From* huzd. *See also* 1 Cor. 16. 2.

HYSSOPO, *wk. sb. f.* hyssop, Skeir. 3. 16.

HW.

HW (HV *in M. and S.,* W *in G.,* WH *in B.*), *the* 24th *letter of the alphabet, denoted by* ☉. *As a numeral, it means* 700. *It answers to the A-S.* HW, *and is pronounced like* WH *in* wby, *when (as sounded by the Scotch)*.

HWA, what; *from* hwas.

HWAD (*also* HWATH), *adv.* whither; — this-hwaduh thadei (*or* thei), whithersoever, Mat. 8. 19; Mk. 6. 10, 56.

HWADRE, *adv.* whither, Jo. 7. 35. [E. *whither*.]

HWADUH, *adv.* whither; *see* this-hwaduh. *From* hwad *and* ub.

HWA'H, *contr. from* bwa uh, everything; *see* hwazuh.

HWAIRBAN, *vb.* (*perf.* hwarb, *pl.* hwaurbnm, *pp.* hwaurbans), *lit.* to throw, throw oneself about; *hence,* to walk, 2 Th. 3. 6, 11. *Der.* bi-; hwairbs *in* hweila-, ga-, unga-; hwarbon. [G. *werfen*; D. *werpen*; E. *warp*.]

HWAIRNEI, *sb. n.* a skull, Mk. 15. 22; *but see* hwairneins. [G. *hirn*; *Cf.* D. *hersen*; Sc. *harns*.]

HWAIRNEINS, *adj.* of a skull, Mk. 15. 22. [*Unless we suppose it a sb.*]

HWAITEIS, *str. sb. m.* (*or* hwaiti, *sb. n.*) wheat, Jo. 12. 24. [G. *waizen*; D. *weit*; E. *wheat*.]

HWAIWA, *adv.* how; h. managa, how many, as many as, 2 Cor. 1. 20; ei h., if anyhow, Rom. 11. 14; that by all means, 1 Cor. 9. 22.

HWAN, *conj.* when, Mat. 25. 38; Lu. 17. 20; *Greek* ποτέ, Phil. 4. 10; *see also* Mat. 7. 14; Mk. 9. 21; Mat. 6. 23; Rom. 11. 12; ibai hwan, nibai hwan, ei hwan ni, lest at any time, Mat. 5. 25; Mk. 4. 12; Lu. 4. 11. [G. *wann*; E. *when*.]

HWANHUN, *adv.* at any time, (*always with* ni); ni h., never, Mat. 7. 23; Lu. 15. 29; Jo. 5. 37; 6. 35.

HWAPJAN*, *vb.* to quench. *Der.* af-, af-hwapnan, un-hwapnands.

HWAPNAN*, *vb. in* af-hwapnan, q. v.

HWAR, *adv.* where; this-hwaruh

thei, wheresoever, Mk. 9. 18; 14. 9. *Der.* hwarjis. [D. *waar;* E. *where.*]

HWARB, threw; *from* hwairban.

HWARBON, *vb.* to go about, walk, Mat. 9. 27; Mk. 11. 27; Jo. 7. 1; 8. 59. *From* hwairban.

HWARJIS, *pron.* who? which? (*out of many*), Mk. 9. 34; 12. 23; — hwarjizuh, every, each, all (*Gk.* ἕκαστος *and* πᾶς), Mat. 27. 14; — ain-hwarjizuh, every one, every, Lu. 4. 40. *From* hwar *and* is.

HWARUH, *adv.* where; *from* hwar *and* uh. See hwar.

HWAS (1), *pron. inter.* (*f.* hwo, *n.* hwa), who? what? which? what sort of? (2) any one, anything. *Cf.* hwarjis *and* hwathar. *Der.* hwashun, hwazuh, hwe, hwaiwa, hwath, hwadre, hwan, hwanhun, hwar, hwaruh, hwarjis, hwarjizuh. [G. *wer;* E. *who;* A. S. *hwa.*]

HWASHUN, any one; ni hwashun, no one, Mat. 9. 16; Mk. 10. 18, 29.

HWASS*, *adj.* sharp; *from* hwatan. *Der.* hwassaba, hwassei.

HWASSABA, *adv.* sharply, Tit. 1. 13.

HWASSEI, *wk. sb. f.* sharpness, severity, Rom. 11. 22.

HWATAN*, *vb.* to whet. *Der.* hwass, hwassaba, hwassei, hwota, hwotjan, gahwotjan. [*Cf.* G. *wetzen;* D. *wetten;* E. *whet.*]

HWATH, HWAD, *adv.* whither, Jo. 8. 14; 12. 35; 13. 36.

HWATHAR, *adj.* whether (of two), which (of two); Mat. 9. 5; Mk. 2. 9; Lu. 5. 23; — hwatharuh, each (of two), Skeir. 5. 22; — ain hwatharuh, each one (of two), Skeir. 3. 5. [E. *whether.*]

HWATHJAN, *vb.* to foam, Mk. 9. 18, 20. See hwatho.

HWATHO, *str. sb. f.* foam, Lu. 9. 39. *From* hwathjan.

HWATHRO, *adv.* from whence, whence, Mk. 6. 2; 8. 4. *See also* Lu. 7. 42.

HWAURBANS, thrown; *from* hwairban.

HWAZUH (*fem.* hwo'h, *neut.* hwa'h), each, every; (*from* hwas *and* uh), Mk. 9. 49; Lu. 2. 23; 6. 30.

HWE, *adv.* how, somewhat, *instr. case of* hwas, 2 Cor. 11. 21. [G. *wie; cf.* E. *why, how.*]

HWEH, *adv.* only, Gal. 6. 12; hweh thatanei, only, Phil. 1. 27; *from* hwe *and* uh.

HWEIHTS, *adj.* light, slight, 2 Cor. 4. 17. *Cf.* leihts.

HWEILA, *str. sb. f.* a while, a time, a season, Mat. 8. 13; 9. 22; 27. 45. *Der.* hweilohun, bweila, hwairbs; hweilan, ga-, ana-; ga-hweilains; hweils, unhweils. [G. *weile;* D. *wijl;* E. *while.*]

HWEILA-HWAIRBS, *adj.* enduring only for a while, Mk. 4. 17; 2 Cor. 4. 17. *From* hweila *and* hwairban.

HWEILAINS*; *see* ga-hweilains.

HWEILAN, *vb.* to pause a while, to cease, Col. 1. 9. *From* hweila. *Der.* ga-, ana-, ga-hweilains.

HWEILOHUN, *adv.* for a while, Gal. 2. 5. *From* hweila *and* hun.

HWEILS*, *adj.* resting, pausing; *in* un-hweils.

HWEITJAN*, *vb.* to whiten; *only in comp.* ga-hweitjan, q. v.

HWEITS, *adj.* white, Mat. 5. 36; Mk. 9. 3; Lu. 9. 29. *Der.* ga-hweitjan, hwaiteis(?). [G. *weiss;* D. *wit;* E. *white.*]

HWE-LAUDS, what, what sort of, 2 Cor. 7. 11.

HWE-LEIKS (Lu. 1. 29), HWILEIKS, what sort of, Mk. 4. 30; Jo. 12. 33. [G. *welcher;* A. S. *hwylc.*]

HWI-LEIKS, what sort of a. *See* hwe-leiks.

HWILFTRI, *str. sb. f.* a bier, Lu. 7. 14.

HWIS, *gen. m. and n. of* hwas.

HWO, *fem. of* hwas, who, any one.

HWOFTULI, *str. sb. f.* boasting, 1 Cor. 5. 7; 2 Cor. 1. 14; 5. 12. *From* hwopan.

HWOH, *fem.* of hwazuh, each, every.

HWOPAN, *vb.* (*perf.* hwaihwop), to boast, Rom. 11. 18; 1 Cor. 4. 7; 13. 3; 2 Cor. 5. 12. *Der.* hwoftuli. [E. *whoop; cf.* D. *hop.*]

HWOTA, *str. sb. f.* a threat, threatening, Eph. 6. 9; Skeir. 2. 3. *Der.* hwotjan, ga-hwotjan.

HWOTJAN, *vb.* to threaten, rebuke, charge, Mk. 10. 48; Lu. 4. 35. *Der.* ga-hwotjan. *From* hwota.

I.

I, *the tenth letter of the alphabet; as a numeral* 10. *It is generally short, like* i *in Engl.* did. *The diphthong* iu *may be sounded as* yu, *or as* ew *in Engl.* new.

IBA, *another form of* ibai.

IBAI, IBA, *conj.* perhaps, *answers in questions to Greek* μή, Mat. 9. 15; Mk. 2. 19; perhaps, that not, *Greek* μή, 2 Cor. 12. 21;
— ibai aufto (μήποτε, μήπως, ἵνα μή, ἵνα μήποτε; εἰ μήτι, μήτι ἄρα), lest, perhaps; lest perhaps, Jo. 7. 26; 2 Cor. 1. 17; Mat. 27. 64;
— ibai aufto ni (μήπως οὐδὲ), lest, Rom. 11. 21;
— ibai ni (μὴ οὐ), Rom. 10. 18;
— ibai hwan (μήποτε), lest, Mat. 5. 25;
— thatainei ibai (μόνον μὴ), only not, Gal. 5. 13.
— ibai hwa (μή τι), lest at all;
— ibai than (μὴ γὰρ);
— aiththau ibai (ἤ);
— ibai ei (μήτι), lest perchance;
— nibai, niba (*i. e.* ni ibai, ni iba), except, unless (εἰ οὐ, εἰ μή, ἐὰν μή);
— nibai aufto, unless perhaps;
— nibai thatei, unless that, except that;
— nibai thau thatei, except however that. *Cf.* jabai. [E. *if.*]

IBDALI, *sb.* descent, Lu. 19. 37. [*It is uncertain whether we should read* ibdaljin *or* iddaljin.] *From* dal.

IBNA, even with, like, Lu. 20. 36. *From* ibns, q. v.

IBNA-LEIKS, *adj.* equal, Skeir. 5. 26. *From* ibns *and* leiks.

IBNA-SKAUNS, *adj.* of like appearance with, Phil. 3. 21. *From* ibns *and* skauns.

IBNASSUS, *str. sb. m.* evenness, equality, 2 Cor. 8. 14; Col. 4. 1. *From* ibns.

IBNS, *adj.* even, flat, Lu. 6. 17; even with, equal, Skeir. 1. 4; 5. 24. *Der.* ibna, ibna-leiks, ibna-skauns, ibnassus, ga-ibnjan. [G. *eben;* D. *effen;* E. *even.*]

IBUKS, *adv.* backwards, Lu. 17. 31; Jo. 6. 66; 18. 6.

IDDALI; see IBDALI.

IDDJA, I went. *From* gaggan.

IDDJEDUM, we went. *From* gaggan.

IDREIGA, *str. sb. f.* repentance, Mk. 1. 4; Lu. 3. 3; 5. 32; inu idreiga (ἀμεταμέλητος), Rom. 11. 29. *Der.* idreigon, ga-idreigon.

IDREIGON, *vb.* (*with and without* sik), to repent, Mat. 11. 20; Mk. 1. 15; 6. 12; Lu. 17. 3. *Der.* ga-idreigon.

IDWEIT, *str. sb. n.* shame, reproach, Lu. 1. 25; 1 Tim. 3. 7. *From* weitan. *Der.* idweitjan.

IDWEITJAN, *vb.* to reproach, Mat. 11. 20; 27. 44; Mk. 15. 32; Lu. 6. 22. *From* weitan. [E. *twit.*]

IFTUMA, *adj.* the one after, the following; iftumin daga, on the morrow, Mat. 27. 62; Mk. 11. 12; Jo. 6. 22. *See* aftuma.

IGGKWAR; *dual poss. pron.* belonging to you two, Mat. 9. 29.

IGGKWARA, *gen. dual of* iggkwis, 1 Cor. 12. 21.

IGGKWIS, IGKWIS, *dat. and acc. dual,* you two, Mat. 9. 29; Mk. 1. 17. *Cf.* izwis. [A. S. *incit.*]

IJA, she (*nom. and acc.*); *from* is.

IK, I; jah ik (κἀγώ), I also; — ikei, I who; — ik im saei, I am he, who.

IM, (I) am; *also* to them, *from* is.

IMMA, to him; *from* is.

IN, *prep.* (*with dat. and acc.*), in, towards, to, for; (*with gen.*) on account of, about, through, by (διά); — in this (or in-uh-this), on this account; — in thizei, because, for the reason that. *It is a common prefix. See below. It also helps to form* inilo, inn, inna, innana, innathro, innuma. [G. D. E. *in.*]

INA, him; *acc. of* is.

IN-AGJAN, *vb.* (*lit.* to strike awe into), to threaten, rebuke, Mat. 9. 30. *See* agis.

IN-AHEI, *wk. sb. f.* soberness, quietness, sobriety, 1 Tim. 2. 9; 2 Tim. 1. 7. *From* aha.

IN-AHS, *adj.* wise, sober, prudent, Rom. 12. 16. *From* aha.

IN-ALJANON, *vb.* to provoke to jealousy, make angry, 1 Cor. 10. 22. *From* aljan.

IN-BRANNJAN, *vb.* to burn, Jo. 15. 6. *From* brinnan.

IN-DROBNAN, *vb.* to be troubled, Jo. 13. 21; 14. 1, 27. *From* drobjan.

IN-FEINAN, *vb.* to pity, Mat. 9. 26; Mk. 1. 41; 8. 2; Lu. 7. 13; *and see* Lu. 1. 78.

IN-GALEIKON, *vb.* to metamorphose, to change into the likeness of, 2 Cor. 3. 18. *From* leiks.

IN-GARDIS, INGARDJA, *sb. or adj.* one of the same household, 1 Cor. 16. 19; Col. 4. 15. *From* gards.

IN-GRAMJAN, *vb.* to anger, make angry, 1 Cor. 13. 5.

INILO, *wk. sb. f.* an excuse, Jo. 15. 22; opportunity of excuse, 2 Cor. 11. 12.

IN-KILTHO, *wk. sb. f.* a pregnant woman, Lu. 2. 5; 1. 36; *see* Lu. 1. 24. *From* kilthei.

IN-KUNS, *adj.* one of the same country, 1 Th. 2. 14. *From* kuni.

INKWIS; *see* iggkwis.

IN-LIUHTJAN, *vb.* to enlighten, Eph. 1. 18; 3. 9. *From* liuhan.

IN-MAIDEINS, *str. sb. f.* a change, exchange, Mk. 8. 37; Skeir. 5. 15. *From* maids.

IN-MAIDJAN, *vb.* to change, exchange, transfigure, Mk. 9. 2; 1 Cor. 15. 51; Phil. 3. 21; Gal. 4. 20. *From* maids.

INN, into; *used as a prefix to verbs; see below; sometimes followed by* at.
INNA, *adv.* into, within; *used as a prefix; see below.*
INNA(T)-GAHTS, *str. sb. f.* a going into, a coming in, appearance, Lu. 1. 29. *From* gaggan.
INNA-GAMELJAN, *vb.* to write in, inscribe, 2 Cor. 3. 3. *From* mel.
INNA-KUNDS, *adj.* of the same household, Mat. 10. 25, 36. *From* kuni.
INNANA, *adv.* within, 2 Cor. 7. 5; *prep. with gen.* within, inside, Mk. 15. 16.
INN-AT-BAIRAN, *vb.* to bear or bring in, Lu. 5. 18, 19. *From* bairan.
INN-AT-GAGGAN, *vb.* to enter, enter into, go into, Mat. 8. 5; 27. 53; Mk. 5. 39. *From* gaggan.
INNATHRO, *adv.* within, Mk. 1. 21, 23; inwardly, Mat. 7. 15.
INN-AT-TIUHAN, *vb.* to bring in, Lu. 2. 27. *From* tiuhan.
INN-GAGGAN, *vb.* to go in, enter, Mat. 7. 13; 8. 8; Lu. 7. 6; 8. 51; i. framis, to go on, Mk. 1. 19.
INN-GALEITHAN, *vb.* to go in, to enter, Mat. 7. 13; Lu. 6. 4; 18. 24; 19. 1. *Der.* mith-.
IN-NIUJITHA, *str. sb. f.* the feast of the dedication, Jo. 10. 22. *From* niujis.
INN-UF-SLIUPAN, *vb.* to slip in, to creep in, Gal. 2. 4.
INNUMA, *adj. comp.* the inner, the inward, Rom. 7. 22; 2 Cor. 4. 16; Eph. 3. 16. *See* inna.
INN-WAIRPAN, *vb.* to cast in, to cast, Jo. 12. 6.
IN-RAUHTJAN, *vb.* to groan, Jo. 11. 33, 38.
INS, them; *pl. acc. m. of* is.

IN-SAHTS, *str. sb. f.* an account, argument, explanation, declaration, Lu. 1. 1; Skeir. 5. 13, 20. *From* sakan.
IN-SAIAN, *vb.* to sow in, Mk. 4. 15.
IN-SAIHWAN, *vb.* to look upon, regard, behold, Mat. 6. 26; Mk. 10. 21; to look round, Mk. 9. 8.
IN-SAILJAN, *vb.* to let down or lower with cords, Mk. 2. 4. *From* sail. [*Cf.* A. S. *sdl.*]
IN-SAKAN, *vb.* to suggest, put in mind of, point out, 1 Tim. 4. 6; Skeir. 4. 14, 24.
IN-SANDJAN, *vb.* to send, Mat. 11. 2; Mk. 5. 12; to send back, Philem. 11. *Der.* mith-.
IN-STANDAN. *vb.* to be instant or urgent, 2 Tim. 4. 2.
IN-SWINTHJAN, *vb.* to strengthen, Eph. 6. 10; Phil. 4. 13; 1 Tim. 1. 12. *From* swinths.
IN-TANDJAN, *vb.* to kindle, burn up, Lu. 3. 17. *From* tindan.
IN-THIS, *conj.* on this account, therefore, Eph. 3. 14.
IN-THIZEI, *conj.* therefore, Rom. 15. 7; 2 Cor. 4. 13.
IN-TRISGAN, *vb.* to engraft, Rom. 11. 24. *See the next.*
IN-TRUSGJAN, *vb.* to engraft, Rom. 11. 17, 19, 23.
IN-TUNDNAN, *vb.* to catch fire, be kindled, burn, 1 Cor. 7. 9. *From* tindan.
INU, INUH, *prep.* in; *followed by the enclitic* u *or* uh.
IN-UH-THIS, therefore, 1 Th. 4. 8.
IN-WAGJAN, *vb.* to stir up, Mk. 15. 11; *refl.* to be troubled, Jo. 11. 33. *From* wigan.
IN-WANDJAN, *vb.* to turn, change, pervert, Gal. 1. 7. *From* windan.
IN-WEITAN, *vb.* to worship, reverence, Mat. 8. 2; Mk. 5. 6; Lu. 4. 7; to salute, Mk. 9. 15.

IN-WIDAN, *vb.* to deny, refuse, Mat. 26. 75; Mk. 8. 34; 14. 72; to reject, frustrate, Mk. 7. 9.

IN-WINDITHA, *str. sb. f.* injustice, Lu. 16. 8; 18. 6; Jo. 7. 18. *From* windan.

IN-WINDS, *adj.* perverse, Lu. 9. 41; unjust, Mat. 5. 45; Lu. 16. 11; 18. 11. *From* windan.

IN-WISAN, *vb.* to be present; *hence,* to be present and gone again, to be just past, Mk. 16. 1.

Is, *pron.* he (*fem.* si, she; *n.* ita, it); *gen.* is (*f.* izos); *dat.* imma (*f.* izai); *acc.* ina, ija, ita; *pl.* eis (*n.* ija); *gen.* ize (*f.* izo); *dat.* im; *acc.* ios, ijos, ija; — izei, he who, *from* is *and* ei; — sa izei, he who.

Is, (thou) art; *from* wisan.

IST, (he) is; *from* wisan.

ITA, it; *from* is.

ITAN, *vb.* (*perf.* at, *pl.* etum, *pp.* itans), to eat, Lu. 15. 16; 16. 21; 17. 27, 28. *Der.* fra-; fra-atjan, uzeta, afetja. [G. *essen;* D. *eten;* E. *eat.*]

ITH, *conj.* but, and, for, now, also, if then; — ith than, but; ith nu, therefore; *cf.* aththan.

IUDAIWISKO, *adv.* in a Jewish manner, Gal. 2. 14.

IUDAIWISKON, *vb.* to Judaize, to live like a Jew, Gal. 2. 14.

IUDAIWISKS, *adj.* Jewish, Tit. 1. 14.

IUMJO, *wk. sb. f.* a crowd, Mat. 8. 1.

IUP, *adv.* up, upwards, aloft. *Der.* iupa, iupana, iupathro. [G. *auf;* D. *op;* E. *up.*]

IUPA, *adv.* above, on high, Gal. 4. 26; Col. 3. 1; from on high, Phil. 3. 14.

IUPANA, *adv.* again, Gal. 4. 9. *From* iup.

IUPATHRO, *adv.* from above, Mat. 27. 51; Mk. 15. 38; Jo. 3. 3. *From* iup.

IUS*, *adj.* easy; *see* iusiza.

IUSILA, *str. sb. f.* an easement, lightening of a load, 2 Cor. 8. 13.

IUSIZA, better; *in phr.* iusiza wisan (διαφέρειν), to be better, to excel, exceed, Gal. 4. 1; *as though from* ius, *light, easy.*

IZAI, to her; *dat. fem. sing. of* is.

IZE, of them; *from* is.

IZEEI, of them that; *from* izei.

IZEI, *pron. rel.* he who, he that; *pl.* they who, they that, *like* eizei.

IZOS, of her; *gen. fem. sing. of* is.

IZWAR, *pos. pron.* your; — izwar misso, of yourselves, of one another (of you), *Greek* ἀλλήλων, Gal. 6. 2. *See* thu.

IZWARA, of you (ὑμῶν); *pl. gen. from* thu.

IZWIS, to you; you; *dat. and acc. pl. of* thu.

IZWIZEI, you that, you who; *from* izwis *and* ei. *See* Gal. 3. 1.

J.

J, *the* 15th *letter of the alphabet. As a numeral, it means* 60. [*Pronounced like Germ.* j, *or Engl.* y *in* yield.]

JA, yes; Mat. 5. 37; 2 Cor. 1. 17. *See* jai. [G. & D. *ja;* E. *yea.*]

JABA; *see* JABAI; Jo. 11. 25.

JABAI, *conj.* if, even if, although; — jab jabni, *or* jabai jab, even

if, 2 Cor. 7. 8; Lu. 18. 4;
— jabai .. aiththau, either .. or;
— jabai swethauh, if only, even
though; — thauh jabai, even if,
Jo. 11. 25; 1 Cor. 7. 21. *Cf.*
ibai.

JAH, *conj.* and, also, for, if, but
(καὶ, γάρ, δέ); *changed in composition to* jab-, jad-, jag-, jal-,
jam-, jan-, jar-, jas-, jath-;
according to the letter following;
jah — jah, both — and.

JAI, *adv.* yes, verily, Mat. 9. 28;
— thannu nu jai (μενοῦνγε, ἄρα
οὖν), Rom. 9. 20; 9. 18; — ith
nu jai (σὺ δέ, ὦ), 1 Tim. 6. 11
(*where* jai *seems to be an interjection*). *See* jah.

JAINA, *fem. of* jains, q. v.

JAINAR, *adv.* there; Mat. 5. 23;
8. 12. *See* jains.

JAINATA, *neut. of* jains.

JAIND, *adv.* there, Jo. 11. 8. [E.
yond.]

JAINDRE, *adv.* there, Lu. 11. 37.
[E. *yonder.*]

JAINDWAIRTHS, *adv.* yonderwards,
thither, Jo. 18. 3.

JAINS, *pron. dem.* that; (*fem.* jaina;
neut. jainata), Mat. 7. 25; 8. 13.
Der. ufar-jaina, jainar, jaind,
jaindwairths, jaindre, jainthro.
[G. *jener;* D. *gene;* E. *yon.*]

JAINTHRO, *adv.* thence, Mat. 5.
23; 9. 9. *From* jains.

JANNI, *conj.* and not; *from* jah
and ni.

JATHTHE — JATHTHE, whether
— or, 1 Cor. 10. 31, &c.

JAU, *conj.* whether, if, Lu. 6. 7;
Jo. 7. 48.

JER, *str. sb. n.* a year, Mk. 5. 25;
Lu. 2. 36; a time, season, Lu.
20. 9; 2 Tim. 3. 1. [G. *jahr;*
D. *jaar;* E. *year.*]

JIUKA, *str. sb. f.* strife, anger, Gal.
5. 20; 2 Cor. 12. 20. *From*
jiukan.

JIUKAN, *vb.* to contend, to fight,
1 Cor. 9. 26; to conquer, Rom.
8. 37. *Der.* ga-, jiuka, waurda-
jiuka, juk, gajuk, gajuko, jukuzi.

JIULEIS, *str. sb. m.* July, *in Goth.
calendar.*

JOTA, *sb.* an iota, jot, Mat. 5. 18.

JU, *adv.* now, already, Mat. 5.
28; Mk. 8. 2; Lu. 3. 9; ju ni
thanamais, now no more, no
longer, Lu. 16. 2. [G. *je;*
A. S. *geo.*]

JUGGA-LAUTHS, *str. sb. m.* a young
lad, a young man, Mk. 14. 51;
16. 5; Lu. 7. 14. *From* juggs
and liudan.

JUGGS, *adj.* young, Mat. 9. 17;
Mk. 2. 22; Lu. 5. 39; 15.
12. *Der.* jugga-lauths, junda.
[G. *jung;* D. *jong;* E. *young.*]

JUHIZA* (*supposed comp. of* juggs),
younger.

JUK, *str. sb. n.* a yoke, a pair,
Lu. 14. 19. *Cf.* jiukan. [G.
joch; D. *juk;* E. *yoke.*]

JUKUZI, *str. sb. f.* a yoke,
Gal. 5. 1; 1 Tim. 6. 1. *From* juk.

JUNDA (*or* JUNDS), *str. sb. f.* youth,
Mk. 10. 20; Lu. 18. 21; 1 Tim.
4. 12. *From* juggs.

JUS, ye; *pl. of* thu, thou; *gen.*
izwara; *dat. and acc.* izwis.
Der. izwar.

JUTHAN, *adv.* already, Mk. 4. 37;
11.11; 13. 28. *From* ju *and* than.

JUZEI, ye who, ye that, Lu. 16.
15; 2 Cor. 8. 10; Gal. 5. 4.
From jus *and* ei.

K.

K, *the eleventh letter of the alphabet. As a numeral, it means* 20. [*Pronounced as in English.*]

KABALLARJA, *the name of a place in the Arezzo document.*

KAISAR, *str. sb. m.* Cæsar, Mk. 12. 14; Lu. 2. 1.

KAISARA-GILD, *str. sb. n.* tribute-money, Mk. 12. 14; *from* gildan.

KAISARIA, Cæsarea, Mk. 8. 27.

KALBO, *wk. sb. f.* a calf, heifer, Skeir. 3. 14. [G. *kalb;* D. *kalf;* E. *calf.*]

KALDS, *adj.* cold, Mat. 10. 42; *neut.* kald, the cold, Jo. 18. 18. [G. *kalt;* D. *koud;* E. *cold.*]

KALKINASSUS, *str. sb. m.* fornication, adultery, Mat. 5. 32; Mk. 7. 21. *From* kalkjo.

KALKJO, *wk. sb. f.* a harlot, whore, Lu. 15. 30. *Der.* kalkinassus.

KANN, I know, I can; *from* kunnan.

KANNJAN, *vb.* to make known, Jo. 17. 26; 1 Cor. 15. 1; 2 Cor. 8. 1. *Der.* ga-, us-.

KAN(N)T, thou knowest; *from* kunnan.

KAPILLON, *vb.* to shave, shear, crop, 1 Cor. 11. 6. *From* Lat. *capillus.*

KARA, *str. sb. f.* care; *hence* kar' ist, *with acc. of pers. and gen. of thing,* it concerns, Jo. 10. 13; 12. 6; *and without* ist, Mk. 4. 38; hwa kara unsis, what is that to us? Mat. 27. 4. [E. *care.*]

KARAN*, *in* ga-karan, q. v.

KARJA*, *another form of* kara (?).

KARKARA, *str. sb. f.* a prison, Mat. 11. 2; 25. 39; Lu. 3. 20. [Lat. *carcer.*]

KARON, *vb.* to be concerned about, 1 Cor. 7. 21. *From* kara.

KARS*, *adj. in* unkars, q. v.

KAS, *str. sb. n.* a vessel, pot (for holding liquids, &c.), Mk. 3. 27; 11. 16; Lu. 8. 16. *Der.* kasja.

KASJA, *wk. sb. m.* a potter, Mat. 27. 7; Rom. 9. 21. *From* kas.

KATILS, *str. sb. m.* a kettle, vessel for water, Mk. 7. 4. [G. *kessel;* D. *ketel;* E. *kettle.*]

KAUPATJAN, *vb.* to strike with the palm of the hand, cuff, Mat. 26. 67; Mk. 14. 65. [E. *cuff.*]

KAUPON, *vb.* to traffic, trade, buy and sell, Lu. 19. 13. [A. S. *ceapian;* G. *kaufen;* D. *koopen; cf.* E. *chapman.*]

KAUREI(NS), *sb. f.* a weight, 2 Cor. 4. 17; *from* kaurs. *Der.* un-.

KAURITHA, *str. sb. f.* a weight, burden, Gal. 6. 2; *from* kaurs.

KAURJAN, *vb.* to lade, burden, Lu. 9. 32; 2 Cor. 1. 8; 5. 4; *from* kaurs. *Der.* ana-, mith-.

KAURN, *str. sb. n.* corn, Mk. 4. 28; Lu. 3. 17; 16. 7. [G. *korn;* D. *koren;* E. *corn.*]

KAURNO, *str. sb. f.* corn, a grain of corn, Mk. 4. 31; Lu. 17. 6; Jo. 12. 24.

KAURS, *adj.* heavy, burdensome, 2 Cor. 10. 10. *Der.* kauritha; kaurjan, ana-, mith-, mith-kauriths, kaureins, unkaureins.

KAUS, I chose; *from* kiusan.

KAUSJAN, *vb.* to prove, test, Lu. 14. 19; 2 Cor. 13. 5; to taste,

Mk. 9. 1; Lu. 9. 27; Jo. 8. 52. *From* kiusan.

KAWTSJO, *wk. sb. f.* put for Lat. cautio *in Neapol. document.*

KEIAN*, *vb.* (*perf.* kai, *pl.* kijum, *pp.* kijans), to produce buds, germinate. *Der.* us-; keinan, us-, mithus-.

KEINAN, *vb.* to spring up, grow (of plants), Mk. 4. 27. *Der.* us-, mithus-. [*Cf.* G. *keimen.*]

KELIKN, *str. sb. n.* a tower, Mk. 12. 1; Lu. 14. 28; an upper chamber, Mk. 14. 15.

KILTHEI, *wk. sb. f.* the womb, Lu. 1. 31. *Der.* inkiltho. [*Cf.* E. *child.*]

KINDINS, *str. sb. m.* a governor, Mat. 27. 2; Lu. 20. 20; kindins wisan, to rule, Lu. 2. 2.

KINNUS, *str. sb. f.* the cheek, Mat. 5. 39; Lu. 6. 29. [G. *kinn*; D. *kin*; E. *chin.*]

KINTUS, *str. sb. m.* a farthing (Lat. *quadrans*), Mat. 5. 26.

KIUSAN, *vb.* (*perf.* kaus, *pl.* kusum, *pp.* kusans), to choose; *also,* to prove, test, 2 Cor. 8. 8; Gal. 6. 4. *Der.* gakiusan, gakusans, ungakusans, uskiusan, kausjan, gakausjan, gakusts, kustus. [G. *kiesen*; D. *kiezen*; O. E. *chese*; E. *choose.*]

KLAHEI*, *in* niuklahei, q. v.

KLAHS*, *in* niuklas, q. v.

KLISMJAN, *vb.* to make a clinking, *or* tinkling noise, 1 Cor. 13. 1.

KLISMO, *wk. sb. f.* a clinking instrument, a cymbal, 1 Cor. 13. 1.

KNIU, *str. sb. n.* (*gen.* kniwis), the knee, Mk. 15. 19; Lu. 5. 8; Rom. 14. 11. *Der.* knussjan. [G. D. *knie*; E. *knee.*]

KNODA (*or* KNODS?), *str. sb. f.* a race, stock, Phil. 3. 5.

KNUSSJAN, *vb.* to kneel, Mk. 10. 17; k. kniwam, to kneel, Mk. 1. 40. *From* knius.

KONS*, *in* aljakons; *see* aljakuns.

KREKS, *str. sb. m.* a Greek, Rom. 10. 12; 1 Cor. 1. 22.

KRIUSTAN, *vb.* (*perf.* kraust, *pl.* krustum, *pp.* krustans), to gnash with the teeth, grind the teeth, Mk. 9. 18. *Der.* krusts.

KROTON*, *vb.* to crush; in gakroton, q. v. [E. *crush.*]

KRUSTS, *str. sb. f.* gnashing of teeth, Mat. 8. 12.

KUBITUS, *str. sb. m.* a company, a number of men reclining together, Lu. 9. 14. *Cf.* kumbjan. [Lat. *cubitus.*]

KUKJAN, *vb. with dat.* to kiss, Mk. 14. 44; Lu. 7. 38; 15. 20. *Der.* bikukjan. [G. *küssen*; D. *kussen*; E. *kiss.*]

KUMBJAN*, *vb.* to lie down, recline. *Der.* ana-, mithana. [Lat. *cumbere.*]

KUNAWEDA, *str. sb. f.* a bond, chain, Eph. 6. 20. *From* widan.

KUNDS*, *in* ga-kunds, q. v.

KUNDS*, *adj.* of a certain kind *or* nature. *Der.* airtha-, guma-, goda-, bimina-, inna-, kwina-.

KUNI, *str. sb. n.* kin, race, generation, tribe, Mat. 11. 16; Mk. 8. 12; 9. 19; Lu. 1. 48; 3. 7. *Der.* aljakuns, inkuns, samakuns, kunds, innakunds, godakunds, gumakunds, kwinakunds, airthakunds, biminakunds. [D. *kunne*; E. *kin, kind.*]

KUNNAINS*, *sb.* knowledge, *in* anakunnains, q. v.

KUNNAN, *vb.* (*first perf. as pres.* kann; *pl.* kunnum; *pt. t.* kuntha; *pp.* kunths), to know, to make known, Mat. 7. 23; Mk. 4. 11; Lu. 4. 34; &c. *Der.* ga-, ana-, at-, fra-, uf-; kannjan, ga-, us-; kunths, un-, us-, fra-, swi-, unswi-; kunthi, un-; swikunthaba, gaswikunthjan. [G. & D. kennen; E. ken, can.]

KUNNUM, we know; from kunnan.

KUNS*, adj. of kin. Der. alja-, in-, sama-.

KUNTHA, I knew; from kunnan.

KUNTHI, str. sb. n. knowledge, Lu. 1. 77; Rom. 10. 2; 1 Cor. 8. 10; 13. 2. From kunnan. Der. un-, uf-.

KUNTHJAN*, in ga-swikunthjan, q. v.

KUNTHS, known, Lu. 2. 44; Jo. 18. 15; k. wisan, to be made known, Eph. 3. 5; pp. of kunnan. Der. un-, us-, swi-, unswi-.

KUSTS*, sb. proof, in ga-kusts, q. v. From kiusan.

KUSTUS, str. sb. m. a proof, test, 2 Cor. 2. 9; 8. 2; 13. 3. From kiusan.

KW.

KW (KV in M., Q in S. and G.), the sixth letter of the Gothic alphabet; as a numeral, it means 6. Pronounced probably like qu in Engl.

KWAINON, vb. to weep, mourn, lament, Mat. 9. 15; 11. 17; Mk. 16. 10; 2 Cor. 12. 21. [G. weinen; D. kwijnen; E. whine.]

KWAIRNUS*, str. sb. a millstone, only in comp. asilu-kwairnus, q. v. [E. quern.]

KWAIRREI, wk. sb. f. gentleness, meekness, 2 Cor. 10. 1; Gal. 5. 23; 6. 1. From kwairrus.

KWAIRRUS, adj. gentle, 2 Tim. 2. 24. Der. kwairrei.

KWAL*, sb. quietness, only in comp. ana-kwal, q. v. [Cf. E. quell.]

KWAM, I came; from kwiman.

KWEMUM, we came; from kwiman.

KWENITHS; see un-kweniths.

KWENJAN*, vb. to espouse, to marry a wife; from kwens. Der. unkweniths.

KWENS, KWEINS, str. sb. f. a woman, a wife, Mat. 5. 31; Mk. 6. 17; 10. 2, &c.; kwen niman, to take a wife, 1 Cor. 7. 28. Der. unkweniths, kwino, kwinakunds, kwineins. [Gk. γυνή; E. quean, queen.]

KWETHUM, we spoke; from kwithan.

KWIMAN, vb. (pt. t. kwam, pl. kwemum, pp. kwumans) to come, arrive, Mat. 5. 17; 6. 10; 7. 15, &c. Often followed by in, ana, at, or hindar with dat. Der. ga-kwiman, ana-kwiman, bi-, faura-, fra-, mith-, us-kwiman; kwums, gakwumths, mith-gakwumths. [G. kommen; D. komen; E. come.]

KWINAKUNDS, adj. female, Gal. 3. 28. From kwens and kuni.

KWINEINS, adj. female, Mk. 10. 6; hence neut. kwinein, a womanly thing, a silly woman, 2 Tim. 3. 6.

KWINO, wk. sb. f. a woman, Mat. 5. 28; 11. 11; 27. 55, &c. Another form of kwens, q. v.

KWISS*, str. sb. f. speech; from kwithan; only in comp. ana-, ga-, thiuthi-, missa-, sama-, waila-, us-kwiss.

KWISTEINS, str. sb. f. destruction,

1 Cor. 5. 5. *Der.* fra-kwisteins; *see* kwistjan.

KWISTJAN, *vb. with dat.* to destroy, Lu. 9. 56. *Der.* fra-, us-, fra-kwistnan, kwisteins, fra-kwisteins. [*Cf.* E. *quash.*]

KWISTNAN*, *vb.* to come to destruction, *in comp.* fra-kwistnan, q. v.

KWITHAN, *vb.* (*pt. t.* kwath, *pl.* kwethum, *pp.* kwithans), to say, speak, name, call, Mat. 5. 21; 7. 22; 8. 4, &c.; — garaihtana sik kwithan, to justify oneself, Gal. 5. 4; — ubil kwithan, to speak evil of one, Mk. 7. 10; — waila kwithan, to speak well of, to praise, Lu. 6. 26. *Der.* ana-, and-, af-, faura-, faur-, fra-, ga-, mith-, us-kwithan; kwithlo, kwiss, ga-, ana-, thiuthi-, missa-, sama, us-, waila-kwiss; un-kwethis. [D. *kouten;* E. *quoth, queath, bequeath. Cf.* G. *kosen.*]

KWITHLO, *sb. n.* a word, a saying, Skeir. 5. 23.

KWITHRS, KWITHREI; *see* laus-kwithrs, laus-kwithrei. *From* kwithus.

KWITHU-HAFTA, *sb. f.* a woman with child, Mk. 13. 17; 1 Th. 5. 3. *From* kwithus *and* baban.

KWITHUS, *str. sb. m.* the womb, Lu. 1. 41, 42; 2. 23; the stomach, 1 Tim. 5. 23. *Cf.* kilthei. *Der.* kwithu-hafta, laus-kwithrs, laus-kwithrei.

KWIUJAN*, *vb.* to quicken, *in comp.* ana-, ga-, mithga-. *From* kwius.

KWIUNAN*, *vb.* to be quickened, become alive, *in comp.* ga-kwiunan. *From* kwius.

KWIUS, *adj.* quick, living, alive, Mk. 12. 27; Lu. 20. 38; Rom. 12. 1; 14. 9. *Der.* ana-kwiujan, ga-kwiujan, mithga-kwiujan, ga-kwiunan. [D. *kwik;* E. *quick.*]

KWRAMMITHRA, *str. sb. f.* moisture, Lu. 8. 6.

KWUMS, *str. sb. m.* coming, arrival, 1 Cor. 15. 23; 16. 17; 2 Cor. 7. 6; 10. 10. *From* kwiman.

KWUMTHS*, *sb. in compound* ga-kwumths, q. v.

L.

L, *the twelfth letter of the Gothic alphabet. As a numeral, it signifies* 30.

LAG, I lay; *from* ligan.

LAGEINS, *str. sb. f.* a laying on (of hands), 2 Tim. 1. 6. *Der.* af-, ana-, faur-lageins. *See* ligan.

LAGGA-MODEI, *wk. sb. f.* long-suffering, Rom. 9. 22; 2 Cor. 6. 6. *From* laggs *and* moths.

LAGGEI, *wk. sb. f.* length, Eph. 3. 18. *From* laggs.

LAGGS, *adj.* long (*only used with ref. to time*), Lu. 8. 27; 18. 4; swa lagga swe, so long as, Mk. 2. 19; hwan lagg mel, how long, Mk. 9. 21. *Der.* laggei, lagga-modei. [G. D. *lang;* E. *long.*]

LAGJAN, *vb.* to lay, set, place, Mk. 6. 56; 10. 16; 15. 19; Lu. 9. 44, &c.; — lagjan ana, to lay upon, Mat. 27. 48; Mk. 5. 23. *Der.* ana-, af-, at-, ga-, faur-, ufar-, us-lagjan; lageins. *Cf.* ligan. [G. *legen;* D. *leggen;* E. *lay.*]

LAIAN, *vb. with dat. (pt. t.* lailo, *pp.* laians), to revile, Jo. 9. 28. [A. S. *leán, leáhan.*]

LAIBA, *str. sb. f.* a thing left, a leaving, remnant, Mk. 8. 8; Rom. 9. 27; *see next word.*

LAIBJAN*, *vb.* to leave, *in comp.* bi-laibjan, q. v.

LAIGAION, *sb.* a legion (*from* Gk. λεγεών), Mk. 5. 9, 15.

LAIGON*, *vb.* to lick, *in comp.* bi-laigon, q. v. [G. *lecken;* D. *likken;* E. *lick.*]

LAIKAN, *vb. (pt. t.* lailaik, *pp.* laikans), to skip *or* leap for joy, Lu. 1. 41, 44; 6. 23. *Der.* bilaikan, laiks. [O. E. *laik,* to play.]

LAIKS, *str. sb. m. (pl.* laikos), a sport, a dance, a dancing, Lu. 15. 25. [*Cf.* E. '*a lark*', i. e. a sport, frolic.]

LAIKTJO, *wk. sb. f.* a lesson, reading; *written in the margin opposite* 1 Cor. 15. 58; 2 Cor. 3. 4; &c. [Lat. *lectio.*]

LAILAIK, I leapt; *from* laikan.

LAILOUN, they reviled; *see* laian.

LAILOT, I let; *from* letan, q. v.

LAIS, *lit.* I have learnt; *hence,* I know; *from* leisan.

LAISAREIS, *str. sb. m.* a teacher, master, Mat. 8. 19; 9. 11; 10. 24; &c. *Der.* witoda-laisareis. *From* leisan.

LAISEIGS, *adj.* apt to teach, 1 Tim. 3. 2; 2 Tim. 2. 24.

LAISEINS, *str. sb. f.* a teaching, doctrine, Mat. 7. 28; Mk. 1. 22; 4. 2. *From* leisan.

LAISJAN, *vb.* to teach, Mat. 5. 19; 7. 29; 9. 35; — laisjan sik, to teach oneself, learn, 2 Tim. 3. 7; — antharleiko *or* aljaleikos l., to teach a different doctrine, 1 Tim. 1. 3; 6. 3; *pp.* laisiths, taught, Jo. 6. 45. *Der.* ga-, us-laisjans, unus-laisiths, laiseigs, laiseins, laisareis. *From* leisan, q. v. [G. *lehren;* D. *leeren.*]

LAISTJAN, *vb.* to follow, (*with acc.*) Mat. 8. 19; Mk. 8. 34; 9. 38; *also used with prep.* afar, Mat. 8. 1; 9. 9; *and with prep.* mith, Lu. 9. 49; (2) to follow after, Lu. 17. 23; Rom. 9. 30. *Der.* afar-, ga-, unbi-laistiths, unfair-laistiths, ga-laista. *Cf.* laists *and* leithan.

LAISTS, *str. sb. m.* a track, footstep, step, way, 2 Cor. 12. 18; Skeir. 2. 23; 5. 7. *Cf.* laistjan *and* leithan. [A. S. *lást.*]

LAITH, I went; *from* leithan.

LAMB, *str. sb. n.* a lamb, a sheep, Mat. 7. 15; 9. 36; Lu. 10. 3; 15. 4. [G. *lamm;* D. *lam;* E. *lamb.*]

LAND, *str. sb. n.* land, country, field, Mk. 1. 5; 6. 1; Lu. 14. 18; 2 Cor. 11. 10. [G. D. E. *land.*]

LAS, I gathered; *from* lisan.

LASIWOSTS, *superl. adj.* most feeble, weakest, 1 Cor. 12. 22; *from* laisiws.

LAISIWS, *adj.* weak, 2 Cor. 10. 10. [*Cf.* A. S. *leas;* E. *loose.*]

LATEI, *wk. sb. f.* a grievous thing, a delay, trouble, Phil. 3. 1. *From* lats.

LATHA-LEIKO, *adv.* very willingly, 2 Cor. 12. 15. *From* lathon *and* leiks.

LATHON, *vb.* to call, invite, Mat. 9. 13; Mk. 2. 17; Lu. 5. 32. *Der.* at-, ga-, lathons, latha-leiko. [G. *laden;* A. S. *laðian.*]

LATHONS, *str. sb. f.* a calling, invitation, Rom. 11. 29; 1 Cor. 7. 20; Eph. 1. 18; consolation,

Ln. 2. 25; redemption, Lu. 2. 38. *From* lathon.

LATJAN, *vb.* to be late, to tarry, Lu. 1. 21. *Der.* ga-, ana-. *From* lats.

LATS, *adj.* slothful, Lu. 19. 22; Rom. 12. 11; Tit. 1. 12. *Der.* latei, latjan, ana-, ga-latjan. [G. *lass*; D. *laat*; E. *late*.]

LAUBJAN, *vb.* to believe, Rom. 9. 33; *from* liuban. *Der.* ga-, us-; ga-laubeins, unga-laubeins, galaubs. [G. *glauben*; D. *gelooven*; O. E. *leve*; E. *believe*.]

LAUBOS, *pl. of* laufs, a leaf, q. v.

LAUDJA, *str. sb. f.* form, (*Greek* μορφή) *in margin of* Gal. 4. 19; *but it should perhaps be* ludjai. *Cf.* ludja.

LAUDS*, LAUTHS*; *see* liudan.

LAUFS (or LAUBS), *str. sb. m.* a leaf; *pl.* laubos, Mk. 11. 13; 13. 28. [G. *laub*; D. *loof*; E. *leaf*.]

LAUGNEI*, *in comp.* ana-laugnei, q. v.

LAUGNIBA*, *in* ana-laugniba, q. v.

LAUGNJAN, *vb.* to lie, deny, Mat. 26. 70; Mk. 14. 70; Lu. 8. 45. *Der.* ga-, liugnja, ana-laugns, ana-laugniba, ana-laugnei. *See* liugan.

LAUHATJAN, *vb.* to lighten, shine as lightning, Lu. 17. 24. *From* liuhan.

LAUHMONI or LAUHMUNI, *str. sb. f.* lightning, Lu. 10. 18; 17. 24; 2 Th. 1. 8. *From* liuhan.

LAUN, *str. sb. n.* pay, reward, thank, Mat. 6. 1; Lu. 6. 32, 33, 34; wages, Rom. 6. 23. *Der.* sigis-laun, launa-wargs, anda-launi. [G. *lohn*; D. *loon*; E. *loan*.]

LAUNA-WARGS, *adj.* thankless, unthankful, 2 Tim. 3. 2. *From* laun *and* wargs.

LAUS, *adj.* empty, Lu. 1. 53; 20. 10; 1 Cor. 15. 14; laus wairthan, to be made vain, 2 Cor. 9. 3; laus wisan, to become vain *or* of none effect, Gal. 5. 4; witodis laus, without law, 1 Cor. 9. 21. *It is used at the end of words like* E. *-less, as in* akrana-laus, fruitless; *also in* andi-, guda-, witoda-; *and at the beginning of* laus-kwithrs, laus-handja, lausa-waurds. *Cf.* liusan, lausjan. [G. *-los*; D. *-loos*; E. *-less*.]

LAUSA-WAURDEI, *wk. sb. f.* empty talk, 1 Tim. 1. 6.

LAUSA-WAURDI, *str. sb. n.* empty talk, 2 Tim. 2. 16.

LAUSA-WAURDS, *adj.* talking vainly, speaking loose and random words, Tit. 1. 10. *From* liusan *and* waurd.

LAUSEINS*; *str. sb. f.* a loosing, *in* us-lauseins, q. v.

LAUS-HANDJA, *adj.* empty-handed. Mk. 12. 3. *From* liusan *and* handus.

LAUSJAN, *vb.* to make of none effect, 1 Cor. 1. 17; to loosen, redeem, deliver, Mat. 6. 13; 27. 43; to exact, Lu. 3. 13; to ask for back again, Lu. 6. 30. *Der.* ga-, us-, us-lauseins. *Cf.* liusan *and* laus. [G. *lösen*; D. *lozen*; E. *loosen*.]

LAUS-KWITHREI, *wk. sb. f.* fasting, 2 Cor. 6. 5; 11. 27. *See next word.*

LAUS-KWITHRS, *adj.* with empty stomach, fasting, Mk. 8. 3. *From* laus *and* kwithus.

LAUTHS*, *str. sb. m.* a lad, *in comp.* jugga-lauths, q. v. *From* liudan.

LEDS*, *adj.* (?); *see* unleds.

LEGUM, we lay; *from* ligan.

LEIBAN*, *vb.* to leave. *Der.* laiba, bi-laibjan, bi-laifs, af-lifnan. *Cf.* liban. [E. *leave*; *cf.* G. *bleiben*; D. *blijven*.]

LEIHTS*, adj. light; see next word. [G. leicht; D. ligt; E. light.]

LEIHTS, str. sb. m. (or perhaps leihtis is merely the gen. of the above), lightness, levity of purpose, 2 Cor. 1. 17.

LEIHWAN, vb. (pt. t. laihw), to lend, Lu. 6. 34, 35; — leihwan sis, to borrow, Mat. 5. 42. [G. leihen; A. S. líhan, whence O. E. lene; E. lend.]

LEIK, str. sb. n. the body, Mat. 5. 29; 6. 22; 10. 28; a dead body, carcase, Mat. 27. 52; Mk. 15. 43; Lu. 17. 37; flesh, Mk. 10. 8; 13. 20. Der. ga-leika, leikeins. Cf. leiks. [G. leiche; D. lijk; E. lich in lich-gate, Lich-field.]

LEIKAINS, str. sb. f. liking, good pleasure, purpose, Eph. 1. 5; 2 Th. 1. 11; 2 Tim. 1. 9. From leikan.

LEIKAN, vb. to please, Jo. 8. 29; 1 Cor. 10. 33. Der. ga-, faura-ga-, ga-leikaith, leikains. [D. lijken; E. like.]

LEIKEI*, in comp. anthar-leikei, q. v. From leiks.

LEIKEINS, adj. bodily, fleshly, 1 Tim. 4. 8; Rom. 7. 14; 2 Cor. 1. 12; 10. 4; 2 Cor. 3. 3. From leik.

LEIKEIS, str. sb. m. (also spelt lekeis, q. v.) a leech, physician, Lu. 4. 23; 5. 31; Col. 4. 14. Der. leikinon, ga-leikinon, leikinassus. [E. leech.]

LEIKINASSUS, str. sb. m. healing, Lu. 9. 11. From leikeis.

LEIKINON, vb. to heal, Ln. 5. 15; 6. 7; 9. 6. See lekinon.

LEIKJAN*, see SILDA-LEIKJAN.

LEIKON*, vb. to liken; in comp. ga-leikon, q. v. [E. liken; cf. G. vergleichen.]

LEIKS*, adj. like. Der. ga-, hwi-, ibna-, liuba-, missa-, sama-, silda-, swa-; alja-leikos, ana-leiko, anthar-leiko, latha-leiko, sama-leiko, waira-leiko; ga-leikon, gaga-leikon, thairga-leikon, inga-leikon, mithga-leikon; anthar-leikei, ga-leiki, man-leika, silda-leikjan, alja-leikoths. [G. gleich; D. lijk; E. like.]

LEIN, str. sb. n. linen, Mk. 14. 51, 52; 15. 6. [G. lein; D. lijn; E. linen; Gk. λίνον.]

LEISAN, vb. (pt. t. lais, pl. lisum, pp. lisans), to learn; whence pt. t. lais, I have learnt, i. e. I know, Phil. 4. 12. Der. laisjan, ga-, us-, unus-laisiths; lubja-leisei, laiseigs, laiseins, laisareis, witoda-laisareis, lists, listeigs. [G. lehren, lernen; D. leeren; E. learn.]

LEISEI*; see LUBJA-LEISEI.

LEITAN; see LETAN.

LEITHAN*, vb. (pt. t. laith, pp. lithans), to go. Der. af-, bi-, ga-, inuga-, mithinuga-, hindar-, thairh-, us-, ufar-. [A. S. líðan; cf. G. begleiten; D. leiden; E. lead.]

LEITHUS; str. sb. m. strong drink, Lu. 1. 15.

LEITILS, adj. (comp. minniza, superl. minnists), little, Mat. 25. 45; Mk. 9. 42; 14. 70; leitil galaubjands, of little faith, Mat. 6. 30; 8. 26. [E. little; D. luttel.]

LEIWJAN, vb. to betray, Jo. 6. 64; another form of lewjan, q. v.

LEKEIS, str. sb. m. (also leikeis, q. v.) a leech, physician, Mk. 2. 17; 5. 25; Lu. 8. 43.

LEKINON, vb. to heal (another spelling of leikinon, q. v.), Lu. 10. 9.

LETAN, vb. (also spelt leitan, Mat. 9. 6; Mk. 15. 9, &c.; pt. t. lailot, pp. letans), to let, permit, suffer, allow, Mat. 8. 22; 27. 49; Mk. 5. 19, &c. *Der.* af-, fra-, us-; and-letnan, af-let, fra-let, fra-lets. [G. *lassen;* D. *laten;* E. *let.*]

LETNAN*, *in* and-letnan, q. v.

LETS*, *adj.* in fra-lets, q. v.

LEW, *str. sb.* (n. ?) occasion, opportunity, Rom. 7. 8, 11; 2 Cor. 5. 12; Gal. 5. 13. *Der.* lewjan, ga-lewjan, fra-lewjan. *Cf.* A. S. *lǽwa,* a traitor.]

LEWJAN, *vb.* (*also* LEIWJAN, Jo. 6. 64), to betray, Mk. 14. 42, 44; Jo. 18. 5. *Der.* ga-, fra-.

LIBAINS, *str. sb. f.* life, Mat. 7. 14; Mk. 9. 43; Lu. 10. 25, &c. *From* liban.

LIBAN, *vb.* to live, Mat. 9. 18; Mk. 5. 23; Lu. 2. 36, &c.; liban taujan, to make to live, to quicken, Jo. 6. 63; liban gataujan, to make alive, Jo. 5. 21; samana liban, to live together, 2 Cor. 7. 3. *Der.* mith-; libains. *Cf.* leiban. [G. *leben;* D. *leven;* E. *live.*]

LIF*, *in* ain-lif, eleven, *and* twa-lif, twelve. [*Either from* leiban, *or, according to Bopp,* lif = Lat. *decem* = ten.]

LIGAN, *vb.* (*pt. t.* lag, *pl.* legum, *pp.* ligans), to lie, Lu. 2. 16; 5. 25; Mk. 1. 30; 2. 4. *Der.* at-, uf-, ligrs, ga-ligri; lagjan, ana-, af-, at-, ga-, us-, ufar-, faur-lagjan; lageins, ana-, af-, bi-, faur-lageins. [G. *liegen;* D. *liggen;* E. *lie.*] *Cf.* lagjan.

LIGINON (?); *see* GA-LIGINON.

LIGRI*, *in* ga-ligri, q. v.

LIGRS, *str. sb. m.* a couch, bed, Mat. 9. 2; Mk. 4. 21; 7. 30; chambering, adultery, Rom. 13. 13. *From* ligan. *Der.* ga-ligri.

LINNAN*, *vb.* to cease. *Der.* af-linnan. [O. E. *lin, blin.*]

LISAN, *vb.* to lease, gather, collect, Mat. 6. 26; 7. 16; Lu. 6. 44. *Der.* ga-lisan, lists. [G. D. *lesen;* E *lease,* to glean.]

LISTEIGS, *adj.* crafty, wily, 2 Cor. 12. 16; Eph. 4. 14. *From* lists.

LISTS, *str. sb. f.* craftiness, wiliness, a wile, Eph. 6. 11. [G. D. *list;* A. S. *list.*]

LITA, *str. sb. f.* pretence, dissimulation, Gal. 2. 13. *Cf.* liutei, lists. *Der.* mit-litjan.

LITEINS, *str. sb. f.* an intercession, prayer (Gk. λιτή), 1 Tim. 2. 1.

LITHUS, *str. sb. m.* a limb, member, Mat. 5. 29; Rom. 7. 5; 12. 4. *Der.* us-litha. *Cf.* leitban. [G. *glied;* D. *lied;* O. E. *lith.*]

LITJAN*, *vb. in* mith-litjan, q. v.

LIUBA-LEIKS, *adj.* lovely, Phil. 4. 8. [G. *lieblich;* E. *lovely.*] *From* liubs *and* leiks.

LIUBAN*, *vb.* to be dear. *Der.* liubs, un-liubs, liuba-leiks; laubjan; ga-, us-; ga-laubeins, un-ga-laubeins, laubs, unga-, filuga-; ga-lubs, gudi-lubs; brothralubo, lubains. *Cf.* liubs.

LIUBS, *adj.* dear, beloved, Mk. 1. 11; 9. 7; 12. 6; Lu. 3. 22. [*Cf.* liuban. [G. *lieb;* D. E. *lief; cf.* E. *love.*]

LIUDAN, *vb.* to grow, spring up, Mk. 4. 29. *Der.* lauths, juggalauths, swa-lauths, hwe-lauths, sama-lauths.

LIUGA, *str. sb. f.* marriage, wedlock, 1 Tim. 4. 3; liugom hafts, wedded, married, 1 Cor. 7. 10. *From* liugan (2).

LIUGAITHS*; *see* UN-LIUGAITHS.

LIUGAN (1) *vb.* (*pt. t.* laug *or* lauh, *pl.* lugum, *pp.* lugans), to lie, tell falsehoods, Rom. 9. 1; 2 Cor. 1. 31; Gal. 1. 20. *Der.* un-liugands, ga-liuga, ga-liuga-apaustaulus, ga-liuga-praufetus, ga-liuga-Christus, liugn, liugna-waurds, liugnja, laugnjan, ga-laugnjan, ana-laugns, ana-laugniba, ana-laugnei. [G. *lügen*; D. *liegen*; E. *lie*.] *Cf.* laugnjan.

LIUGAN (2), *vb.* (*pt. t.* liugaida), to marry, to take a wife, Mat. 5 32; Mk. 10. 11; 12. 25; *pass.* to be married, take a husband, Mk. 10. 12; 1 Cor. 7. 9, 28. *Der.* ga-liugan, un-liugaiths, liuga.

LIUGN, *str. sb. n.* a lie, Jo. 8. 44; Eph. 4. 25. *From* liugan (1).

LIUGNA-PRAUFETUS, *sb. m.* a false prophet, Mat. 5. 15.

LIUGNA-WAURDS, *adj.* speaking lies, 1 Tim. 4.2. *From* liugan (1) *and* waurds.

LIUGNJA, *wk. sb. m.* a liar, Jo. 8. 44, 55; 1 Tim. 1. 10; Tit. 1. 12. *From* liugan (1).

LIUHADEI, *sb. f.* light, illumination, 2 Cor. 4. 4, 6. *From* liuhan.

LIUHADEINS, *adj.* full of light, bright, Mat. 6. 22. *From* liuhan.

LIUHAN*, *vb.* to enlighten. *Der.* liuhadei, liuhadeins, liuhath, liuhtjan, ga-liuhtjan, in-liuhtjan, lauhatjan, lauhmuni. *Cf.* liuhtjan. [G. *leuchten*; D. *lichten*.]

LIUHATH, *str. sb. n.* (*gen.* liuhadis), light, Mat. 5. 16; 6. 23; 10. 27, &c. *From* liuhan. [G. D. *licht*; E. *light*; *cf.* O. E. *lowe*.]

LIUHTJAN, *vb.* (*also spelt* liutjan, Mat. 5. 15), to be bright, shine, Mat. 5. 15, 16; Jo. 5. 35; 2 Cor. 4. 4, 6. *From* liuhan.

LIUSAN*, *vb.* to lose. *Der.* fra-liusan, fra-lusnan, fra-lusts, laus (q. v.), lausjan, ga-lausjan, us-lausjan, us-lauseins. [G. *verlieren*; D. *verliezen*; E. *lose*; O. E. *lese*.]

LIUTA, *wk. sb. m.* a dissembler, hypocrite, Mat. 6. 2; Mk. 7. 6; Lu. 6. 42. *From* liutan, *and cf.* lita.

LIUTAN*, *vb.* to dissemble. *Der.* liuta, liuts, un-liuts, liutei, luton, us-luton. [*Cf.* A. S. *lytig*.]

LIUTEI, *wk. sb. f.* deceit, pretence, hypocrisy, Mk. 7. 22; 12. 15; 1 Tim. 4. 2; us liutein taiknjan sik, to feign oneself, Lu. 20. 20. *From* liutan.

LIUTHAREIS, *str. sb. m.* a singer, Ezra 2. 41; Nehem. 7. 1. *From* liuthon.

LIUTHON, *vb.* to sing, Rom. 15. 9. *Der.* liuthareis. [G. D. *lied*; E. *lay* (a song).]

LIUTS, *adj.* deceitful, 2 Tim. 3. 13.

LOFA, *wk. sb. m.* the flat *or* palm of the hand; slabs lofin, a buffet, Jo. 18. 22; 19. 3; — lofam slahan, to strike with the palms of the hands, Mat. 26. 27; Mk. 14. 65. [O. E. *and* Sc. *loof*.]

LOS, *sb. f.* rest (?) [*a proposed reading in* 1 Tim. 2. 2; *there seems nothing to support it*].

LUBAINS, *str. sb. f.* hope, Rom. 15. 13. *From* liuban.

LUBAN*, to hope (?); *see* lubains.

LUBI*, *str. sb. n.* sorcery(?). *Der.* lubja-leisei. [A. S. *lib*.]

LUBJA-LEISEI, *wk. sb. f.* witchcraft, Gal. 5. 20.

LUBO*, *wk. sb. f.* love; *in* brothra-lubo, q. v.

LUDJA, *str. sb. f.* the face, Mat. 6. 17. [A. S. *wlite?*]

LUFTUS, *str. sb. m.* the air, 1 Cor. 9. 26; Eph. 2. 2; 1 Th. 4. 17. [G. *luft*; D. *lucht*; O. E. *lift*.]

LUKAN*, *vb.* to lock. *Der.* ga-, us-; ga-luknan, us-luknan; us-luk, us-lukns. [D. *luiken*; E. *lock*.]

LUKARN, *str. sb. n.* a light (Lat. *lucerna*), Mat. 6. 22; Mk. 4.

21; Lu. 8. 16; Jo. 5. 35. *Der.* lukarna-statha.

LUKARNA-STATHA, *wk. sb. m.* a candlestick, Mat. 5. 15; Mk. 4. 21; Lu. 8. 16. *From* lukarn *and* staths.

LUKNS*, *in* us-lukns, q. v.

LUSTON, *vb.* to desire, Mat. 5. 28; *from* lustus.

LUSTS*, *in* fra-lusts, q. v.

LUSTUS, *str. sb. m.* lust, desire, Mk. 4. 19; Jo. 8. 44; Rom. 7. 7, &c.; — us lustum, without desire, freely, willingly, Philem. 14. *Der.* un-lustus, lustu-sams, luston, us-luston.

LUSTU-SAMS, *adj.* longed for, much desired, Phil. 4. 1. *From* lustus.

LUTON, *vb.* to betray; *pres. pt.* lutonds, *as sb.* a betrayer, deceiver, Tit. 1. 10. *Der.* us-luton. *See* liutan.

M.

M, the thirteenth letter of the Gothic alphabet. [*As a numeral, it means* 40.]

MAGAN, *vb.* (*old pt. t. as pres.* mag, *pt. t.* mahta, *pp.* mahts), to be able, Mat. 5. 36; 6. 24; 7. 18, &c.; — mag wairthan, it is possible, it may be, Rom. 12. 18. *Der.* ga-magan, mahts, un-mahts, ana-mahts, ana-mahtjan, mahteigs, un-mahteigs. [G. *mögen*; D. *vermögen*; E. *may, might*.]

MAGATHEI, *wk. sb. f.* virginity, maidenhood, Lu. 2. 36. *From* magus.

MAGATHS, *str. sb. f.* a virgin, maid, Lu. 1. 27. *From* magus. *Der.* magathei. [G. *magd*; D. *maagd*; E. *maid*.]

MAGULA, *wk. sb. m.* a little boy, Jo. 6. 9. *From* magus.

MAGUS, *str. sb. m.* a boy, child, Lu. 2. 43; 9. 42; 15. 26. *Cf.* magaths, mawi.

MAHEI, *sb. f.* modesty, 1 Tim. 2. 9. [*But it should perhaps be* inahei, q. v.]

MAHTEIGS, *adj.* mighty, great, Lu. 1. 49, 52; possible, Mk. 9. 23; 10. 27. *Der.* unmahteigs. *From* magan. [G. *mächtig*; D. *magtig*.]

MAHTJAN*, *vb. in* ana-mahtjan, q. v.

MAHTS, *adj.* possible, Mk. 14. 5; Jo. 3. 4 (*where we find* maht wesi, it might have been, *and* mahts ist, it is possible); mahta was, was able, could, Lu. 8. 43. *From* magan.

MAHTS, *str. sb. f.* might, power, strength, Mat. 6. 13; Mk. 5. 30; Lu. 1. 17; a wonder, miracle, Mat. 7. 22; 11. 20. *Der.* ana-, un-. *From* magan. [G. *macht*; D. *magt*.]

MAIDEINS*; *see* in-maideins.

MAIDJAN, *vb.* to change about, to change deceitfully, to corrupt, 2 Cor. 2. 17. *From* maids. *Der.* inmaidjan, inmaideins.

MAIDS*, *adj.* changeable (?), *the supposed root of* ga-maids, maidjan, in-maidjan, in-maideins. [*Cf.* G. *meiden*, to shun.]

MAIHSTUS, *str. sb. m.* a mixen, dunghill (*lit.* dung), Lu. 14. 35. [A. S. *meox*; G. *mist*.]

MAIL, *sb. n.* (?) a spot, blemish, Eph. 5. 27. [Lat. *macula*; E. *mole*: G. *maal*.]

MAIMAIT, he cut; *from* maitan.
MAIMBRANA (μεμβράνα) *str. sb. m.* a membrane, parchment, 2 Tim. 4. 13.
MAINDS*, *adj.; see* af-mainds.
MAINS*, *adj.* mean, common. *Der.* ga-mains, ga-mainja, ga-mainjan, gaga-mainjan, ga-mainei, ga-mainduths, ga-mainths. [E. *mean;* Germ. *ge-mein;* D. *ge-meen.*]
MAIS (μᾶλλον), *adv.* more, rather, Mat. 6. 26; Mk. 5. 26; Jo. 12. 43; — mais thamma, so much the more, Mk. 7. 36; — mais frathjan (ὑπερφρονεῖν), to think more highly, Rom. 12. 3; — filaus mais, *or* filu mais, much more; — thana mais, more still, longer, Mk. 5. 35; — ni thanamais, no more; — ju thanamais, any longer, Lu. 16. 2. [Lat. *magis;* G. *mehr;* D. *meer.*]
MAIST, *adv.* at most, 1 Cor. 14. 27.
MAISTS, *superl. adj.* the greatest, Mk. 4. 32; 9. 34; Lu. 9. 46; *as a sb.* a chief man, man of rank, Mk. 6. 21; — maists gudja, the high priest, Jo. 18. 24. *Cf.* mais *and* maiza. [E. *most;* G. *meist;* D. *meest.*]
MAITAN, *vb.* (*pt. t.* maimait, *pp.* maitans), to cut, cut off, cut down, Mk. 11. 8. *Der.* af-, bi-, us-, bimait, unbimait, ga-maitano, unbimaitans. [*Cf.* G. *messer;* Lat. *metere.*]
MAITHMS, *str. sb. m.* a gift, Corban, Mk. 7. 11. [A. S. *maðm.*]
MAIZA, *comp. adj.* (*f.* maizei, *n.* maizo), greater, Mat. 11. 11; Mk. 12. 31; — maizo, *as adv.* more, Lu. 9. 13. *See* mais, maists.
MALAN, *vb.* to grind in a mill, Lu. 17. 35. *Der.* malo, malma,

malwjan. [G. *zermalmen; cf.* E. *meal.*]
MALMA, *wk. sb. m.* sand, Mat. 7. 26; Rom. 9. 27. [A. S. *mealm.*]
MALO, *wk. sb. f.* a moth, Mat. 6. 19, 20.
MALSKS*; *see* untila-malsks.
MALTEINS*; *see* ga-malteins.
MALTJAN*, *vb.* to melt, dissolve; *see* ga-malteins.
MALWJAN, *vb.* to grind down (*cf.* malan); *hence, pp.* gamalwiths, contrite, Lu. 4. 18. See malan.
MAMJAN*, MAMPJAN, MAMNJAN, *or* MAMINJAN, *vb.* to deride, *as root of* bi-mampjan, q. v. [*Cf.* G. *mummen;* D. *mommen;* E. *mummer.*]
MAMMO, *wk. sb. f.* flesh, Col. 1. 22.
MAMMONA, *wk. sb. m.* Mammon, Mat. 6. 24; Lu. 16. 13.
MAN, I mean, I think; *see* minan.
MAN*, a man; *see* manna. *Der.* ga-man, man-leika.
MANAGDUTHS, *str. sb. f.* abundance, 2 Cor. 8. 2. *See* manags.
MANAGEI, *wk. sb. f.* a crowd, multitude, the people, Mk. 3. 7; Lu. 2. 13; Jo. 6. 1. *See* manags. [G. *menge.*]
MANAG-FALTHS, *adj.* manifold, Lu. 18. 30; Eph. 3. 10.
MANAGJAN, *vb.* to multiply, 2 Cor. 9. 10; to make to increase, 1 Th. 3. 12.
MANAGNAN, *vb.* to abound, 2 Cor. 4. 15; Eph. 3. 10; 2 Th. 1. 3. *Der.* us-managnan.
MANAGS, *adj.* much, many, Mat. 7. 13; 8. 1; Mk. 1. 34; *compar.* managiza, more, Mat. 5. 37; Jo. 10; *sup.* managists; *hence,* swa-manags swe, as many as; hwai-wa manags, however many; hwan manags, how many. *Der.* managei, manag-duths, managjan, managnan, us-managnan.

MANA-MAURTHJA, *wk. sb. m.* a homicide, murderer, Jo. 8. 44. *From* manna *and* maurthr.

MANA-RIGGWS; *see* un-mana-riggws.

MANA-SETHS, MANA-SEDS, *str. sb. f.* a multitude, Lu. 9. 13; the world, Mk. 14. 9; Lu. 9. 25; Jo. 1. 29, &c. *From* manna *and* seths.

MANAULI, *str. sb. n.* the shape or fashion of a man, Phil. 2. 8.

MANLEIKA, *wk. sb. m.* the image or likeness (of a man), Mk. 12. 16; Lu. 20. 24; 1 Cor. 15. 49. *From* manna *and* leiks.

MANNA, *wk. sb. m.* a man, Mat. 5. 16; Mk. 1. 17; Lu. 1. 25, &c.; ni manna *or* manna ni, nobody, Mat. 6. 24. *Der.* manna-hun, ala-mans, mannisks, manniskodus, ga-man, manauli, manleika, mana-seths, mana-maurthja, un-mana-riggws. [G. D. *mensch, man.*]

MANNA, *sb.* manna, Jo. 6. 31, 49, 58.

MANNA-HUN, *adj.* any one; ni m., no one, Mat. 1. 44; 8. 26; 9. 9.

MANNISKODUS, *str. sb. m.* humanity, Skeir. 6. 12.

MANNISKS, *adj.* human, 1 Cor. 4. 3; Jo. 12. 43; Skeir. 6. 10. *From* manna.

MANS, *nom. pl. of* manna (*gen.* manne, *dat.* mannam), men.

MANWI, *sb. n.* the cost, price (of a thing), Lu. 14. 28. *Cf.* manwitha *and* manwus.

MANWITHA, *str. sb. f.* preparation, Eph. 6. 15. *From* manwus.

MANWJAN, *vb.* to prepare, Mat. 25. 41; Mk. 1. 3; Lu. 1. 17. *Der.* ga-manwjan. *From* manwus.

MANWUBA, *adv.* in readiness, 2 Cor. 10. 6.

MANWUS, *adj.* ready, Mk. 14. 15; Lu. 14. 17; Jo. 7. 6. *Der.* manwuba, un-manwus, manwi, manwitha, manwjan, ga-manwjan, fauraga-manwjan, faura-manwjan.

MAREI, *wk. sb. f.* the sea, Mat. 8. 18; Mk. 1. 16; Lu. 17. 6; — faur marein, near the sea, Lu. 6. 17; — hindar marein, across the sea, Mk. 5. 1. [E. *mere*; G. & D. *meer.*]

MARI-SAIWS, *str. sb. m.* the sea, Lu. 8. 22. *From* marei *and* saiws.

MARKA, *str. sb. f.* border-country, coast, Mat. 8. 34; Mk. 5. 17; 7. 31. *Der.* ga-marko. [E. *marches, mark, margin*; G. *mark*; D. *merk*; Lat. *margo.*]

MARKREITUS, *str. sb. m.* a pearl, 1 Tim. 2. 9. [A. S. *meregrot;* Gk. μαργαρίτης.]

MARTYR, *sb.* (*wrongly (?) spelt* matyr), a martyr, *in the Gothic calender.*

MARZEINS, *str. sb. f.* stumbling block, offence, Gal. 5. 11. *Der.* af-, ga-, frathja-marzeins.

MARZJAN, *vb.* to offend, hinder, cause to stumble, Mat. 5. 29; Mk. 9. 43. *Der.* af-, ga-; marzeins, af-, ga-, frathja-marzeins. [E. *mar.*]

MAT, I measured; *from* mitan.

MATHA, *wk. sb. m.* a worm, Mk. 9. 44, 46, 48. [G. & D. *made*; A. S. *maðu.*]

MATHL, *str. sb. n.* a market, market-place, Mk. 7. 4. *Der.* fauramathli, faura-mathleis, mathljan, mathleins. [A. S. *meðel,* talk; O. E. *mele,* to talk.]

MATHLEINS, *str. sb. f.* discourse, speech, Jo. 8. 43. *From* mathl.

MATHLJAN, *vb.* to speak, talk, Jo. 14. 30. *From* mathl. [O. E. *medle, mele,* to talk.]

MATI-BALGS, *str. sb. m.* a meat-bag, wallet, scrip, Mk. 6. 8; Lu. 9. 3; 10. 4.

MATJAN, *vb.* to eat, Mat. 25. 42; Mk. 2. 26; Lu. 4. 2, &c. *Der.* ga-, mith-matjan. *From* mats.

MATS, *str. sb. m.* (*pl.* mateis), meat, food, Mk. 7. 19; Lu. 3. 11; 9. 13. *Der.* matjan, ga-, mith-matjan, nahta-mats, undaurni-mats, mati-balgs.

MAUDEINS, *str. sb. f.* remembrance, Skeir. 6. 4 (*where M. has* ufarmaudeinai). *Der.* ga-maudeins. *From* maudjan.

MAUDJAN, *vb.* to remind, Skeir. 6. 5. *Der.* ga-maudjan, maudeins, ga-maudeins. *Cf.* munan.

MAUJOS, *gen. of* mawi, q. v.

MAURGINS, *str. sb. m.* morning, Mk. 11. 20; 15. 1; Jo. 18. 28; du maurgina, to-morrow, 1 Cor. 15. 32. [G. D. *morgen.*]

MAURGJAN*, *in* ga-maurgjan, q. v.

MAURNAN, *vb.* to mourn; *hence*, to be anxious *or* troubled about, Mat. 6. 25; Phil. 4. 6.

MAURTHR, *str. sb. n.* murder, Mk. 7. 21; 15. 7; Gal. 5. 21. *Der.* maurthrjan, mana-maurthja. [G. *mord;* D. *moord.*]

MAURTHRJA*, *wk. sb. m.* a murderer, *in comp.* mana-maurthrja.

MAURTHRJAN, *vb.* to murder, kill, Mat. 5. 21; Lu. 18. 20. *From* maurthr.

MAWI, *str. sb. f.* (*gen.* maujos), a maid, maiden, damsel, Mat. 9. 24; Mk. 5. 42; 6. 22 [O. E. *may*.]

MAWILO, *wk. sb. f.* a young maiden, damsel, Mk 5. 41.

MEGS, *str. sb. m.* son-in-law, Nehem. 6. 18. [A. S. *mago*.]

MEINA, of me (*gen. of* ik), Mat. 10. 37; Mk. 8. 35.

MEINS, *possess. pron.* mine, Mat. 7. 21; Mk. 1. 11.

MEKEIS, *or* MEKI, *sb.* a sword, Eph. 6. 17. [Gk. μάχαιρα; A. S. *mece*.]

MEL, *str. sb. n.* (1) time, Mk. 9. 21; Lu. 1. 57; Jo. 12. 35; (2) *pl.* writings, scriptures, Mk. 12. 24; Lu. 4. 21; Jo. 5. 47. *Der.* meljan, ana-, ga-, fauraga-, uf-, ufar-, faura-meljan; gameleins, gilstra-meleins, ufarmeleins, ufar-meli. [A. S. *mǽl*.]

MELA, *wk. sb. m.* a measure, a bushel, Mk. 4. 21.

MELEINS*, *str. sb. f.* writing. *Der.* ga-, gilstra-, ufar-meleins.

MELI*; *see* ufar-meli.

MELJAN, *vb.* to write, Mk. 10. 4; Lu. 1. 3; 16. 7. *Der.* ana-, ga-, fauraga-, faura-, uf-, ufar-meljan. *See* meleins.

MENA, *wk. sb. m.* the moon, Mk. 13. 24. *Der.* menoths. [G. *mond;* D. *maan*.]

MENOTHS, *str. sb. m.* a month, Lu. 1. 24; 4. 25; Gal. 4. 10. [G. *monat;* D. *maand*.]

MEREI*, *in* waja-merei, q. v.

MEREINS, *str. sb. f.* a preaching, 1 Cor. 15. 14; Tit. 1. 3. *From* merjan.

MERITHA, *str. sb. f.* fame, report, Mat. 9. 26; Mk. 1. 28; Lu. 4. 14, 37. *From* merjan.

MERJAN, *vb.* to proclaim, announce, noise abroad, Mat. 9. 35; Mk. 1. 4; Lu. 1. 65; to preach the gospel, 1 Cor. 15. 1; Gal. 1. 23. *Der.* us-, waila-, waja-; us-mernan, waila-mers, waja-merei, mereins, wailamereins, waja-mereins, meritha. [*Cf.* G. *mähre;* D. *maar;* A. S. *mǽrsian*.]

MERJANDS, *pres. pt. of* merjan; *hence*, a herald, a preacher, 1 Tim. 2. 7; 2 Tim. 1. 11.

MES, *str. sb. n.* a table, Mk. 11. 15; a dish, 'charger', Mk. 6.

25; dal uf mesa, a ditch *or* receptacle for a wine-vat, Mk. 12. 1. [A. S. *myse;* E. *mess?*]

MET*, *in* us-met, q. v.

MID, *prep.* with, Lu. 7. 11; *another form of* mith, q. v.

MIDJA, *adj.* middle, in the midst, Mk. 9. 36; Lu. 2. 46; Jo. 7. 14. *Der.* midja-sweipains, midjun-gards, miduma, midumonds, [G. *mittel;* D. *middel.*]

MIDJA-SWEIPAINS, *str. sb. f.* the flood, deluge, Lu. 17. 27. *From* midja *and* sweipan.

MIDJUN-GARDS, *str. sb. m.* the inhabited earth, the earth, the world, Lu. 2. 1; 4. 5. Rom. 10. 18. [A. S. *middan-geard.*]

MIDUMA, *str. sb. f.* the midst, Mk. 3. 3; Lu. 8. 7; 10. 3.

MIDUMONDS, *pt. pres. as sb.* a mediator, 1 Tim. 2. 5.

MIK, me; *acc. of* ik.

MIKILABA, *adv.* greatly, very much, Phil. 4. 10.

MIKILDUTHS, *str. sb. f.* greatness, Skeir. 4. 12, 14.

MIKILEI, *wk. sb. f.* greatness, Lu. 1. 49; 9. 43; Eph. 1. 19.

MIKILJAN, *vb.* to magnify, extol, glorify, praise, Lu. 1. 46; 2. 20; 4. 15. *Der.* ga-mikiljan.

MIKILNAN, *vb.* to be enlarged *or* magnified, 2 Cor. 10. 15.

MIKILS, *adj.* mickle, great, much, Mat. 5. 19; 7. 27, &c. *Der.* mikilaba, mikilduths, mikilei, mikiljan, mikilnan, mikil-thuhts. [A. S. *mycel.*]

MIKIL-THUHTS, *adj.* high-thoughted, proud, Lu. 1. 51.

MILDITHA, *str. sb. f.* mildness, mercy, pity, Phil. 2. 1.

MILDS*, *adj.* mild. *Der.* un-milds, friathwa-milds, milditha.

MILHMA, *wk. sb. m.* a cloud, Mk. 9. 7; 13. 26; Lu. 9. 34.

MILITH, *str. sb. n.* honey, Mk. 1. 6. [Lat. *mel.*]

MILITON, *vb.* to be a soldier, serve as soldier, Lu. 3. 14. [Lat. *militare.*]

MILUKS, *sb. f.* milk, 1 Cor. 9. 7.

MIMZ, *sb. n.* flesh, meat, 1 Cor. 8. 13.

MINAN*, *vb.* (*pt. t.* man, *pp.* munans), to mean, mind, think. *Der.* ga-minthi, ana-minds, munan, ga-munan, muns, ga-munds, uf-munnan, ufar-munnon. [G. *meinen;* D. *meenen.*]

MINDS*, *in* ana-minds, q. v.

MINNIZA, *compar. adj.* more minute, smaller, less, Mat. 11. 11; Mk. 15. 40; Lu. 7. 28; — minnizo gataujan, to be behind, 2 Cor. 11. 5. *From* mins.

MINNISTS, *superl. adj.* most minute, smallest, least, Mat. 5. 19; Mk. 4. 31; Lu. 9. 48. *From* mins.

MINS, MINZ, *adv.* less, 2 Cor. 12. 15; 1 Tim. 5. 9. *Der.* minniza, minnists, minznan. [G. D. *minder.* *Cf.* E. *mince.*]

MINZNAN, *vb.* to grow less, decrease, Jo. 3. 30.

MIS, to me, *dat. of* ik.

MISSA-, *a prefix, like Engl.* mis-. *Der.* missadeds, missa-kwiss, missa-leiks, missa-taujands. *See* Appendix.

MISSO (ἀλλήλων), *adv.* reciprocally, *gen. after a pers. pron.* one another, Mk. 1. 27; 4. 41.

MITADJO, *wk. sb. f.* measure, Lu. 6. 38.

MITAN, *vb.* (*pt. t.* mat, *pl.* metum, meitum, *pp.* mitans), to mete, measure, Mk. 4. 24; Lu. 6. 38. *Der.* ga-, us-; miton, ufar-miton, mitons, ga-mitons; us-met, mitadjo, mitaths. [G. *messen;* D. *meten.*]

MITATHS, MITADS, *str. sb. f.* a measure, a bushel, Mk. 4,

24; Lu. 6. 38; 16. 7. *From* mitan.

MITH, *prep.* (*spelt* mid *in* Lu. 7. 11), *with dat.* with, amongst, together with, through, by, near, in reply to. *Very common as a prefix verbal meaning* together with; Gk. σύν. [G. *mit;* D. *met.*]

MITH-ANAKUMBJAN, *vb.* to lie down together with, to recline at meat with, Mat. 9. 10; Mk. 2. 15; Lu. 7. 49.

MITH-ARBAIDJAN, *vb.* to labour together with, Phil. 4. 3; to suffer evils together with, 2 Tim. 1. 8.

MITH-FAGINON. *vb.* to rejoice with, Lu. 1. 58; 15. 6, 9.

MITH-FRAHUNTHANS, *pt. pt. as from vb.* mith-frahinthan, a fellow-prisoner, Col. 4. 10; Philem. 23.

MITH-GADAUTHNAN, *vb.* to die with, 2 Tim. 2. 11.

MITH-GAGGAN, *vb.* (*pt. t.* mithiddja *and* mididdja), to go with, Mk. 15. 41; Lu. 7. 11.

MITH-GAKWIUJAN, *vb.* to quicken together with, Eph. 2. 5; Col. 2. 13. *From* kwius.

MITH-GAKWUMTHS, *str. sb. f.* a gathering together, *a proposed reading in* 2 Th. 2. 1.

MITH-GALEIKON, *vb.* to imitate, Phil. 3. 17.

MITH-GANAWISTRON, *vb.* to bury with, Col. 2. 12. *From* naus.

MITH-GARDA-WADDJUS, *str. sb. f.* a partition wall, Eph. 2. 14. *From* gards *and* waddjus.

MITH-GASATJAN, *vb.* to set together, make to sit together, Eph. 2. 6. *From* sitan.

MITH-GASINTHA, *wk. sb. m.* one who is sent together with a companion, 2 Cor. 8. 19. *From* sinthan.

MITH-GASWILTAN, *vb.* to die with, 2 Cor. 7. 3. *From* swiltan.

MITH-GATIMRJAN, *vb.* to build together, Eph. 2. 22.

MITH-GATIUHAN, *vb.* to draw away with one, carry away with, Gal. 2. 13. *From* tiuhan.

MITH-GAWISAN, *vb.* to be amongst, remain with, Rom. 12. 16. *From* wisan.

MITH-INNGALEITHAN, *vb.* to go in with, Jo. 18. 15.

MITH-INSANDJAN, *vb.* to send with, 2 Cor. 8. 22; 12. 18.

MITH-KAURJAN, *vb.* (*lit.* to load with), *in phrase* mith-kauriths dauthau is, being made conformable unto his death, Phil. 3. 10. *See* kaurs.

MITH-KWIMAN, *vb.* to come with, go with, Jo. 6. 22; 11. 33.

MITH-KWITHAN, *vb.* to contradict, be contrary, strive together, Skeir. 5. 6.

MITH-LIBAN, *vb.* to live with, 2 Tim. 2. 11.

MITH-LITJAN, *vb.* to dissemble with, Gal. 2. 13. *From* lita.

MITH-MATJAN, *vb.* to eat with, Lu. 15. 2; 1 Cor. 5. 11.

MITH-NIMAN, *vb.* to receive, Mat. 11. 4.

MITH-RODJAN, *vb.* to speak with, Lu. 9. 30.

MITH-SANDJAN, *vb.* to send with, 2 Cor. 8. 18.

MITH-SATJAN, *vb.* to remove, 1 Cor. 13. 2. *From* sitan.

MITH-SKALKINON, *vb.* to serve with, Phil. 2. 22. *From* skalks.

MITH-SOKJAN, *vb.* to dispute, Mk. 8. 11.

MITH-STANDAN, *vb.* to stand near, be with, Lu. 9. 32.

MITH-THAN, *conj.* whilst, Skeir. 2. 4; then, Skeir. 2. 9; still, Skeir. 2. 17.

MITH-THAN-EI (*spelt* mith-thane, Lu. 2. 43), *conj.* when, whilst, Mat. 9. 18; Lu. 4. 40.

MITH-THIUDANON, *vb.* to reign with, 1 Cor. 4. 8; 2 Tim. 2. 12.

MITH-URRAISJAN, *vb.* to raise up together, Eph. 2. 6. *From* reisan.

MITH-URREISAN, *vb.* to rise up with, Col. 2. 12; 3. 1.

MITH-USHRAMJAN, *vb.* to crucify with, Mat. 27. 44; Mk. 15. 32; Gal. 2. 20. *From* hramjan.

MITH-USKEINAN, *vb.* to spring up with, grow up with, Lu. 8. 7. *From* keian.

MITH-WEITWODJAN, *vb.* to bear witness with, Rom. 9. 1. *From* weitan *and* wods.

MITH-WISAN, *vb.* to be with, to be beside, stand by, 2 Tim. 4. 16.

MITH-WISSEI, *wk. sb. f.* conscience, Rom. 9. 1; 1 Cor. 8. 10; 10. 25. *From* weitan.

MITH-WITAN, *vb.* to be conscious of, 1 Cor. 4. 4. *From* weitan.

MITON, *vb.* to measure; *hence,* to weigh a matter, consider, reason upon, think over, think. Mat. 9. 4; Mk. 2. 8; to look to, mind, Rom. 8. 5; Phil. 2. 4; to intend, 2 Cor. 1. 17. *Der.* ufarmiton. *See* mitan.

MITONS, *str. sb. f.* a measuring; *hence,* a reasoning, consideration, thought; Mat. 9. 4; Lu. 5. 22; 6. 8. *Der.* ga-mitons. *From* mitan.

MIZDO, *wk. sb. f.* meed, reward, Mat. 5. 46; 6. 2; Mk. 9. 41. [*Cf.* Gk. μισθός; E. *meed.*]

MODAGS, *adj.* moody, wroth, angry, Mat. 5. 22; Lu. 15. 28.

MODEI*, *wk. sb. f.* mood. *Der.* lagga-modi, muka-modei.

MODS, *str. sb. m.* moodiness, anger, wrath, Mk. 3. 5; Lu. 4. 28. *Der.* modags, lagga-modei, muka-modei. [G. *muth;* D. *moed;* E. *mood.*]

MOSTA, I must, I could; *from* motan.

MOTA, *str. sb. f.* toll, custom, Mat. 9. 9; Mk. 2. 14; Rom. 13. 7. *Der.* motareis, motastaths. [G. *mauth.*]

MOTAN*, *vb.* (*pt. t.* mosta), to be able to, be obliged to. *Der.* gamotan. [A. S. *motan;* O. E. *mot;* E. *must;* G. *müssen;* D. *moeten.*]

MOTAREIS, *str. sb. m.* a receiver of custom, toll-taker, publican, Mat. 5. 47; 9. 10, 11; &c. *From* mota.

MOTA-STATHS, *str. sb. m.* a toll-place, place for receipt of custom, Lu. 5. 27. *From* mota and staths.

MOTJAN*, *vb.* to meet. *Der.* gamotjan, withra-gamotjan. [E. *meet;* D. *ont-moeten.*]

MUKA-MODEI, *wk. sb. f.* meekness of mood, meekness, 2 Cor. 10. 1. *See* mods.

MUKS*, *adj.* meek. *Der.* mukamodei.

MUL*, *str. sb. n.* the muzzle, mouth. *Der.* faur-muljan. [G. *maul;* D. *muil.*]

MULDA, *str. sb. f.* dust, Mk. 6. 11; Lu. 9. 5. *Der.* muldeins. [E. *mould;* D. *mul.*]

MULDEINS, *adj.* earthy, 1 Cor. 15. 47.

MULJAN*, *vb.* to muzzle; see faurmuljan.

MUNAN, *vb.* (*pt. t.* munaida), to be minded, consider, Jo. 12. 10; to intend, Lu. 10. 1; 19. 4.

MUNDITHA*, *in* aina-munditha, q. v. *From* munths.

MUNDON, *vb.* to mind, mark, observe, Phil. 3. 17. *Der.* mundrei. *Cf.* minan. [A. S. *mundian;* E. *mind.*]

MUNDREI, *wk. sb. f.* a mark, a goal, Phil. 3. 14.

MUNNAN*, *vb. in* uf-munnan, q. v.

MUNNON*, vb. in ufar-mannon, q. v.

MUNS, str. sb. m. (pl. muneis), mind, meaning, intention, device, 2 Cor. 2. 11; mind, purpose, will, Rom. 9. 11; Eph. 3. 11; readiness, 2 Cor. 8. 11, provision, Rom. 13. 14. Der. ga-munds, uf-munnan, ufar-munnon.

Cf. minan. [E. mind, meaning; G. meinung.]

MUNTHS, str. sb. m. (also munth, n. 2 Cor. 6. 11), the mouth, Lu. 1. 64; 4. 22; 6. 45, &c.; munth fair-waipjan, to bind the mouth, muzzle, 1 Tim. 5. 18. Der. aina-munditha. [E. mouth; G. mund; D. mond.]

N.

N, the fourteenth letter of the Gothic alphabet. As a numeral, it means 50.

NADRS, str. sb. (m.?) an adder, viper, Lu. 3. 7. [A. S. næddre; O. E. nadder; G. natter; D. adder.]

NAGLJAN*, vb. to nail; see ga-nagljan.

NAGLS*, str. sb. m. a nail. Der. ga-nagljan. [G. D. nagel.]

NAHAN*, vb. (pres. t. nah, pt. t. nauhta, pp. nauhts), to suffice, be enough. Der. bi-, ga-, ga-nauha, ga-nohs, ge-nohjan, ga-nohnan. [G. genügen; cf. D. genoeg; D. enough.]

NAHTA-MATS, str. sb. m. (lit. night-meat), an evening meal, supper, Mk. 6. 21; Lu. 14. 12, Jo. 12. 2.

NAHTS, str. sb. f. night, Mk. 4. 27; Lu. 5. 5; 6. 12, &c. Der. nahta-mats, anda-nahti. [G. D. nacht.]

NAITEINS, str. sb. f. blasphemy, Mk. 2. 7; 3. 28; Lu. 5, 21.

NAITJAN*, vb. to revile, blaspheme. Der. ga-naitjan, naiteins. [Cf. A. S. næting, a chiding.]

NAKWADEI, wk. sb. f. nakedness, Rom. 8. 35; 2 Cor. 11. 27.

NAKWATHS, adj. (gen. nakwadis), naked, Mat. 25. 38; Mk. 14. 51; nakwaths wisan, to be naked, 1 Cor. 4. 11; nakwaths wairthan, to suffer shipwreck, 1 Tim. 1. 19. [G. nackt; D. naeckt.]

NAM, I took; from niman.

NAMNJAN, vb. to name, call, Lu. 6. 13, 14; 9. 10; Eph. 2. 11. Der. ga-namnjan. From namo.

NAMO, wk. sb. n. (pl. namna, gen. namne, dat. namnan), Mat. 6. 9; 7. 22; 10. 41, &c. Der. namnjan, ga-namnjan. [G. name; D. naam.]

NANTHJAN*, vb. to dare. Der. ana-, ga-nanthjan. [A. S. nédan.]

NARDUS, str. sb. m. nard, spikenard, Jo. 12. 3. [G. νάρδος.]

NASEINS, NASSEINS, str. sb. f. salvation, Lu. 1. 69; 2. 30; 19. 9.

NASJAN, vb. to save, Mat. 8. 25; 27. 49; Mk. 3. 4, &c. Der. ga-nasjan. From nisan.

NASJANDS, pres. p. as sb. the Saviour, Lu. 1. 47; 2. 11; Eph. 5. 23.

NATI, str. sb. n. a net, Mk. 1. 16, 18; Lu. 5. 2. [G. netz; D. net.]

NATJAN, vb. to wet, make wet, water, wash, Lu. 7. 38. Der. ga-natjan. [G. nass, netzen; D. nat.]

NAUMBAIMBAIR, *sb.* November, *in Gothic calendar.*

NAUDI-BANDI, *str. sb. f.* a fetter, Mk. 5. 3. 4; 2 Tim. 1. 16. *From* nauths *and* bindan.

NAUDI-THAURFTS, *adj.* necessary, 2 Cor. 9. 5; Skeir. 2. 20. *From* nauths *and* thaurban.

NAUH, *adv.* still, yet, Mat. 27. 63; Lu. 14. 22; ni nauh *or* nauh ni, not yet, not as yet, Mk. 4. 40. [G. *noch.*]

NAUH-THAN, NAUH-THANUH, *adv.* still, yet; — ni nauh-than, not yet, Jo. 6. 17; 11. 30.

NAUHUTH-THAN, *adv.* besides, as well, moreover, Lu. 14. 26.

NAUS, *sb. m.* (*pl.* naweis), a dead man, Lu. 7. 15, 22; 9. 60.

NAUTHJAN, *vb.* to force, to compel, Lu. 14. 23; 16. 16. *Der.* ana-.

NAUTHS, *str. sb. f.* (*gen.* naudis), need, necessity, 2 Cor. 6. 4; 9. 7; 12. 10. [G. *noth*; D. *nood.*]

NAWIS, *adj.* dead, Rom. 7. 8. *Der.* ga-nawistron, mith-gana-wistron (*as if from* nawistr*, *sb.* a grave).

NE, *adv.* nay, no, Mat. 5. 37; Lu. 1. 60; Jo. 7. 12; not, Jo. 18. 40. [E. *nay*; G. *nein.*]

NEHW, *adv.* near, Lu. 15. 25. *Der.* nehwa, nehwis, nehwjan, at-nehwjan, nehwundja. [A. S. *neah*; G. *nahe*; D. *na.*]

NEHWA, *adv.* near, Mk. 13. 28; Jo. 6. 4; 7. 2.

NEHWIS, *compar. adv.* nearer, Rom. 13. 11.

NEHWJAN, *vb.* to draw near, Lu. 15. 1. *Der.* at-nehwjan. *From* nehw.

NEHWUNDJA, *wk. sb. m.* a neighbour, Mat. 5. 43; Mk. 12. 31; Lu. 10. 27; another, Rom. 13. 8.

NEI, *adv.* not, 2 Cor. 3. 8. *Cf.* ne.

NEIPAN*, *vb.*; *see* nipjan.

NEITH, *str. sb. n.* envy, Mat. 27. 18; Mk. 15. 10; Gal. 5. 21; in-neitha wisan, to envy, Gal. 5. 26. *Der.* anda-neiths. [G. *neid*; D. *nijd*; A. S. *nið.*]

NEMEIGS*, *adj. in* anda-nemeigs, q. v.

NEMS*, *in* anda-nems, q. v.

NETHLA, *str. sb. f.* a needle, Mk. 10. 25; Lu. 18. 25. [G. *nadel*; D. *naald.*]

NI, *conj.* nor, not; Mat. 5. 17, 42, &c.; nist, is not; ni waiht, no whit, nothing; ni manna, no man; ni aiw, never; ni ju, no more; ei ni, that not; niba, if not; nih, not, nor. [A. S. & O. E. *ne.*]

NIBA, NIBAI, *conj.* if not, except, Mat. 5. 20; Mk. 3. 27; 7. 3; 8. 14. *From* ni *and* iba *or* ibai.

NIDWA, *str. sb. f.* rust, Mat. 6. 19, 20.

NIH, *conj.* nor (*sometimes* nith *before* th *following, and* nis *before* s *following*), Mat. 10. 34; Lu. 20. 16, 40; nih — nih, neither — nor, Mat. 5. 35, 36.

NIH-THAN, *conj.* neither, nor (*also spelt* nith-than), Mat. 9. 17; Lu. 6. 43. *From* nih *and* than.

NIMAN, *vb.* to take, take away, receive, Mat. 5. 40; Mk. 7. 27; 8. 6, &c. *Der.* and-, at-, af-, bi-, dis-, ga-, mith-, us-, fra-; anda-nems, anda-nemeigs, anda-numts, arbi-numja. [G. *nehmen*; D. *nemen*; O. E. *nim.*]

NIPJAN*, *vb. or* NEIPAN? to vex? *Der.* ga-nipnan.

NIPNAN*, *vb. see* ga-nipnan.

NISAN*, *vb.* to heal. *Der.* ga-nisan, ga-nists, nasjan, ga-nasjan, naseins. [G. *genesen*; D. *genezen*; A. S. *genesan.*]

NIST, is not, Mat. 10. 24; *from* ni *and* ist.

NITHAN, *vb.* to help, Phil. 4. 3. [A. S. *nit*, useful.]

NITHJIS, *str. sb. m.* a kinsman, Lu. 14. 12; Jo. 18. 26; Rom. 16. 21. *Der.* ganithjis, nithjo. [G. *neffe*; D. *neef*; E. *nephew*.]

NITHJO, *wk. sb. f.* a cousin, Lu. 1. 36. [E. *niece*.]

NITH-THAN; see nih-than.

NIU, *conj.* not (*gen. in asking a question*), Mat. 6. 26; 7. 22; 27. 13; niu aiw, never, Mk. 2. 25; niu hwan, if perchance, 2 Tim. 2. 25; niu aufto, whether or not, Lu. 3. 15. *From* ni and uh.

NIUHSEINS, *str. sb. f.* visitation, Lu. 19. 44.

NIUHSJAN*, *vb.* to visit. *Der.* biniuhsjan, niuhseins. [A. S. *neósian*.]

NIUJAN*, *vb.* to renew, *in* ana-niujan, q. v.

NIUJIS, *adj.* new, Mat. 9. 17; 27. 60; Mk. 1. 27. *Der.* ana-niujan, ana-niujitha, in-niujitha, niujitha, nin-klahs. [G. *neu*; D. *nieuw*.]

NIUJITHA, *str. sb. f.* newness, Rom. 7. 6.

NIU-KLAHEI, *wk. sb. f.* weakness of faith, faint-heartedness, Skeir. 7. 7. *From* niujis and klahs.

NIU-KLAHS, *adj.* new-born, young, infantine, Lu. 10. 21; 1 Cor. 13. 11; Gal. 4. 1.

NIUN, *num.* nine, Lu. 15. 4; 17. 17. [G. *neun*; D. *negen*.]

NIUNDA, *ord. adj.* ninth, Mat. 27. 45; Mk. 15. 33.

NIUN-HUNDA, nine hundred, Ezra 2. 16.

NIUNTEHUND, ninety, Ezra 2. 16; Lu. 15. 4, 7.

NIUTAN, *vb.* to receive joy from, Philem. 20; to obtain, Lu. 20. 35. *Der.* ga-niutan, nuta, un-nutis. [G. *nützen*, *geniessen*; D. *geneiten*; A. S. *neótan*, to use, enjoy.]

NOTA, *wk. sb. m.* stern, hinder part of a ship, Mk. 4. 38.

NU, *adv.* now, Mat. 26. 65. &c.; fram himma nu, from henceforth, Lu. 5. 10; fram thamma nu, from henceforth, 2 Cor. 5. 16; tho nu hweila, the present time, 2 Cor. 8. 14; tho nu ald, this present world, 2 Tim. 4. 10; ath-than nu, wherefore, Rom. 7. 12; ith in thizei nu, but because therefore, Skeir. 1. 26; nu sai *or* sai nu, see now, now therefore, Eph. 2. 19. [G. *nun*; D. *nu*; E. *now*.]

NU'H, NUH, then (*in questions*), Mk. 12. 9; Jo. 18. 37. *From* nu and uh.

NUMJA*, *wk. sb. m.* a taker, *in* arbi-numja, q. v.

NUMTS*, *str. sb. f. in* anda-numts, q. v.

NUNU, *adv.* therefore, Mat. 10. 26, 31.

NUTA, *wk. sb. m.* a fisher, catcher of fishes, Mk. 1. 17; a catcher of men, Lu. 5. 10. *From* niutan.

NUTIS*, *adj.* useful; *see* un-nutis.

O.

O, the 25th and last letter of the Gothic alphabet. *As a numeral, it means* 800. *Answers generally Greek* ω, *seldom to* o *or* ου. *It is to be regarded as essentially long; and to be sounded probably like* o *in* gold.

O, *interj.* O! Oh! Mk. 9. 19; Gal. 3. 1; ho! ah! Mk. 15. 29.

OGAN, *vb.* (*pres.* og, *pt. t.* ohta, *pl.* ohtedum), to fear, *with acc.* Mat. 9. 8; 10. 28; Mk. 5. 15; *refl.* to fear, be afraid of, Mat. 10. 26; Mk. 4. 41. *Der.* ogjan. *From* agan.

OGJAN, *vb.* to terrify, frighten, Nehem. 6. 19.

OHTEIGO; *see* uhteigo.

ON*, breathed out; *pt. t. of* anan; *in comp.* uz-on, q. v. *Cf.* anan.

OSANNA, Hosannah, Mk. 11. 9; Jo. 12. 23.

P.

P, the 17th letter of the Gothic alphabet. *As a numeral, it means* 80. [*Nearly all words beginning with* P *are Greek*]

PAIDA (χιτών), *str. sb. f.* a coat, outer body-garment, Mat. 5. 40; Mk. 6. 9; Lu. 3. 11. *Der.* ga-paidon. [A. S. *pád*.]

PAINTEKUSTE (πεντηκοστή), Pentecost, 1 Cor. 16. 8.

PAPA, *sb.* a bishop, *in Gothic calendar.*

PARAKLETUS, *sb.* the Paraclete, comforter, Jo. 14. 16; 15. 26; 16. 7.

PARASKAIWE (παρασκευή), *sb.* the day of the preparation, Mat. 27. 62; Mk. 15. 42.

PAURPURA (*spelt* paurpaura, Lu. 16. 19), *sb.* purple, Mk. 15. 17, 20. *Der.* paurpuron.

PAURPURON, *vb.* to clothe in purple; *pt. pass.* paurpuroths, clothed in purple. Jo. 19. 2, 5.

PEIKA-BAGMS, *str. sb. m.* (*lit.* a pitch-tree, a pine-tree), a palm-tree, Jo. 12. 13.

PISTIKEINS (πιστικός), *adj.* genuine, pure, Jo. 12. 3.

PLAPJA, *str. sb. f.* a street, Mat. 6. 5. [M. *proposes to read* platja.]

PLATS, *str. sb. m.* a patch, new piece put in, Mat. 9. 16; Mk. 2. 21; Lu. 5. 36.

PLINSJAN, *vb.* to dance, Mat. 11. 17; Mk. 6. 22; Lu. 7. 32.

PRAGGAN*, *vb.* to press. *Der.* ana-praggan. [D. *prangen.*]

PRAITORIA, PRAITAURIA, *sb.* Pretorium, Jo. 18. 28; 19. 9.

PRAITORIAUN, *sb. the same*, Mk. 15. 16; Jo. 18. 28.

PRAIZBYTAIREI, *wk. sb. f.* (*spelt* praizbyterei, 1 Tim. 5. 19), the presbytery, the elders, 1 Tim. 5. 19; Tit. 1. 5.

PRAIZBYTAIREIS, *str. sb. m.* a presbyter, a priest, 1 Tim. 4. 14.

PRAUFETEIS (προφῆτις), *sb. f.* a prophetess, Lu. 2. 36.

PRAUFETI, *sb. n.* a prophecy, 1 Cor. 13. 8.
PRAUFETJA, *wk. sb. m.* a prophecy, 1 Cor. 13. 2; 14. 22; 1 Th. 5. 20.
PRAUFETJAN, *vb.* to prophesy, Mat. 7. 22; Mk. 7. 6; Lu. 1. 67.
PRAUFETUS, *sb.* (PRAUFETES *in* Mat. 10. 41; Mk. 6. 15; 11. 32), a prophet, Mat. 5. 17; 7. 12, &c. *Der.* galiuga-praufetus, liugna-praufetus, praufeteis, praufetja, praufetjan, praufeti.
PSALMA, PSALMO, *sb. f.* a psalm, Lu. 20. 42; 1 Cor. 14. 26; Eph. 4. 8.
PUGGS ($\beta\alpha\lambda\lambda\acute{a}\nu\tau\iota o\nu$), *sb. m.* a purse, Lu. 10. 4.
PUND, *str. sb. n.* a pound, Jo. 12. 3. [G. *pfund;* D. *pond.*]

Q.

Q, *the sixth letter of the Gothic alphabet, denoted in* Bosworth, Schulze, *and* Gabelentz *by* Q, *and in* Massmann *by* KV, *is denoted in this volume by* KW. *See* KW.

R.

R, the 18th letter of the Gothic alphabet. *As a numeral, it means* 100.
RABBAUNEI ($\dot{\rho}\alpha\beta\beta ov\nu\acute{\iota}$), Rabboni, Mk. 10. 51.
RABBEI ($\dot{\rho}\alpha\beta\beta\acute{\iota}$), Rabbi, Mk. 9. 5; 11. 21; Jo. 6. 25.
RAGIN, *str. sb. n.* a rule; *hence,* opinion, judgment, 1 Cor. 7. 25; advice, 2 Cor. 8. 10; ordinance, decree, Col. 2. 14; dispensation, Col. 1. 25. *Der.* raginon, ga-raginon, ragineis, fidur-ragineis.
RAGINEIS, *str. sb. m.* a counsellor, Rom. 11. 34; Mk. 15. 43; a governor, guardian, Gal. 4. 2.
RAGINON, *vb.* to rule, govern, Lu. 2. 2; 3. 1. [*Cf.* Lat. *regere;* G. *regieren.*]
RAHNJAN, *vb.* to reckon, count up, Lu. 14. 28; to number, Mk. 15. 28; Rom. 8. 36; to compute, think, Phil. 2. 6; — wairthana rahnjan, to consider worthy, Lu. 7. 7; to impute, 2 Cor. 5. 19. *Der.* ga-, faura-. [G. *rechnen;* D. *rekenen.*]
RAHTON, *vb.* to relate to, 2 Cor. 9. 1. *Cf.* rikan.
RAIDEINS*; *see* ga-raideins.
RAIDJAN, *vb.* to appoint, Skeir. 3. 14; raihtaba raidjan, to divide rightly, 2 Tim. 2. 15. *Der.* ga-raidjan. *From* raids.
RAIDS*, *adj.* set, appointed, ready. *Der.* ga-raids, raidjan, ga-raidjan, ga-raideins. [E. *ready.*]
RAIHTABA, *adv.* rightly, Lu. 7. 43; 10. 28; 20. 21; straight-

way, Mk. 7. 35; r. gaggan, to walk uprightly, Gal. 2. 14. *From* raihts.

RAIHTIS, *conj.* (*always used in the position of an enclitic*), for, Mat. 9. 5; 11. 18; but however, Rom. 10. 18; however, indeed, Mk. 4. 4; swe raihtis, just as, 2 Cor. 8. 7. *From* raihts.

RAIHTS, *adj.* right, straight, Mk. 1. 3; Lu. 3. 4, 5; righteous, 2 Tim. 4. 8. *Der.* raihtaba, ga-raihts, ga-raihtaba, ga-raihtei, un-ga-raihtei, ga-raihtitha, ga-raihtjan, at-ga-raihtjan, ga-raihteins, raihtis. [G. *recht*; D. *regt*.]

RAIP*, *sb.* a rope, string; *see* skauda-raip. [G. *reif*; D. *reep*.]

RAISJAN, *vb.* to raise, Rom. 9. 17. *Der.* ur-, mithur-. *From* reisan.

RAKA (ῥακά), Mat. 5. 22.

RAKJAN*, *vb.* to reach, to stretch. *Der.* uf-rakjan. *From* rikan.

RANN, I ran; *from* rinnan.

RANNEINS*, *sb.* a running; *see* ufar-ranneins.

RANNJAN*, *vb.* to cause to run. *Der.* ur-rannjan, ufar-ranneins. *From* rinnan.

RASTA, *str. sb. f.* rest; *hence*, a stage of a journey, a mile, Mat. 5. 41.

RATHJAN*, *vb.* to speak, tell. *Der.* rathjo, ga-rathjan. *Cf.* rodjan.

RATHJO, *wk. sb. f.* a number, Jo. 6. 10; Rom. 9. 27; account, Lu. 16. 2; Rom. 14. 2. [Lat. *ratio.*]

RATHS, *adj.* ready, easy; *compar.* rathiza, easier, Lu. 18. 25. *Cf.* raids.

RATJAN, *vb.* to appoint, 1 Th. 3. 3. [M. *reads* satidai, *from* satjan.]

RAUBON*, *vb.* to reave, rob. *Der.* bi-raubon. [G. *rauben*; Lat. *rapere*.]

RAUDS, *adj.* red, Skeir. 3. 16. [G. *roth*; D. *rood*.]

RAUHTJAN*, *vb.* to be angry. *Der.* in-rauhtjan.

RAUPJAN, *vb.* to reap; *hence*, to pluck, Mk. 2. 23; Lu. 6. 1. [G. *raufen*, *rupfen*; D. *rapen*; E. *reap*.]

RAUS, *str. sb. n.* a reed, Mat. 11. 7; 27. 48; Mk. 15. 19; Lu. 7. 24. [G. *rohr*.]

RAZDA, *str. sb. f.* a speech, a tongue, language, Mat. 26. 73; Mk. 14. 70; Rom. 14. 11. [A. S. *reord*.]

RAZN, *str. sb. n.* a house, Mat. 5. 15; 7. 24; Lu. 6. 48. *Der.* ga-razna, ga-razno. *Cf.* hus, gards. [A. S. *ræsen*.]

REDAN*, *vb.* to counsel, provide, think of. *Der.* ga-redan, fauragaredan, und-redan, ur-redan, ga-redaba. *Cf.* rathjan, rodjan.

REIKEI*, *sb.* danger; *see* bi-reikei.

REIKI, *str. sb. n.* power, authority, Lu. 20. 20; Rom. 8. 38; 1 Cor. 15. 24. *From* reiks. [E. *-ric* in *bishopric*.]

REIKINON, *vb.* to rule, govern, Mk. 10. 42; Jo. 14. 30; Rom. 15. 12.

REIKISTA, *superl. adj.* most powerful; *hence*, *as sb.* a prince, Mk. 3. 22; — reikista gudja, the high-priest, Jo. 18. 22. *See* reiks.

REIKS, *adj.* mighty, chief, having authority, honourable, Nehem. 6. 17; *hence*, *as sb.* a chief, ruler, Mat. 9. 18; Lu. 18. 18; Jo. 7. 26. *Der.* reikista, reiki, reikinon, fritha-reiks. [G. *reich*, a kingdom; D. *rijk*; A. S. *ric*.]

REIRAN, *vb.* to tremble, Mat. 27. 51; Mk. 5. 43; Lu. 8. 47. *Der.* reiro. [*Cf.* G. *rühren*.]

REIRO, *wk. sb. f.* a trembling, Mk. 16. 8; an earthquake, Mat. 27. 54.

REISAN*, *vb.* to rise. *Der.* ur-, mithur-; ur-rists; raisjan, ur-, mithur-raisjan.

REKS*, *adj.* in danger; *see* bi-reks.

RIGGWS*, *adj. in comp.* unmana-riggws, q. v.

RIGN, *str. sb. n.* rain, Mat. 7. 25, 27. *Der.* rignjan. [G. & D. *regen*.]

RIGNJAN, *vb.* to rain, Mat. 5. 45; Lu. 17. 29.

RIKAN, *vb.* (*pt. t.* rak, *pl.* rekum, *pp.* rikans) to reach; *hence*, to collect, heap up, Rom. 12. 20. *Der.* uf-rakjan, bi-reks, bi-reiki. [G. *reichen;* D. *reiken;* E. *reach.*]

RIKWIS, RIKWIZ, *str. sb. n.* darkness, Mat. 6. 23; 8. 12; 27. 45, &c. *Der.* rikwizeins, rikwizjan. [*Cf.* G. *rauch;* E. *reek;* O. E. *roke,* a mist.]

RIKWIZEINS, *adj.* roky, misty, dark, Mat. 6. 23; darkened, Eph. 4. 18.

RIKWIZJAN, *vb.* to become dark, to be darkened, Mk. 13. 24.

RIMIS, *str. sb. n.* rest, quietness, 2 Th. 3. 12.

RINNAN, *vb.* (*pt. t.* rann, *pl.* runnum, *pp.* runnans), to run, Mk. 5. 6; to go out, Lu. 8. 33; to come out, Mat. 8. 28; to flow, Jo. 7. 38; — samath rinnan, to run together, Mk. 9. 25. *Der.* and-, at-, bi-, duat-, ga-, du-, fair-, faur-, fra-, und-, ur-; blotha-rinnandei, rinno, runs, ga-runs, ur-runs, ga-runjo, ur-rannjan, afar-rinneins. [G. D. *rennen.*]

RINNO, *wk. sb. f.* that which flows, a brook, Jo. 18. 1.

RISTS*, *str. sb. f.* a rising; *see* ur-rists.

RIUDS*, *adj.* honourable, worthy. *Der.* ga-riuds, ga-rindi, ga-riudjo.

RIUREI, *wk. sb. f.* corruption, 1 Cor. 15. 50; Gal. 6. 8; Col. 2. 22. *Der.* un-riurei. *From* riurs.

RIURJAN, *vb.* to corrupt, 1 Cor. 15. 33.

RIURS, *adj.* mortal, 2 Cor. 4. 11; temporal, 2 Cor. 4. 18; corruptible, 1 Cor. 9. 25; corrupt, Eph. 4. 22; — riurs wairthan, to be corrupted, 2 Cor. 11. 3. *Der.* riurei, un-riurei, un-riurs, riarjan. [*Cf.* A. S. *hreosan*, to rush, fall.]

RODJAN, *vb.* to speak, Mat. 9. 18; Mk. 1. 34; 2. 2, &c. *Der.* unrodjands, bi-rodjan, mith-rodjan, bi-rodeins. [G. *reden;* D. *raden;* A. S. *rædan;* O. E. *rede.*]

ROHSNS, *str. sb. f.* a hall, Mat. 26. 69; Mk. 14. 66; Jo. 18. 15.

RUGKS*, *adj.*; *see* ur-rugks.

RUMA, *wk. sb. f.* Rome, 2 Tim. 1. 17.

RUMONEIS, *pl. sb.* Romans.

RUMS, *str. sb. m.* room, space, place, Lu. 2. 7; *Der.* rums, ur-rumnan. [G. *raum;* D. *ruim.*]

RUMS, *adj.* roomy, large, broad, Mat. 7. 13.

RUNA, *str. sb. f.* a rune, a mystery, Mk. 4. 11; Lu. 8. 10; Rom. 11. 25; counsel, Mat. 27. 1; Lu. 7. 30. *Der.* ga-runi, bi-runains.

RUNS, *str. sb. m.* a running, an issue, Mk. 5. 25; Lu. 8. 43; a course, 2 Tim. 4. 7; — run ga-waurkjan sis, to run down violently, Mat. 8. 32. *Der.* ga-runs, ur-runs. *From* rinnan.

S.

S, the 19th letter of the Gothic alphabet. *As a numeral, it means* 200.

SA, *dem. pron.* this (*f.* so, *n.* thata); also (2) *as def. art.* the; (3) *pers. pron.* he, *pl.* thai, they (*f.* thos). *Der.* sa'h, sa-ei. *See also under* thata. [A. S. *se, seo, that.*]

SABAN, *sb. n.* fine linen, Mat. 27. 59. [A. S. *saban.*]

SABBATO, *sb. m. indecl.* the Sabbath, Mk. 2. 27, 28; sabbato-dags, the Sabbath-day, Mk. 1. 21.

SABBATUS, *str. sb. m.* (*gen. pl.* sabbate, -o; *dat.* -um, -im), the Sabbath, Mk. 2. 24; 3. 4; 16. 1. *Der.* sabbato, afar-sabbatus.

SADS; *see* SATHS.

SA-EI, *rel. pron.* that, who (*f.* so-ei or sei, *n.* thatei). *From* sa *and* ei.

SAGGKWJAN, *vb.* to make to sink, 1 Tim. 6. 9. *From* siggkwan.

SAGGKWS, *str. sb. m.* a sinking, the quarter of sun-set, the west, Mat. 8. 11. *From* siggkwan.

SAGGWS, *str. sb. m.* song, singing, Lu. 15. 25; Eph. 5. 19; — saggws boko, reading, 1 Tim. 4. 13.

SA'H, *contr. from* sa *and* uh, *dem. pron.* (*f.* soh, *n.* thatuh), and this, and that; this, that.

SAHTS*, *str. sb. f.* a seeking, searching? *Der.* ga-, in-, fri-, gafrisahtjan, gafrisahtnan. *From* sakan.

SAHW, I saw; *from* saihwan.

SAI, *adv.* see! lo! behold! Mat. 8. 2; 9. 10; 10. 28; sai nu, see now, now, therefore, Eph. 2. 19; nu sai, now, Rom. 7. 6; sai jau, see whether, Jo. 7. 48. *Cf.* saihwan.

SAIAN, SAIJAN, *vb.* (*pt. t.* saiso, *pp.* saians), to sow, Mat. 6. 26; Mk. 4. 3; 4. 14. *Der.* insaian. [G. *säen;* D. *zaaijen.*]

SAIHS, *num.* six, Mk. 9. 2; Lu. 4. 25. *Der.* saihs-tigjus, saihsta.

SAIHS-TIGJUS, sixty, 1 Tim. 5. 9.

SAIHSTA, *adj.* the sixth, Mat. 27. 45; Mk. 15. 33.

SAIHWAN, *vb.* (*pt. t.* sahw, *pl.* sehwum, *pp.* saihwans), to see, Mat. 8. 4; Mk. 5. 6; Lu. 2. 15, &c.; s. faura, to beware of, Mk. 12, 38. *Der.* and-, at-, bi-, ga-, us-, duga-, usga-, in-, thairh-; unsaihwands, ungasaihwans. [G. *sehen;* D. *zien.*]

SAIJAN; *see* SAIAN.

SAIL*, *str. sb. n.* a cord, rope. *Der.* in-sailjan. [A. S. *sál;* G. *seil;* D. *zeel.*]

SAINJAN, *vb.* to delay, wait, tarry, 1 Tim. 3. 15. [*Cf.* A. S. *sǽne,* slow.]

SAIR, *str. sb. n.* sorrow, 1 Tim. 6. 10; travail, 1 Th. 5. 3. [E. *sore, sorrow;* A. S. *sár.*]

SAISLEP, slept; *from* slepan.

SAISO, sowed; *from* saian.

SAIWALA, *str. sb. f.* (ψυχή) the soul, the life, Mat. 6. 25; 10. 39; Mk. 3. 4, &c. *Der.* samasaiwals. [G. *seele;* D. *ziel.*]

SAIWS, *str. sb. m.* the sea, a lake, Lu. 5. 1, 2. *Der.* mari-saiws. [G. *see;* D. *zee.*]

SAIZLEP, slept; *from* slepan. *See also* saislep.

SAKAN, *vb.* (*pt. t.* sok, *pp.* sakans), to rebuke, Mk. 10. 13; Lu. 19. 39; to strive, dispute, Jo. 6. 52; 2 Tim. 2. 24. *Der.* and-, anain-, ga-, in-, us-; unandsakans, sakjis, sakjo; sahts, gasahts, in-sahts, fri-sahts, ga-frisahtjan, ga-frisahtnan, un-sahtaba; sokjan, ga-sokjan, mithsokjan, us-sokjan, sokns, unandsoks, sokeins, sokareis. See sokjan. [A. S. *sacan;* E. *sake* in *forsake.*]

SAKJIS, *str. sb. m.* a brawler, striker, 1 Tim. 3. 3. *From* sakan.

SAKJO, *wk. sb. f.* strife, 2 Tim. 2. 23. *From* sakan. [A. S. *sacu.*]

SAKKUS, *str. sb. m.* a sack, sackcloth, Mat. 11. 21; Lu. 10. 13. [G. *sack;* D. *zak.*]

SALBON, *vb.* to salve, anoint, Mat. 6. 17; Lu. 7. 46; Jo. 11. 2. *Der.* ga-salbon, salbons. [G. *salben;* D. *zalven.*]

SALBONS, *str. sb. f.* ointment, salve, Jo. 12. 3.

SALDRA, *sb. f.* jesting, Eph. 5. 4.

SALITHWA, *str. sb. f. (only in pl.* salithwos), a mansion, Jo. 14. 2, 23; guest-chamber, Mk. 14. 14; a lodging, Philem. 22.

SALJAN, *vb.* (1) to dwell, abide, remain, Mk. 6. 10; Lu. 9. 4; Jo. 10. 40. *Der.* us-saljan, salithwos. [A. S. *sal;* G. *saal;* D. *zaal,* a hall.]

SALJAN, *vb.* (2) to bring an offering, to sacrifice, Mk. 14. 12; 1 Cor. 10. 20; to 'burn incense' (A. V.), Lu. 1. 9; — thatei galiugam saljada, that which is offered to idols, 1 Cor. 10. 19; — hunsla saljan, to offer a sacrifice, do service, Jo. 16. 2. *Der.* ga-saljan. [A. S. *syllan;* whence E. *sell.*]

SALT, *str. sb. n.* salt, Mk. 9. 49; Lu. 14. 34; Col. 4. 6. *Der.* saltan, un-saltans. [G. *salz;* D. *zout.*]

SALTAN, *vb.* to salt, Mk. 9. 49.

SAMA, SA SAMA, *adj.* the same, Mat. 5. 46; 27. 44; Mk. 10. 10, &c.; (2) *in comp.* together. *Der.* sama-frathjis, -kuns, -kwiss, -lauds, -leiks, -saiwals; lustusams, samana, samath. [*Cf.* O. E. *sam,* together; G. *samt, zusammen.*]

SAMA-FRATHJIS, *adj.* like-minded, Phil. 2. 2. *From* sama *and* frathjan.

SAMA-KUNS, *adj.* kindred, of the same kin, Rom. 9. 3. *From* sama *and* kuni.

SAMA-KWISS, *str. sb. f.* concord, agreement, 2 Cor. 6. 15, 16. *From* sama *and* kwithan.

SAMA-LAUDS, *adj.* as much, an equal share, Lu. 6. 34.

SAMA-LEIKO, *adv.* equally, likewise, Mk. 12. 21; 15. 31; Lu. 6. 26.

SAMA-LEIKS, *adj.* alike, agreeing together, Mk. 14. 56, 59. *From* sama *and* leiks.

SAMANA, *adv.* together, in the same place, Lu. 17. 35; 1 Cor. 14. 23. *From* sama.

SAMA-SAIWALS, *adj.* of one accord, Phil. 2. 2.

SAMATH, *adv.* to the same place, together, 1 Cor. 7. 5; — s. gagaggan, to come together, 1 Cor. 5. 4; — s. rinnan, to run together. *From* sama.

SAMJAN, *vb.* to please, Col. 3. 22; *refl.* to please oneself, to 'make a fair show' (A. V.), Gal. 6. 12. [A. S. *seman;* whence E. *seem, seemly.*]

SANDJAN, *vb.* to send, Lu. 20. 11; Jo. 5. 37; 6. 38. *Der.* ga-, fauraga-, in-, mithin-, mith-, us-. *From* sinthan. [G. *senden;* D. *zenden.*]

SARWA, *sb. n. pl.* arms, armour, Rom. 13. 12; panoply, whole armour, Eph. 6. 11, 13. [A. S. *searo.*]

SATANA, SATANAS, *sb.* Satan, Mk. 1. 13; 3. 23; 8. 33, &c.

SATEINS, *str. sb. f.* natural disposition, nature, Eph. 2. 3 (*a gloss for* wistai.). *Der.* af-, ga-, us-. *From* sitan.

SATHAN*, *vb.* (*pt. t.* soth, *pp.* satbans), to be full. *Der.* saths.

SATHS, SADS, *adj.* (*gen.* sadis), full, Lu. 6. 25; 1 Cor. 4. 8; s. wairthan, to be filled, to be full, Mk. 7. 27; 8. 8; sath itan, to eat enough, be filled, Lu. 16. 21; to fill one's belly, Lu. 15. 16. *Der.* soth, ga-sothjan. [G. *satt*; A. S. *sæd*; E. *sated.*]

SATJAN, *vb.* to set, place, put, Mk. 4. 21; Lu. 8. 16; to set *or* plant (trees), Lu. 17. 28; 1 Cor. 9. 7; — satiths wisan, to be set, made, ordained, 1 Tim. 1. 9; — niuja satiths, one newly planted, a novice, 1 Tim. 3. 6. *Der.* and-, at-, af-, bi-, ga-, mitbga-, fauraga-, mitb-, us-; sateins, af-, ga-, us-sateins. *From* sitan. [G. *setzen*; D. *zetten*; E. *set.*]

SAUDS: *see* SAUTHS.

SAUHTS, *str. sb. f.* sickness, disease, Mat. 8. 17; 9. 35; Mk. 1. 34. *From* siukan.

SAUIL, *str. sb. n.* the sun, Mk. 1. 32; 13. 24. *Cf.* sunna. [Lat. *sol.*]

SAULJAN*, *vb.* to soil, sully. *Der.* bi-sauljan, bi-saulnan, bi-sauleins.

SAULS, *str. sb. f.* (*pl.* sauleis), a pillar, Gal. 2. 9; 1 Tim. 3. 15. [G. *säule*; D. *zuil*; A. S. *sýl*; E. *sill.*]

SAUN, *str. sb. n.* (?) a ransom, Mk. 10. 45. *Der.* us-sauneins. [G. *sühne.*]

SAUR, *sb. m.* a Syrian, Lu. 2. 2; 4. 27.

SAURA, *sb. f.* Syria, Gal. 1. 21.

SAURGA, *str. sb. f.* sorrow, grief, Mk. 4. 19; Lu. 8. 14; Jo. 16. 20. *Der.* saurgan. [G. *sorge*; D. *zorg.*]

SAURGAN, *vb.* to sorrow, to be grieved, to be anxious about, Mat. 6. 28; Jo. 16. 20; 2 Cor. 6. 10.

SAURINI-FYNIKISKA, *sb. f.* a Syro-Phœnician, Mk. 7. 26.

SAUTHA, *str. sb. f.* subject of discourse, theme, 1 Cor. 15. 2.

SAUTHS, SAUDS, *str. sb. m.* a sacrifice, Rom. 12. 1; Eph. 5. 2; a holocaust, burnt-offering, Mk. 12. 33.

SEDS*, *sb.* seed? *Der.* manaseths. *Cf.* saian. [*A word of doubtful existence.*]

SEHWUM. we saw; *from* saihwan.

SEI, *contr. from* so-ei, she who. *See* sa-ei.

SEINA, *gen. sing. and pl. of third pers. pron.* his, their, Jo. 16. 32; — seina misso, one another, Lu. 7. 32; — seinai gairnai, lovers of themselves, *a gloss to* sik frijondans, 2 Tim. 3. 2. *Cf.* sik, sis.

SEINS, *poss. pron.* his, theirs, their, Mat. 5. 22; 6. 2. &c. [G. *sein*; D. *zijn.*]

SEITEINS, *another form of* SINTEINS, 2 Cor. 11. 28; *see* sinteins.

SEITHU, *adv.* late, Mat. 27. 57; Jo. 6. 16. *Der.* thana-seiths. [A. S. *sið*; O. E. *sith.*]

SELEI, *wk. sb. f.* goodness, Rom. 11. 22; 2 Cor. 6. 6; Eph. 5. 9. *Der.* un-selei. *From* sels.

SELS, *adj.* good, kind, Lu. 8. 15; Eph. 4. 32; — sels wisan, to be kind, 1 Cor. 13. 4. *Der.* unsels, selei, un-selei. [A. S. *sél*; whence E. *silly.*]

SENEIGS, *another form of* SINEIGS, q. v., 1 Tim. 5. 1, 2.

SETHS*; *see* SEDS.

SI, *pers. pron. f.* she. *From* is. [E. *she*; G. *sie*.]

SIBIS*, *adj.* related, akin, friendly. *Der.* un-sibis, sibja, un-sibja, frasti-sibja, ga-sibjon. [O. E. *sib.*]

SIBJA, *str. sb. f.* relationship; suniwe sibja, the adoption of sons, adoption as sons, Gal. 4. 5. *Der.* frasti-sibja, un-sibja.

SIBUN, *num.* seven, Mk. 8. 5; 12. 20; 16. 9. [G. *sieben*; D. *zeven.*]

SIBUN-TEHUND, *num.* seventy, Lu. 10. 1, 17.

SIDON, *vb.* to meditate on, 1 Tim. 4. 15. *From* sidus.

SIDUS, *str. sb. m.* a custom, manner, 1 Cor. 15. 33; 2 Tim. 3. 10. [G. *sitte.*]

SIFAN, *vb.* to rejoice, be glad, Jo. 8. 56; Rom. 15. 10; Gal. 4. 27. [A. S. *sifian.*]

SIGGKWAN, SIGKWAN, *vb.* (*pt. t.* saggkw, *pp.* suggkwans), to sink, Lu. 5. 7; to set (of the sun), Lu. 4. 40. *Der.* dis-, ga-, saggkwjan, ufsaggkwjan, saggkws. [G. *sinken*; D. *zinken.*]

SIGGWAN, *vb.* (*pt. t.* saggw, *pl.* suggwum, *pp.* suggwans), to sing, Eph. 5. 19; to read aloud, Lu. 4. 16; 2 Cor. 3. 15; to read, Eph. 3. 4. *Der.* us-, saggws. [G. *singen*; D. *zingen.*]

SIGIS, *str. sb. n.* victory, 1 Cor. 15. 54. *Der.* sigis-laun. [A. S. *sige*; G. *sieg*; D. *zege.*]

SIGIS-LAUN, *str. sb. n.* the reward or crown of victory, prize, 1 Cor. 9. 24; Phil. 3. 14. *From* sigis and laun.

SIGKWAN: *see* SIGGKWAN.

SIGLJAN, *vb.* to seal, 2 Cor. 1. 22. *Der.* ga-, faur-, siglo.

SIGLO, *wk. sb. n.* a seal, 1 Cor. 9. 2; 2 Tim. 2. 19. [G. *siegel*; D. *zegel*; A. S. *sigel.*]

SIJAU, I may be; *from* wisan.

SIJUM, SIUM, we are; *see* wisan.
SIJUTH, SIUTH, ye are; *see* wisan.
SIK, *acc. of pers. pron.* him. [G. *sich.*]
SIKLS, *str. sb. m.* a shekel, Neh. 5. 15.
SILAN*, *vb.*; *see* ana-silan. [Lat. *silere.*]

SILBA, *pron.* self; — is silba, he himself, Lu. 5. 1; — thata silbo, this very thing, Rom. 13. 6; — sein silbins, his own, Lu. 14. 26. *Der.* silba-siuneis, silba-wileis, silba-wiljands. [G. *selber*; D. *zelf.*]

SILBA-SIUNEIS, *sb. m.* an eye-witness, Lu. 1. 2. *From* silba and siuns.

SILBA-WILEIS, *adj.* willing of oneself, 2 Cor. 8. 3. *From* silba and wiljan.

SILBA-WILJANDS, willing of one's own accord, 2 Cor. 8. 17. *Cf.* preceding word.

SILD*, *adv.* seldom. *Der.* silda-leiks, silda-leikjan. [*Cf.* G. *selten.*]

SILDA-LEIKJAN, *vb.* to wonder, Mat. 8. 10; 9. 8; Mk. 5. 20; to wonder at, Lu. 7. 9.

SILDA-LEIKS, *adj.* wonderful, Mk. 12. 11; Jo. 9. 30; 2 Cor. 11. 14.

SILUBR, *str. sb. n.* silver, silver money, Mat. 27. 5; Lu. 19. 15, 23. *Der.* silubreins. [G. *silber*; D. *zilver.*]

SILUBREINS, *adj.* of silver, Mat. 27. 3, 9; 2 Tim. 2. 20.

SIMLE, *adv.* once, at one time, Rom. 7. 9; Gal. 1. 23; 2. 6. [A. S. *symle* (?); Lat. *semel.*]

SINAPS, *sb. m.* mustard, Mk. 4. 31; Lu. 17. 6. [A. S. *senepe*; Gk. σίναπι.]

SIND, they are; *see* wisan.
SINDO*, *adv. in comp.* us-sindo, q. v.

SINEIGS, SENEIGS, *adj.* old, Lu. 1. 18; elder, 1 Tim. 5. 1. *From* sins.

7*

SINISTA, *sup. adj.* the eldest, Mat. 27. 1, 3; Mk. 7. 3; 8. 31. *From* sins.
SINS*, *adj.* old; *whence superl.* sinista. [*Cf.* Lat. *senex.*]
SINTEINO, *adv.* ever, always, continually, Mk. 14. 7; Lu. 15. 31.
SINTEINS, *adj.* (*spelt* seiteins *in* 2 Cor. 11. 28), daily, Mat. 6. 11; Skeir. 3. 10. *Der.* sinteino.
SINTH, *str. sb. (n.?)* a journey; *hence* a time; *in the phrases* ainamma sintha, once; twaim sintham, twice, &c.; *also* antharamma sintha, a second time; *see* Mk. 14. 72; 2 Cor. 11. 25.
SINTHAN*, *vb.* (*pt. t.* santh, *pl.* sunthum, *pp.* sunthans), to go, wander. *Der.* sinth, ga-sintha, mithga-sintha, us-sindo, sandjan, ga-sandjan, fauraga-sandjan, in-sandjan, mithin-sandjan, mith-sandjan, us-sandjan. *See* sandjan. [A. S. *siðian.*]
SIPONEIS, *str. sb. m.* a pupil, disciple, Mat. 8. 18; 9. 10, 11, &c. *Der.* siponjan.
SIPONJAN, *vb.* to learn, to be a disciple, Mat. 27. 57.
SIS, *dat. of pron. pers.* to him.
SITAN, *vb.* (*pt. t.* sat, *pl.* setum, *pp.* sitans), to sit, Mat. 9. 9; 16. 26; 27. 19, &c. *Der.* and-, bi-, ga-, dis-, us-; sitls, andasets; satjan, ga-, fauraga-, mithga-, af-, at-, and-, bi-, mith-, us-satjan; sateins, ga-, af-, ussateins. [G. *sitzen;* D. *zitten.*]
SITLS, *str. sb. m.* a settle, seat, Mk. 11. 15; a throne, Col. 1. 16; a nest, Mat. 8. 20; Lu. 9. 58. *From* sitan. [E. *settle.*]
SIUJAN, *vb.* to sew, Mk. 2. 21. [Lat. *suere;* E. *sew.*]
SIUKAN, *vb.* (*pt. t.* sauk, *pl.* sukum, *pp.* sukans), to be sick, to be ill, to be diseased, Lu. 7. 2; 2 Cor. 11. 29; 12. 10. *Der.* siuks, siukei, sauhts.

SIUKEI, *wk. sb. f.* sickness, disease, Jo. 11. 4; 2 Cor. 11. 30; 12. 9.
SIUKS, *adj.* sick, ill, diseased, Mat. 25. 39; Lu. 10. 9; Jo. 6. 2; — siuks wisan, to fall sick, be sick, Jo. 11. 3. [G. *siech;* D. *ziek.*]
SIUNS, *str. sb. f.* the sight, Lu. 4. 19; 7. 21; sight, seeing, 2 Cor. 5. 7; a sight, a vision, Lu. 1. 22; an appearance, outward shape, form, Lu. 3. 22; 9. 29. *Der.* ana-, unana-siunaba, silba-siuneis. [A. S. *sien.*]
SIUTH, ye are; *see* sijuth. *From* wisan.
SKABAN, *vb.* to shave, 1 Cor. 11. 6. *Der.* bi-skaban. [G. *schaben;* D. *schaven.*]
SKADUS, *str. sb. m.* a shade, shadow, Mk. 4. 32; Lu. 1. 79; Col. 2. 17. *Der.* ga-skadweins, ufar-skadwjan. [G. *schatten;* D. *schaduw.*]
SKAFTJAN, *vb.* to shape; *hence,* sk. sik, to shape one's course, to be about to do, Jo. 12. 4. *From* skapjan.
SKAFTS*, *str. sb. f.* a shaping, making. *Der.* ga-, ufar-.
SKAIDAN, *vb.* (*pt. t.* skaiskaid), to divide, sever, separate, put asunder, Mk. 10. 9; to set at variance, Mat. 10. 35; *refl. and neut.* to depart, 1 Cor. 7. 10, 15. *Der.* ga-, af-, dis-; ga-skaidnan, ga-skaidei. [G. & D. *scheiden;* O. E. *shed.*]
SKAIDEI*, *wk. sb. f.* separation; *in comp.* ga-skaidei, q. v.
SKAIDNAN*; *see* ga-skaidnan.
SKAIN, shone; *from* skeinan.
SKAISKAID. divided; *from* skaidan.
SKAL, shall; *from* skulan.
SKALJA, *str. sb. f.* a scale; *hence,* a tile, Lu. 5. 19. [G. *schale;* D. *schaal;* E. *shell, scale.*]

SKALKINASSUS, *str. sb. m.* service, Rom. 9. 4; bondage, Gal. 5. 1; s. galiugagude, idolatry, Gal. 5. 20; Eph. 5. 5; Col. 3. 5. *From* skalks.

SKALKINON, *vb.* to serve, Mat. 6. 24; Lu. 15. 29; 16. 13; to be in bondage, Gal. 4. 3. *Der.* mith-.

SKALKS, *str. sb. m.* a servant, Mat. 8. 9; 10. 24; Mk. 10. 44, &c. *Der.* ga-skalki, skalkinon, mith-skalkinon, skalkinassus. [G & D *schalk*; A. S. *scealc*.]

SKAMAN, *vb. refl. with gen.* to be ashamed of, be ashamed, Mk. 8. 38; Lu. 9. 26; 16. 3. *Der.* ga-skaman. [G. *schämen*; D. *schamen*.]

SKANDA, *str. sb. f.* shame, Phil. 3. 19. *Cf.* skaman. [G. & D. *schande*; O. E. *shend*, to put to shame.]

SKAPJAN*, *vb.* to shape, make. *Der.* ga-skapjan, ga-skafts, ufar-skafts, skaftjan. [G. & D. *schaffen*.]

SKATHIS, *str. sb. n.* scathe, wrong-doing, wrong. 2 Cor. 12. 13.

SKATHJAN, *vb.* (*pt. t.* skoth, *pp.* skatbans), *with dat.* to do scathe to, do wrong to, Col. 3. 25. *Der.* ga-skathjan, skathis, ska-thuls. [G. & D. *schaden*.]

SKATHULS, *adj.* hurtful, harmful, 1 Tim. 6. 9; Col. 3. 25.

SKATTJA, *wk. sb. m.* a money-changer, Mk. 11. 15; Lu. 19. 23.

SKATTS, *str. sb. m.* money, Mat. 27. 6; Lu. 9. 3; 20. 24; a pound (Gk μνᾶ), Lu. 19. 16. [G. *schatz*; D. *schat*; A. S. *sceat*.]

SKAUDA-RAIP, *sb.* a shoe-latchet (*lit.* a shoe-rope?), Mk. 1. 7; Lu. 3. 16.

SKAUDS*, *sb.* (*of uncertain meaning*) a shoe(?) *Der.* skauda-raip. *See* skohs.

SKAUNEI*; *see* gutha-skaunei.

SKAUNS, *adj.* formed, well formed; hence, beautiful, Rom. 10. 15. *Der.* ibna-skauns, gutha-skaunei. [G. *schön*; D. *schoon*; A. S. *sciene*, *sceone*; *cf.* E. *sheen*.]

SKAURO*; *see* winthi-skauro.

SKAURPJO, *sb. f.* a scorpion, Lu. 10. 19. [Gk. σκορπίος.]

SKAUTS, *str. sb. m.* the hem of a garment, Mat. 9. 20; Mk. 6. 56; Lu. 8. 44. [A. S. *sceata*.]

SKAWJAN*, *vb.* to look at, see. *Der.* us-skawjan, un-skaws, us-skaws. [G. *schauen*; D. *schouwen*; A. S. *sceawian*; E. *shew*.]

SKEIMA, *wk. sb. m.* a light, a torch, a lantern, Jo. 18. 3. [*Cf.* E. *shimmer*.]

SKEINAN, *vb.* to shine, Lu. 9. 29; 17. 24; 2 Cor. 4. 6. *Der.* bi-skeinan. [G. *scheinen*; D. *schijnen*.]

SKEIREINS, SKEREINS, *str. sb. f.* a making sheer *or* clear, an explanation, interpretation, 1 Cor. 12. 10; 14. 26.

SKEIRJAN*, *vb.* to interpret, make clear. *Der.* ga-.

SKEIRS, *adj.* clear, evident, easily understood, Skeir. 4. 12; 5. 7. [G. *schier*; E. *sheer*.]

SKEREINS; *see* SKEIREINS.

SKEWJAN, *vb.* to go along, Mk. 2. 23.

SKILDUS, *str. sb. m.* a shield, Eph. 6. 16. [G. D. *schild*.]

SKILJA, *wk. sb. m.* a butcher; at skiljam, from the butchers, *i. e.* in the shambles, 1 Cor. 10. 25.

SKILLIGGS, *str. sb. m.* a shilling, in *Neap. document*.

SKIP, *str. sb. n.* a ship, boat, Mat.

8. 23; Mk. 1. 19; Lu. 5. 2; us-fairthon gataujan us skipa, to suffer shipwreck, 2 Cor. 11. 25. [G. *schiff;* D. *schip.*]

SKIUBAN*, *vb.* (*pt. t.* skauf, *pl.* skubum, *pp.* skubans), to push, shove. *Der.* af-skiuban. [G. *schieben;* D. *schuiven.*]

SKIUBAN*, *vb.* to scour. *Der.* winthi-skauro, skura. [G. *scheuer;* D. *schuren.*]

SKOF, shaved; *from* skaban.

SKOHS, *str. sb. m.* a shoe, sandal, Mat. 3. 11; Mk. 1. 7; Lu. 3. 16. *Der.* ga-skohs, ga-skoh. [G. *schuh;* D. *schoen.*]

SKOHSL. *str. sb. n.* an evil spirit, demon, Mat. 8. 31; Lu. 8. 27; 1 Cor. 10. 20. [A. S. *scucca.*]

SKOTH, did harm, did wrong: *from* skathjan.

SKREITAN*, *vb.* (*pt. t.* skrait, *pl.* skritum, *pp.* skritans), to shred, to tear. *Der.* dis-skreitan, dis-skritnan. [G. *schroten.*]

SKUFTS, *str. sb. m.* (or skuft, *n.*) the hair of the head, Lu. 7. 38, 44; Jo. 11. 2; 12. 3. [G. *schopf.*]

SKUGGWA, *wk. sb. m.* a mirror, 1 Cor. 13. 12.

SKULA, *wk. sb. m.* a debtor, Mat. 6. 12; Gal. 5. 3; liable to, in danger of, Mat. 5. 22; Mk. 3. 29; — skula wisan, to be a debtor, to owe, Rom. 13. 8; Philem. 18. 19; — thatei skulans sijaima, that for which we owe, our debts, Mat. 6. 12; — dulgis skula, a debtor, Lu. 7. 41. *Der.* fai-hu-skula. *From* skulan.

SKULAN, *vb.* (*pres.* skal, *pt. t.* skulda, *pp.* skulds), to owe, Lu. 7. 41; 16. 5; to be obliged to do, Lu. 17. 10; Jo. 13. 14; to be about to be (*like* E. *shall*), Mat. 11. 14; Lu. 1. 66. *Der.* skulds, skuldo, skula, faihu-skula. [G. *sollen;* D. *zullen;* E. *shall, should.*]

SKULDO, *sb. n.* a debt, a due. Rom. 13. 7.

SKULDRS*, *sb.* in *comp.* spai-skuldrs, q. v.

SKULDS, *adj.* owing; *hence,* skulds wisan, to be owing, to owe, to be obliged to do, to be permitted to do, to be about to do, Mat. 27. 6; Lu. 15. 32; 19. 11.

SKULUM, we ought. we should; *from* skulan.

SKURA, *str. sb. f.* a shower; — skura windis, a storm of wind, Mk. 4. 37; Lu. 8. 23. *Cf.* skinran.

SKYTHUS, *sb. m.* a Scythian, Col. 3. 11.

SLAHALS, *str. sb. m.* a striker, 1 Tim. 3. 3; Tit. 1. 7. *From* slahan.

SLAHAN, *vb.* (*pt. t.* sloh, *pp.* slahans), to strike, beat, hit, Mat. 26. 68; Mk. 15. 19; Lu. 18. 13; — lofam slaban, to strike with the palms of the hands, to buffet, Mat. 26. 67; Mk. 14. 65. *Der.* af-slahan, slahs, slahals, slauhts. [G. *schlagen;* E. *slay;* D. *schlaan.*]

SLAHS, *str. sb. m.* (*pl.* slaheis), a stroke, stripe, 2 Cor. 6. 5; 11. 23; a plague, Mk. 5. 29; Lu. 7. 21; — slahs lofin, a buffet, Jo. 18. 22; 19. 3. *From* slahan.

SLAIHTS, *adj.* slight; *hence,* smooth, Lu. 3. 5. [G. *schlecht, schlicht;* D. *slecht;* E. *slight.*]

SLAUHTS, *str. sb. f.* slaughter, Rom. 8. 36. [G. *schlachten.*]

SLAUPJAN*, *vb. see* af-slaupjan; *from* sliupan.

SLAUTHJAN*. *vb.* to cause to slide. in *comp.* af-slauthjan. q. v. *From* sliuthan.

SLAUTHNAN*; see af-slauthnan.

SLAWAN, vb. to be silent, be still, Mk. 9. 34; Lu. 19. 40; pres. pt. slawands, quiet, 1 Tim. 2. 2. Der. ana-, ga-. [A. S. slawian, to be inert, slow.]

SLEITHA, str. sb. f. loss, Phil. 3. 7, 8. Der. sleithei, ga-sleithjan.

SLEITHEI, wk. sb. f. danger, peril, Rom. 8. 35.

SLEITHIS, adj. (pl. sloidjai), dangerous, perilous, 2 Tim. 3. 1; dangerous, fierce. Mat. 8. 28. From sleitha.

SLEPAN, vb. (pt. t. saislep or saizlep, pl. saislepum, pp. slupans), to sleep, fall asleep, Mat. 8. 24; 9. 24; Mk. 4. 27. Der. ana-, ga-, sleps. [G. schlafen; D. slapen.]

SLEPS, str. sb. m. sleep, Lu. 9. 32; Jo. 11. 13; Rom. 13. 11.

SLINDAN*, vb. (pt. t. sland, pp. slundans), to devour, gulp down. Der. fra-slindan. [G. schlingen; D. slinden.]

SLIUPAN, vb. (pt. t. slaup, pl. slupum, pp. slupans), followed by in, to slip into, to creep into, 2 Tim. 3. 6. Der. uf-, inouf-, af-slaupjan. [G. schlüpfen; D. slippen.]

SLIUTHAN*, vb. to slide, glide. Der. af-slauthjan, af-slauthnan. [G. schleudern.]

SLOH, struck; from slahan.

SMAIRTHR, str. sb. n. fatness, Rom. 11. 17. [Cf. E. smear.]

SMAKKA, wk. sb. m. a fig, Mat. 7. 16; Mk. 11. 13; Lu. 6. 44.

SMAKKA-BAGMS, str. sb. m. a figtree, Mk. 11. 13; Lu. 19. 4.

SMALISTA, superl. adj. smallest, least, 1 Cor. 15. 9.

SMALS, adj. small, little; superl. smalista, q. v. [G. schmal; D. smal.]

SMARNA, str. sb. f. dung, Phil. 3. 8. Cf. smairthr, maibstus.

SMEITAN*, vb. to smear, smudge. Der. bi-, ga-. [G. schmiessen; D. smetten; A. S. besmitan.]

SMITHA*. wk. sb. m. a smith. Der. aiza-smitha, ga-smithon. [G. schmied; D. smid.]

SMYRN, str. sb. n. myrrh; — mith smyrna, mingled with myrrh, Mk. 15. 23. [Gk. σμύρρον.]

SNAGA, wk. sb. m. a garment. Mat. 9. 16; Lu. 5. 36.

SNAIWS, str. sb. m. snow, Mk. 9. 3. [G. schnee; D. sneeuw.]

SNARPJAN*, vb. to bite, nip. Der. at-snarpjan.

SNAU, went; from sniwan.

SNEITHAN, vb. to cut, to reap, Mat. 6. 26; Lu. 19. 21; 2 Cor. 9. 6. Der. uf-sneithan. [G. schneiden; D. snijden; A. S. snidan.]

SNEWUM, we went; from sniwan.

SNIUMJAN, vb. to hasten, make haste, Lu. 2. 16; 19. 5; 1 Th. 2. 17. Der. ga-. sniumundo. Cf. sniwan.

SNIUMUNDO, adv. with haste, quickly, Mk. 6. 25; Lu. 1. 39; compar. sniumundos, with more haste (more carefully, A. V.), Phil. 2. 28. Cf. sniwan. [A. S. sneome.]

SNIWAN, vb. (pt. t. snau, pl. snewum and sniwum, pp. sniwans), to go, proceed, Jo. 15. 16; 1 Cor. 9. 25; to come, come hastily, 1 Th. 2. 16. Der. duat-, faurbi-, ga-, faur-. [A. S. snedwan.]

SNORJO, wk. sb. f. a woven basket, a basket, 2 Cor. 11. 33. [Cf. G. schnur; E. snare.]

SNUTREI, wk. sb. f. wisdom, 1 Cor. 1. 17, 19.

SNUTRS, adj. wise, Lu. 10. 21; 1 Cor. 1. 19. [A. S. snoter.]

So, *fem. of* sa, she, this.

Soei, *fem. of* saei, she that.

Sok, rebuked; *from* sakan.

Sokareis, *str. sb. m.* a disputer, 1 Cor. 1. 20; *see* sakan.

Sokeins, *str. sb. f.* a question, Jo. 3. 25; Skeir. 3. 13. *From* sakan.

Sokjan, *vb.* to seek, desire, long for, Mk. 1. 37; 3. 32; 8. 11; to question with, dispute, Mk. 1. 27; 9. 10; — samana sokjan, to talk together, discuss, Mk. 12. 28. *Der.* ga-, mith-, us-; sokns, sokeins, sokareis. [G. *suchen*; D. *zoeken*; E. *seek.*] *See* sakan.

Sokns, *str. sb. f.* a seeking out, a question, 1 Tim. 1. 4; 6. 4; 2 Tim. 2. 23.

Soth, *str. sb. n. or* soths, *str. sb. m.* a satisfying, Col. 2. 23. *From* sathan.

Spaikulatur, *sb.* a spy, 'executioner' (A. V.), Mk. 6. 27. [Lat. *speculator.*]

Spaiskuldrs, *sb.* spittle, Jo. 9. 6. *From* speiwan.

Spaiw, spat; *from* speiwan.

Spann, spun; *from* spinnan.

Sparwa, *wk. sb. m.* a sparrow, Mat. 10. 29, 31.

Spaurds, *sb. f.* a stadium, a furlong, Jo. 6. 19; 11. 18; 1 Cor. 9. 24 (*where it is spelt* sprauds). [G. *spur*; A. S. *spyrd.*]

Speds, speids, spids, *adj.* late; *compar.* spediza, the latter, Mat. 27. 64; *superl.* spedists, spedumists, the last, Mk. 12. 6; Jo. 6. 40. [G. *spät*; D. *spade.*]

Speiwan, *vb.* (*pt. t.* spaiw, *pl.* spiwum, *pp.* spiwans), to spit, Mat. 26. 27; Mk. 7. 33; 10. 34. *Der.* and-, bi-, ga-, spaiskuldrs. [G. *speien*; D. *spuijen*; E. *spew.*]

Spilda, *str. sb. f.* a writing-tablet, tablet, Lu. 1. 63; 2 Cor. 3. 3. *Cf.* spillon.

Spill, *str. sb. n.* a fable, tale, myth, 1 Tim. 1. 4; 4. 7; 2 Tim. 4. 4. *Der.* spilla, spillon, ga-spillon, thiuth-spillon, us-spillon, unus-spilloths. [E. *spell, go-spel.*]

Spilla, *wk. sb. m.* a teller forth, proclaimer of the *good-spell* or Gospel, a preacher, Skeir. 1. 26.

Spillon, *vb.* to tell a tale, narrate, Mk. 5. 16; 9. 9; to tell or bring tidings, Lu. 2. 10; to preach the good-*spell* or Gospel, Rom. 10. 15. *Cf.* spill, spilla.

Spinnan, *vb.* (*pt. t.* spann, *pl.* spunnum, *pp.* spunnans), to spin, Mat. 6. 28. [G. D. *spinnen.*]

Sprauds; *see* spaurds.

Sprauto, *adv.* quickly, soon, Mat. 5. 25; Mk. 9. 39; Jo. 11. 29, &c.

Spyreida, *wk. sb. m.* a large basket, Mk. 8. 8, 20. [Gk. σπυρίς.]

Stabs, *str. sb. m.* a letter; *hence,* an element, rudiment, Gal. 4. 3, 9; Col. 2. 20. [G. *stab*; A. S. *stæf*; E. *staff.*]

Stads; *see* staths.

Staig, mounted, went up; *from* steigan.

Staiga, *str. sb. f.* a path, way, high-way, Mk. 1. 3; Lu. 3. 4; 14. 21. *From* steigan.

Stainahs, *adj.* stony, Mk. 4. 5, 16. *From* stains.

Staineins, *adj.* stony, 2 Cor. 3. 3.

Stainjan, *vb.* to stone, Jo. 10. 32, 33; 2 Cor. 11. 25.

Stains, *str. sb. m.* a stone, rock, Mat. 27. 60; Mk. 5. 5; 12. 10; — stainam wairpan, to stone, Mk. 12. 4; — stainam af-wairpan, to stone, Lu. 20. 6; Jo. 11. 8. Der. waihsta-stains, stainahs, staineins, stainjan. [G stein; D. steen.]

STAIRNO, wk. sb. f. a star, Mk. 13. 25. [G. stern; D. ster.]

STAIRO, wk. sb. f. a barren woman, Lu. 1. 7, 36; Gal. 4. 27. [Gk. στεῖρος.]

STAKS, str. sb. m. a mark, stigma, Gal. 6. 17. From stikan.

STALDAN*, vb. to own, possess. Der. ga-, and-; and-stald, aglaitga-stalds.

STAMMS, adj. stammering, with an impediment in the speech, Mk. 7. 32. [G. stammeln; D. stamelen.]

STANDAN, vb. (pt. t. stoth, pp. stothans?), to stand, stand firm, Mk. 6. 5; 26. 73; 27. 11, &c. Der. and-, af-, at-, bi-, ga-, in-, mith-, us-, twis-, faura-; afga-stothans, unga-stothans, ga-stothanan; af-stass, us-stass, twis-stass, faur-stasseis; ana-stodjan, du-stodjan, ana-stodeins, aftra-ana-stodeins. Cf. staths. [G. stehen; D. staan.]

STATHS, str. sb. m. (spelt stads, Lu. 14. 22; pl. stadeis), a stead, a place, Mk. 1. 35; 16. 6; room, Lu. 14. 22; an inn, Lu. 2. 7; land, shore, Mk. 4. 1; Lu. 5. 3; — jainis stadis, the other side (of the lake), Mk. 4. 35. Der. bunsla-staths, mota-staths, lukarna-statba, anda-stathjis, Cf. standan. [G. statt; D. stad.]

STAUA, str. sb. f. judgment, Mat. 5. 21; 11. 22; Mk. 6. 11; a law-suit, matter for trial, 1 Cor. 6. 1. Der. staua, anda-staua, staua-stols, stojan, ga-stojan.

STAUA, wk. sb. m. a judge, Mat. 5. 25; Lu. 18. 2, 6.

STAUA-STOLS, str. sb. m. the judgment-seat, Mat. 27. 19; Rom. 14. 10; 2 Cor. 5. 10.

STAURKJAN*, vb. to dry up, wither (transitive). Der. ga-staurknan, q. v. [G. stark; D. sterk; E. stark, starch.]

STAURRAN*, vb. to murmur. Der. and-staurran.

STAUTAN, vb. (pt. t. staistaut, pp. stautans), to strike, smite, Mat. 5. 39; Lu. 6. 29. [G. stossen; D. stooten; cf. E. stoke.]

STEIGAN, vb. to mount, go up, ascend, Jo. 7. 14; 10. 1. Der. at-, ga-, ufar-, us-; staiga. [G. steigen; D. stijgen; O. E. sty; cf. E. stairs, stirrup.]

STIBNA, str. sb. f. a voice, Mat. 27. 46; Mk. 1. 3; 5. 7. [G. stimme; D. stem; O. E. steven.]

STIGGAN*, vb. to sting, stick, pierce, thrust. Der. us-. Cf. stikan.

STIGGKWAN, vb. to strike, smite, thrust; — st. withra, to make war against, Lu. 14. 31. Der. bi-, ga-, ga-staggkwjan, bi-stuggkws. Cf. stautan, stiggan.

STIKAN*, vb. to stick, prick. Der. stiks, staks, hlethra-stakeins. [G. stechen; D. steken.]

STIKLS, str. sb. m. a cup, Mat. 10. 42; Mk. 7. 4; 9. 41. [O. N. stikill.]

STIKS, str. sb. m. a point, a moment (of time), Lu. 4. 5. From stikan.

STILAN, vb. to steal, Mat. 6. 20; Jo. 10. 10. [G. stehlen; D. stelen.]

STIUR, str. sb. m. a steer, calf, Lu. 15. 23, 27, 30. [G. & D. stier.]

STIURJAN, vb. to steer, govern; hence, to establish, Rom. 10. 3; to affirm, 1 Tim. 1. 7. [G. steuern; D. sturen.]

STIURS*, adj. rightly steered, well-ordered. *Der.* us-stiuriba, us-stiurei, stiurjan.

STIWITI, *str. sb. n.* enduring, endurance, patience, 2 Cor. 1. 6; 6. 4; 2 Th. 1. 4.

STODEINS*, STODJAN*; *see* standan.

STOJAN, *vb.* (*pt. t.* stauida), to judge, Lu. 6. 37; 7. 43; 19. 22. *From* staua.

STOLS, *str. sb. m.* a stool, seat, throne, Mat. 5. 34; Lu. 1. 32. *Der.* staua-stols. [G. *stuhl*; D. *stoel.*]

STOMA, *wk. sb. m.* substantial grounds, sound cause, 'confidence' (A. V.), 2 Cor. 9. 4; 11. 17.

STOTH, stood; *from* standan.

STRAUJAN, *vb.* to strew, straw, Mk. 11. 8; to prepare, Mk. 14. 15. *Der.* uf-. [G. *streuen*; D. *strooijen.*]

STRIKS, *str. sb. m.* a stroke, flourish of the pen, a tittle, Mat. 5. 18. [G. *strich*; D. *streek.*]

STUBJUS, *str. sb. m.* dust, Lu. 10. 11. [G. *staub*; D. *stof.*]

STUGGKWS*, *sb.* a bit. *Der.* bi-stuggkws. *From* stiggkwan.

SUKWNS, *str. sb. m.* the stomach, 1 Tim. 5. 23.

SUKWON*, *vb.* to season; *see* ga-sukwon. *Cf.* supon.

SULJA, *str. sb. f.* a sole of a shoe, a sandal, Mk. 6. 9. *Der.* ga-suljan. [G. *sohle*; D. *zool.*]

SUMAN, *adv.* once, on a time, Rom. 11. 30; Gal. 1. 23; Eph. 2. 3; partly, in part, 1 Cor. 13. 9. *From* sums.

SUMS, *adj.* (*f.* suma, *n.* sumata), some one, some, Mat. 9. 3; 27. 47; one, Mk. 14. 43; — bi sumata, in part, Rom. 11. 25; — sums — sumsuh, the one — the other, Mk. 12. 5; Rom. 9. 21. *Der.* suman.

SUNDRO, *adv.* asunder, alone, privately, Mk. 4. 10; 7. 33; Lu. 9. 10. [G. *sonder*; D. *zonder.*]

SUNIS*, *adj.* sooth, true. *Der.* sunja, sunjaba, sunjai-frithas, sunjeins, sunjon, ga-sunjon, sunjons. [E. *sooth?*]

SUNJA, *adv.* soothly, verily, truly, Lu. 9. 27; Jo. 17. 3.

SUNJA, *str. sb. f.* the sooth, the truth, Mk. 5. 33; 12. 14, 32; bi sunjai, truly, verily, Mat. 26. 73.

SUNJABA, *adv.* truly, verily, 1 Th. 2. 13.

SUNJAI-FRITHAS, *sb.* a proper name in the Neap. document.

SUNJEINS, *adj.* true, Mk. 12. 14; Jo. 7. 18; 8. 13.

SUNJON, *vb.* to verify, put in the right; *refl.* to put oneself in the right, to excuse oneself, 2 Cor. 12. 19.

SUNJONS, *str. sb. f.* a setting oneself right, an apology, defence, answer, 2 Cor. 7. 11; Phil. 1. 17; 2 Tim. 4. 16.

SUNNA, *wk. sb. m.* the sun, Mk. 4. 6; 16. 2. *Cf.* sauil. [G. *sonne*; D. *zon.*]

SUNNO, *wk. sb. f.* the sun, Mat. 5. 45; Lu. 4. 40. *See* sunna.

SUNS, *adv.* soon, at once, immediately, Mat. 8. 3; 26. 74; 27. 48. *Der.* suns-aiw, sunsei, bi-sunjane.

SUNS-AIW, *adv.* soon, immediately, straightway, Mk. 3. 6; 5. 29; 6. 25.

SUNS-EI, *adv.* as soon as, when, Lu. 1. 44; 19. 41.

SUNUS, *str. sb. m.* a son, Mat. 5. 45; 8. 12; 9. 15, &c. [G. *sohn*; D. *zoon.*]

SUPON, *vb.* to season, Mk. 9. 50. *Der.* ga-supon. *Cf.* sukwon.

SUTHJON, SUTHJAN, *vb.* to soothe;

hence, to long to be soothed, to itch, 2 Tim. 4. 3.

SUTIS, *adj.* sweet; *hence*, patient, 1 Tim. 3. 3; peaceable, 1 Tim. 2. 2; *compar.* sutiza, more tolerable, Mat. 11. 24; Mk. 6. 11; Lu. 10. 12. *Der.* unsuti. [G. *süss*; D. *zoet*.]

SWA, *conj.* so, just so, also, Mat. 5. 16; Jo. 13. 15; swa jah *or* jah swa, so also, 1 Cor. 12. 12; swa samaleiko, in like manner, 1 Cor. 11. 25. *Der.* swab, swa-u, swaei, swa-lauds, swa-leiks, swe, swe-kunths, swi-kunths, swaswe. [G. *so*; D. *zo*.]

SWAEI, *conj.* so that. that, Mk. 1. 27; as, Lu. 3. 23. *From* swa *and* ei.

SWAGGWJAN*, *vb.* to swing about. *Der.* af-swaggwjan.

SWAH, *conj.* so, also, so too, Lu. 14. 33. *From* swa *and* uh.

SWAIHRA, *wk. sb. m.* father-in-law, Jo. 18. 13. [G. *schwieger*; A. S. *sweor*.]

SWAIHRO, *wk. sb. f.* mother-in-law, Mat. 8, 14; 10. 35; Mk. 1. 30; Lu. 4. 38. *Cf.* swaihra.

SWAIRBAN°, *vb.* to wipe. *Der.* af-, bi-. *Cf.* sweipan.

SWA-LAUDS, *adj.* so much, such, Mat. 8. 10; Jo. 14. 9; swalaud melis swe, as long as, Gal. 4. 1. *Cf.* hwe-lauds.

SWA-LEIKS, *adj.* such, Mat. 9. 8; Mk. 4. 33; 6. 2; swaleiks swe, such as, 2 Cor. 12. 20.

SWALLEINS*, *str. sb. f.* a swelling. *Der.* uf-swalleins. *From* swillan.

SWALLJAN*, to cause to swell. *Der.* uf-swalleins. *See* swillan.

SWALT, died; *from* swiltan.

SWAMM, swam; *from* swimman.

SWAMMS, SWAMS, *str. sb. m.* a sponge, Mat. 27. 48; Mk. 15. 36. [G. *schwamm*; D. *zwam*; A. S. *swamm*.]

SWARAN, *vb.* to swear, Mat. 5. 34; Mk. 6. 23; Lu. 1. 73. *Der.* bi-, ufar-, ufar-swara. [G. *schwören*; D. *zweren*.]

SWARE, SWAREI, *adv.* without a cause, in vain, Mat. 5. 22; Mk. 7. 7; Gal. 2. 21.

SWARTIZL, *str. sb. n.* that which is black, ink, 2 Cor. 3. 3.

SWARTS, *adj.* black, Mat. 5. 36. [G. *schwarz*; D. *zwart*; E. *swart*. *swarthy*.]

SWASWE, *conj.* as, just as, as it were, in like manner as; *from* swa *and* swe.

SWA-U, *adv.* so? thus? (*in asking a question*). Jo. 18. 22. *From* swa *and* uh.

SWE, *conj.* as, just as. *Cf.* swa. swa-swe.

SWEGNITHA, *str. sb. f.* (*spelt* swignitha, Lu. 1. 44), joy, Lu. 1. 14, 44.

SWEGNJAN, *vb.* (*spelt* swignjan, Jo. 5. 35), to rejoice. triumph, Lu. 1. 47; 10. 21; Col. 3. 15. [*Cf.* A. S. *swegan*, *swegian*.]

SWEIBAN, *vb.* to cease, Lu. 7. 45. *Der.* unsweibands.

SWEIN, *str. sb. n.* a swine, pig, Mat. 8. 30; Mk. 5. 11; Lu. 8. 32. [G. *schwein*; D. *zwijn*.]

SWEIPAINS*; *see* midja-sweipains.

SWEIPAN*, *vb.* to sweep. *Der.* midja-sweipains.

SWE-KUNTHS; *see* swi-kunths.

SWERAINS, *str. sb. f.* honour, 2 Tim. 2. 20. *From* swers. [M. *reads* swerein.] *Cf.* unswerains.

SWERAN, *vb.* to honour, esteem. glorify, Mk. 7. 6; Lu. 18. 20; Jo. 12. 23. *Der.* ga-, un-; swerains. un-swerains. *From* swers.

SWEREI*, wk. sb. f. honour. Der. all-, un-.
SWERITHA, str. sb. f. honour, Col. 2. 23; 1 Th. 4. 4; 1 Tim. 1. 17. Der. un-. From swers.
SWERS, adj. heavy, weighty; hence, grave, honoured, Phil. 2. 29; honoured, dear, Lu. 7. 2. Der. un-, sweritha, un-sweritha, all-swerei, un-swerei, sweran, ga-sweran, un-sweran, swerains, un-swerains. [G. schwer; D. zwaar; A. S. swǽr.]
SWES, adj. one's own, Mk. 15. 20; Lu. 6. 44; Jo. 10. 3.
SWES, sb. n. one's own property, one's substance, Lu. 15. 13, 30. See the preceding. [A. S. swǽs.]
SWETHAUH, conj. however, but, although; — swethaub ni, not as if, Rom. 9. 6.
SWIBLS, str. sb. m. brimstone, Lu. 17. 29. [G. schwefel; D. zwavel. A. S. swefel.]
SWIGGWAN*, vb. to swing. Der. af-swaggwjan. [G. schwingen.]
SWIGLJA, wk. sb. m. a piper, flute-player, Mat. 9. 23.
SWIGLJON, vb. to pipe, play the flute, Mat. 11. 17; Lu. 7. 32. Der. swiglja. [A. S. swég.]
SWIGNITHA; see swegnitha.
SWIGNJAN; see swegnjan.
SWIKNABA, adv. sincerely, Phil. 1. 16.
SWIKNEI, wk. sb. f. meekness, simplicity, purity, Gal. 5. 23; 1 Tim. 5. 2; 2 Cor. 11. 3.
SWIKNEINS, str. sb. f. purification, Jo. 3. 25.
SWIKNITHA, str. sb. f. purity, 2 Cor. 6. 6; 1 Tim. 4. 12.
SWIKNS, adj. pure, innocent, Mat. 27. 4; 2 Cor. 11. 2; 1 Tim. 2. 8; 5. 23. Der. swiknaba, swiknei, swikneins, swiknitha.
SWIKUNTHABA, adv. openly, manifestly, Mk. 8. 32; Jo. 11. 14; 1 Tim. 4. 1. From swikunths.

SWI-KUNTHS, adj. (spelt swekunths, Lu. 8. 17), manifest, evident, Mk. 6. 14; Lu. 8. 17; Rom. 10. 20. Der. un-; swikunthaba, ga-swikunthjan. From kunnan.
SWILLAN*, vb. (pt. t. swall, pp. swullans), to swell. Der. swalljau, uf-swalleins. [G. schwellen; D. zwellen.]
SWILTAN, vb. to die, Lu. 8. 42. Der. ga-, mithga-; swultawairthja. [A. S. sweltan.]
SWIMMAN*, vb. to swim. Der. swumsl. [G. schwimmen.]
SWINTHEI, wk. sb. f. strength, Lu. 1. 51; Eph. 1. 19; 6. 10.
SWINTHJAN, vb. to use force (?), Nehem. 5. 16. Der. ga-, in-,
SWINTHNAN, vb. to grow strong, become strong, Lu. 1. 80; 2. 40.
SWINTHS, adj. strong, powerful, healthful, whole, Mat. 3. 11; Mk. 1. 7; Lu. 3. 16; compar. swinthoza. Der. swinthei, swinthjan, ga-swinthjan, in-swinthjan, swinthnan, ga-swinthnan. [A. S. swið.]
SWISTAR, sb. f. a sister, Mk. 3. 32; Lu. 14. 26; Jo. 11. 1. [G. schwester; D. zuster.]
SWOGATJAN, vb. to sigh, groan, 2 Cor. 5. 2, 4.
SWOGJAN*, vb. to sigh. Der. gaswogjan, swogatjan, uf-swogjan.
SWULTA-WAIRTHJA, adj. about to die, lying at the point of death, Lu. 7. 2. From swiltan and wairthan.
SWUMSL, SWUMFSL, str. sb. n. a swimming-bath, pool, Jo. 9. 7, 11.
SYNAGOGA-FATHS, str. sb. m. the ruler of a synagogue, Mk. 5. 22.
SYNAGOGE, sb. f. a synagogue, Mk. 1. 21; 6. 2; Lu. 4. 16. Der. synagoga-faths.
SYRIA, sb. Syria, Lu. 2. 2.

T.

T, the twentieth letter of the Gothic alphabet. As a numeral, it means 300.

Tagl, *str. sb. n.* hair, Mat. 5. 36; 10. 30; Mk. 1. 6. [A. S. *tægel*; E. *tail*.]

Tagr, *str. sb. n.* a tear, Mk. 9. 24; Lu. 7. 38; 2 Cor. 2. 4. *Der.* tagrjan. [G. *zähre*; D. *traan*; Gk. δάϰρυ.]

Tagrjan, *vb.* to weep, Jo. 11. 35.

Taheins*; *in comp.* dis-taheins, q. v.

Tahjan, *vb.* to tear, rend, Mk. 1. 26; 9. 20; Lu. 9. 39; to disperse, 2 Cor. 9. 9. *Der.* dis-tahjan, dis-taheins. *Cf.* tiuhan.

Taihsws, *adj.* the right, on the right hand, Mat. 5. 29; Mk. 14. 47; Lu. 6. 6; *fem.* taihswo, the right hand, Mat. 6. 3; Mk. 10. 37. [Gk. δεξιός.]

Taihswa, *wk. sb. f.* the right hand, Mk. 16. 5; Col. 3. 1. *Cf.* taihswo, *fem. of* taihsws.

Taihun, *num.* ten, Mk. 10. 41; Lu. 14. 31; 15. 8. *Der.* fidwor-, fimf-; taihunda, fimfta-taihunda, taihun-taihund, taihuntaihundfalths. [G. *zehn*; D. *tien*.]

Taihunda, *ord. adj.* the tenth, Lu. 18. 12.

Taihun-taihund, taihun-tehund, *num.* a hundred, Lu. 15. 4; 16. 6, 7.

Taihuntaihund-falths, *adj.* a hundred-fold, Mk. 10. 30; Lu. 8. 8. *From* falthan.

Taikneins*, *in comp.* us-taikneins, q. v.

Taiknjan, *vb.* to betoken, point out, shew, Mk. 14. 15; 1 Tim. 6. 15; *refl.* to shew oneself as, feign to be, Lu. 20. 20. *From* taikns.

Taikns, *str. sb. f.* a token, sign, wonder, miracle, Mk. 8. 11; Lu. 2. 12; Jo. 6. 2. *Der.* taiknjan, ga-taiknjan, us-taiknjan, us-taikneins. [G. *zeichen*; D. *teeken*.]

Tainjo, *wk. sb. f.* a basket of twigs, a light basket, Mk. 8. 19; Lu. 9. 17; Jo. 6. 13. *From* tains. *Cf.* spyreida.

Tains, *str. sb. m.* a twig, sprig, branch, Jo. 15. 2. *Der.* weina-tains, tainjo. [G. *zain*; D. *teen*; A. S. *tán*.]

Tairan*, *vb.* to tear. *Der.* ga-, dis-; ga-taura, ga-taurths, aftaurnan, ga-taurnan, dis-taurnan. [G. *zehren*.]

Taitrarkes, *sb.* a tetrarch, Lu. 3. 19; 9. 7.

Tals*, *adj.* teachable. *Der.* untals. *From* tilan.

Talzeins, *str. sb. f.* doctrine, 2 Tim. 3. 16. *From* tilan.

Talzjan, *vb.* to teach, instruct, 2 Cor. 6. 9; 2 Tim. 2. 25; to warn, Col. 1. 28. *Pres. pt. as sb.* a teacher, master, instructor, Lu. 5. 5; 8. 24; 9. 33. *Der.* ga-, talzeins. *From* tilan.

Tamjan*, *vb.* to tame; *in comp.* ga-tamjan, q. v. *From* timan.

Tandjan, *vb.* to kindle, light, Lu. 8. 16; 15. 8. *Der.* ga-. in-; tundnan, in-tundnan. *From* tindan.

TANI*, sb. n. a token? Der. faura-tani. Cf. taikns.
TARHJAN*, vb.; see ga-tarhjan.
TARMJAN, vb. to break forth, Gal. 4. 27.
TARNJAN*, vb. to hide. Der. ga-tarnjan. [Cf. A. S. dearn.]
TASS*, adj. well-ordered. Der. ungatass, ungatassaba. [Cf. Gk. τάσσειν.]
TAUH, pt. t. of tiuban, q. v.
TAUHEI*, in comp. us-taubei, q. v. From tiuhan.
TAUHTS*, sb. a drawing forth, in comp. us-tauhts. q. v. From tiuhan.
TAUI, str. sb. n. (gen. tojis) a work, deed, thing made or created. Jo. 8. 41; Rom. 12. 4; Col. 3. 9; working, Eph. 3. 7. Cf. ti-wan, taujan. [G. that; D. daad.]
TAUJAN, vb. (pt. t. tawida), to do, make, Mat. 5. 46; 8. 9; 9. 28, &c.; to finish, Jo. 5. 36. Common in various phrases, where it means to do, cause, make. Der. ga-taujan, missa-taujands, taui, ubil-tojis, fulla-tojis; tewa, tewi, ga-tewjan, un-ga-tewiths. [G. thun; D. doen.]

TAURA*, TAURTHS*; see ga-taura. ga-taurths.
TAURNAN*. vb. to become torn. Der. af-, dis-, ga-. From tairan.
TAWEI, do thou; imp. of taujan.
TAWIDA, did; pt. t. of taujan.
TEHUND, num. answers to E. -ty, G. -zig; as in sibun-tehund, seventy, ahtau-tehund, eighty, niun-tehund, ninety, taihun-tehund, a hundred. See taihun.
TEIHAN*, vb. (pt. t. taih, pp. tai-hans), to teach, shew, announce, declare. Der. ga-tei-han, faura-gateihan. Cf. taikns. [E. teach.]
TEIKAN, another form of tekan. q. v.
TEKAN, vb. (pt. t. taitok, pp. te-kans), to touch, Mk. 5. 30; Lu. 7. 39; 8. 45. Der. at-tekan. [E. touch; Lat. tangere.]
TEWA, str. sb. f. arrangement, order, 1 Cor. 15. 23. From tiwan.
TEWI, str. sb. n. an order, rank, company, 1 Cor. 15. 6. [The reading is very uncertain.]
TEWJAN*, vb. to put in order, place, arrange. Der. ga-tew-jan, tewa, tewi. From tiwan.

[For the rest of the words beginning with T see further on, according to the alphabetical order.]

TH.

TH, the ninth letter in the Gothic alphabet. As a number, it means 9. [This letter answers to the A. S. thorn-letter (þ), which is used by some editors to represent it.]
THADEI, adv. where, wheresoever, whither, Mk. 6. 55; 14. 14; Jo. 6. 62; thiswaduh thadei, whither-soever, Mat. 8. 19; Mk. 6. 56.
THAGKJAN, THAGGKJAN, vb. (pt. t. thahta, pp. thahts), to think, consider, reason, Mk. 2. 6; Lu. 3. 15; to consult, Lu. 14. 31;

to doubt, debate, Jo. 13. 22. *Der.* and-thagkjan, bi-thagkjan, anda-thahts, ga-thagki, thagks. [G. & D. *denken.*]

THAGKS, *str. sb. m.* thank, thanks, Lu. 17. 9. [*Spelt* thank *in the* MS.]

THAHAINS, *str. sb. f.* silence, 1 Tim. 2. 12.

THAHAN, *vb.* to be silent, be still, Mk. 3. 4; 14. 61; Lu. 1. 20. *Der.* ga-thahan, thahains. [Lat. *tacere.*]

THAHO, *wk. sb. f.* clay, Rom. 9. 21. [G. *thon*; A. S. *po.*]

THAI, the; *pl. nom. masc. of article* sa, so, thata.

THAIM, to the; *pl. dat. of article.*

THAIRH, *prep.* through, by, by means of, Mk. 6. 2; Lu. 1. 78, &c. *For verbs with* thairh, *as prefix, see below.* [G. *durch*; D. *door.*]

THAIRH-ARBAIDJAN, *vb.* to toil throughout, Lu. 5. 5.

THAIRH-BAIRAN, *vb.* to carry through, Mk. 11. 16.

THAIRH-GAGGAN, *vb.* to go through, come through, Mk. 2. 23; Lu. 2. 15; 9. 6; to go round, 1 Tim. 5. 13.

THAIRH-GALEIKON, *vb.* to transfer in a figure, 1 Cor. 4. 6.

THAIRH-LEITHAN, *vb.* to go through, go along, Mat. 9. 9; Lu. 4. 30; 18. 25.

THAIRH-SAIHWAN, *vb.* to see through, behold as in a glass, 2 Cor. 3. 18.

THAIR-WAKAN, *vb.* to keep watch throughout, keep watch, Lu. 2. 8; 6. 12.

THAIRH-WISAN, *vb.* to remain throughout, stay, continue, Jo. 9. 41; Rom. 11. 22; Col. 1. 23.

THAIRKO, *wk. sb. n.* a hole through any thing, the eye of a needle, Mk. 10. 25; Lu. 18. 25. *From* thairh.

THAIRSAN*, *vb.* (*pt. t.* thars, *pl.* thaursum, *pp.* thaursans), to dry up, thirst, be parched. *Der.* ga-thairsan, thaursus, ga-thaursnan, thaursjan, af-thaursjan, thaurstei. [G. *dürren, dürsten*; D. *dorsten*; E. *thirst.*]

THAMMA, to the, *dat. s. m. & n. of the art.* sa, so, thata.

THAMMEI, to whom, to that which. *dat. sing. m. & n. of* sa-ei.

THAN, *adv.* (1) then, thereupon, Mat. 7. 23; 9. 15, &c.; (2) when, whenever, as long as, Mat. 6. 2; 9. 15; *conj.* (3) but, and, however, therefore, for, for also, although; — jah than, for also, however, although; — ei-than, therefore; — mith-than, meanwhile, now; — mith-thanei, whilst; — nauh-than, still however; — ni nauh-than, not any longer, never; — ju-than, now, already; — juthan ni, no more, no longer; — ath-than, but; — thanuh, then, but, and, therefore, then; — thanuh-than, then however, then also; — than-ei, when, since; — thande *or* thandei, if, but if, since, so long as; — than-nu, for, therefore. [G. *dann, denn*; D. *dan*; E. *then.*]

THANA, the; *acc. s. m. of* sa.

THANA-MAIS, *adv.* more, still, further, Mk. 5. 35; 14. 63; ni thana-mais, no more, no longer, Lu. 16. 2.

THANA-SEITHS, *adv.* more, longer; ni thana-seiths, no longer, Mk. 9. 8; 10. 8; 11. 14.

THANDE, THANDEI, *conj.* if, since, because, Mat. 6. 30; Lu. 2. 30; whilst, Jo. 12. 35.

THAN-EI, him who, whom; *acc. s. m. of* sa-ei.

THANEI, *conj.* since; jah thanei, inasmuch as, Mat. 25. 40.

THANJAN*, *vb.* to stretch; *in comp.* uf-thanjan. *From* thinan.

THANKJAN, THANKS; *see* thagkjan, thagks.

THANNU, *conj.* therefore, then, so that, for, Rom. 10. 17; Mat. 7. 20; Mk. 14. 6; — thannu nu, thannu nu jai, therefore, Rom. 9. 16, 18; — thannu than, so then, Rom. 7. 3. *From* than *and* nu.

THANS, the; *acc. m. pl. of* sa.

THANUH, *conj. and adv.* (*spelt* thanuth *before* th *following*), then, Mat. 8. 26; but, Mat. 9. 25; and, Mk. 10. 13; therefore, Mk. 12. 6; — thanuh than *or* thanuth than, then therefore, then also, Jo. 11. 14; — thanuh than swethauh, nevertheless, Jo. 12. 42.

THANUH, *pron.* this, *acc. m. s. of* sa'h.

THANZEI, *rel. pron.* whom, *acc. pl. m. of* sa-ei.

THANZUH, *pron.* these, and these, *acc. pl. m. of* sa'h.

THAR, *adv.* there, Mat. 6. 20; Lu. 9. 4.

THARBA, *wk. sb. m.* a beggar, Mk. 10. 21; Jo. 12. 5, 6. *Der.* ala-tharba. *From* thaurban.

THARBA, *str. sb. f.* want, need, lack, 2 Cor. 8. 14; 11. 9; Phil. 4. 11, 12. *From* thaurban.

THARBAN*, *vb.*; *see* ga-tharban.

THARBJAN*, *vb.*; *see* ga-tharbjan.

THARBS, *adj.* needy, in want, Lu. 9. 11; necessary, Phil. 2. 25.

THAREI, *adv.* where, Mat. 6. 19; Mk. 2. 4; Lu. 4. 16.

THARIHIS (ἀγνάφου), *gen. case of adj.* new (?), Mat. 9. 16.

THARUH, *adv.* there, Mat. 6. 21; but, Mk. 10. 20; behold, Mat. 9. 18; — tharuh sai, and behold, Lu. 7. 12; — tharuh than, but, Lu. 8. 23.

THATA (*neut. of* sa), the, that, this; *whence* thatainei, thatei, thatuh. [E. *that;* G. *das;* D. *dat.*]

THATAIN, that one, that only, one thing only, Jo. 9. 25; Rom. 9. 10; Gal. 3. 2. *From* thata *and* ains.

THATAINEI, THATAINE, *adv.* only, Mat. 5. 47; 8. 8; Mk. 5. 36.

THATEI, *rel. pron. neut.* that which, which, what; — *also conj.* that, because, if; bi thatei, because, Lu. 19. 11; — afar thatei, after that, Mk. 1. 14; — und thatei, until, Rom. 11. 25. *From* thata *and* ei.

THATHRO, THATHROH, *adv.* thence, Lu. 4. 9; after that, thenceforth, Lu. 16. 16.

THATHRO-EI, *adv.* from whence, Phil. 3. 20.

THATIST (*for* thata ist), that is to say, Mk. 7. 2; this is, Jo. 6. 29.

THATUH, *neut. of* sa'h, q. v.

THAU, THAUH, *conj.* though, than, however, Mat. 9. 5, &c.; — ei thau, or else, Lu. 14. 32. *Cf.* swethauh.

THAUHJABAI, THAUHJABA, even if, Jo. 11. 25; 1 Cor. 7. 21.

THAURBAN, *vb.* (*pt. t. as pres.* tharf, *pl.* thaurbum, *pt. t.* thaurfta), to need, want, lack, Mat. 6. 8; 9. 12; Mk. 2. 17. *Der.* ga-thaurbs, thaurfts, naudi-thaurfts, tharbs, tharba, ala-tharba, ga-tharban, ga-tharbjan. [G. *bedürfen;* D. *derven;* A. S. *pearfan.*]

THAURFTS, *adj.* needy, necessary, 1 Cor. 12. 22; profitable, 2 Tim. 3. 16. *Der.* naudi-thaurfts.

THAURFTS, *str. sb. f.* need, Lu. 19. 34; Phil. 2. 25; profit, Lu. 9. 25. *Cf.* Eph. 5. 4. *From* thaurban.

THAURNEINS, *adj.* thorny, made of thorns, Mk. 15. 17; Jo. 19. 5.

THAURNUS, *str. sb. m.* a thorn, Mat. 7. 16; Mk. 4. 7; Lu. 6. 44. *Der.* thaurneins. [G. *dorn;* D. *doorn.*]

THAURP, *str. sb. n.* a field, Neh. 5. 16. [G. *dorf;* D. *dorp;* E. *thorpe.*]

THAURSJAN, *vb.* to thirst; *only impers. as* thaurseith mik, I thirst, Jo. 6. 35; 7. 37; thaursiths wisan, to be thirsty, 1 Cor. 4. 11. *Der.* af-thaursjan, ga-thaursnan, thaurstei. *From* thairsan.

THAURSTEI, *wk. sb. f.* thirst, 2 Cor. 11. 27. [G. *durst;* D. *dorst.*]

THAURSUS, *adj.* dry, withered, parched up, Mk. 11. 20; Lu. 6. 6. *From* thairsan. [G. *dürr;* D. *dor.*]

THE, *instrumental case of* sa, so, thata. *Der.* bi-the, du-the, jaththe, the-ei. [A. S. *þi, þy.*]

THE-EI, *conj.* that; — ni the-ei *or* nih the-ei, not that, that not, Jo. 6. 38; 12. 6.

THEI, *conj.* that, Mat. 6. 26, &c.

THEIGAINS, *sb.* silence, *a reading for* thahains, 1 Tim. 2. 12. [*Almost illegible in the MS.*]

THEIHAN, *vb.* to thrive, increase, advance, Lu. 2. 52; Col. 2. 19; 1 Tim. 4. 15. *Der.* ga-, ufar-. [G. *gedeihen;* D. *gedijen;* O. E. *the.*]

THEIHS, *str. sb. n.* time, season, Rom. 13. 11; 1 Th. 5. 1.

THEIHWO, *wk. sb. f.* thunder, Mk. 3. 17; Jo. 12. 29.

THEINA, (1) of thee, (2) thine *(fem.).*

THEINATA, thine *(neuter).*

THEINS, *poss. pron.* thine.

THEWIS, *str. sb. n.* a slave, servant, Col. 3. 22; 4. 1. *From* thiwan. [A. S. *þeów.*]

THINAN*, *vb.* to stretch, extend, make thin. *Der.* af-thanjan.

[G. *dehnen;* A. S. *þenian; cf.* E. *thin;* G. *dünn;* D. *dun.*]

THINSAN*, *vb.* to draw. *Der.* atthinsan. *Cf.* thinan.

THIS, of the; *m. and n. gen. sing. of* sa, so, thata.

THIS-HUN, *adv.* chiefly, especially, Gal. 6. 10; 1 Tim. 4. 10; 5. 8.

THIS-HWADUH, *adv.* wheresoever, Mat. 18. 19; Mk. 6. 56; Lu. 9. 57.

THIS-HWARUH, *adv.* wheresoever, Mk. 9. 18; 14. 9.

THIS-HWAZUH, *pron.* whoever; — this-hwazuh ei, whoever, Mk. 11. 23; — this-hwazuh thei, *or* this-hwazuh saei, whosoever, Mat. 10. 33; Jo. 15. 16.

THIUBI, *str. sb. n.* a theft, Mk. 7. 22. *From* thiubs.

THIUBJO, *adv.* like a thief, secretly, Jo. 11. 28; 18. 20.

THIUBS, *str. sb. m.* a thief, Mat. 6. 19; Lu. 19. 46; Jo. 10. 8. [G. *dieb;* D. *dief.*]

THIUDA, *str. sb. f.* a people, a nation; *in pl.* the Gentiles, Mat. 6. 32; Mk. 10. 42; 11. 17. *Der.* Gut-thiuda, thiudisko, thiudans, thiudan-gardi, thiudanon, miththiudanon, thiudinassus. [A. S. *peód.*]

THIUDAN-GARDI, *str. sb. f.* a kingdom, Mat. 5. 19; 6. 13; 7. 21; a king's house, king's court, Lu. 7. 25. *From* thiuda *and* gards.

THIUDANON, *vb.* to rule, reign, Lu. 1. 33; 19. 14, 27. *Der.* mith-. *From* thiuda.

THIUDANS, *str. sb. m.* a king, Mat. 5. 35; 11. 8; 25. 40. *From* thiuda.

THIUDINASSUS, *str. sb. m.* a kingdom, Mat. 6. 10; Mk. 9. 1; a kingship, reign, Lu. 3. 1. *From* thiuda.

THIUDISKO, *adv.* after the manner of Gentiles, Gal. 2. 14. *From* thiuda.

THIU-MAGUS, *str. sb. m.* a servant, Mat. 8. 6; Lu. 1. 54; 7. 7. *From* thius *and* magus.

THIUS, *str. sb. m.* a servant, Lu. 16. 13; *pl.* thiwos, Nehem. 5. 16. *From* thiwan. *Cf.* thewis.

THIUTH, *str. sb. n* good, Lu. 1. 53; 6. 45; Rom. 7. 18; — thiuth taujan, to do good, Mk. 3. 4; Lu. 6. 9. *Der.* thiutheigs, thiutheins, thiuthjan, thiuth-spillon, un-thiuth, thiuthi-kwiss.

THIUTHEIGS, *adj.* good, Mat. 7. 18; Mk. 10. 17; Lu. 6. 45; blessed, Mk. 14. 61; Lu. 1. 68.

THIUTHEINS, *str. sb. f.* goodness, 2 Thess. 1. 11; a blessing, Eph. 1. 3.

THIUTHI-KWISS, *str. sb. f.* a blessing, 1 Cor. 10. 16.

THIUTHJAN, *vb. with dat. and acc.* to bless, Mk. 10. 16; 11. 9; Lu. 1. 28. *Der.* ga-, un-.

THIUTH-SPILLON, *vb.* to tell *or* bring glad tidings, Lu. 3. 18; *cf.* 8. 1. *From* thiuth *and* spill.

THIWADW, *str. sb. n.* service, slavery, Gal. 4. 24.

THIWAN*, *vb.* to be a slave, serve. *Der.* ana-, ga-, thiwadw, thius, thiu-magus, thiwi, thewis. [A. S. *peówian.*]

THIWI, *str. sb. f.* a maid-servant, handmaid, Lu. 1. 38; Mk. 14. 66; Jo. 18. 17.

THIZAI, to this, to her; *dat. f. s. of* sa.

THIZAI-EI, to her whom, to that which, to whom, to which.

THIZE, of the, of them; *g. pl. m. and n. of* sa.

THIZE-EI, of them who, of those that, of whom, of which, *m. and n. g. pl. of* sa-ei.

THIZO, of them, of those, *g. pl. f. of* sa.

THIZO-EI, of them who, of those that, of whom, of which, *g. pl. f. of* sa-ei.

THIZOS, of her, of that; *g. s. f. of* sa.

THIZOZEI, of her who, of that which, of whom, of which, *g. s. f. of* sa-ei.

THLAHSJAN, *vb.* to terrify, 2 Cor. 10. 9. *Der.* ga-thlahsnan. *Cf.* thliuhan.

THLAIHAN*, *vb.* to cherish, fondle. *Der.* ga-thlaihan, ga-thlaihts. [*Cf.* Gk. θέλγειν.]

THLAKWUS, *adj.* flaccid, tender, Mk. 13. 28. [*Cf.* G. *flau;* Lat. *flaccus.*]

THLAUHS, *str. sb. m.* flight, Mk. 13. 18. *From* thliuhan.

THLEIHSL, *str. sb. n.;* see threihsl.

THLIUHAN, *vb.* to flee, fly, Mat. 10. 23; Lu. 3. 7; Jo. 10. 5. *Der.* af-, ga-, untha-, thlauhs. [G. *fliehen;* D. *vliegen.*]

THO, her, it, this, the, that, *acc. f. s. and acc. n. pl. of* sa.

THOEI, her who, that which, whom, which, *acc. f. s. and acc. n. pl. of* sa-ei.

THOS, them, the; *acc. f. pl. of* sa.

THOZEI, them that, those which, which, *acc. f. pl. of* sa-ei.

THRAFSTEINS, *str. sb. f.* consolation, comfort, Rom. 15. 5.

THRAFSTJAN, *vb.* to console, comfort, Jo. 11. 31; to exhort, Lu. 3. 18; to terrify, Neh. 6. 14 (*which must be wrong*); *refl.* to take courage, be of good cheer, Mat. 9. 2; Mk. 10. 49. *Der.* ana-, ga-, thrafsteins, ga-thrafsteins. [G. *trösten;* D. *troosten; Cf.* E. *trust.*]

THRAGJAN, *vb.* to run, Mat. 27. 48; Mk. 15. 36; Lu. 15. 20. *Der.* bi-. [A. S. *prægian; cf.* A. S. *prah;* O. E. *throw.*]

THRAIHNS*, *str. sb. m.* a throng, heap. *Der.* faihu-thraihns. *From* threihan.

THRAMSTEI, *wk. sb. f.* a locust, Mk. 1. 6.

THRAS*, *adj.* quick, rash. *Der.* thrasa-balthei.

THRASA-BALTHEI, *wk. sb. f.* audacity, presumption, Skeir. 5. 11.

THRASK, thrashed; *from* thriskan.

THRASK*, *sb. in comp.* ga-thrask, q. v.

THREIHAN, *vb.* to throng, crowd round, press upon, Mat. 7. 14; Mk. 3. 9; 5. 24; — *pp.* thraihans, troubled, 2 Cor. 4. 8. *Der.* ga-, threihsl, faihu-thraihns. [G. *drängen*; D. *dringen*; O. E. *thring*.]

THREIHSL, *str. sb. n.* distress, 2 Cor. 12. 10. *From* threihan. [*Another reading for* threihslam *is* thleihslam.]

THREIS, *num.* (*neut.* thrija, *gen.* thrije, *dat.* thrim, *acc.* thrins), three, Mat. 27. 63; Mk. 8. 2; Lu. 1. 56. *Der.* threis-tigjus, thrija-hunda, thridja, thridjo. [G. *drei*; D. *drie*.]

THREIS-TIGJUS, *num.* (*gen.* thrije-tigiwe, *acc.* thrins-tiguns), thirty, Mat. 27. 3; Lu. 3. 23.

THRIDJA, *adj.* the third, Mat. 27. 64; Mk. 9. 31; 12. 21.

THRIDJO, *adv.* for the third time, 2 Cor. 12. 14; 13. 1.

THRIJA-HUNDA, *neut. pl.* three hundred, Mk. 14. 5.

THRIM, THRINS; *see* threis.

THRISKAN, *vb.* (*pt. t.* thrask, *pl.* thruskum, *pp.* thruskans), to thresh, thrash, 1 Cor. 9. 9; 1 Tim. 5. 18. *Der.* ga-thrask. [G. *dreschen*; D. *dorschen*.]

THRIUTAN*, *vb.* to urge, trouble, threaten. *Der.* us-, thruts-fill. [G. *verdriessen*; A. S. *preatian*; E. *threaten*.]

THROTHEINS*, *sb.* use, exercise; *in comp.* us-throtheins, q. v.

THROTHJAN, *vb.* to exercise, 1 Tim. 4. 7. *Der.* us-, us-throtheins.

THRUTS-FILL, *str. sb. n.* leprosy, Mat. 8. 3; Mk. 1. 42; Lu. 5. 12; — thr. habands, a leper, Mat. 8. 2; Mk. 1. 40. *From* thriutan *and* fill.

THRUTS-FILLS, *adj.* leprous, a leper, Mat. 11. 5; Lu. 4. 27; 7. 22. *From* thriutan *and* fill.

THU, *pers. pron.* thou; *gen.* theina, *dat.* thus, *acc.* thuk. [G. *du.*]

THUEI, thou who; *from* thu *and* ei.

THUGKJAN, THUGGKJAN, *vb.* to think, suppose, intend, seem, Mk. 10. 42; Lu. 8. 18; Jo. 16. 2; *impers.* thugkeithmis, me thinks, it seems to me, I suppose, Mat. 26. 65; Lu. 19. 11. *Der.* bauh-thuhts, mikil-thuhts, thuhtus. [G. *dünken*; G. & D. *denken*.]

THUHTUS, *str. sb. m.* thought, wisdom, Col. 2. 23; conscience, 1 Cor. 10. 28. *From* thugkjan.

THUK, thee; *acc. of* thu.

THUKEI, thee who; *acc. of* thuei.

THULAINS, *str. sb. f.* sufferance, patience, Lu. 8. 15; Rom. 15. 4; suffering, 2 Cor. 1. 5. *Der.* us-. *From* thulan.

THULAN, *vb.* to tolerate, suffer, put up with, endure, Mk. 9. 19; Lu. 9. 41; 1 Cor. 13. 7. *Der.* ga-, us-; thulains, us-thulains. [G. & D. *dulden*; O. E. *thole*; *cf.* E. *tolerate*.]

THUS, to thee; *dat. of* thu.

THUSUNDI, *num.* a thousand, Mk. 5. 13; 8. 9; Lu. 9. 14; — fimf thusundjos, five thousand, Lu. 9. 14; — twa thusundja, two thousand, Ezra 2. 15. *Der.* thusundi-faths. [G. *tausend*; D. *duizend*.]

THUSUNDI-FATHS, *str. sb. m.* a leader of a thousand men, Mk. 6. 21; Jo. 18. 12.

THUT-HAURN, *str. sb. n.* a horn, trumpet, 1 Cor. 15. 52; 1 Th. 4. 16. [A. S. *peótan;* G. *tuten;* cf. D. *toethoren;* E. *toot.*]

THUT-HAURNJAN, *vb.* to blow the trumpet, 1 Cor. 15. 52.

THUZEI, to thee to whom; *see* thus. *From* thu *and* ei.

THWAHAN, *vb.* (*pt. t.* thwoh, *pp.* thwahans), to wash, Mat. 6. 17; Jo. 13. 14; to wash oneself, Jo. 9. 7. *Der.* af-, bi-, us-; un-thwahans, thwahl. [A. S. *pweán.*]

THWAHL, *str. sb. n.* a washing, Eph. 5. 26; Skeir. 2. 8.

THWAIRHEI, *wk. sb. f.* anger, wrath, Rom. 9. 22; 12. 19; strife, 2 Cor. 12. 20.

THWAIRHS, *adj.* angry, Lu. 14. 21; Eph. 4. 26; Tit. 1. 7. *Der.* thwairhei. [A. S. *pweorh;* cf. E. *thwart.*]

THWASTITHA, *str. sb. f.* safety, Phil. 3. 1.

THWASTJAN*, *vb.* to secure; *in comp.* ga-thwastjan.

THWASTS*, *adj.* secure, safe. *Der.* thwastitha, ga-thwastjan.

THYMIAMA (θυμίαμα), *sb.* incense, offering of incense, Lu. 1. 10, 11.

T (continued).

[For other words beginning with T, see above, according to the alphabetical order.]

TIGUS, *num.* ten; *whence pl. nom.* tigjus, *gen.* tigiwe, Lu. 3. 23; *dat.* tigum, 1 Tim. 5. 9; *acc.* tiguns, Lu. 7. 41. *Der.* twai-, threis-, fidwor-, fimf-, saihs-. [E. -*ty;* G. -*zig.*]

TILABA*; *see* ga-tilaba.

TILAN*, *vb.* to suit, fit. *Der.* tils, ga-tils, ga-tilaba, untila-malsks, and-tilon, un-tals, talzjan, tal-zeins. [*Cf.* A. S. *til,* suitable; *tilian,* to prepare, till; E. *till.*]

TILON*, *vb.; see* and-tilon, ga-tilon, gaga-tilon. *From* tilan.

TILS, *adj.* suitable, fit; — til du wrohjan, fit for accusing, an accusation, Lu. 6. 7. *Der.* ga-tils, ga-tilaba. *From* tilan. [A. S. *til.*]

TIMAN*, *vb.* to tame. *Der.* ga-timan, ga-tamjan, ga-temiba. [G. *ziemen, zähmen;* D. *temmen.*]

TIMBRJAN; *see* TIMRJAN.

TIMREINS, *str. sb. f.* a building, Rom. 14. 19; 1 Cor. 14. 26; 2 Cor. 10. 8. *Der.* ga-timreins.

TIMRJA, *wk. sb. m.* a builder, Mk. 12. 10; Lu. 20. 17.

TIMRJAN, *vb.* (*spelt* timbrjan *in* Lu. 14. 28), to build, Lu. 6, 48; 14. 30; 17. 28. *Der.* ana-, ga-, mithga-, timrja, timreins, ga-timreins, ga-timrjo. [G. *zim-mern;* D. *timmeren;* A. S. *tim-brian;* cf. E. *timber.*]

TINDAN*, *vb.* to burn. *Der.* tand-jan, ga-tandjan, in-tandjan, tund-nan, in-tundnan. [*Cf.* E. *tinder;* G. *zünden.*]

TIUHAN, *vb.* (*pt. t.* tauh, *pl.* tau-hum, *pp.* tauhans), to tow, tug, pull; *hence* to lead, Lu. 4. 1;

18. 40; Jo. 18. 28; to guide, Lu. 6. 39; to lead away, Mk. 14. 44. *Der.* at-, inn-at, af-, bi-, ga-, mithga-, us-, us-tauhts, us-taubei. [G. *ziehen;* A. S. *teón.*]

TIWAN*, *vb.* to be ready. *Der.* taujan, ga-taujan, missa-taujands, taui, ubil-tojis, fulla-tojis, tewa, tewi, ga-tewjan, ungatewiths. [*Cf.* A. S. *tawian.*]

TOJIS, *gen. case of* taui, q. v. *Cf.* ubil-tojis, fulla-tojis.

TRAUAINS, *str. sb. f.* trust, confidence, 2 Cor. 1. 15; 3. 4; boldness, 2 Cor. 7. 4; Phil. 1. 20.

TRAUAN, *vb.* to trow, be persuaded, 2 Tim. 1. 5; to trust (*followed by* du *or* in), Mat. 27. 43; Lu. 18. 9; 2 Cor. 1. 9. *Der.* ga-trauan, trauains, trausti. *Cf.* triggws. [E. *trow, true, trust;* G. *treu, trauen;* D. *trouw.*]

TRAUSTI, *str. sb. n.* a covenant, Eph. 2. 12. [E. *trust.*]

TRIGGWA, *str. sb. f.* a covenant, Lu. 1. 72; Rom. 9. 4; 11. 27. *Cf.* trausti.

TRIGGWABA, *adv.* truly, assuredly, confidently, Lu. 20. 6; Phil. 1. 25.

TRIGGWS, *adj.* true, faithful, Lu. 16. 10; 19. 17; 1 Cor. 4. 2. *Der.* un-, triggwa, triggwaba. *Cf.* trauan.

TRIGO, *wk. sb. f.* grief, sorrow, 2 Cor. 9. 7.

TRIMPAN*, *vb.* to tramp, tread. *Der.* ana-trimpan. [G. *trampeln;* D. *trappen.*]

TRISGAN*, *vb.* to graft. *Der.* in-, trusgjan, in-trusgjan.

TRIU, *str. sb. n.* (*gen.* triwis), a tree; *hence* a piece of wood, a staff, Mk. 14. 43, 48. *Der.* triweins, weina-triu.

TRIWEINS, *adj.* made of a tree, wooden, 2 Tim. 2. 20.

TRUDAN, *vb.* to tread, tread upon, Lu. 10. 19; to tread as in a winepress, Lu. 6. 44. *Der.* ga-trudon. [G. *treten;* D. *treden.*]

TRUSGJAN*, *vb.* to graft. *Der.* in-trusgjan. *Cf.* trisgan.

TRUSNJAN*, *vb.* to sprinkle. *Der.* ufar-trusnjan.

TUGGL, *str. sb. n.* a star? *as gloss to* stabim, elements, Gal. 4. 3. [A. S. *tungel.*]

TUGGO, *wk. sb. f.* a tongue, Mk. 7. 33; Lu. 1. 64. [G. *zunge;* D. *tong.*]

TULGITHA, *str. sb. f.* safety, 1 Th. 5. 3; a stronghold, 2 Cor. 10. 4; a stay, sure foundation, 1 Tim. 3. 15. *From* tulgus.

TULGJAN, *vb.* to confirm, establish, 2 Cor. 2. 8; 1 Th. 3. 13. *Der.* ga-.

TULGUS, *adj.* steadfast, sure, 1 Cor. 15. 58; 2 Tim. 2. 19. *Der.* tulgjan, ga-tulgjan, tulgitha.

TUNDNAN, *vb.* to burn, 2 Cor. 11. 29. *Der.* in-. *From* tindan.

TUNTHUS, *str. sb. m.* a tooth, Mat. 5. 38; 8. 12; Mk. 9. 18. [G. *zahn;* D. *tand.*]

TUZ-WERJAN, *vb.* to doubt, Mk. 11. 23. *From* tus (*a derivative of* twai?) *and* werjan.

TWADDJE, *gen. of* twai, two.

TWA-HUNDA, *num.* two hundred, Jo. 6. 7.

TWAI, *num.* (*fem.* twos, *neut.* twa, *gen.* twaddje, *dat.* twaim, *acc.* twans, twos, twa), two, Mat. 6. 24; 27. 51; Mk. 5. 13. *Der.* tweihnai, twa-lif, twai-tigjus, twa-hunda, twis, tus? [G. *zwei;* D. *twee.*]

TWAI-TIGJUS, *num.* twenty, Lu. 14. 31.

TWALIB-WINTRUS, adj. twelve years' old, Lu. 2. 42.
TWA-LIF, num. twelve (spelt twalib, Lu. 2. 42; 8. 1), Mat. 10. 1; 11. 1, &c. [G. zwölf; D. twaalf.]
TWEIFLEINS, str. sb. f. doubting, 1 Tim. 2. 8; disputation, Rom. 14. 1.
TWEIFLJAN, vb. to make doubtful, Skeir. 6. 10.
TWEIFLS, str. sb. m. doubt, Skeir. 2. 13. [G. zweifel; D. twijfel.]
TWEIHNAI, pl. adj. two apiece, Lu. 9. 3. From twai.
TWIS-STANDAN, vb. to depart from one, bid farewell to, 2 Cor. 2. 13. From twai and standan.
TWIS-STASS, str. sb. f. a standing aloof from, sedition, Gal. 5. 20. From twai and standan.
TYRA, sb. f. Tyre, Mk. 3. 8; Lu. 10. 14.
TYRUS, adj. a Tyrian, Mat. 11. 22; Mk. 7. 24, 31.

U.

U, the sixteenth letter of the Gothic alphabet. As a numeral, it means 70. It is probably equivalent to oo in cool; or, if unaccented, to oo in foot.
U, an enclitic used in asking a question, as in skuld-u ist, is it lawful, Mk. 3. 4; sometimes found in the middle of a word; thus ga-u-laubjats is put for ga-laubjats-u, do ye believe, Mat. 9. 28. Cf. ub.
UBILABA, adv. evilly, ill, Mk. 2. 17; Jo. 18. 23.
UBILS, adj. evil, ill, bad, useless, Mat. 5. 37; 6. 13; Mk. 7. 23; — ubil haban, to be ill, Mat. 8. 16; — ubil kwithan, to speak evil against, to curse, Mk. 7. 10; — ubil waurdjan, to speak evil of, Mk. 9. 39. Der. ubilaba, ubiltojis, ubil-waurds. [G. übel.]
UBIL-TOJIS, adj. as sb. a malefactor, evildoer, Jo. 18. 30; 2 Tim. 2. 9.
UBIL-WAURDS, adj. evilspeaking, railing, 1 Cor. 5. 11.
UBIZWA, str. sb. f. a porch, Jo. 10. 23. [A. S. efese; E. eaves.]
UB-UH; put for uf-uh, from uf and uh.
UF, prep. with dat. and acc. under, beneath, in the time of. Occurs as a prefix in numerous compounds. [Gk. ὑπό; Lat. sub.]
UF-AITHIS, adj. under an oath, Neh. 6. 18.
UFAR, prep. with dat. and acc. over, above, beyond. Occurs as a prefix in numerous compounds. [G. über; D. & E. over.]
UFARASSJAN, vb. to abound, overflow, redound, 2 Cor. 4. 15; 9. 8, 12; 1 Tim. 1. 14.
UFARASSUS, str. sb. m. overflow, abundance, superfluity, 2 Cor. 8. 14; 10. 15; — ufarassau haban, to have in abundance, Lu. 15. 17; Phil. 2. 12.
UFAR-FULLEI, wk. sb. f. overfullness, abundance, Lu. 6. 45.
UFAR-FULLJAN, vb. to fill to overflowing, 2 Cor. 7. 4; to abound, 1 Cor. 15. 58.
UFAR-FULLS, adj. full to overflowing, Lu. 6. 38.
UFAR-GAGGAN, vb. to go over, transgress, Lu. 15. 29; to go beyond, overreach, 1 Th. 4. 6.
UFAR-GIUTAN, vb. to pour over, make to run over, Lu. 6. 38.

UFAR-GUDJA, *wk. sb. m.* a chief-priest, Mk. 10. 33.
UFAR-HAFJAN, *vb.* to heave *or* lift over, to exalt, 2 Th. 2. 4.
UFAR-HAFNAN, *vb.* to be heaved *or* lifted over, to be exalted, 2 Cor. 12. 7.
UFAR-HAMON, *vb.* to put on clothes over, to be clothed upon (A. V.), 2 Cor. 5. 2.
UFAR-HAUHJAN, *vb.* to exalt over, to lift up, 1 Tim. 3. 6.
UFAR-HAUSEINS, *str. sb. f.* a hearing over, disregarding, disobedience, 2 Cor. 10. 6.
UFAR-HIMINAKUNDS (ἐπουράνιος), *adj.* heavenly, 1 Cor. 15. 48.
UFAR-HLEITHRJAN, *vb.* to dwell upon, rest upon, 2 Cor. 12. 9.
UFAR-HUGJAN, *vb.* to think over highly, to be exalted above measure, 2 Cor. 12. 7.
UFAR-JAINA, *adv.* in places beyond, beyond, 2 Cor. 10. 16.
UFAR-LAGJAN, *vb.* to lay upon; *pass.* to lie upon, Jo. 11. 38.
UFAR-LEITHAN, *vb.* to pass over, Mat. 9. 1.
UFAR-MELEINS, *str. sb. f.* superscription, Mk. 12. 16.
UFAR-MELI, *str. sb. n.* superscription, Mk. 15. 26; Lu. 20. 24.
UFAR-MELJAN, *vb.* to write over, Mk. 15. 26.
UFAR-MITON, *vb.* to cause to be forgotten, to put away from remembrance (?), Skeir. 3. 17.
UFAR-MUNNON, *vb.* to forget, Mk. 8. 14; Phil. 3. 14; to disregard, Phil. 2. 30.
UFARO, *adv.* above, thereon, Jo. 11. 38; *prep. with gen.* upon, Lu. 10. 19; *with dat.* over, above, Lu. 19. 19; Jo. 3. 31.
UFAR-RANNEINS, *str. sb. f.* an over-sprinkling, besprinkling, Skeir. 3. 10.

UFAR-SKADWJAN, *vb.* to overshadow, Mk. 9. 7; Lu. 1. 35; 9. 34.
UFAR-SKAFTS, *str. sb. f.* the first fruit, Rom. 11. 16. *From* skapjan.
UFAR-STEIGAN, *vb.* to mount up, grow up, Mk. 4. 7.
UFAR-SWARA, *wk. sb. m.* an overswearer, a perjured man, 1 Tim. 1. 10.
UFAR-SWARAN, *vb.* to overswear, forswear, Mat. 5. 33.
UFAR-THEIHAN, *vb.* to surpass, supersede, Skeir. 3. 21.
UFAR-TRUSNJAN, *vb.* to besprinkle, Skeir. 3. 16.
UFAR-WAHSJAN, *vb.* to over-wax, grow exceedingly, 2 Th. 1. 3.
UFAR-WISAN, *vb.* to be over, exceed, surpass, 2 Cor. 3. 9; Phil. 4. 7; to be set over, to be higher, Rom. 13. 1.
UF-BAULJAN, *vb.* to puff up; *pass.* to be highminded, 2 Tim. 3. 4.
UF-BLESAN, *vb.* to blow up, puff up; *pass.* to be puffed up, 1 Cor. 4. 6; 13. 4; Col. 2. 18.
UF-BRIKAN, *vb.* to reject, Mk. 6. 26; to despise, Lu. 10. 16; 1 Th. 4. 8; *see* 1 Tim. 1. 13.
UF-BRINNAN, *vb. neut.* to be burnt up, be scorched, Mk. 4. 6.
UF-DAUPJAN, *vb.* to dip into, dip in, Jo. 13. 26; to baptize, Lu. 3. 21; 7. 29.
UF-GAIRDAN, *vb.* to undergird, gird about, Eph. 6. 14.
UF-GRABAN, *vb.* to dig under, dig through, Mat. 6. 19, 26.
UF-HABAN, *vb.* to bear up, sustain, Lu. 4. 11.
UF-HAUSEINS, *str. sb. f.* a hearing under, regard, obedience, 2 Cor. 7. 15; 10. 5; subjection, 1 Tim. 2. 11. *Cf.* ufar-hauseins.
UF-HAUSJAN, *vb.* to hear under, to obey, submit to, Mat. 8. 27; Mk. 1. 27; Lu. 2. 51. *Cf.* ufar-hauseins.

UF-HLOHJAN, *vb.* to make rejoice; *pass.* to rejoice, laugh, Lu. 6. 21. *From* hlahjan.

UF-HNAIWEINS, *str. sb. f.* a bending under, subjection, Gal. 2. 5.

UF-HNAIWJAN, *vb.* to make to bend under, to put under, make subject, 1 Cor. 15. 27; Eph. 1. 22; Phil. 3. 21.

UF-HROPJAN, *vb.* to cry out, Mk. 1. 23; 9. 24; Lu. 4. 33.

UFJO, *wk. sb. f.* a superfluous thing, 2 Cor. 9. 1. *Cf.* ufar.

UF-KUNNAN, *vb.* (*pt. t.* uf-kuntha), to know, recognise, Mk. 5. 29; Lu. 7. 39; Jo. 6. 69.

UF-KUNTHI, *str. sb. n.* knowledge, Eph. 1. 17; 4. 13; Col. 1. 10.

UF-LIGAN, *vb.* to lie under; hence to faint, Mk. 8. 3; to fail, Lu. 16. 9.

UF-MELJAN, *vb.* to subscribe, *Neap. and Arezzo documents.*

UF-MUNNAN, *vb.* to remember (?), Phil. 2. 28. *Read* uf-kunnands.

UF-RAKJAN, *vb.* to stretch out, Mat. 8. 3; Mk. 1. 41; 3. 5; *pass.* to become uncircumcised, 1 Cor. 7. 18.

UF-SAGGKWJAN, *vb.* to swallow up, 1 Cor. 15. 54.

UF-SLIUPAN, *vb.* to slip under, to withdraw privily, Gal. 2. 12.

UF-SNEITHAN, *vb.* to kill, Lu. 15. 23; Jo. 10. 10; 1 Cor. 5. 7. *From* sneithan, to cut.

UF-STRAUJAN, *vb.* to spread or strew under, to spread, Lu. 19. 36.

UF-SWALLEINS, *str. sb. f.* a swelling up, swelling, 2 Cor. 12. 20. *From* swillan.

UF-SWOGJAN, *vb.* to sigh deeply, Mk. 8. 12.

UFTA, *adv.* oft, often, Mk. 5. 4; Jo. 18. 2; 2 Cor. 8. 22; — thizo ufta sauhte, frequent infirmities, 1 Tim. 5. 23.

UFTAHARI, *a name; Neap. document.*

UF-THANJAN, *vb. refl.* to stretch out, 2 Cor. 10. 14; to stretch after, Phil. 3. 14. *From* thinan.

UFTO, *adv.* perhaps, Mat. 27. 64; Lu. 20. 13. [*Probably an error for* aufto, q. v.]

UF-WOPJAN, *vb.* to cry out, speak aloud, Lu. 1. 42; 8. 8; 18. 38.

UGGK, UGK, *dual acc.* us two, both of us, Eph. 6. 22.

UGGKIS, UGKIS, *dual dat.* for us two, Mk. 10. 35; Jo. 17. 21; *also acc.* Mat. 9. 27; Lu. 7. 20.

UH, *conj.* but, and; *an enclitic particle like the Latin* que; *it takes the form* uth *before* th, ul *before* l (2 Cor. 7. 8), uk *before* k (1 Cor. 7. 16); *also a demonstrative particle, like Latin* ce, *as in* sah, *put for* sa-uh; *also, an indefinite particle, as in* hwazuh, *put for* hwas uh. *Hence the forms* tharuh, thanuh, hwatharuh, sumanuh, &c.; *also* swah, hwah, &c., *for* swa uh, hwa uh, &c.

UHT*, *sb.?* early time, right season? *Der.* uhteigs, uhteigo, un-uhteigo, uhtiugs, uhtwo. [A. S. *uhta*, early morn.]

UHTEDUN, *put for* ohtedun, they feared, Mk. 11. 32; *from* ogan.

UHTEIGO, OHTEIGO, *adv.* in season, at a fit time, 2 Tim. 4. 2. *Der.* un-uhteigo.

UHTEIGS, *adj.* at leisure for, having opportunity for, 1 Cor. 7. 5. *From* uht?

UHTIUGS, *adj.* at leisure, having a fit opportunity for, 1 Cor. 15. 12. *Cf.* uhteigs.

UHTWO, *wk. sb. f.* early morn, Mk. 1. 35. [A. S. *uhta.*]

ULBANDUS, *str. sb. m.* a camel,

Mk. 1. 6; 10. 25; Lu. 18. 25. [A. S. *olfend;* E. *elephant.*]

UN-, *a negative prefix, like English* un-. [G. *un-*; D. *on-.*]

UN-AGANDS, *pres. pt. (as from* unagan), fearless, without fear, 1 Cor. 16. 10; Phil. 1. 14.

UN-AGEI, *wk. sb. f.* fearlessness; *dat.* un-agein, without fear, Lu. 1. 74.

UN-AIRKNS, *adj.* unholy, 1 Tim. 1. 9; 2 Tim. 3. 2.

UN-AIWISKS, *adj.* that needeth not to be ashamed, 2 Tim. 2. 15.

UN-ANASIUNABA, *adv.* invisibly, Skeir. 8. 2.

UN-ANDHULITHS, *pp. (as from* unandhuljan), not uncovered, 2 Cor. 3. 14.

UN-ANDSAKANS, *pp. (as from* unandsakan), irrefragable, irrefutable, Skeir. 6. 14.

UN-ANDSOKS, *adj.* that cannot be spoken against, irrefutable, Skeir. 6. 12.

UN-ATGAHTS, *adj.* inaccessible, unapprochable, 1 Tim. 6. 16.

UN-BAIRANDEI, *fem. adj.* barren, that beareth not, Gal. 4. 27.

UN-BAIRANDS, *adj.* not bearing, Lu. 3. 9; Jo. 15. 2.

UN-BARNAHS, *adj.* without children, childless, Lu. 20. 28, 29, 30.

UN-BAURANS, *pp. (as from* un *and* baurans), *pp. of* bairan, unborn, not born, Skeir. 5. 20.

UN-BEISTEI, *wk. sb. f.* want of leaven, unleavened bread, 1 Cor. 5. 8.

UN-BEISTOTHS, *adj.* unleavened, 1 Cor. 5. 7.

UN-BILAISTITHS, *pp. (as from* un *and* bilaistjan), not to be traced, not to be found out, Rom. 11. 33.

UN-BIMAIT, *str. sb. n.* uncircumcision, Col. 2. 13.

UN-BIMAITANS, *pp. (as from* un *and* bimaitan), uncircumcised, Eph. 2. 11.

UN-BRUKS, *adj.* unprofitable, Lu. 17. 10; Skeir. 1. 2.

UND, *prep. with dat.* in return for, for, Mat. 5. 38; Rom. 12. 17; *more often with acc.* unto, until, as far as, up to, Lu. 2. 15; Mk. 6. 23; — und hwan filu, how much, Mat. 10. 25. *Also in compounds, where it perhaps once takes the form* untha; *see* unthathliuhan. [E. *unto?*]

UNDAR, *prep. with acc.* under, Mk. 4. 21. *Der.* undaro, undaraists, undarleija. [G. *unter;* D. *onder.*]

UNDARAISTS, *superl. adj.* undermost, lowest, Eph. 4. 9.

UNDARLEIJA, *superl. adj.* lowest, least, Eph. 3. 8; *but for* undarleijin *M. reads* undaraistin. *Cf.* undaraists.

UNDARO, *prep. with dat.* Mk. 6. 11; 7. 28.

UNDAURNI-MATS, *str. sb. m.* undernmeat, morning meal, Lu. 14. 12. [A. S. & O. E. *undern.*]

UND-GREIPAN, *vb.* to grip, lay hold of, Mk. 1. 31; 12. 8; 15. 21; Jo. 18. 12.

UN-DIWANEI, *wk. sb. f.* deathlessness, immortality, 1 Cor. 15. 53; 1 Tim. 6. 16.

UN-DIWANS, *adj.* undying, immortal, 1 Tim. 1. 17.

UND-REDAN, *vb.* to provide, Sk. 6. 13.

UND-RINNAN, *vb.* to fall to one's share, Lu. 15. 12.

UN-FAGRS, *adj.* unthankful, Lu. 6. 35.

UN-FAIRINODABA, *adv.* unblameably, 1 Th. 2. 20.

UN-FAIRINS, *adj.* blameless, unblameable, 1 Th. 3. 13; 5. 23; Col. 1. 22. *See* us-fairins.

UN-FAIRLAISTITHS, *pp. (as from* un *and* fairlaistjan), unsearchable, Eph. 3. 8. *Cf.* unbilaistiths.

UN-FAURS, *adj.* not sober, not staid in behaviour, a tattler, 1 Tim. 5. 13. *Cf.* ga-faurs.

UN-FAURWEIS, *adj.* un-premeditated, Skeir. 3. 14. *From* weis.
UN-FRATHJANDS, *adj.* without understanding, foolish, Rom. 10. 19.
UN-FREIDEINS, *str. sb. f.* not taking care of, neglect, Col. 2. 23. *Cf.* ga-freideins.
UN-FROTHS, *adj.* without understanding, foolish, 2 Cor. 11. 16; Eph. 5. 17; Gal. 3. 1.
UN-GAFAIRINONDS, *pres. pt. (as from* un *and* gafairinon) blameless, 1 Tim. 3. 2; Tit. 1. 6.
UN-GAFAIRINOTHS, *pp. (as from* un *and* gafairinon) blameless, 1 Tim. 3. 10; 5. 7; Tit. 1. 7.
UN-GAHABANDS (*with* sik), *pres. pt. (as from* un *and* gababan) not restraining, incontinent, 2 Tim. 3. 3.
UN-GAHOBAINS, *str. sb. f.* incontinency, 1 Cor. 7. 5.
UN-GAHWAIRBS, *adj.* unruly, Tit. 1. 6, 10; disobedient, 2 Tim. 3. 2.
UN-GAKUSANS, *pp. (as from* un *and* gakiusan) unchosen, not elect, reprobate, 2 Cor. 13. 5; Tit. 1. 16. *From* kiusan.
UN-GALAUREINS, *str. sb. f.* unbelief, Mk. 6. 6; 9. 24; Rom. 11. 20. *From* liuban.
UN-GALAUBJANDS, *pres. pt. (as from* un *and* galaubjan) unbelieving, Mk. 9. 19; Lu. 9. 41; Rom. 10. 21.
UN-GALAUBS, *adj.* not dear, worthless, Rom. 9. 21.
UN-GARAIHTEI, *wk. sb. f.* unrighteousness, 2 Cor. 6. 14.
UN-GASAIHWANS, *pp. (as from* un- *and* gasaihwan) not seen, invisible, 2 Cor. 4. 4; Col. 1. 15; 1 Tim. 1. 17.
UN-GASTOTHANS, *pp.*, *or* UN-GASTOTHS, *adj.* without fixed abode, unsettled, 1 Cor. 4. 11.
UN-GATASS, *adj.* unruly, 1 Th. 5. 14.

UN-GATASSABA, *adv.* not according to rule, disorderly, 2 Thess. 3. 6, 11.
UN-GATEWITHS, *pp. (as from* un *and* gatewjan) disorderly, 2 Thess. 3. 8.
UN-GAWAGITHS, *pp. (as from* un *and* gawagjan) immoveable, 1 Cor. 15. 58. *From* wigan.
UN-HABANDS, *pres. pt. (as from* un *and* haban) not having, that hath not, Lu. 3. 11; 19. 26; 1 Cor. 11. 22.
UN-HAILI, *str. sb. n.* want of health, sickness, Mat. 9. 12, 35.
UN-HAILS, *adj.* not hale, sick, weak, Lu. 5. 31; 9. 2; 1 Cor. 11. 30.
UN-HANDUWAURHTS, *adj.* not handwrought, not made with hands, Mk. 14. 58. *From* waurkjan.
UN-HINDARWEIS, *adj.* unfeigned, 2 Cor. 6. 6; 1 Tim. 1. 5.
UN-HRAINEI, *wk. sb. f.* uncleanness, Col. 3. 5.
UN-HRAINITHA, *str. sb. f.* uncleanness, 2 Cor. 12. 21; Gal. 5. 19; Eph. 4. 19.
UN-HRAINS, *adj.* unclean, Mk. 1. 23; 6. 7; Lu. 4. 33; unpolished, rude, 2 Cor. 11. 6.
UN-HULTHA, *wk. sb. m.* an evil spirit, unclean spirit, devil, Lu. 4. 35; 8. 29; Mat. 25. 41.
UN-HULTHO, *wk. sb. f. the same as* un-hultha, Mat. 7. 22; 9. 33; Mk. 1. 34. *From* hilthan.
UN-HUNSLAGS, *adj.* truce-breaking, 2 Tim. 3. 3. *From* hunsl.
UN-HWAPNANDS, *pres. pt. (as from* un *and* hwapnan) unquenchable, Mk. 9. 43; Lu. 3. 17.
UN-HWEILS, *adj.* without rest, ceaseless, continual, Rom. 9. 2.
UN-KARJA, *adj.* careless, neglectful, Mk. 4. 15; 1 Tim. 4. 14.

UN-KAUREINS, *str. sb. f.* a refraining from being a burden; — in allaim un-kaureinom, in all things that are without charge; *see* 2 Cor. 11. 9.

UNKJA, *wk. sb. m.(?)* an ounce, *Arezzo document*. [Lat. *uncia*.]

UN-KUNNANDS, *pres. pt. (as from* un *and* kunnan*)* ignorant, Rom. 10. 3; Skeir. 2. 12; 4. 5.

UN-KUNTHI, *str. sb. n.* ignorance, 1 Cor. 15. 34.

UN-KUNTHS, *pp. (as from* un *and* kunnan*)* unknown, 2 Cor. 6. 9; Gal. 1. 22.

UN-KWENITHS, *pp. (as from* un *and* kwenjan*)* unmarried, 1 Cor. 7. 8. *From* kwens.

UN-KWETHIS, *adj.* unspeakable, 2 Cor. 12. 14.

UN-LEDI, *str. sb. n.* poverty, 2 Cor. 8. 2, 9.

UN-LEDS, *adj.* poor, Mat. 11. 5; Mk. 14. 5; Lu. 4. 18.

UN-LIUBS, *adj.* not beloved, Rom. 9. 25.

UN-LIUGAITHS, *pp. (as from* un *and* liugan*)* unmarried, 1 Cor. 7. 11.

UN-LIUGANDS, *as pres. pt.* not lying, truthful, Tit. 1. 2.

UN-LIUTS, *adj.* without dissimulation, unfeigned, Rom. 12. 9; 2 Tim. 1. 5.

UN-LUSTUS, *str. sb. m.* displeasure; in unlustau wairthan, to be discouraged, Col. 3. 21.

UN-MAHTEIGS, *adj.* unmighty, weak, Rom. 14. 1; 1 Cor. 4. 10; impossible, Mk. 10. 27; Lu. 18. 27. *From* magan.

UN-MAHTS, *str. sb. f.* unmight, weakness, Mat. 8. 17; 2 Cor. 12. 5; Gal. 4. 13. *From* magan.

UN-MANA-RIGGWS, *adj.* inhuman, fierce, 2 Tim. 3. 3.

UN-MANWUS, *adj.* unprepared, 2 Cor. 9. 4.

UN-MILDS, *adj.* not mild, without natural affection, 2 Tim. 3. 3.

UN-NUTIS, *adj.* useless, unprofitable, foolish, 1 Tim. 6. 9. *From* niutan.

UN-RIUREI, *wk. sb. f.* incorruption, 1 Cor. 15. 50; Eph. 6. 24; 2 Tim. 1. 10.

UN-RIURS, *adj.* incorruptible, imperishable, 1 Cor. 9. 25; 15. 52.

UN-RODJANDS, *pres. pt. (as from* un *and* rodjan*)* not speaking, speechless, dumb, Mk. 7. 37; 9. 17, 25.

UNS, *pron.* us. *From* ik. [G. *uns*.]

UN-SAHTABA, *adv.* without controversy, 1 Tim. 3. 16. *From* sakan.

UN-SAIHWANDS, *pres. pt. (as from* un *and* saihwan*)* not seeing, blind, Jo. 9. 39.

UN-SALTANS, *pp. (as from* un *and* saltan*)* unsalted, Mk. 9. 50.

UNSAR, *pron. poss.* our. [G. *unser*.]

UN-SELEI, *wk. sb. f.* wickedness, evil, injustice, unrighteousness, Mk. 7. 22; Lu. 20. 23; Eph. 6. 12.

UN-SELS, *adj.* wicked, unholy, Mat. 5. 39; 6. 23; Mk. 7. 22.

UN-SIBIS, *adj.* lawless, impious, a transgressor, Mk. 15. 28; 1 Tim. 1. 9.

UN-SIBJA, *sb.* iniquity, Mat. 7. 23.

UNSIS, *pron.* to us, us; *from* ik.

UN-SUTI, *str. sb. n.* lack of peace, a tumult, 2 Cor. 6. 5.

UN-SWEIBANDS, *pres. pt. (as from* un *and* sweiban*)* not ceasing, Eph. 1. 16; 1 Thess. 2. 13; 5. 17.

UN-SWERAINS, *sb. f.* dishonour, 2 Tim. 2. 20. *See* un-swerei.

UN-SWERAN, *vb.* to treat shamefully, maltreat, dishonour, Lu. 20. 11; Jo. 8. 49.

UN-SWEREI, *wk. sb. f.* shame, dishonour, 2 Cor. 6. 8.

UN-SWERITHA, *str. sb. f.* shame, 2 Cor. 11. 21.
UN-SWERS, *adj.* without honour, Mk. 6. 4; 1 Cor. 4. 10.
UN-SWIKUNTHS, *adj.* unknown, unevident, Skeir. 6. 1. *From* kunnan.
UN-TALS, *adj.* unlearned, 2 Tim. 2. 23; indocile, disobedient, Lu. 1. 17; 1 Tim. 1. 9. *From* tilan.
UNTE, *conj.* until, as long as, whilst, Mat. 5. 18; Jo. 9. 4; for, because, Mat. 6. 14; since, because that, Mk. 1. 34. *Cf.* und.
UNTHA-THLIUHAN, *vb.* to flee out, escape, 2 Cor. 11. 33; 1 Th. 5. 3. *From* und (?) *and* thliuban; *but cf.* D. ontvliegen.
UN-THIUDA, Rom. 10. 19; *see* thiuda.
UN-THIUTH, *str. sb. n.* evil, Rom. 9. 11; 12. 21; — unthiuth taujan, to do evil, Mk. 3. 4; Lu. 6. 9.
UN-THIUTHJAN, *vb.* to devote to evil, to curse, Rom. 12. 14.
UN-TWAHANS, *pp.* (*as from* un *and* thwaban) unwashen, Mk. 7. 2.
UN-TILAMALSKS, *adj.* rash, headstrong, foolish, 2 Tim. 3. 4. *From* tilan *and* malsks. [*Cf.* A. S. *malscra*.]
UN-TRIGGWS, *adj.* untrue, unjust, Lu. 16. 10.
UN-UFBRIKANDS, *pres. pt.* without giving offence, 1 Cor. 10. 32. *From* brikan.
UN-UHTEIGO, *adv.* at an unfit time, out of season, 2 Tim. 4. 2.
UN-USLAISITHS, *pp.* (*as from* un *and* uslaisjan) uninstructed, that hath never learnt, Jo. 7. 15. *From* leisan.
UN-USSPILLOTHS, *pp.* (*as from* un *and* usspillon) unspeakable, 2 Cor. 9. 15; unsearchable, Rom. 11. 33.
UN-WAHS, *adj.* blameless, Lu. 1. 6.
UN-WAIRTHABA, *adv.* unworthily, 1 Cor. 11. 27, 29.

UN-WAMMEI, *wk. sb. f.* the being without blemish, purity, sincerity, 1 Cor. 5. 8.
UN-WAMMS, *adj.* without spot, 1 Tim. 6. 14; without reproach, Eph. 1. 4; 5. 27.
UN-WAURSTWO, *wk. sb. f.* an unworking woman, an idle woman, 1 Tim. 5. 13. *From* waurkjan.
UN-WEIS, *adj.* unlearned, 1 Cor. 14. 23; ignorant, 2 Cor. 1. 8; 1 Th. 4. 13.
UN-WENIGGO, *adv.* unexpectedly, on a sudden, 1 Th 5. 3. *From* wens.
UN-WEREINS, *str. sb. f.* unendurance; *hence* indignation, 2 Cor. 7. 11. *From* werjan.
UN-WERJAN, *vb.* to be unable to endure, to be displeased, Mk. 10. 14, 41.
UN-WIS, *adj.* uncertain, 1 Cor. 9. 26. [*Cf.* G. *gewiss*; O. E. *i-wis*.]
UN-WITANDS, *pres. pt.* unknowing, ignorant, 2 Cor. 2. 11; 1 Tim. 1. 13.
UN-WITI, *str. sb. n.* ignorance, Eph. 4. 18; foolishness, Mk. 7. 22; 2 Tim. 3. 9.
UN-WITS, *adj.* without understanding, foolish, Mk. 7. 18; 2 Cor. 11. 19; 12. 6; ignorant, 1 Cor. 10. 1. *From* weitan.
UN-WUNANDS, *pres. pt.* joyless, very sad, Phil. 2. 26. [*Cf.* G. *wonne*.]
UR-, *the form which* us *assumes before* r *following; see* us.
UR-RAISJAN, *vb.* (*spelt* us-raisjan, Lu. 8. 24), to raise up, Mk. 1. 31; Lu. 1. 69; Jo. 5. 21; to rouse up, wake, Mat. 8. 25; *pass.* to arise, Jo. 6. 18. *Der₂* mithurreisjan. *From* reisan.
UR-RANNJAN, *vb.* to make to run out, make to rise (of the sun), Mat. 5. 45. *From* rinnan.

UR-REDAN, *vb.* to make ordinances, Col. 2. 20.

UR-REISAN, *vb.* to arise, Mat. 8. 15; 9. 5; Mk. 4. 39. *From* us *and* reisan.

UR-RINNAN, *vb.* to go out, come out, come forth, Mk. 4. 3; 8. 11; Jo. 15. 26; to rise (of the sun), Mk. 4. 6; to spring up, Mk. 4. 5; to fall (as a lot), Lu. 1. 9.

UR-RISTS, *str. sb. f.* arising, resurrection, Mat. 27. 53. *From* us *and* reisan.

UR-RUGKS, *adj.* reprobate? [*A marginal gloss to* barna batizis (children of wrath), *is* ur-rugkai; Eph. 2. 3.]

UR-RUMNAN, *vb.* (*also* us-rumnan, 2 Cor. 6. 11), to spread out, be enlarged, 2 Cor. 6. 11, 13. *From* us *and* rums.

UR-RUNS, *str. sb. m.* a running out, departure, decease, Lu. 9. 31; day-spring, Lu. 1. 78; east, Mat. 8. 11; the draught, Mk. 7. 19.

US, *prep. with dat.* out, out of, from, forth from, Mk. 1. 11; 7. 15; Lu. 17. 34. *It changes into* ur *before* r; *and into* uz *in* uz-u *and* uz-uh, Gal. 3. 2; Mk. 11. 30. [A. S. *ut;* E. *out;* G. *aus;* D. *uit.*]

US-AGJAN, *vb.* to frighten utterly; *pp.* usagiths, sore afraid, Mk. 9. 6. *From* agan.

US-AGLJAN, *vb.* to trouble exceedingly, to weary out, Lu. 18. 5.

US-AIWJAN, *vb.* to last out, continue, endure, 1 Cor. 15. 10. *[Not in the Greek.]*

US-ALTHAN, *vb.* to grow old; *pp.* usalthans, old, antiquated, 1 Tim. 4. 7.

US-ANAN, *vb.* (*pt. t.* uzon), to breathe out, expire, Mk. 15. 37, 39.

US-BAIRAN, *vb.* to bear out, carry out, 1 Tim. 6. 7; to bear, Mat. 8. 17; to bring forth, Lu. 6. 45; to answer, Mk. 11. 14.

US-BALTHEI, *wk. sb. f.* impudent speech, perverse disputing, 1 Tim. 6. 5.

US-BAUGJAN, *vb.* to sweep out, sweep, Lu. 15. 8. [*Cf.* G. *fegen.*]

US-BEIDAN, *vb.* to expect, abide for, 1 Cor. 16. 11; Phil. 3. 20; Lu. 2. 38; to abide, bear long with, Lu. 18. 7; Rom. 9. 22.

US-BEISNEI, *wk. sb. f.* long abiding *or* enduring of, long-suffering, Gal. 5. 22; Col. 3. 12; 1 Tim. 1. 16.

US-BEISNEIGS, *adj.* long-abiding, long-suffering, 1 Cor. 13. 4; 1 Th. 5. 14.

US-BEISNS, *str. sb. f.* abiding, expectation, Phil. 1. 20; long-abiding, long-suffering, Eph. 4. 2; Col. 1. 11. *From* beidan.

US-BIDJAN, *or* US-BIDAN, *vb.* to pray for, wish exceedingly, Rom. 9. 3.

US-BLIGGWAN, *vb.* to beat exceedingly, scourge, Lu 18. 33; Jo. 19. 1; to beat (with rods), 2 Cor. 11. 25.

US-BLOTEINS, *str. sb. f.* an entreaty, 2 Cor. 8. 4. *From* blotan.

US-BRAIDJAN, *vb.* to broaden out, stretch forth, Rom. 10. 21.

US-BRUKNAN, *vb.* to be broken out *or* off, Rom. 11. 17, 19, 20.

US-BUGJAN, *vb.* to buy out, buy, Mat. 27. 7; Mk. 15. 46; 16. 1.

US-DAUDEI, *wk. sb. f.* diligence, Rom. 12. 8; 2 Cor. 7. 11; perseverance, Eph. 6. 18.

US-DAUDJAN, *vb.* to be diligent, Gal. 2. 10; Eph. 4. 3; to strive, fight, Jo. 18. 36; Col. 1. 29.

US-DAUDO, *adv.* diligently, urgently, Lu. 7. 4; 1 Tim. 4. 16; 2 Tim. 1. 17.

Us-DAUDS, *adj.* diligent, 2 Cor. 8. 17, 22.

Us-DREIBAN, *vb.* to drive out, send away, Mat. 9. 25; Mk. 5. 10; 6. 13.

Us-DRIUSAN, *vb.* to fall out, fall away, Gal. 5. 4; to fail, Rom. 9. 6.

Us-DRUSTS, *str. sb. f.* a falling away, a hollow way, rough way, Lu. 3. 5.

Us-FAIRINS, *adj.* blameless, Phil. 3. 6.

Us-FARTHO, *wk. sb. f.* a faring out, a journey out, egress; *hence* usfarthon gataujan us skipa, to suffer shipwreck, 2 Cor. 11. 25.

Us-FILH, *str. sb. n.* a hiding altogether, a burial, Mat. 27. 7; Mk. 14. 8.

Us-FILHAN, *vb.* to hide completely, bury, Lu. 9. 59, 60.

Us-FILMEI, *wk. sb. f.* amaze, Mk. 16. 8; Lu. 5. 26.

Us-FILMS, *adj.* amazed, Mk. 1. 22; Lu. 9. 43.

Us-FLAUGJAN: see *Appendix*.

Us-FODEINS, *str. sb. f.* food, nourishment, 1 Tim. 6. 8.

Us-FRAISAN, *vb.* to tempt greatly, tempt, 1 Th. 3. 5.

Us-FRATWJAN, *vb.* to make wise, 2 Tim. 3. 15. [*For* us-frathwjan?] *From* frathjan.

Us-FULLEINS, *str. sb. f.* fulness, Rom. 13. 10; Gal. 4. 4; Eph. 1. 10.

Us-FULLJAN, *vb.* to fill completely, fill up, fill, fulfil, Mat. 5. 17; Lu. 1. 23; Jo. 7. 8.

Us-FULLNAN, *vb.* to become full, to be filled, to be fulfilled, Mat. 8. 17; Mk. 1. 15; Lu. 1. 23.

Us-GAGGAN, *vb.* to go out, come out, go forth, go up, Mat. 5. 26; Mk. 1. 26; Jo. 6. 15, &c.

Us-GAISJAN, *vb.* to make aghast; *hence pass.* to be beside oneself, Mk. 3. 21. *From* geisan.

Us-GASAIHWAN, *vb.* (*pt. t.* us-gasahw) to perceive, Gal. 2. 14. *From* saihwan.

Us-GEISNAN, *vb.* to be aghast, be amazed, Mk. 2. 12; 5. 42; 10. 26.

Us-GIBAN, *vb.* to give away, give, restore, pay, Mat. 5. 26; Mk. 12. 17; Lu. 4. 20.

Us-GILDAN, *vb.* to pay back, render, 1 Th. 5. 15; Lu. 14. 12, 14.

Us-GRABAN, *vb.* to dig out, Mk. 12. 1; to break through, Mk. 2. 4; to pluck out, Gal. 4. 15.

Us-GRUDJA, *wk. adj. only in phr.* us-grudja wairthan, to faint, Lu. 18. 1; 2 Cor. 4. 1; Gal. 6. 9. [*Cf.* E. *grudge*.]

Us-GUTNAN, *vb.* to be poured out, to gush out, Mat. 9. 17; Mk. 2. 22; Lu. 5. 37. [*Cf.* E. *gush*.]

Us-HAFJAN, *vb.* to heave up, lift, take up, Mk. 2. 12; Lu. 5. 24; 6. 20.

Us-HAHAN, *vb. refl.* to hang oneself, Mat. 27. 5.

Us-HAISTS, *adj.* very poor, in great want, 2 Cor. 11. 8 (9).

Us-HAITAN, *vb.* to call forth; *hence* to provoke, Gal. 5. 26.

Us-HAUHJAN, *vb.* to exalt, Mat. 11. 23; Lu. 1. 52; 10. 15.

Us-HAUHNAN, *vb.* to be exalted, be glorified, 2 Th. 1. 12.

Us-HINTHAN, *vb.* to take captive, lead captive, Eph. 4. 8.

Us-HLAUPAN, *vb.* to leap up, rise quickly, Mk. 10. 50.

Us-HRAINJAN, *vb.* to cleanse out, purge out, 1 Cor. 5. 7.

Us-HRAMJAN, *vb.* to crucify, Mat. 26. 2; Mk. 15. 13; Jo. 19. 6.

Us-HRISJAN, *vb.* to shake out, shake off, Mk. 6. 11.

Us-HULON, *vb.* to hollow out, Mat. 27. 60.

Us-kannjan, *vb.* to make known, Rom. 9. 22; to commend, 2 Cor. 5. 12. *From* kunnan.

Us-keian (Us-kijan?), *vb.* to produce; *pass.* to spring up, Lu. 8. 6.

Us-keinan, *vb.* to spring up, grow up, Lu. 8. 8; to produce, put forth, Mk. 13. 28.

Us-kiusan, *vb.* to choose out; to reject, Mk. 8. 31; Lu. 9. 22; to thrust out, Lu. 4. 29; to test, 1 Th. 5. 21.

Us-kunths, *pp.* (*as from* us-kunnan) made known, evident, manifest, Mat. 9. 33; Lu. 6. 44; Jo. 7. 4.

Us-kwiman, *vb.* to kill, destroy, Mk. 6. 19; 8. 31; Lu. 19. 27. *Cf.* us-kwistjan.

Us-kwiss, *str. sb. f.* an out-speaking; *hence* an accusation, charge, Tit. 1. 6.

Us-kwistjan, *vb.* to destroy, kill, Mk. 3. 4; 9. 22; 12. 9. *Cf.* us-kwiman.

Us-kwithan, *vb.* to proclaim, Mk. 1. 45.

Us-lagjan, *vb.* to lay on, to lay upon, Mk. 14. 46; Lu. 9. 62; 15. 5; Jo. 7. 30. *From* ligan.

Us-laisiths, *pp.* instructed, Eph. 4. 21; 1 Th. 4. 9.

Us-laubjan, *vb.* to permit, suffer, Mat. 8. 21; Mk. 5. 13; Lu. 8. 32; to command, Mat. 27. 58.

Us-lauseins, *str. sb. f.* an out-loosing, deliverance, redemption, Lu. 1. 68; Eph. 4. 30. *From* liusan.

Us-lausjan, *vb.* to loosen out, pluck up, Lu. 17. 6; to deliver, 2 Th. 3. 2; *refl.* to make oneself mean, Phil. 2. 7.

Us-leithan, *vb.* to come out, go out, Mat. 8. 28; Mk. 5. 21; Jo. 7. 3; to pass away, Mat. 5. 18.

Us-letan, *vb.* to leave out, shut out, exclude, Gal. 4. 17.

Us-litha, *wk. sb. m.* one with useless limbs, a paralytic person, Mat. 8. 6; 9. 2; Mk. 2. 3; Lu. 5. 18.

Us-lukan, *vb.* to unlock, open, Jo. 9. 14; 10. 3; Lu. 2. 23; to unsheathe (a sword), Mk. 14. 47; Jo. 18. 10.

Us-luknan, *vb.* to become unlocked, to be opened, to open, Mat. 9. 30; Lu. 1. 64; Jo. 9. 10.

Us-lukns, *adj.* unlocked, opened, Mk. 1. 10.

Us-luks *or* Us-luk, *sb.* an opening, Eph. 6. 19.

Us-lunein; *see* Us-sauneins.

Us-luston, *vb.* to deprive of one's desire, to deceive, Eph. 5. 6. [*Unless we read* us-luto.]

Us-luton, *vb.* to deceive, 1 Tim. 2. 14; Rom. 7. 11; 2 Cor. 11. 3. *From* liutan.

Us-maitan, *vb.* to cut away, cut off, Mat. 7. 19; Lu. 3. 9; Rom. 11. 22.

Us-managnan, *vb.* to abound exceedingly, 2 Cor. 8. 2.

Us-merjan, *vb.* to speak out, proclaim, Mat. 9. 31.

Us-mernan, *vb.* to be proclaimed, get noised abroad, Lu. 5. 15.

Us-met, *str. sb. n.* manner of life, 'conversation', Eph. 4. 22; 1 Tim. 4. 12; 2 Tim. 3. 10; commonwealth, Eph. 2. 12. *From* mitan.

Us-mitan, *vb.* to live as citizens, to behave, 2 Cor. 1. 12; Eph. 2. 3; Phil. 1. 27; — uswiss usmitan, to live dissolutely, to err, 2 Tim. 2. 18.

Us-niman, *vb.* to take away, Mk. 4. 15; 6. 29; to take, Mat. 8. 17; 27. 9; Lu. 17. 34.

Us-raisjan, *vb.* to awake, Lu. 8. 24. *See* ur-raisjan.

Us-rumnan, *vb.* to be enlarged, 2 Cor. 6. 11. *See* ur-rumnan.

Us-saihwan, *vb.* to look up, Mk. 7. 34; to regain one's sight

Mat. 11. 5; Mk. 8. 25; to look on, Mk. 3. 5.

Us-sakan, *vb.* to communicate to, make to participate in, Gal. 2. 2.

Us-saljan, *vb.* to stay as a guest, Lu. 19. 7.

Us-sandjan, *vb.* to send out, send forth, Mat. 9. 38; Mk. 1. 43. *From* sinthan.

Us-sateins, *str. sb. f.* nature, Eph. 2. 3. [*A gloss to* wistai.] *From* sitan.

Us-satjan, *vb.* to set on, place upon, Lu. 19. 35; to set, plant, Mk. 12. 1; Lu. 17. 6; to send out, Lu. 10. 2.

Us-sauneins, *str. sb. f.* reconciliation, Skeir. 1. 6. [*But we should read* us-luneiп, redemption.]

Us-siggwan, *vb.* to read, Mk. 2. 25; Lu. 6. 3; 10. 26.

Us-sindo, *adv.* especially, Philem. 16.

Us-sitan, *vb.* to sit up, Lu. 7. 15.

Us-skawjan, *vb. pass.* or *refl.* to awake, re-awake, 1 Cor. 15. 34; 2 Tim. 2. 26.

Us-skaws, *adj.* wakeful;— us-skaws wisan, to awake, 1 Th. 5. 8.

Us-sokjan, *vb.* to seek out, search, Jo. 7. 52; to judge, 1 Cor. 4. 3; 9. 3; 14. 24.

Us-spillon, *vb.* to tell out, to publish, Lu. 8. 39; to relate, Lu. 9. 10.

Us-standan, *vb.* to stand up, rise up, Mat. 9. 9; Mk. 1. 35; Lu. 1. 39; to go out, Mk. 6. 1; to rise again, Mk. 8. 31.

Us-stass, *str. sb. f.* a rising up, resurrection, Mk. 12. 18; Jo. 11. 24; a rising again, Lu. 2. 34.

Us-steigan, *vb.* to mount up, go up, Mk. 3. 13; Lu. 5. 19; Jo. 6. 62; *see also* Jo. 6. 17.

Us-stiggan, *vb.* to pluck out, put out, Mat. 5. 29.

Us-stiurei, *wk. sb. f.* excess, riot, Eph. 5. 18; Tit. 1. 6.

Us-stiuriba, *adv.* riotously, Lu. 15. 13.

Us-taikneins, *wk. sb. f.* a proof, token, 2 Cor. 8. 24; Phil. 1. 28; a shewing, Lu. 1. 80.

Us-taiknjan, *vb.* to give a token of, shew, Rom. 9. 22; to appoint, Lu. 10. 1; 1 Cor. 4. 9; brotheigana us-taiknjan, to cause to triumph, 2 Cor. 2. 14.

Us-tauhei, *wk. sb. f.* a making perfect, perfecting, Eph. 4. 12. [*But read* us-tauhtai.]

Us-tauhts, *str. sb. f.* a completion, performance, Lu. 1. 45; perfection, Col. 3. 14; end, Rom. 10. 4. *From* tiuhan.

Us-thriutan, *vb.* to threaten, use despitefully, Mat. 5. 44; to trouble, Mk. 14. 6; Lu. 18. 5.

Us-throtheins, *str. sb. f.* exercise, 1 Tim. 4. 8.

Us-throthjan, *vb.* to exercise; *pass.* to be accustomed, to be well instructed, Phil. 4. 12.

Us-thulains, *str. sb. f.* patience, Col. 1. 11; patient waiting for, 2 Th. 3. 5.

Us-thulan, Us-thuljan, *vb.* to have patience, put up with, Rom. 12. 12; 2 Cor. 11. 1; to forbear, 1 Th. 3. 1; 2 Tim. 2. 24.

Us-thwahan, *vb.* to wash, Lu. 5. 2; Jo. 13. 12, 14.

Us-tiuhan, *vb.* to lead out, Mk. 1. 12; 8. 23; to finish, Mat. 10. 23; Lu. 4. 2; to pay (tribute), Rom. 13. 6.

Us-wagjan, *vb.* to stir up, excite, 2 Cor. 9. 2; to toss about, Eph. 4. 14. *From* wigan.

Us-wahsans, *pp. from* us-wahsjan, grown up, of full age, Jo. 9. 21.

Us-WAHSJAN, *vb.* to wax to one's full size; *in pp.* us-wahsans.
Us-WAHSTS, *str. sb. f.* a waxing out, increase, Eph. 4. 16.
Us-WAIRPAN, *vb.* to cast out, Mat. 7. 22; 8. 12; Mk. 5. 40; to reject, Mk. 12. 10; to cast off, Rom. 13. 12; to cast upon, Lu. 19. 35.
Us-WAKJAN, *vb.* to wake up, awake from sleep, Jo. 11. 11. *From* wakan.
Us-WALTEINS, *str. sb. f.* a subverting, 2 Tim. 2. 14; ruin, Lu. 6. 49. *From* waltjan.
Us-WALTJAN, *vb.* to overturn, overthrow, Mk. 11. 15; 2 Tim. 2. 18; to subvert, Tit. 1. 11.
Us-WALUGJAN, *vb.* to carry about, turn about, Eph. 4. 14. *[See* us-flaugjan *in the Appendix.]*
Us-WANDI, *str. sb. n.* a turning aside, Eph. 4. 14. *From* windan. *[But we should read* uswandeinai, *as if from* us-wandeins.*]*
Us-WANDJAN, *vb.* to turn aside, 1 Tim. 1. 6; to turn oneself away, Mat. 5. 42. *From* windan.
Us-WAURHTS, *str. sb. f.* justice, righteousness, 2 Cor. 9. 9, 10.
Us-WAURHTS, *adj.* just, righteous, Mat. 9. 13; Mk. 2. 17; Lu. 14. 14; — us-waurthana domjan, to justify, Mat. 11. 19; Lu. 10. 29.
Us-WAURKJAN, *vb.* to work mightily, to work, Eph. 6. 13; Col. 1. 29.
Us-WAURPA, *str. sb. f.* a casting away, Rom. 11. 15; a thing cast away, 1 Tim. 4. 4; an outcast, 'one born out of due time', 1 Cor. 15. 8.
Us-WEIHS, *adj.* unholy, profane, 1 Tim. 1. 9; 4. 7; 2 Tim. 2. 16.
Us-WENA, *adj.* without hope, Eph. 4. 19; — ni waibtais uswenans (*lit.* not expecting nothing), expecting nothing, Lu. 6. 35. *[See* S.; G. & L. *wrongly omit the negative force of* us.*]*
Us-WINDAN, *vb.* to wind in and out, to plait, Mk. 15. 17; Jo. 19. 2.
Us-WISS, *adj.* loose, dissolute, 2 Tim. 2. 18; *see* us-mitan. *From* widan.
Us-WISSI, *str. sb. n.* looseness, dissoluteness, vanity, Eph. 4. 17. *From* widan.
UT, *adv.* out, Mat. 9. 32; Mk. 11. 19; Jo. 18. 29.
UTA, *adv.* out, without, Mat. 26. 69; Mk. 1. 45; 3. 31.
UTANA, *adv. and prep. with gen.* out, out of, Mk. 8. 23; Jo. 9. 22; — sa utana unsar manna, our outer man, 2 Cor. 4. 16.
UTATHRO, *adv.* from without, Mk. 7. 15, 18.
UT-BAIRAN, *vb.* to bear out, carry out, Lu. 7. 12.
UT-GAGGAN, *vb.* to go out, come out, Mk. 7. 15; Jo. 10. 9.
UZ-ETA, *wk. sb. m.* a manger (*lit.* a thing to eat out of), Lu. 2. 7, 12, 16. *From* us *and* itan.
UZ-ON, *pt. t. of* us-anan, q. v.
UZ-U, UZ-UH, (*comp. of* us *and the enclitic* u *or* uh), whether from, Mk. 11. 30; — uz-uh allis, for out, Lu. 6. 45.

W (Y).

W, the 21st letter of the Gothic alphabet. As a numeral, 400. It is both a consonant and a vowel. As a consonant, it seems altogether equivalent to the English *w*; as a vowel, it resembles the Welsh *w*, or *oo* in *moon*; thus *triggws* would be pronounced *tring-oos*. [*German editors represent this letter by* v, *and in some Greek words, where it has a vowel sound, write* y, *as in* byssus, *which might well be written* bwssus.]

Waddjus*, *str. sb. m.* a wall; *in comp.* baurgs-, grundu-, mithgarda-. [A. S. *wåh*; *cf.* E. *wattle*.]

Wadi, *str. sb. n.* a pledge, earnest, 2 Cor. 1. 22; 5. 5; Eph. 1. 14. *Der.* wadja-bokos, ga-wadjon. *From* widan. [O. E. *wed*.]

Wadja-bokos, *sb. pl.* (*lit.* pledgebooks), a bond, handwriting, Col. 2. 14.

Waggari, *str. sb. n.* a pillow, Mk. 4. 38. [*Cf.* O. E. *wang*, the cheek; A. S. *wangere*, a pillow.]

Waggs, *str. sb. m.* a field; *hence* Paradise, 2 Cor. 12. 4. [A. S. *wang*.]

Wagjan, *vb.* to wag, shake, Mat. 11. 7; Lu. 7. 24; 2 Th. 2. 2. *Der.* af-, ga-, in-, us-, ungawagiths. *From* wigan. [G. D. *bewegen*.]

Wahs*, *adj.* weak (?). *Der.* unwahs, q. v. [G. *schwach* (?); E. *weak* (?).]

Wahsjan, *vb.* (*pt. t.* wohs, *pp.* wahsans), to wax, grow, increase, Mat. 6. 28; Mk. 4. 8; Lu. 1. 80. *Der.* ufar-, us-wahsts, us-wahsans, wahstus. [G. *wachsen*; D. *wassen*.]

Wahstus, *str. sb. m.* a waxing, growth, increase, stature, Lu. 2. 52; 19. 3; Mat. 6. 27; Eph. 4. 13. *From* wahsjan.

Wahtwo, *wk. sb. f.* watch, Lu. 2. 8. *From* wakan.

Wai, *interj.* woe! Mk. 13. 17; Lu. 6. 24; 10. 13. *Der.* wai-dedja, wai-fairhwjan, waja-merjan, waja-merei, waja-mereins. [Gk. οὐαί; Lat. *væ*.]

Waian, *vb.* (*pt. t.* waiwo, *pp.* waians), to blow (as the wind does), Mat. 7. 25; Jo. 6. 18. [G. *wehen*.]

Waibjan*, *vb.* to weave, wind. *Der.* bi-waibjan. *From* weiban.

Wai-dedja, *wk. sb. m.* a woedoer, evil-doer, malefactor, robber, Mat. 27. 44; Mk. 11. 17; Lu. 10. 30. *From* wai *and* deds.

Wai-fairhwjan, *vb.* to lament loudly, wail greatly, Mk. 5. 38. *From* wai *and* fairhwus.

Waihjo, *wk. sb. f.* a fighting, contention, 2 Cor. 7. 5. *From* weigan.

Waihsta, *wk. sb. m.* a corner, Mat. 6. 5; Mk. 12. 10; Lu. 20. 17. *Der.* waihsta-stains.

Waihsta-stains, *str. sb. m.* a corner-stone, Eph. 2. 20.

Waihts, *str. sb. f.* (*also* waiht, *neut.*), a whit, a thing, Lu. 1. 1; a whit, slight appearance, 1 Th. 5. 22; — in thizozei waihtais, for this cause, Eph. 3. 1; — ni waiht *or* waiht ni, no whit, naught, nothing, not at all, Mat. 10. 26; 27. 12. [E. *whit, aught; cf. naught, not.*]

WAILA, *adv.* well, Mk. 1. 11; 7. 6; 12. 28; — waila frathjan, to think soberly, Rom. 12. 3; — waila hugjan, to agree, Mat. 5. 25; — waila kwithan, to speak well of, praise, Lu. 6. 26; — waila merjan, to proclaim, to preach the gospel, Mat. 11. 5; 2 Cor. 1. 19; — waila wisan, to fare well, be merry, Lu. 15. 23. *See also* waila-kwiss, waila-mereins, waila-wizns. [G. *wohl*; D. *wel*.]

WAILA-DEDS, *str. sb. f.* a benefit, 1 Tim. 6. 2.

WAILA-KWISS, *str. sb. f.* a well-saying, blessing, 2 Cor. 9. 5. *From* kwithan.

WAILA-MEREINS, *str. sb. f.* good report, 2 Cor. 6. 8; preaching the gospel, 1 Cor. 1. 21. *From* merjan.

WAILA-MERJAN; *see* WAILA.

WAILA-MERS, *adj.* of good report, Phil. 4. 8.

WAILA-WIZNS, *str. sb. f.* food, Skeir. 7. 13. *See* wizon.

WAINAGS, WAINAHS, *adj.* unhappy, miserable, wretched, Rom. 7. 24. *Perhaps from* wai.

WAINEI, *adv.* if only, would that, 1 Cor. 4. 8; 2 Cor. 11. 1; Gal. 5. 12.

WAIPJAN*, *vb.* to bind. *Der.* faur-waipjan. *Cf.* weipan.

WAIPS, *str. sb. m.* a crown, Jo. 19. 5; 1 Cor. 9. 25; Phil. 4. 1. *From* weipan. [E. *wisp*.]

WAIR, *str. sb. m.* a man, Mat. 7. 24; Mk. 6. 20; Lu. 7. 20. [A. S. *wer*; Lat. *vir*; *cf.* E. *wertwolf*.]

WAIRA-LEIKO, *adv.* in a manly manner, 1 Cor. 16. 13.

WAIRDUS, *str. sb. m.* a host, Rom. 16. 23. [G. *wirth*; D. *waard*.]

WAIRILO, *wk. sb. f.* a lip, Mk. 7. 6; 1 Cor. 14. 21. [A. S. *weler*.]

WAIRPAN, *vb. (pt. t.* warp, *pl.* waurpum, *pp.* waurpans, *with acc. and dat.; also with preps.* af, ana, in); to cast, Mat. 5. 29; Mk. 1. 16; 4. 26; to throw, let down (a net), Lu. 5. 5; to cast stones, stone, Jo. 10. 31; *cf.* Mk. 12. 4. *Der.* at-, af-, ga-, inn-, fra-, us-, us-waurpa. [E. *warp*; G. *werfen*; D. *werpen*.]

WAIRS, *adv.* worse, Mk. 5. 26; *also* wairsiza, worser, worse, Mat. 9. 16; 27. 64.

WAIRTHABA, *adv.* worthily, Eph. 4. 1; Phil. 1. 27; Col. 1. 10.

WAIRTHAN, *vb. (pt. t.* warth, *pl.* waurthum, *pp.* waurthans), to become, to happen, come to pass, Mat. 5. 18; Lu. 1. 14; to be, Mat. 5. 22; Jo. 10. 16; *also as auxiliary verb*, Mat. 8. 24, &c. *Der.* fra-wairthan, ga-wairthi, ga-wairtheigs, gaga-wairthjan, gaga-wairthnan. *Cf.* wairths. [G. *werden*; D. *worden*; O. E. *worth*].

WAIRTHIDA, *str. sb. f.* worth, worthiness, sufficiency, 2 Cor. 3. 5; Skeir. 5. 23.

WAIRTHON, *vb.* to reckon the worth of, value, Mat. 27. 9.

WAIRTHS, -wards. *Der.* ana-, and-, jaind-, withra-, fram-wairthis.

WAIRTHS, *adj.* worth, worthy, Mat. 8. 8; Mk. 1. 7; Lu. 3. 16; — wairthana briggan, to make worthy, 2 Cor. 3. 6. *See next word.*

WAIRTHS, *str. sb. m.* worth, a price, high sum of money, 1 Cor. 7. 23. *Der.* wairths, wairthaba, un-wairthaba, wairthida, and-wairthi, wairthon. [E. *worth*; G. *werth*; D. *waarde*.]

WAIT, I know, he knows; *from* weitan.

WAITEI, *adv.* whether, perhaps, Jo. 18. 35; 1 Cor. 16. 6.

WAJA-MEREI, *wk. sb. f.* blasphemy, Jo. 10. 33. *See next word.*

WAJA-MEREINS, *str. sb. f.* evil report, 2 Cor. 6. 8; blasphemy, Mat. 26. 65; Mk. 7. 22; 14. 64.

WAJA-MERJAN, *vb.* to blaspheme, Mat. 9. 3; Mk. 3. 28; 15. 29.

WAKAN, *vb.* (*pt. t.* wok, *pp.* wokans), to wake, watch, 1 Cor. 16. 13; Col. 4. 2; 1 Th. 5. 6. *Der.* du-, thairh-; us-wakjan, ga-waknan, wahtwo, wokains. [G. *wachen;* D. *waken.*]

WALDAN, *vb.* to wield, govern; garda waldan, to guide a house, 1 Tim. 5. 14; — garda waldands, householder, Mat. 10. 25; Lu. 14. 21; (2) to make proper use of, be thrifty with, be content with, Lu. 3. 14. *Der.* ga-, all-waldands, waldufni. [E. *wield;* G. *walten.*]

WALDUFNI, *str. sb. n.* power, might, authority, Mat. 7. 29; 8. 9; Mk. 1. 22. *From* waldan.

WALEINS*, *sb.*; *see* ga-waleins.

WALIS, *adj.* chosen, true, Phil. 4. 3; 1 Tim. 1. 2; Tit. 1. 4; beloved, Col. 3. 12; 2 Tim. 2. 1. *Der.* ga-walis. *From* waljan.

WALJAN, *vb.* to choose, Phil. 1. 22; 2 Cor. 5. 8. *Der.* ga-waljan, ga-waleins, walis, ga-walis. [G. *wählen;* O. E. & Sc. *wale.*]

WALTJAN, *vb.* to beat upon, dash against, Mk. 4. 37. *Der.* us-waltjan, us-walteins. [A. S. *wealtian;* *cf.* A. S. *wealcan;* E. *walk;* G. *wälzen.*]

WALUGJAN*, *vb.* to reel about; *in comp.* us-walugjan. [*Cf.* A. S. *wealtian.*]

WALUS, *str. sb. m.* a staff, Lu. 9. 3.

WALWISON, *vb.* to wallow, Mk. 9. 20.

WALWJAN*, *vb.* to roll. *Der.* at-, af-, faur-, walwison. [Lat. *volvere;* A. S. *wealwian;* E. *wallow.*]

WAMBA, *str. sb. f.* the belly, womb, Mk. 7. 19; Lu. 1. 15; 2. 21; Tit. 1. 12. [G. *wamme.*]

WAMM, *str. sb.* (*n.* ?) a spot, Eph. 5. 27. *Der.* ga-wamms, un-wamms, un-wammei, ana-wammjan. *From* wimman. [O. E. *wem.*]

WAMMS*, *adj.* spotted; *in comp.* ga-, un-.

WANAINS, *str. sb. f.* a waning, diminishing, Rom. 11. 12.

WANDEINS*, *sb.* a wending, turning; *in comp.* ga-wandeins.

WANDJAN, *vb.* to wend, turn, Mat. 5. 39; *refl.* to turn one-oneself about, Lu. 7. 9. *Der.* af-, at-, bi-, ga-, in-, us-; ga-wandeins, us-wandi. *From* windan.

WANDUS, *sb. m.* a wand, rod, 2 Cor. 11. 25.

WANINASSUS, *str. sb. m.* a waning, defect, that which is lacking, 1 Cor. 16. 17; 1 Th. 3. 10.

WANS, *adj.* waning, lacking, wanting, Tit. 1. 5; — wan wisan, to lack, Mk. 10. 21; Lu. 18. 22; — fidwortigjus, ainamma wanai, forty save one, 2 Cor. 11. 24. *Der.* waninassus, wanains. [E. *want, wane;* G. *wahn; cf.* E. *vain;* Lat. *vanus.*]

WARDJA, *wk. sb. m.* a guard, Mat. 27. 65.

WARDJAN*, *vb.* to ward (?). *Der.* fra-wardjan. *See* wards.

WARDS*, *sb.* a warder, warden, guardian. *Der.* daura-wards, daura-warda, daura-wardo, wardja, fra-wardjan. [G. *warten.*]

WAREI, *wk. sb. f.* wariness, craftiness, 2 Cor. 4. 2.

WARGITHA, *str. sb. f.* condemnation, Rom. 8. 1; 13. 2; 2 Cor. 3. 9. *See* wargs.

WARGS*, *str. sb. m.* an accursed

man, an evildoer. *Der.* launa-wargs, wargitha, ga-wargjan, ga-wargeins. [A. S. *werig;* O. E. *warie,* to curse.]

WARJAN, *vb.* to bid to beware, to forbid, Mk. 9. 38; 10. 14; Lu. 6. 29. *From* wars.

WARMJAN, *vb.* to warm, cherish, Eph. 5. 29; *refl.* to warm oneself, Mk. 14. 54; Jo. 18. 18.

WARMS*, *adj.* warm. *Der.* warmjan. [G. D. *warm.*]

WARS, *adj.* wary, 1 Th. 5. 6. *Der.* warei, warjan.

WARTH, became, was; *from* wairthan.

WAS, was; *from* wisan.

WASJAN, *vb.* to vest, clothe, Mat. 6. 31; 25. 38; *pp.* wasids, clothed, Mat. 11. 8. *Der.* and-, ga-, ga-waseins, wasti. [Lat. *vestire.*]

WAST, wast; *from* wisan.

WASTI, *str. sb. f.* vesture, clothing, Mat. 5. 40; 9. 20; Mk. 5. 27. *Cf.* wasjan.

WATO, *wk. sb. n.* (*pl.* watna), water, Mat. 8. 32; 10. 42; Mk. 1. 8. [G. *wasser;* E. & D. *water.*]

WAURD, *str. sb. n.* a word, Mat. 5. 37; 7. 24; 8. 16. *Der.* anda-, gabaurthi-, waurda-jiuka, lausawaurds, liugna-waurds, ubilwaurds, anda-waurdi, ga-waurdi, lausa-waurdi, aglaiti-waurdei, dwala-waurdei, lausa-waurdei, filu-waurdei, waurdahs, waurdjan, and-waurdjan, filu-waurdjan, fra-waurdjan. [G. *wort;* D. *woord.*]

WAURDAHS, *adj.* verbal, literal, Skeir. 4. 18.

WAURDA-JIUKEI, *str. sb. f.* a strife about words, 1 Tim. 6. 4.

WAURDEI*, *wk. sb. f.* speech, speaking. *Der.* aglaiti-, dwala-, filu-, lausa-. *See* waurd.

WAURDI*, *str. sb. n.* speech. *Der.* ga-, anda-, lausa-.

WAURDJAN, *vb.* to speak, talk; waurdjan ubil, to speak evil, Mk. 9. 39.

WAURDS*, *adj.* speaking. *Der.* lausa-, liugna-, ubil-.

WAURHTA, wrought. *From* waurkjan.

WAURHTS; *see* waurkjan.

WAURKI*, *str. sb. n.* work. *See* ga-waurki, faihu-ga-waurki.

WAURKJAN, *vb.* (*pt. t.* waurhta, *pl.* waurhtedum, *pp.* waurhts), to work, do, make, Mk. 1. 3; Lu. 3. 4; Jo. 6. 10, &c.; *neut.* to work, become operative, Mk. 6. 14. *Der.* ga-, fair-, fra-, us-; ga-waurki, faihu-ga-waurki, handu-waurhts, unhanduwaurhts, fra-waurhts, us-waurhts, waurstw, waurstwa, alla-waurstwa, ga-waurstwa, un-waurstwo, waurstwei, waurstweigs, waurstwja. [G. *wirken;* D. *werken.*]

WAURMS, *str. sb. m.* a serpent, Lu. 10. 19; 2 Cor. 11. 3. [O. E. *worm;* G. *wurm;* D. *worm.*]

WAURPANS; *pp. of* wairpan.

WAURSTW, *str. sb. n.* a work, deed, Mat. 5. 16; Mk. 14. 6; Jo. 5. 36, &c.; working, energy, Eph. 1. 19; 4. 16. *From* waurkjan.

WAURSTWA, *wk. sb. m.* a worker, workman, labourer, 1 Tim. 5. 18. *Der.* ga-, alla-, unwaurstwo.

WAURSTWEI, *wk. sb. f.* a working, doing, Eph. 4. 19.

WAURSTWEIGS, *adj.* full of work, effectual, 1 Cor. 6. 19; 2 Cor. 1. 6; Gal. 2. 8; 5. 6. *From* waurkjan.

WAURSTWJA, *wk. sb. m.* a workman, labourer, Mat. 9. 37; Mk. 12. 1; Lu. 10. 2; — airthos waurstwja, husbandman, 2 Tim. 2. 6. *Cf.* waurstwa.

WAURTHANS, *pp. of* wairthan.

WAURTS, *str. sb. f.* a wort, a root, Mk. 4. 6; Lu. 3. 9; 8. 13; — uslausjan us waurtim, to pull up by the roots, Lu. 17. 6. [G. *wurzel;* D. *wortel.*]

WEGS, *str. sb. m.* a wagging, violent movement; *hence* a tempest (σεισμός), Mat. 8. 24; raging, violent movement, Lu. 8. 24; *pl.* wegos (*dat. pl.* wegim), waves, Mat. 8. 24; Mk. 4. 37. *Cf.* wigan, wagjan. [G. *woge;* E. *wave.*]

WEHS; *see* WEIHS.

WEIBAN*, *vb.* (*pt. t.* waif, *pl.* webum, *pp.* wibans), to weave. *Der.* bi-waibjan. [G. *weben;* D. *weven.*]

WEIGAN, WEIHAN, *vb.* (*pt. t.* waih, *pl.* wigum, *pp.* wigans), to fight, strive, contend, 1 Cor. 15, 32; 2 Tim. 2. 14. *Der.* and-, waihjo, and-waihjan, wigans. [E. *vie;* A. S. *wig.*]

WEIHA, *wk. sb. m.* a priest; — auhumists weiha, chief priest, Jo. 18. 13. *From* weihs.

WEIHABA, *adv.* holily, 1 Th. 2. 10. *From* weihs.

WEIHAN, *vb.* to consecrate, sanctify, make holy, Jo. 17. 17, 19; 1 Cor. 7. 14. *Der.* ga-weihan, weihnan. *From* weiha.

WEIHAN, *vb.* to strive, contend; *see* weigan.

WEIHITHA, *str. sb. f.* holiness, sanctification, 2 Cor. 7. 1; 1 Th. 3. 13; 4. 3; Eph. 4. 24; 1 Tim. 2. 15.

WEIHNAN, *vb.* to become holy, to be hallowed, Mat. 6. 9. *From* weihan.

WEIHS, *adj.* holy, Mat. 3. 11; 27. 52; Mk. 1. 8, &c.; sanctified, Jo. 17. 19. *Der.* weihaba, weiha, weihan, ga-weihan, weihnan, weihitha, us-weihs. [A. S. *wig.*]

WEIHS, *str. sb. n.* a wick, *i. e.* a town, village, Mk. 6. 6; 8. 23; Jo. 7. 42; the country, Lu. 8. 34. [A. S. *wic;* Lat. *vicus.*]

WEIN, *str. sb. n.* wine, Mat. 9. 17; Mk. 2. 22; Lu. 1. 15. *Der.* weina-basi, weina-gards, weina-tains, weina-triu, wein-drugkja, wein-nas. [G. *wein;* D. *wijn.*]

WEINA-BASI, *str. sb. n.* a wineberry, grape, Mat. 7. 16; Lu. 6. 44.

WEINA-GARDS, *str. sb. m.* a vineyard, Mk. 12. 1; Lu. 20. 9.

WEINA-TAINS, *str. sb. m.* a vinebranch, Jo. 15. 4.

WEINA-TRIU, *str. sb. n.* a vine-tree, vine, Jo. 15. 1; *pl.* a vineyard, 1 Cor. 9. 7.

WEIN-DRUGKJA, *wk. sb. m.* a winedrinker, wine-bibber, Lu. 7. 34. *From* drigkan.

WEIN-NAS, *str. sb. m.* a drunkard, 1 Tim. 3. 3; Tit. 1. 7. [*But* Uppström *reads* weinuls.]

WEIPAN, *vb.* (*pt. t.* waip, *pp.* wipans), to crown, 2 Tim. 2. 5. *Der.* waips, wipja, faur-waipjan. [*Cf.* E. *wipe* (?).]

WEIS, we; *from* ik; *cf.* wit. *See* Mat. 6. 12; 9. 14, &c. [G. *wir;* D. *wij;* E. *we.*]

WEIS*, *adj.* wise, prudent. *Der.* hindar-, unhindar-, un-, unfaur-fulla-, bindar-weisei, ga-weison, fulla-weisjan, ga-fulla-weisjan. *Cf.* weitan, witan. [G. *weise;* D. *wijs.*]

WEITAN*, *vb.* (*pt. t.* wait, *pl.* witum, *pp.* witans), to see, *whence* witan, *vb.* (*pres.* wait) to know; *cf.* Gk. οἶδα *from* ἰδεῖν. *Der.* in-, fra-; id-weit, fra-weit;

id-weitjan, fair-waitjan, fair-weitl, weit-wods; *and see* witan. [Lat. *videre*; *cf*. E. *eye-wit-ness*.]

WEIT-WODEI, *wk. sb. f.* witness, 2 Cor. 1. 12; 2 Th. 1. 10; Tit. 1. 13. *See next word.*

WEIT-WODEINS, *str. sb. f.* witness, Skeir. 6. 19.

WEIT-WODI, *str. sb. n.* witness, testimony, 2 Tim. 2. 2.

WEIT-WODITHA, *str. sb. f.* (*spelt* weit-wodida, Jo. 3. 32), witness, testimony, Mat. 27. 13; Mk. 1. 44; 6. 11; — weitwoditha habands, having a witness, being well reported of, 1 Tim. 5. 10.

WEIT-WODJAN, *vb.* to witness, to testify, Lu. 4. 22; Jo. 3. 26; 5. 36; galiug weit-wodjan, to bear false witness, Mk. 14. 56. *Der.* mith-weitwodjan.

WEITWODS, *str. sb. m.* a witness, Mat. 26. 65; Mk. 14. 63; 2 Cor. 1. 23.

WENJAN, *vb.* to ween, hope, expect, Lu. 6. 34; Jo. 5. 45; Rom. 15. 12. *Der.* ga-, faura-; *see* wens. [G. *wähnen*; D. *wanen*; E. *ween*.]

WENS, *str. sb. f.* a weening, expectation, hope, Rom. 12. 12; 15. 4; 2 Cor. 1. 6. *Der.* wenjan, ga-wenjan, faura-wenjan, us-wena, un-weniggo. *Cf.* wenjan.

WEPNA, *str. sb. n. pl.* weapons, Jo. 18. 3; 2 Cor. 6. 7; 10. 4. [G. *waffen*, *wappen*; D. *wapen*.]

WEREKA, *wk. sb. m.* a proper name in the Gothic calendar.

WEREINS*, *str. sb. f.* forbearance. *Der.* un-wereins. *See* werjan.

WERJAN*, *vb.* to wear, endure, forbear. *Der.* un-werjan, tuz-werjan, un-wereins. [G. *währen*; E. *wear*.]

WESEI*, *wk. sb. f.* existence, state. *Der.* balwa-wesei.

WESUM, we were. *From* wisan.

WIDAN*, *vb.* (*pt. t.* wath, *pl.* wedum, *pp.* widans), to bind. *Der.* ga-, in-; ga-wiss, dis-wiss, us-wiss, us-wissi, wadi, wadjabokos, ga-wadjon, kuna-weda. [E. *wed*, *withy*; G. *wiede*.]

WIDUWAIRNS, *adj.* orphaned, comfortless, Jo. 14. 18.

WIDUWO, WIDOWO, *wk. sb. f.* a widow, Lu. 2. 37; 4. 25; 7. 12. [G. *wittwe*; D. *weduwe*.]

WIGA-DEINA (*or* WIGA-DEINO), *sb. f.* a thistle, Mat. 7. 16.

WIGAN*, *vb.* (*pt. t.* wag, *pl.* wegum, *pp.* wigans), to make to wag, to move, shake. *Der.* ga-, wagjan, ga-wagjan, un-gawagiths, af-wagjan, in-wagjan, us-wagjan, wegs. [G. *bewegen*.]

WIGANS, *sb. m.* war, Lu. 14. 31. *From* weigan.

WIGS, *str. sb. m.* a way, Mat. 5. 25; 7. 13; 8. 28, &c. *Der.* fram-wigis, wiga-deina (?). [G. & D. *weg*.]

WIKO, *wk. sb. f.* a week, Lu. 1. 8. [*Such seems to be the meaning, and not a* turn; *see* S. *and note in* G. & L.]

WILDA, would; *from* wiljan.

WILJA, *wk sb. m.* the will, Mat. 6. 10; 7. 21; Mk. 3. 35; wish, desire, Rom. 10. 1; *and see* Lu. 2. 14. *From* wiljan.

WILJA-HALTHEI, *wk. sb. f.* a respecting of persons, Eph. 6. 9; Col. 3. 25; 1 Tim. 5. 21. *From* wilja *and* hilthan.

WILJAN, *vb.* irregular (*pres.* wiljau, *pt. t.* wilda, *pl.* wildedum), to will, wish, Mat. 5. 40; 8. 2; Mk. 1. 40; — silba wiljands, of his own accord, 2 Cor. 8. 17. *Der.* wilja, wilja-halthei, ga-wileis, silba-wileis, ana-wiljei. [G. *wollen*; D. *willen*.]

WILJA-RITH, *sb. m.* a proper name in the Neap. document.

WILEIS*, *adj.* willing. *Der.* ga-, silba-.

WILTHEIS, *adj.* wild, uncultivated, Mk. 1. 6; Rom. 11. 17, 24. [G. D. & E. *wild.*]

WILWAN, *vb.* (*pt. t.* walw, *pp.* wulwans), to take by force, Mk. 3. 27; Jo. 6. 15; — wilwands, ravening, Mat. 7. 15. *Der.* dis-, fra-; wilws, wulwa; *and cf.* wulfs.

WILWS, *adj.* extortionate, Lu. 18. 11; 1 Cor. 5. 10, 11.

WIMMAN*, *vb.* to blemish. *Der.* wamm, ga-wamms, un-wamms, un-wammei, ana-wammjan. *See* wamm.

WINDAN*, *vb.* (*pt. t.* wand, *pl.* wundum, *pp.* wundans), to wind. *Der.* bi-, duga-, us-; in-winds, in-winditha; wandjan, af-, at-, bi-, ga-, in-, us-wandjan; ga-wandeins, us-wandi. [G. & D. *winden.*]

WINDS, *str. sb. m.* the wind, Mat. 7. 25; 8. 26; Mk. 4. 37. [G. D. & E. *wind.*]

WINJA, *str. sb. f.* pasture, Jo. 10. 9.

WINNA, *str. sb. f.* (*or* WINNO, *wk. sb. f.*) passion, inordinate affection, Col. 3. 5; *pl.* passions, Rom. 7. 5; Gal. 5. 24. *Cf.* wunns. *From* winnan.

WINNAN, *vb.* (*pt. t.* wann, *pp.* wunnans), to suffer, Mk. 8. 31; 9. 12; Lu. 9. 22; — aglons winnan, to suffer afflictions, 1 Tim. 5. 10. *Der.* ga-, winna, winno, wunns. [A. S. *winnan;* whence E. *win.*]

WINTHI-SKAURO, *wk. sb. f.* a winnowing fan, Lu. 3. 17. *From* winthjan *and* skiuran; *cf.* skura.

WINTHJAN*, *vb.* to winnow. *Der.* winthi-skauro, dis-winthjan. *Cf.* winds. [A. S. *windwian.*]

WINTRUS, *str. sb. m.* a winter, Mk. 13. 18; Jo. 10. 22; a year (*in reckoning*), Mat. 9. 20; Lu. 2. 42; 8. 42. [G. D. E. *winter.*]

WIPJA, WIPPJA, *str. sb. f.* a crown, Mk. 15. 17; Jo. 19. 2. *Cf.* waips. *From* weipan.

WIS*, *adj.* certain. *Der.* un-wis, q. v. [G. *gewiss;* O. E. *Iwis.*]

WIS, *str. sb. n.* a calm, Mat. 8. 26; Mk. 4. 39; Lu. 8. 24. *Cf.* wisan, wizon.

WISAN, *vb.* (*pres.* im, is, ist, sijum, sijuth, sind; *pt. t.* was, wast, was, wesum, wesuth, wesun; *pres. cond.* sijau, *pt. cond.* wesjau) to be, Mat. 6. 30; Mk. 8. 1; Lu. 20. 27, &c.; to dwell, remain, continue, Lu. 10. 7; 19. 5; Jo. 5. 38, &c.; — waila wisan, to be merry, Lu. 15. 23; 16. 19. *Der.* ga-, mithga-, at-, bi-, faura-, in-, mith-, thairh-, ufar-; wists; *cf. also* wis, wizon. [*Cf.* G. *war;* D. E. *was.*]

WISS*, *str. sb. f.* a binding, joining. *Der.* ga-, dis-, us-wiss. *From* widan.

WISSEI*, *wk. sb. f.* knowledge, science. *Der.* mith-wissei. *From* witan.

WISTS, *str. sb. f.* being, existence; *hence* nature, Rom. 11. 24; Gal. 4. 8; Eph. 2. 3. *From* wisan.

WIT, we two; *cf.* ik *and* weis. [A. S. *wit.*]

WITAINS*, *str. sb. f.* a watching; *in comp.* at-witains. *From* witan, to watch.

WITAN (1), *vb.* (*pres.* wait, *pt. t.* wissa), to know, Mat. 6. 8; 9. 4; Mk. 2. 10, &c.; to learn, Gal. 3. 2. *Der.* mith-witan, un-witands, waitei, un-wits, fulla-wits, un-witi, witubni, witoth, drauhti-witoth, witoda-fasteis, witoda-laisareis, witoda-laus, witodeigo, mith-wissei. *Cf* weitan. [G. *wissen;* D. *weten;* E. *wit, weet, wot, wist.*]

WITAN (2), *vb.* (*pt. t.* witaida), to watch, observe, Mat. 27. 54; Mk. 3. 2; Jo. 9. 16; to keep watch, Lu. 2. 8; 2 Cor. 11. 32. *Der.* at-witains. *Cf.* weitan.

WITHON, *vb.* to shake, wag, Mk. 15. 29. [G. *wedeln.*]

WITHRA, *prep. with acc.* over against, against, in return for, in reply to, for; to, towards, near, Mk. 4. 1; Lu. 8. 12; 1 Cor. 13. 12. *Der.* withra-gaggan, withra-gamotjan, withra-wairths. [G. *wider;* D. *weder;* A. S. *wið;* E. *with* in *withstand.*]

WITHRA-GAGGAN, *vb.* to go to meet, Jo. 11. 20.

WITHRA-GAMOTJAN, *vb.* to go to meet, Jo. 12. 13.

WITHRA-WAIRTHS, *adj.* opposite, that which is over against, Mk. 11. 2; Lu. 8. 26; 19. 30;—thata withra-wairtho, contrariwise, Gal. 2. 7. *From* wairthan.

WITHRUS, *str. sb. m.* a wether, a lamb, Jo. 1. 29. [G. *widder.*]

WITI*, *str. sb. n.* wit, knowledge. *Der.* un-witi. [E. *wit.*]

WITODA-FASTEIS, *adj.* a guardian of the law, lawyer, Lu. 7. 30; 10. 25. *From* witoth *and* fastan.

WITODA-LAISAREIS, *str. sb. m.* a teacher of the law, Lu. 5. 17; 1 Tim. 1. 7.

WITODA-LAUS, *adj.* lawless, without law, 1 Cor. 9. 21; 1 Tim. 1. 9. *From* witoth *and* liusan.

WITODEIGO, *adv.* lawfully, 1 Tim. 1. 8; 2 Tim. 2. 5. *From* witoth.

WITOTH, *str. sb. n.* law, Mat. 5. 17; 7. 12; Lu. 2. 22, &c. *Der.* drauhti-witoth, witoda-laisareis, witoda-laus, witoda-fasteis, witodeigo. *From* witan.

WITS*, *adj.* witty, knowing. *Der.* un-wits, fulla-wits. *From* witan.

WITUBNI, *str. sb. n.* knowledge, Rom. 11. 33; 1 Cor. 8. 11.

WITUM, we know; *from* witan.

WIZON, *vb.* to live, 1 Tim. 5. 6. *Cf.* wisan. *Der.* anda-wizn, waila-wizns, ga-wizneigs.

WLAITON, *vb.* to look round about, Mk. 5. 32.

WLEITAN*, *vb.* (*pt. t.* wlait, *pl.* wlitum, *pp.* wlitans), to look. *Der.* anda-wleizns, wlaiton, wlits, wlizjan. [A. S. *wlitan.*]

WLITS, *str. sb. m.* the face, Mk. 14. 65; Jo. 11. 44; 2 Cor. 3. 7; likeness, form, Phil. 2. 7. [A. S. *wlite.*]

WLIZJAN, *vb.* to smite in the face; hence (*like* Gk. ὑπωπιάζειν) to bring into subjection, 1 Cor. 9. 27.

WODS*, *adj.* the root of weitwods (*meaning uncertain*).

WODS, *adj.* mad, possessed, Mk. 5. 15, 16, 18. [G. *wuth;* D. *woede;* O. E. *wood.*]

WOHS, wox, waxed, grew, Lu. 1. 80. *From* wahsjan.

WOKAINS, *str. sb. f.* watching, 2 Cor. 6. 5; 11. 27. *From* wakan.

WOKRS, *str. sb. m.* increase, usury, Lu. 19. 23. *Cf.* wahsjan. [G. *wucher;* D. *woeker;* A. S. *wocer;* O. E. *okyre.*]

WONDON*, *vb.* to wound; *in comp.* ga-wondon, *another spelling of* ga-wundon.

WOPJAN, *vb.* to cry aloud, cry out, call, Mk. 1. 3; Lu. 3. 4; Jo. 11. 28; to call to, address aloud,

Lu. 7. 32. *Der.* at-, uf-. [E. *whoop, weep.*]

WOTHS, WOTHIS, *adj.* good, sweet, pleasant; — dauns wothi, a sweet savour, 2 Cor. 2. 15; Eph. 5. 2.

WRAIKWS, *adj.* wry, crooked, Lu. 3. 5.

WRAK, persecuted; *from* wrikan.

WRAKA, *str. sb. f.* a wreaking (vengeance), persecution, Mk. 10. 30; 2 Tim. 3. 11.

WRAKJA, *str. sb. f.* the same as wraka, Mk. 4. 17; Rom. 8. 35; 2 Th. 1. 4; — wrakja winnan, to suffer persecution, Gal. 6. 12.

WRAKJAN, *vb.* to persecute, Phil. 3. 6. *From* wrikan.

WRAKS, *str. sb. m.* a persecutor, 1 Tim. 1. 13. *From* wrikan.

WRATODUS, *str. sb. m.* a journeying, voyaging, 2 Cor. 11. 26.

WRATON, *vb.* to go, journey, Lu. 2. 41; 8. 1; 1 Cor. 16. 6.

WREKEI, *wk. sb. f.* persecution, 2 Cor. 12. 10. *From* wrikan.

WRIGGAN*, *vb.* to wring, press closely. *Der.* wruggo.

WRIKAN, *vb.* to wreak (anger on), to persecute, Mat. 5. 44; Jo. 15. 20; Rom. 12. 14. *Der.* ga-, fra-; wraks, wraka, wrakja, wrakjan, wrekei. [G. *rächen;* D. *wreken;* E. *wreak.*]

WRISKWAN*, *vb.* to produce fruit, *in comp.* ga-wriskwan, q. v.

WRITHUS, *str. sb. f.* a herd, Lu. 8. 33. [A. S. *wréd,* a wreath, band, flock.]

WRITS, *str. sb. m.* a stroke of a pen, Lu. 16. 17. [*Cf.* E. *write.*]

WROHJAN, *vb.* to accuse, Mat. 27. 12; Mk. 3. 2; Lu. 6. 7; Jo. 5. 45. *Der.* fra-, wrohs. [E. *bewray;* G. *rügen.*]

WROHS, *str. sb. f.* accusation, Jo. 18. 29; 1 Tim. 5. 19.

WRUGGO, *wk. sb. f.* that which compresses *or* encloses, a net, snare, 2 Tim. 2. 26. *From* wriggan.

WULAN, *vb.* to well up, boil; *hence* to be fervent, Rom. 12. 11; to fester, 2 Tim. 2. 17. [A. S. *weallan;* E. *well; cf. boil.*]

WULFILA, *sb.* Ulphilas, Ulfilas.

WULFS, *str. sb. m.* a wolf, Mat. 7. 15; Lu. 10. 3; Jo. 10. 12. [Lat. *vulpes;* G. & D. *wolf.*]

WULLA, *str. sb. f.* wool, Skeir. 3. 16.

WULLAREIS, *str. sb. m.* one who whitens wool, a fuller, Mk. 9. 3. *From* wulla.

WULTHAGS, *adj.* gorgeous, Lu. 7. 35; honourable, 1 Cor. 4. 10; glorious, 2 Cor. 3. 7; Eph. 5. 27; wonderful, strange, Lu. 5. 26. *From* wulthus.

WULTHRIS, *adv. compar.* of more consequence; — ni mais mis wulthris ist, is of no more consequence to me, Gal. 2. 6.

WULTHRS, *str. sb. f.* consequence; ni mais mis wulthrais ist, Gal. 2. 6. (*Another reading; see preceding word.*)

WULTHRS, *adj.* (*compar.* wulthriza) of worth, of consequence; — wulthriza wisan, to be of more worth, Mat. 6. 26.

WULTHUS, *str. sb. m.* glory, Mat. 6. 13; Mk. 8. 38; 10. 37, &c. *Der.* wulthags, wulthris, wulthrs. [A. S. *wuldor.*]

WULWA, *str. sb. f.* robbery, Phil. 2. 6. *From* wilwan.

WUNAN*, *vb.* to be glad. *Der.* unwunands. [*Cf.* G. *wonne;* A. S. *wyn.*]

WUNDON*, *vb.* to wound; *see* ga-wundon. *From* wunds.

WUNDS, *adj.* wounded; — haubith wundan briggan, to wound in the head, Mk. 12. 4. *Der.* wundufni, ga-wundon, ga-wondon.

WUNDUFNI, *str. sb. f.* a wound, a plague, Mk. 3. 10.

WUNNS, *str. sb. f.* affliction, suffering, 2 Tim. 3. 11. *From* winnan.

Y.

Y is sometimes used to denote the vowel sound of W, the Gothic character being the same for both. It is chiefly used in Greek proper names. The sound is that of *oo* in *moon* or in *wool.*

Z.

Z, the seventh letter of the Gothic alphabet. As a numeral, 7.

APPENDIX.

[The following words were accidentally omitted in their proper places.]

AF-GASTOTHANS (*pp. as from* af-gastandan), unsettled, unreasonable, 2 Th. 3. 2. [M. *reads* af ungastothanaim.]

AF-LEITAN, *vb.* to forgive, Mat. 9. 6; Lu. 5. 20; to put away (a wife), Lu. 16. 18; *see* af-letan.

AF-MAUITHS, *pp.* wearied out, Gal. 6. 9. [*Read* af-mauidai, *not* af-maindai.]

AIHTS, *str. sb. f.* possessions, goods, wealth, 1 Cor. 13. 3; 2 Cor. 12. 14. [*Only in the plural.*]

ALL-BRUNSTS; *see* ALA-BRUNSTS.

ANA-HNEIWAN, *vb.* to bend down, Mk. 1. 7.

ANA-KUNNAINS, *str. sb. f.* reading, 2 Cor. 3. 14.

ANA-LAUGNS, *adj.* secret, Mk. 4. 22; Lu. 8. 17; 1 Cor. 4. 5. *From* liugan (1).

ANDA-SET, *str. sb. n.* an abomination, Lu. 16. 15. [*Or it is the neuter of* anda-sets, q. v.]

ANNUH; *see* AN.

ATISKS *or* ATISE, *sb. m. or n.* a cornfield, Mk. 2. 23; Lu. 6. 1.

DAURA-WARDA, *str. sb. f.* a female doorkeeper, Jo. 18. 16.

DAURA-WARDO, *wk. sb. f.* the same; Jo. 18. 17.

DAURA-WARDS, *str. sb. m.* a doorkeeper, porter, Jo. 10. 3; Ezra 2. 42; Nehem. 7. 1.

DRAUHTINASSUS, *str. sb. m.* warfare, 2 Cor. 10. 4.

DRAUHTINON, *vb.* to war, go to war, 1 Cor. 9. 7; 2 Cor. 10. 3; 2 Tim. 2. 4. *From* driugan.

DRAUHTI-WITOTH, *str. sb. n.* fight, warfare, 1 Tim. 1. 18. *From* driugan *and* witoth.

DROBNA, *str. sb. m.* a tumult, 2 Cor. 12. 20.

DROBNAN, *vb.* to be shaken, 2 Th. 2. 2. [*But the reading is uncertain.*]

DUHWE, DUHTHE, DUTHE, DUTHEI, DUTH-THE; *see under* du.

FAIHO (Mk. 10. 23); *see* faihu.

FAIHU-FRIKEI, *wk. sb. f.* covetousness, Mk. 7. 22; Eph. 4. 19; 5. 3.

FAIHU-FRIKS, *adj.* covetous, Lu. 16. 14; 1 Cor. 5. 10; Eph. 5. 5.

FAIHU-GAIRNEI, *sb. f.* 'filthy lucre's sake' (A. V.), covetousness, Tit. 1. 11.

FAIHU-GAIRNS, *adj.* covetous, 2 Tim. 3. 2.

FAIHU-GAWAURKI, *str. sb. m.* gain, 1 Tim. 6. 5.
FAIHU-GEIGAN (*not* faihu-geironjan), *vb.* to covet, Rom. 13. 9.
FAIHU-GEIGO, *sb. f.* covetousness, Col. 3. 5; 1 Tim. 6. 10. *[The form* faihu-geiro *is wrong.]*
FAIHU-SKULA, *wk. sb. m.* a debtor, Lu. 16. 5. *Cf.* dulgis skula, Lu. 7. 41.
FAIHU-THRAIHNS, *str. sb. m.* riches, wealth, Mammon, Lu. 16. 9, 11, 13. *From* threihan.
FAIRRATHRO, *adv.* from far, Mk. 5. 6; 8. 3; 11. 13.
FAUR-DOMEINS, *str. sb. f.* prejudice, partiality, 1 Tim. 5. 21.
FIMFTA-TAIHUNDA, *adj.* fifteenth, Lu. 3. 1.
FLAUHTS, *adj.* arrogant; *read* flauhtai, *not* flautandans, Gal. 5. 26.
FRA-LEWJAN, *vb.* to betray, 2 Tim. 3. 4.
FRAM-ALDROZA, *compar. of* fram-aldrs, q. v.
GABIGJAN, *vb.* to enrich, 2 Cor. 6. 10.
GABIGNAN, *vb.* to be rich, Lu. 1. 53; 2 Cor. 9. 11.
GALIUGA-GUTH, *sb.; pl.* galiuga-guda, false gods, idols, 1 Cor. 8. 10; Eph. 5. 5; Col. 3. 5.
GALIUGA-WEITWODS, *sb. m.* a false witness, Mk. 10. 19; Lu. 18. 20; 1 Cor. 15. 15.
GA-TAURTHS, *str. sb. f.* destruction, 2 Cor. 10. 4; 13. 10. *From* tairan.
GA-WONDON, *vb. for* ga-wundon, q.v.
GILSTRA-MELEINS, *str. sb. f.* (*lit.* a tax-writing), an enrolment for taxation, Lu. 2. 2.
GUTH-BLOSTREIS, *str. sb. m.* a worshipper of God, Jo. 9. 31.
HROPS; *read* hrops, *not* hropi, Eph. 4. 31.
KUNA-WIDA; *read* kuna-widom, *not* kuna-wedom, Eph. 6. 20.
KWAIRRUS; *read* kwairrus, *not* airknis, 1 Tim. 3. 3.
KWITHANO; *a better reading for* kwithlo.
LUN; *a better reading for* saun.
MISSA-DEDS, *str. sb. f.* a misdeed, sin, Mat. 6. 14; Mk. 11. 25; Rom. 11. 11.
MISSA-KWISS, *str. sb. f.* a mis-saying; *hence,* a dissension, Jo. 7. 43; 9. 16; 10. 19.
MISSA-LEIKS, *adj.* various, divers, Mk. 1. 34; Lu. 4. 40; 2 Tim. 3. 6.
MISSA-TAUJANDS, *pt. pres.,* a misdoer, transgressor, Gal. 2. 18.
SAKULS; *a better reading for* sakjis.
UFAR-MAUDEIN; *see* MAUDEINS.
US-FLAUGJAN, *vb.; read* us-flaugidai, *not* us-walujidai.

NOTE. *The above corrections are chiefly from Uppström. He denies the existence of the following words:* — af-mainds; airknis (*read* kwairrus); all-brunsts; ana-kwal (*read* ana-silan); at-bairhtjan (*read* at-augida); biari; faihu-geiro; faihu-geironjan; flautands; ga-bindi (*read* ga-binda); ga-dikis (*read* ga-digis); gairuni (*read* gairnein); ga-sukwon (*read* ga-supon); hropi; kuna-weda; los; nawis (*see* naus); kwithlo; sakjis; saun; uf-munnands; un-gastothans; us-sauneins; us-tauhei; us-walugjan; us-wandi; weinnas.

AN OUTLINE

OF

MŒSO-GOTHIC GRAMMAR.

AN OUTLINE
OF
MŒSO-GOTHIC GRAMMAR.

ALPHABET.

𐌰	a	1	𐌽	n	50
𐌱	b	2	𐌲	j (y)	60
𐌲	g	3	𐌿	u	70
𐌳	d	4	𐍀	p	80
𐌴	e	5	𐍂	r	100
𐌿	kw (kv, q)	6	𐍃	s	200
𐌶	z	7	𐍄	t	300
𐌷	h	8	𐍅	w (v), y	400
𐌸	th (þ)	9	𐍆	f	500
𐌹 ï	i	10	𐍇	ch (x)	600
𐌺	k	20	𐍈	hw (hv, w, wh)	700
𐌻	l	30	𐍉	o	800
𐌼	m	40			

REMARKS. For *kw* Massmann writes *kv*, and Schulze, Uppström, Gabelentz and Löbe, Stamm, and Dr. Bosworth write *q*.

For *th* many editors use the thorn-letter (þ).

For *j*, Dr. Bosworth and Mr. Cockayne write *y*.

For *w*, German editors write *v*.

Ch is the Greek χ, and is sometimes denoted by *x*.

For *hw* Massmann and Stamm write *hv*, Gabelentz and Löbe write *w*, and Dr. Bosworth writes *wh*.

The Roman letters which I have used to replace the Gothic ones will be found very convenient to all who use Massmann's text, as the only change I have made in it is to write *w* for *v*, and consequently *kw*, *hw* for *kv*, *hv*. This one change was well worth making, because *w*, *kw*, *hw* represent the probable sounds of the Gothic letters, which *v*, *kv*, *hv* certainly do not.

ADDITIONAL SIGNS. For the number 90, Ulfilas used a modification of the Greek *koppa*, like the sign for *kw* with the second stroke lengthened; and for 900 he used a sign (↑), resembling a barbed arrow-head, which took the place of the Greek *sampi*.

SOUNDS OF THE LETTERS. Most of the consonants have the same sounds as in English, *g* being always *hard*, like the *g* in *give*. *Ch* is also hard and guttural. Also, *gg*, *gk*, are sounded like *ng*, *nk*, as in Greek; hence *aggilus* is an *angel*, *drigkan* is to *drink*. *J* has the *German* sound, like *j* in the German word *ja*, or the English *y* in *yea*; indeed, *y* would have been used to represent it, but for the fact that this introduces yet another change from Massmann's edition, and *y* is moreover used by German editors to represent the vowel-sound of *w* in some Greek words. This vowel-sound (the Greek υ) I believe to have been like *oo* in *moon*, or, if unaccented, like *oo* in *foot*, with which compare the Welsh sound of *w*. Dr. Bosworth gives it the sound of *oy*, I do not know why. For the vowel-sounds, it seems most convenient to give *a* the sound of *a* in *father*; *e* (which is almost always *long*) has the sound of *a* in *fate*; *i* (generally *short*) is like *i* in *pin*; *o* has the *long* sound of *o* in *note*; *u* is like *u* in *mule* or *bull*. To *au* we may give the sound of *aw* in *law*; to *ai* that of long *i*, as in *pride*, but somewhat broader; to *ei* the sound of *i* in *pride*, whilst *iu* may resemble *ew* in *new*.

DECLENSIONS OF NOUNS.

There are *two* declensions, one called the *strong* or *vowel* declension, the other the *weak* or *consonantal* declension. The latter is distinguished by the insertion of an *n* in many cases, as though this were required to *strengthen* it. The first of these is further subdivided into the A-declension, I-declension, and U-declension, the datives plural of which end in *am* (*om*), *im*, and *um* respectively.

I. STRONG DECLENSION.

A-form.

Thus are declined *m. fisks* (a fish); *f. giba* (a gift); *n. waurd* (a word).

Sing.	Plu.	Sing.	Plu.
N. fisk—*s*	fisk—*os*	N. gib—*a*	gib—*os*
G. fisk—*is*	fisk—*e*	G. gib—*os*	gib—*o*
D. fisk—*a*	fisk—*am*	D. gib—*ai*	gib—*om*
A. fisk	fisk—*ans*	A. gib—*a*	gib—*os*
V. fisk	fisk—*os*	V. gib—*a*	gib—*os*

Sing.	Plu.
N. waurd	waurd—*a*
G. waurd—*is*	waurd—*e*
D. waurd—*a*	waurd—*am*
A. waurd	waurd—*a*
V. waurd	waurd—*a*

I-form.

Thus are declined *m. balgs* (a bag); *f. ansts* (grace).

Sing.	Plu.	Sing.	Plu.
N. balg—*s*	balg—*eis*	N. anst—*s*	anst—*eis*
G. balg—*is*	balg—*e*	G. anst—*ais*	anst—*e*
D. balg—*a*	balg—*im*	D. anst—*ai*	anst—*im*
A. balg	balg—*ins*	A. anst	anst—*ins*
V. balg	balg—*eis*	V. anst	anst—*eis*

U-form.

Thus are declined *m. sunus* (a son); *f. handus* (hand); *n. faihu* (fee, property).

Sing.	Plu.	Sing.	Plu.
N. sun—*us*	sun—*jus*	N. hand—*us*	hand—*jus*
G. sun—*aus*	sun—*iwe*	G. hand—*aus*	hand—*iwe*
D. sun—*au*	sun—*um*	D. hand—*au*	hand—*um*
A. sun—*u*	sun—*uns*	A. hand—*u*	hand—*uns*
V. sun—*au (u)*	sun—*jus*	V. hand—*au (u)*	hand—*jus*

	Sing.	Plu.
N.	faih—*u*	(*wanting*).
G.	faih—*aus*	
D.	faih—*au*	
V.	faih—*u*	
A.	faih—*u*	

It will be observed that *sunus* and *handus* are declined *exactly alike*; and *faihu* follows them closely.

NOTES. 1. To the A-form belong some masculine words in -*jis* and -*eis*, in which a *j* is introduced in the stem in some cases. They are declined thus, taking as examples *harjis*, a host; *hairdeis*, a shepherd.

Sing.	Plu.	Sing.	Plu.
N. harj—*is*	harj—*os*	N. haird—*eis*	hairdj—*os*
G. harj—*is*	harj—*e*	G. haird—*eis*	hairdj—*e*
D. harj—*a*	harj—*am*	D. hairdj—*a*	hairdj—*am*
A. hari	harj—*ans*	A. haird	hairdj—*ans*
V. hari	harj—*os*	V. haird	hairdj—*os*

2. Some variations are found from the above forms; thus *sunaus* is nom. sing. in Lu. 4. 3; *dauthus* is gen. sing. in Lu. 1. 79; *wegim* (not *wegam*) is the dat. plu. of *wegs* in Mat. 8. 24.

3. Neuters in *i*, such as *kuni* (kin), are declined like *waurd*, with a change of the *i* into *j* in the gen. and dat. sing., and in the plural. Thus:— *kuni, kunj-is, kunj-a, kuni, kuni*; pl. *kunj-a, -e, -am, -a, -a*. Similarly, in masculines in *-ius* and neuters in *-iu*, as *thius* (a servant), *kniu* (a knee), the *u* becomes a *w* in the same cases.

4. In like manner the feminine nouns *bandi* (a band), *sunja* (truth), are to be compared with *giba*, and are declined:— *bandi, bandj-os, -ai, bandi, bandi*; pl. *band-jos, -o, -om, -os, -os*; also *sunj-a, -os, -ai, &c.*

5. *Brothar, fadar, dauhtar, swistar* (brother, father, daughter, sister) resemble in some cases the declination of *sunus*. They are thus declined:

	Sing.	Plu.
N.	brothar	brothr—*jus*
G.	brothr—*s*	brothr—*e*
D.	brothr	brothr—*um*
A.	brothar	brothr—*uns*
V.	brothar	brothr—*jus*

6. The present participles of verbs, when used as substantives, partly follow the declension of *fisks*; such as *gibands* (a giver), *daupjands* (the Baptist). But the dat. sing. is *giband*, not *gibanda*, and the plural is *giband-s, -e, -am, -s, -s*. And see p. 294.

7. *Menoths* (a month) somewhat resembles *gibands;* we find *sing. nom.* menoths, *gen.* menoths, *dat.* menoth, *pl. dat.* menothum, *acc.* menoths.

8. The feminine nouns *baurgs* (a town), *alhs* (temple), *brusts* (breast), *mitaths* (measure), *dulths* (feast), *miluks* (milk), *nahts* (night), *spaurds* (stadium), *waihts* (a whit, thing), are anomalous, being but slightly inflected; as *sing. nom. and gen.* baurgs, *dat., acc., voc.* baurg; *pl. nom. acc. voc.* baurgs, *gen.* baurge, *dat.* baurgim. *Dulths* and *waihts* are also found declined as *ansts*, and the *dat. pl.* nahtam occurs in Mk. 5. 5.

9. Other slight exceptions are best observed by practice.

II. WEAK OR CONSONANTAL DECLENSION.

The typical forms are those of *m.* hana (a cock); *f.* tuggo, managei (tongue, multitude); *n.* hairto (a heart); wato (water).

A. Masculine Nouns.

N. han—*a*		*Pl.* han—*ans*	
G. han—*ins*		han—*ane*	
D. han—*in*		han—*am*	
A. han—*an*		han—*ans*	
V. han—*a*		han—*ans*	

B. Feminine Nouns.

N. tugg—*o*	*Pl.* tugg—*ons*	manag—*ei*	*Pl.* manag—*eins*
G. tugg—*ons*	tugg—*ono*	manag—*eins*	manag—*eino*
D. tugg—*on*	tugg—*om*	manag—*ein*	manag—*eim*
A. tugg—*on*	tugg—*ons*	manag—*ein*	manag—*eins*
V. tugg—*o*	tugg—*ons*	manag—*ei*	manag—*eins*

C. Neuter Nouns.

N. hairt—*o*	*Pl.* —*ona*	wat—*o*	*Pl.* —*na*
G. hairt—*ins*	—*ane*	wat—*ins*	—*ne*
D. hairt—*in*	—*am*	wat—*in*	—*nam*
A. hairt—*o*	—*ona*	wat—*o*	—*na*
V. hairt—*o*	—*ona*	wat—*o*	—*na*

The pl. dat. *watnam* is to be considered irregular; it should rather be *watam*.

REMARKS. The chief exceptions are *manna* (a man), *fon* (fire); which are thus declined. Manna, mans, mann, mannan, manna; pl. nom. and acc. both manns *and* mannans, gen. manne, dat. mannam. *Nom.* fon, *gen.* funins, *dat.* funin, *acc.* fon; no plural.

A few extra examples are here added by way of illustration.

I. Strong declension. A-form. Masc. nouns, *dags* (day), *hlaifs* (a loaf), *hunds* (a hound), *laufs* (a leaf), *stains* (a stone), *fugls* (a fowl, bird); all like *fisks*. Fem. nouns, *airtha* (earth), *hairda* (a herd), *halba* (a half), *saiwala* (soul), *staua* (judgment), *aglitha* (trouble), all like *giba*. Neut. nouns, *agis* (awe), *ahs* (ear of corn), *akran* (fruit), *barn* (child), *bloth* (blood), *daur* (door), like *waurd*; also *badi* (bed), *ga-waurdi* (speech), *wadi* (pledge), &c., like *kuni*; for which see note 3.

I-form. Masc. *arms* (arm), *barms* (bosom), *gards* (house), *bruthfaths* (bridegroom), *frasts* (child). Fem. *alths* (old age), *dails* (a part), *mahts* (might), *magaths* (maiden), *faheths* (joy).

U-form. Masc. *airus* (messenger), *auhsus* (ox), *skadus* (shadow), *wintrus* (winter), *fotus* (foot). Fem. *asilus* (ass), *kinnus* (chin), *writhus* (flock). Neut. *gairu* (thorn). Like *bandi* are *akwizi* (axe), *haithi* (field), *haiti* (command), *fraistubni* (temptation); see note 4. Like *sunja* are *wrakja* (persecution), *brakja* (strife), *halja* (hell), *sibja* (relationship).

II. Weak declension. Masc. *ahma* (spirit), *atta* (father), *bloma* (flower), *guma* (man), *staua* (a judge), *aurtja* (gardener), *baurgja* (citizen). Fem. *gatwo* (street), *dauro* (door), *sunno* (sun), *fauho* (fox), all like *tuggo*; and *aithei* (mother), *bairhtei* (brightness), *balthei* (boldness), *hauhei* (height), like *managei*. Neut. *augo* (eye), *auso* (ear), *barnilo* (child), *sigljo* (seal), like *hairto;* and *namo* (name) like *wato*.

ADJECTIVES.

There are two declensions: (1) the *strong* or *vowel* declension, used without the article, and to which belong possessive pronouns and the words *fulls, halbs, alls, ganohs, swaleiks, jains, anthar, sums, &c.;* and (2) the *weak* or *consonantal* declension, used with the article (or without it, but chiefly when the meaning is *definite* or *demonstrative*), and to which belong comparatives, ordinals (except *anthar*), and present participles.

I. STRONG DECLENSION.

Blinds (blind); *m.* blinds, *f.* blinda, *n.* blind *or* blindata, is thus declined.

Sing.	N.	blind—*s*	—*a*	(—*ata*)
	G.	blind—*is*	—*aizos*	—*is*
	D.	blind—*amma*	—*ai*	—*amma*
	A.	blind—*ana*	—*a*	(—*ata*)
Pl.	N.	blind—*ai*	—*os*	—*a*
	G.	blind—*aize*	—*aizo*	—*aize*
	D.	blind—*aim*	—*aim*	—*aim*
	A.	blind—*ans*	—*os*	—*a*

Words in *-is*, as *midis*, *sutis* are declined in a *similar* manner.

N. midi—*s*	midj—*a*	midi (midj—*ata*)
G. midj—*is*	midj—*aizos*	midj—*is*, &c.

U-form.

Hardus (hard).

Sing.	N.	hard—*us*	—*us*	—*u* (-*jata*)
	G.	hardj—*is*	—*aizos*	—*is*
	D.	hardj—*amma*	—*ai*	—*amma*
	A.	hardj—*ana*	—*a*	—*ata* (hardu)
Pl.	N.	hardj—*ai*	—*os*	—*a*, &c.

This resembles *blinds* except in introducing the *j*.

11. WEAK DECLENSION.

Sa blinda (the blind).

Sing.	N. V.	blind—*a*	—*o*	—*o*
	G.	blind—*ins*	—*ons*	—*ins*
	D.	blind—*in*	—*on*	—*in*
	A.	blind—*an*	—*on*	—*o*
Pl.	N. V.	blind—*ans*	—*ons*	—*ona*
	G.	blind—*ane*	—*ono*	—*ane*
	D.	blind—*am*	—*om*	—*am*
	A.	blind—*ans*	—*ons*	—*ona*

REMARKS. 1. Some exceptions will be found; thus, the feminine of *ainaha* takes the irregular form *ainoho*.
2. The weak declension of adjectives is exactly like that of weak nouns; compare *hana*, *tuggo*, and *hairto*.
3. The declension here called *weak* answers to what in A. S. grammars is often called the *definite* one.

Degrees of comparison. The comparative degree is formed by adding *-oza* or *iza* (Eng. *-er*) to the stem; thus *blind-s* (blind) gives *blind--oza (blind-er)*, and *hard-us* (hard) gives *hard-iza*. *Blindoza* follows the weak declension. Both comparative adjectives and present participles active (which are also of the weak declension except in the nominative masculine) follow *managei*, not *tuggo*, in the *feminine*. The superlative follows both declensions, and is known by the insertion of *-ist-* (Eng. *-est*). Thus, from *smals* (small), is formed *smalists*, *sa smalista* (smallest, the smallest).

The following are irregular:

Gods, batiza, batists;	*Eng.* good, better, best.
Ubils, wairsiza, wairsists;	evil, worse, worst.
Mikils, maiza, maists;	mickle, more, most.
Leitils, minniza, minnists;	little, (less, least).
Altheis, aldiza, sinista;	old, older, (oldest).
Juggs, juhiza, juhists (?);	young, younger, youngest.

Numerals. Ains (one), is declined like a strong adjective; in the plural, it signifies *sole*, *only*. Twai (two), is declined thus: *nom.* twai, twos, twa; *gen.* twaddje; *dat.* twaim; *acc.* twans, twos, twa. Threis (three) makes *nom.* threis, threis, thrija; *gen.* thrije; *dat.* thrim; *acc.* thrins, thrins, thrija. Of fidwor (four) is found also the *dat.* fidworim. The numbers following are fimf, saihs, sibun, ahtau, niun (*gen.* niune), taihun, ainlif, twalif (*dat.* ainlibim, twalibim), threis-taihun, fidwor-taihun, &c. The Eng. *-ty* is denoted by *-tigus*, declined like *handus*, and therefore forming a plural *-tigjus*. Hence we get, twai-tigjus, threis-tigjus, &c., for 20, 30, &c.; but only up to 60. 70, 80, 90, 100 are sibun-tehund, ahtau-tehund, niun-tehund, taihun-tehund. 200, 300, &c., are twa hunda, thrija hunda, fidwor hunda, &c. 1000 is thusundi, *pl.* thusundjos *and* thusundja, *dat.* thusundjom.

Ordinals. Fruma, *fem.* frumei (the first), admits of the degrees of comparison *frumoza*, *frumists*; compare Eng. *fore*, *former*, *foremost*. Anthar, anthara, anthar (the second). Bai, *neut.* ba, *dat.* baim, *acc.* bans, *neut.* ba (both). The next are thridja, fidwortha (?), fimfta, saihsta, sibunda (?), ahtuda, niunda, taihunda.

PRONOUNS.

The personal pronouns are *ik*, I; *thu*, thou; of which the *dual* forms are found *wit*, we two; *jut (?)*, ye two.

N. V. ik	*Dual.*	wit	*Pl.*	weis
G. meina		ugkara		unsara
D. mis		ugkis		unsis, uns.
A. mik		ugkis, ugk		unsis, uns.
N. V. thu	*Dual.*	(jut)	*Pl.*	jus
G. theina		igkwara		izwara
D. thus		igkwis, iggkwis		izwis
A. thuk		igkwis, iggkwis		izwis

Also a reflexive form of the third personal pronoun is found in oblique cases. *Gen.* seina, *dat.* sis, *acc.* sik.

Again we find the third personal pronoun in all three genders, as *is, si, ita* (he, she, it).

N. is	si	ita	*Pl.* eis	ijos	ija
G. is	izos	is	ize	izo	ize
D. imma	izai	imma	im	im	im
A. ina	ija	ita	ins	ijos	ija

Possessive Pronouns. *Meins* (mine), *theins* (thine), *seins* (his) are declined like strong adjectives; as also are *unsar* (our), *izwar* (your). *seins* (their); and a dual form is found in the second person, *dat. sing. fem.* in Mat. 9. 29. 'Bi galaubeinai *iggkwarai* wairthai iggkwis', according to the faith *of you two* be it done unto you two.

Demonstrative Pronouns. *Sa, so, thata* (this, that) is also used as a *definite article.*

N. sa	so	thata	*Pl. N.* thai	thos	tho
G. this	thizos	this	*G.* thize	thizo	thize
D. thamma	thizai	thamma	*D.* thaim	thaim	thaim
A. thana	tho	thata	*A.* thans	thos	tho
I. the	the	the			

The *instrumental* case, *the*, occurs in the words *du-the* or *duth-the*, *bi-the*, *the-haldis*; compare *hwe* from *hwas*, and the A. S. *thi* or *thy*.

Sa is often followed by *uh*, and is then contracted into *sa'h*. Thus:—

					Pl.			
N.	sah	soh	thatuh			thaih	thozuh	thoh
G.	thizuh	thizozuh	thizuh			thizeh	thizoh,	thizeh
D.	thammuh	thizaih	thammuh			thaimuh	thaimuh	thaimuh
A.	thanuh	thoh	thatuh			thanzuh	thozuh	thoh

His (this) is only found in dat. masc. *himma*, and acc. masc. and neut. *hina, hita*, in the singular number.

Jains (yon, that) is declined like a strong adjective.

Sama (the same), and *silba* (self), are declined like weak adjectives; *swaleiks* (such) and *swalauds* (such) like strong adjectives.

Relative Pronouns. The relative is formed by help of the particle *ei* that, as, *thuei* (thou that); and especially by *ei* following *sa*, such forms as *thata-ei*, *thamma-ei* being contracted into *thatei, thammei*. In the feminine, both *soei* and *sei* are found.

Interrogative Pronouns. *Hwas*, fem. *hwo*, neut. *hwa* or *hwata* (who, what).

					Pl.			
N.	hwas	hwo	hwa			hwai	hwos	hwo
G.	hwis	hwizos	hwis			hwize	hwizo	hwize
D.	hwamma	hwizai	hwamma			hwaim	hwaim	hwaim
A.	hwana	hwo	hwa			hwans	hwos	hwo
I.	hwe	hwe	hwe					

The plural forms given are merely conjectural, and do not appear. The *instrumental* case, *hwe*, occurs in *du-hwe*, *hwe-lauds*, *hwe-leiks*; also *hweh* is found for *hwe-uh*.

Hwathar (whether, which of two) only appears in the *nom. sing.* We also find *hwatharuh*, *ainhwatharuh*.

Hwarjis (which, of more than two) is declined like a strong adjective, *gen.* hwarjis, *dat.* hwarjamma, *acc.* hwarjana; *pl. nom.* hwarjai, *acc.* hwarjans. With *-uh* added, it becomes *hwarjiz-uh*; we also find *ain-hwarjizuh*.

Hwe-leiks (what sort of), and *hwe-lauds* (what sort of), are declined as strong adjectives; compare *swa-leiks* (such) and *swa-lauds* (such).

Other pronominal forms. *Sums* (some) is like a strong adjective; *ains-hun* (any one) makes *fem.* aino-hun, *neut.* ain-hun; *gen. m. & n.* ainis-hun; *dat. m. & n.* ainumme-hun; *f.* ainai-hun; *acc.* ainno-hun, aino-hun, ain-hun.

Hwas-hun (any one) follows the declination of *hwas*; so also does *hwaz-uh* (every one).

Hwathar-uh, ain-hwathar-uh (each of two), are declined like *hwathar*; and *hwarjiz-uh, ain-hwarjizuh* (each, every) like *hwarjis*.

VERBS.

The *numbers* are *three*, singular, dual and plural. Dual forms are scarce.

Besides the infinitive, the *moods* are *three*, viz. indicative, conjunctive, and imperative.

The *tenses* are but *two*, *present* and *past*; the *future* being expressed by the present, as in Anglo-Saxon.

Verbs are of three forms, *active*, *passive*, and *middle*; the passive is partly formed by help of the past participle with *wisan* or *wairthan*; of the middle form but a few traces remain.

The conjugations are of two forms, *strong* and *weak*. Strong verbs change the vowel in the past tense, as *giban*, to give, past tense *gaf*, I gave; or else employ reduplication like Greek verbs, so that from *haldan*, to hold, is formed the past tense *haihald*, I held. Weak verbs have in the past tense the ending *-da*.

The following is a general scheme of endings for *all* verbs in the *active* voice.

INDICATIVE.

		Present	*Past (strong)*	*Past (weak)*
Sing.	1.	—a, —o	—	—da
	2.	—s	—t	—des
	3.	—th	—	—da
Dual.	1.	—os	—u	—dedu
	2.	—ts	—uts	—deduts
Plu.	1.	—m	—um	—dedum
	2.	—th	—uth	—deduth
	3.	—nd	—un	—dedun

CONJUNCTIVE.

Sing.	1.	—au, —o	—jau	—dedjau
	2.	—s	—eis	—dedeis
	3.	—ai, —o	—i	—dedi
Dual.	1.	—wa		
	2.	—ts	—eits	—dedeits
Plu.	1.	—ma	—eima	—dedeima
	2.	—th	—eith	—dedeith
	3.	—na	—eina	—dedeina

IMPERATIVE.

Dual. 2. —ts   *Pl.* 1. —m   2. —th.

INFINITIVE.

—an *(strong)*; —jan, —an, —on *(weak)*.

PRESENT PARTICIPLE.

—ands *(strong)*; —jands, —ands, —onds *(weak)*.

PAST PARTICIPLE PASSIVE.

—ans *(strong)*; —iths, —aiths, —oths *(weak)*.

I. ACTIVE VOICE. FIRST CONJUGATION.

Strong verbs, without reduplication.

As a good example, take the verb *rinnan*, to run.

INDICATIVE.

	Present		Past	
Sing. 1.	rinn	—*a*	rann	
2.		—*is*	rann	—*t*
3.		—*ith*	rann	
Dual. 1.		—*os*	runn	—*u*
2.		—*ats*	runn	—*uts*
Plu. 1.		—*am*	runn	—*um*
2.		—*ith*	runn	—*uth*
3.		—*and*	runn	—*un*

CONJUNCTIVE.

	Present		Past	
Sing. 1.	rinn	—*au*	runn	—*jau*
2.		—*ais*		—*eis*
3.		—*ai*		—*i*
Dual. 1.		—*aiwa*		—*eiwa*
2.		—*aits*		—*eits*
Plu. 1.		—*aima*		—*eima*
2.		—*aith*		—*eith*
3.		—*aina*		—*eima*

IMPERATIVE.

Sing. 2. rinn.   *Dual.* 2. rinn —ats.   *Plu.* 1. rinn —am.   2. rinn —ith.

PRESENT PARTICIPLE ACTIVE.

rinn —ands.

PAST PARTICIPLE PASSIVE.

runn —ans.

It will here be observed, that the *stem-form*, which in the present is *rinn*-, becomes *rann*- in the past tense singular, and *runn*- in the past tense dual and plural, and in the passive participle. Hence the first conjugation has been subdivided by Gabelentz and Löbe into six, and by Massmann into five divisions. Adopting the classification of the former, we have the following scheme for the vowels of the stem-forms.

	INFIN.	PAST SING.	PAST PLU.	PASS. PART.
1.	i	a	u	u
2.	i	a	e	u
3.	i	a	e	i
4.	ei	ai	i	i
5.	iu	au	u	u
6.	a	o	o	a

The first persons sing. and plu. of the past tense and the passive participle thus furnish the principal forms requisite for conjugating the verb, and hence are in general given in the glossary, as *rinnan* (*pt.* rann, *pl.* runnum, *pp.* runnans). Other verbs of the *first* class are *brinnan*, to burn, *bindan*, to bind, *finthan*, to find, *siggwan*, to sing, *drigkan*, to drink, &c.

Second class. Ex. *niman*, to take; *pt. t.* nam, nemum; *pp.* numans. Other verbs are *kwiman*, to come, *stilan*, to steal, *bairan*, to bear (*pt. t.* bar, *pl.* berum, *pp.* baurans), and *brikan*, to break.

Third class. Ex. *ligan*, to lie; *pt. t.* lag, legum; *pp.* ligans. So also *giban*, to give, *kwithan*, to say, *sitan*, to sit, *lisan*, to gather, *saihwan*, to see (*pt. t.* sahw, *pl.* sehwum, *pp.* saihwans), &c.

Fourth class. Ex. *steigan*, to mount, climb; *pt. t.* staig, *pl.* stigum, *pp.* stigans. So also *beidan*, to bide, *beitan*, to bite, *leisan*, to teach, *leithan*, to go, *dreiban*, to drive, &c.

Fifth class. Ex. *driusan*, to fall; *pt. t.* draus, *pl.* drusum, *pp.* drusans. So also *kiusan*, to choose, *biugan*, to bend, *liugan*, to lie, *tiuhan*, to tug, *sliupan*, to slip, &c.

Sixth class. Ex. *slahan*, to strike; *pt. t.* slob, *pl.* slobum, *pp.* slahans. So also *swaran*, to swear, *faran*, to fare, *dragan*, to draw, *wakan*, to watch, *graban*, to grave, dig, &c.

REMARKS. 1. Even with these numerous subdivisions, some exceptional forms occur. Thus *standan* (to stand) belongs to class 6, but the past tense is *stoth*, not *stond*, and the past part. *stothans*.

2. Classes 2 and 3 only differ in the form of the past participle. Class 4 only differs from class 3 in having the long diphthongs *ei* and *ai* (as in *steigan, staig*), in place of the vowels *i* and *a* (as in *ligan, lag*); and in putting *i* for *e* in the past tense dual and plural.

II. ACTIVE VOICE. SECOND CONJUGATION.

Strong verbs, taking the reduplication.

The reduplication is formed by repeating the initial consonants of the words before the diphthong *ai*; thus from *haldan, fraisan, skaidan* are formed *hai-hald, fai-frais, skai-skaid*.

There are two principal classes of verbs in this conjugation: (1) those which merely use the reduplication, and (2) those which not only use the reduplication, but change the vowel in the stem-form.

First class. Ex. *hahan*, to hang; *pt. t.* haihah, *pl.* haibaihum, *pp.* habans. So also *fahan*, to take, *haldan*, to hold, *fraisan*, to tempt, *skaidan*, to part, *haitan*, to bid, *slepan*, to sleep.

Second class. Ex. *tekan*, to touch; *pt. t.* taitok, *pl.* taitokum, *pp.* tekans. So also *gretan*, to weep, *letan*, to let, *blesan*, to blow, *saian*, to sow, &c.

NOTE. In all verbs of this conjugation the *pp.* merely adds *s* to the infinitive.

III. ACTIVE VOICE. WEAK CONJUGATION OF VERBS.

There are three classes of verbs, (1) those in which the *pt. t.* ends in -*ida*, and the *pp.* in -*iths*; (2) those in which these end in -*aida*, -*aiths*; (3) those with the endings -*oda*, -*oths*.

First class. To this class belong all verbs of which the infinitive ends in -*jan*, as *lagjan*, to lay.

INDICATIVE.

	Present		Past
Sing.	lag—*ja*		lag—*ida*
	—*jis*		—*ides*
	—*jith*		—*ida*
Dual.	—*jos*		—*idedu*
	—*jats*		—*ideduts*
Plu.	—*jam*		—*idedum*
	—*jith*		—*ideduth*
	—*jand*		—*idedum*

CONJUNCTIVE.

	Present		Past
Sing.	lag—*jau*		lag—*idedjau*
	—*jais*		—*idedeis*
	—*jai*		—*idedi*
Dual.	—*jaiwa*		—*idedeiwa*
	—*jaits*		—*idedeits*
Plu.	—*jaima*		—*idedeima*
	—*jaith*		—*idedeith*
	—*jaina*		—*idedeina*

IMPERATIVE.

Sing. 2. lag—*ei*.   Dual. 2. lag—*jats*.   Plu. 1. lag—*jam*
                                                    2.   —*jith*.

ACTIVE PRESENT PARTICIPLE.

lag—*jands*.

PASSIVE PAST PARTICIPLE.

lag—*iths*.

One peculiar exception must be particularly noticed. Some verbs in -*jan*, as *sokjan* (to seek), depart from the above form in the second and third pers. sing. and second pers. pl. of the indicative present, and in the second pers. sing. and pl. of the imperative; instead of *j* they use *e* in these persons. Thus the present indicative of *sokjan* is *sok-ja*, -*eis*, -*eith*; -*jos*, -*jats*; -*jam*, -*eith*, -*jand*. The imperative is *sok-ei*; -*jats*; -*jam*, -*eith*.

Like *lagjan* are conjugated all verbs with a *short* stem-syllable, or in which the stem-syllable terminates in a *vowel* or *diphthong*, such as *wal-jan*, to choose, *hram-jan*, to crucify, *satjan*, to set, *nas-jan*, to save, *wrak-jan*, to persecute; also *sto-jan*, to judge, *straujan*, to strew, *tau-jan*, to do, the preterites of which are *stauida*, *strawida*, *tawida*, and a few others less common, as *afdau-jan*, *ana-niujan*, *gakwiu-jan*, *siu-jan*.

Like *sokjan* are conjugated verbs with *long* vowels in the stem-syllable, or short vowels made *long by position*; as, *mel-jan*, to write, *mer-jan*, to proclaim, *dom-jan*, to deem, *fod-jan*, to feed, *draib-jan*, to drive, *haus-jan*, to bear, *gaskeir-jan*, to explain, *snium-jan*, to hasten; also *balth-jan*, to dare, *sand-jan*, to send, *full-jan*, to fill, *airz-jan*, to err, *andwaurd-jan*, to answer; to which must be added *mikil-jan*, *rikwiz-jan*, *audag-jan*, *manag-jan*, *lauhat-jan*, *swogat-jan*, *framath-jan*, *gabig-jan*, *glitmun-jan*, *us-walug-jan*, some of which might have been expected to follow *lagjan*.

Second class. Ex. *haban*, to have.

INDICATIVE.

	Present	Past
Sing.	hab—*a*	hab—*aida*
	—*ais*	—*aides*
	—*aith*	—*aida*
Dual.	—*os*	—*aidedu*
	—*aths*	—*aideduts*
Plu.	—*am*	—*aidedum*
	—*aith*	—*aideduth*
	—*and*	—*aidedun*

CONJUNCTIVE.

	Present	Past
Sing.	hab—*au*	hab—*aidedjau*
	—*ais*	—*aidedeis*
	—*ai*	—*aidedi*
Dual.	—*aiwa*	—*aidedeiwa*
	—*aits*	—*aidedeits*
Plu.	—*aima*	—*aidedeima*
	—*aith*	—*aidedeith*
	—*aina*	—*aidedeina*

IMPERATIVE.

hab—*ai*;   —*ats*;   —*am*, —*aith*.

PRESENT PARTICIPLE.

hab—*ands*.

PAST PARTICIPLE.

hab—*aiths*.

Some of the principal verbs like *haban* are:—skaman, hahan, thahan, slawan, waldan, blandan, arman, fastan, fijan, hlifan, thulan, munan, sweran, blotan, aistan, bauan, trauan, hweilan, weihan, leikan, liugan, jiukan.

Third class. The infinitive ends in -*on*, as *spillon*, to tell, proclaim.
Indicative present: spill-*o*, -*os*, -*oth*; -*os*, -*ots*; -*om*, -*oth*, -*ond*.
Conjunctive present: spill-*o*, -*os*, -*o*, &c.
Indicative past: spill-*oda*, -*odes*, -*oda*, &c.

Compare the general scheme on p. 297.

IV. VERBS ENDING IN -nan.

Verbs ending in -*nan* have a passive or neuter signification, as *fullnan*, to become full, *and-bundnan*, to become unbound, *aflifnan*, to be left remaining, *gahailnan*, to become whole, *gawaknan*, to become awake, to wake, &c. They are *weak* verbs, declined like *lagjan* (writing *n* for *j*) in the present indicative and conjunctive, and like *spillon* in the past tense. Thus the past tense of *fullnan* is *fullnoda*. The second person singular imperative is *fulln*.

PASSIVE VOICE.

There is a general form only for the present tense, the past tense being formed by help of the past participle.

General scheme.

INDICATIVE.		CONJUNCTIVE.
Sing.	—da	—dau
	—za	—zau
	—da	—dau

	INDICATIVE.	CONJUNCTIVE.
Plu.	—nda	—ndau
	—nda	—ndau
	—nda	—ndau

These endings are to be added to the infinitive, after removing *n*. Thus from *haitan*, *waurkjan*, *kroton*, we get *haita-da*, *waurkja-da*, *kroto-da*, and so on. In the conjunctive mood, verbs in *-an*, *-jan* make *-aidau*, *-jaidau*, and verbs in *-on* make *-odau*.

MIDDLE VOICE.

Of this there are but a few traces, following the form of *passive* verbs. Thus we find *lausjadau*, let him deliver ($\dot{\rho}\upsilon\sigma\acute{\alpha}\sigma\vartheta\omega$, Mat. 27. 43); *atsteigadau*, let him come down ($\varkappa\alpha\tau\alpha\beta\acute{\alpha}\tau\omega$, Mat. 27. 42); *liugandau*, let them marry ($\gamma\alpha\mu\eta\sigma\acute{\alpha}\tau\omega\sigma\alpha\nu$, 1 Cor. 7. 9). To these Gabelentz and Löbe add a few more instances, which Massmann denies. The proof that there ever was a middle voice is indeed small.

ANOMALOUS AND AUXILIARY VERBS.

The following verbs are, some of them, of frequent occurrence and considerable importance.

The following *twelve* verbs use as a present an old preterite form, from which again a second *weak* preterite is formed. Compare the use of the Greek $ol\delta\alpha$ in a *present* sense. *Daursan* only occurs in the compound *gadaursan*, and *nahan* only in *binahan*, *ganahan*.

1. *Magan*, to be able. Pres. sing. *mag*, pl. *magum*; pt. t. *mahta*, pp. *mahts*. (Eng. *may, might*.)

2. *Kunnan*, to know. Pres. sing. *kann*, pl. *kunnum*; pt. t. *kuntha*, pp. *kunths*. (Eng. *ken, can, could*.)

3. *Thaurban*, to need. Pres. sing. *tharf*, pl. *thaurbum*; pt. t. *thaurfta*, pp. *thaurfts*. (A. S. *pearfan*. O. E. *tharf*.)

4. *Daursan*, to dare. Pres. sing. *dars*, pl. *daursum*; pt. t. *daursta*, pp. *daursts*. (Eng. *dare, durst*.)

5. *Munan*, to think, intend. Pres. sing. *man*, pl. *munum*; pt. t. *munda*, pp. *munds*. (A. S. *mynan*. O. E. *min*. Eng. *mean, mind*.)

6. *Skulan*, to owe, be obliged to do. Pres. sing. *skal*, pl. *skulum*; pt. t. *skulda*, pp. *skulds*. (Eng. *shall, should*.)

7. *Nahan*, to suffice. Pres. sing. *nah* (impersonal); pt. t. *nauhta*, pp. *nauhts*. (*Cf*. Eng. *enough*.)

8. *Witan*, to see, know. Pres. sing. *wait*, pl. *witum*; pt. t. *wissa*, pp. *wits* (?). (Eng. *wit, wot, wist*.)

9. *Aigan*, to own, have. Pres. sing. *aih*, pl. *aigum*; pt. t. *aihta*, pp. *aihts*. (Eng. *own*. O. E. *owe*.)

10. *Dugan*, to profit, avail. Pres. sing. *daug* (impersonal); pt. t. *dauhta*, pp. *dauhts*. (A. S. *dugan*. O. E. *dowthe*. Sc. *dow*; cf. *doughty*.)

11. A conjectural verb, *Motan*, to be able. Pres. sing. *mot*, pl. *motum*; pt. t. *mosta*, pp. *mosts*. (O. E. *mot*. Engl. *must*.)

12. *Ogan*, to be in awe. Pres. sing. *og*, pl. *ogum*; pt. t. *ohta*, pp. *ohts*.

The present tenses of these verbs follow the inflections of *rann*, the pt. t. of *rinnan*, of the first conjugation of *strong* verbs. The past tenses are like the past tenses of *weak* verbs. It may be remarked that *not all* of the above forms are *really found*.

To these may be added the verb *wiljan*, to wish, only found in the past tense *wilda* (Eng. *would*), and in the conjunctive (or *optative*) mood, viz. wil-jau, -eis, -i; -eiwa, -eits; -eima, -eith, -eina.

Gaggan, to go, makes the past tense *iddja*, of the *weak* form; once the past tense *gaggida* occurs, in Lu. 19. 12.

Wisan, to be, has in the dual and plural of the *present* tense the inflections of a *past* tense.

INDICATIVE.

	Present	Past
Sing.	im	was
	is	wast
	ist	was
Dual.	siju	wesu
	sijuts	wesuts
Pl.	sijum	wesum
	sijuth	wesuth
	sind	wesun

CONJUNCTIVE.

	Present	Past
Sing.	sijau	wesjau
	sijais	weseis
	sijai	wesi
Dual.	sijaiwa	weseiwa
	sijaits	weseits
Pl.	sijaima	weseima
	sijaith	weseith
	sijaina	weseina

Wisan, in the sense *to remain*, is also found conjugated regularly, like *ligan*, Conj. I., class 3.

Used with past participles, *wisan* forms the past tenses of passive verbs; as, *gasuliths was ana staina*, was founded upon a rock, Mat. 7. 25.

Wairthan, to become. Pt. t. *warth*, pl. *waurthum*, pp. *waurthans*, is a regular verb, like *rinnan*. It is also used, like *wisan*, to form the past tenses of passive verbs, as, *thanuh than usdribana warth so managei*, when therefore the multitude was driven out, Mat. 9. 25.

Briggan, to bring, makes the past tense *brahta*, brought, conjugated as a *weak* verb.

Haban, to have, has been conjugated above: *see* weak verbs, second class, p. 302.

ADVERBS.

The common adverbial ending of adverbs formed from adjectives is *-aba*, *-iba*, or *-uba*; as, *baitrs*, bitter, *baitraba*, bitterly; *arneis**, sure, *arniba*, surely; *hardus*, hard, *harduba*, hardly, also spelt *hardaba*. Another common ending is *-o*, as *uhteigs*, seasonable, *uhteigo*, seasonably.

The more common adverbs are these.

1) *Of time*. *Sunsaiw*, immediately, *air*, early, *anaks*, at once, *than*, *thanuh*, then, when, *ju*, *juthan*, already, *nauh*, *nauhthan*, still, *nu*, now, *bithe*, then, when, *simle*, once, *ufta*, oft, *seithu*, late, *sinteino*, ever, *suman*, once, *suns*, soon, *aftra*, again, *hwan*, when.

2) *Of place*. *Her*, here, *tharuh*, there, *tharei*, where, *hwar*, *hwarei*, where, *jainar*, yonder, *aljar*, elsewhere, *ufaro*, above, *undaro*, beneath, *aftana*, *aftaro*, behind, *uta*, without, *inna*, within, *fairra*, far, *nehwa*, near, *faura*, before, *iup*, up, *dalath*, down, &c.; also *hwadre*, whither, *jaindre*, thither, *hidre*, hither, &c.; also *innathro*, from within, *utathro*, from without, *iupathro*, from above, *fairrathro*, from afar, *allathro*, from all sides, *aljathro*, elsewhere.

3) *Of quality, &c.* *Swa*, so, *hwe*, how, *hweh*, only, *ne*, no, *ja*, *jai*, yes, *aufto*, perhaps, *sunja*, truly, *allis*, altogether, *frumist*, first, *aiw*, ever, &c. Also *waila*, well; *ubilaba*, ill; *wairs*, worse; *filu*, much; *mais*, more; *maist*, most; *leitil*, little; *mins*, less.

PREPOSITIONS.

With the dative: *alja*, except, *af*, off, from, *fram*, from, *faura*, before, *mith*, with, *us*, out; also *du*, to (which also takes the accusative only once).

With the accusative: *and*, along, at, *faur*, for, before, *inuh*, without, *thairh*, through, *undar*, under, *withra*, against.

With both accusative and dative: *ana*, on, *at*, at, *afar*, after, *bi*, by, *du*, to, *hindar*, behind, *und*, unto, *uf*, under, *ufar*, over.

With genitive, dative, and accusative: *in*, in, on account of. *Faur* is also found with the genitive in the words *faurthis*, *faurthizei*, before, first.

Bi and *du* are also found with the instrumental case, as in *bi-the*, *du-the*.

CONJUNCTIONS.

The conjunctions are (1) copulative, as *jah*, and, *-uh*, and, *nih*, and not; (2) disjunctive, as *aiththau*, or, *andizuh — aiththau*, either — or, *jaththe — jaththe*, whether — or; (3) denoting opposition, as *ith*, than, *aththan*, *ak*, *akei*, but, however; (4) causal, as *allis*, *auk*, *unte*, *raihtis*, for; (5) expressing a conclusion, as *thanuh*, *tharuh*, *eithan*, *nu*, *thannu*, therefore, now; (6) conditional, as *jabai*, if, *niba*, if not, except; (7) expressing concession, as *thau*, *thauhjabai*, though, even if, *swethauh*, however; (8) final, as *ei*, *thatei*, *theei*, that, *swaei*, *swaswe*, so that, so as that; (9) of comparison, as *hwaiwa*, how, *swe*, as, so, *swaswe*, so as, as; (10) of time, as *swe*, just as, *than*, *thande*, when, then, as long as, *bithe*, *miththanei*, whilst, *sunsei*, as soon as, *faurthizei*, before that.

INTERJECTIONS.

These are, *O*, oh! *wai*, woe! *sai*, see! *hiri*, come thou hither! *hirjaths*, come here, you two! *hirjith*, come ye hither!

SYNTAX.

A good short syntax will be found in Stamm's Ulfilas. The constructions present little difficulty. The most remarkable one is the use of the *dative absolute*, corresponding to that of the *ablative absolute* in Latin.

A LIST OF ENGLISH WORDS,

THE ETYMOLOGY OF WHICH IS ILLUSTRATED BY COMPARISON WITH MŒSO-GOTHIC.

A LIST OF ENGLISH WORDS,

THE ETYMOLOGY OF WHICH IS ILLUSTRATED BY COMPARISON WITH MŒSO-GOTHIC.

[*A few Anglo-Saxon and Old English (or provincial English) words are included in this list. The Anglo-Saxon words are marked with an* ASTERISK, *the old or provincial words with an* OBELUS. *Mœso-Gothic words marked with an* ASTERISK *are root-words which are not actually found. Words included in square brackets, not being Saxon-English, may perhaps be considered as out of place here; they are merely added by way of illustration. More remote analogies are not noticed. Some, even, that are inserted, are very doubtful.*]

A, AN, *ains*.
ABAL* (strength), *cf. abrs*.
ABIDE; *see* BIDE.
AC† (but), *ak*.
[ACID, *cf. akeit.*]
ACORN, *akran?*
ACRE, *akrs*.
ADDER; *see* NEDDER.
AFRAID, *faurhts*.
AFT; *cf. aftuma, afta*.
AFTER, *afar, aftra, afta, aftaro*.
[AGE; *cf. aiws.*]
AGHAST; *cf. usgaisjan*.
AGTE, AHTE (goods), *aihts*.
AILING, *agls*.
ALL, *alls*.
AM, *im*.
AMMBOHHT† (servant), *andbahts*.
AND† (breath); *cf. anan*.
AND-* (prefix), *and-*.
ANFALD† (onefold), *ainfalths*.
ANGE* (anxious), *aggwus*.
ANGE* (sorrow), *aggwitha*.
ANGER; *see* ANGE.

ANSWER; *cf. and* and *swaran*.
[ANXIOUS, *aggwus.*]
[ANXIETY, *aggwitha.*]
ARK, *arka*.
ARM, *arms*.
ARRFETH† (difficult); *cf. arbaiths*.
ARROW, *arhwazna*.
ASH (cinder), *azgo*.
ASHAMED, to be, *gaskaman sik, skaman sik*.
ASS, *asilus*.
[ASSEMBLE; *cf. samana, samath.*]
ASUNDER, *sundro*.
AT, *at*.
ATHWART; *cf. thwairhs*.
AUGHT, *aiw* and *waihts*.
AWAKE; *see* WAKE.
AWE, *agis*.
AWE, *vb., agjan*.
AWN, *ahana*.
AWRY; *see* WRY.
AYE, *aiw*.
AYND† (breath), *cf. anan*.
AXE, *akwizi*.

BAG, *balgs*.
BAIRN, *barn*.
BALE, *sb.*, *cf. balwos*(?).
BAND, *bandi*.
BANE, *banja*.
BAR-LEY, *baris*.
BARM† (bosom), *barms*.
[BARON; *cf. wair*.]
BARROW (mound); *cf. bairgan*.
BAY (of the sea); *cf. biugan*.
BE-, *bi-*.
BEAM, *bagms*.
BEAR, *vb.*, *bairan*.
BEAR (children), *gabairan*.
BEAR† (barley), *baris*.
BECOME; *cf. bikwiman*.
BED, *badi*.
BEDE† (prayer), *bida*.
BEDE† (to pray), *bidjan*.
BEDESMAN; *see* BEDE.
BEGET† (acquire), *bigitan*.
BEGIN, *duginnan*.
BEGIRD, *bigairdan*.
BEHEST; *see* HEST.
BEHIND, *hindar*.
BELIEF, *galaubeins*.
BELIEVE, *laubjan*, *galaubjan*.
BELLOWS, *cf. balgs*.
BELLY, *cf. balgs*.
BEORG* (mountain), *bairgs*.
BEREAVE, *biraubon*.
BERRY, *basi*.
BESET, *bisatjan*.
BESPIT, *bispeiwan*.
BEST, *batists*.
BETE†(to amend), *botjan*; *see* BOOT.
BETHINK, *bithaggkjan*.
BETOKEN, *taiknjan*, *ga-taiknjan*.
BETTER, *batiza*.
BEWARE, *cf. warjan*.
BEWRAY, *cf. wrohjan*, *frawrohjan*.
BID (to order), *biudan*.
BID (to pray), *bidjan*.
BIDDER† (beggar), *bidagwa*.
BIDDING-PRAYER; *cf. bida*.
BIDE, *beidan*, *gabeidan*.
BIGHT; *cf. biugan*.

BIND, *bindan*, *gabindan*.
BIRTH, *gabaurths*.
BITE, *beitan*.
BITTER, *baitrs*.
BLAST; *cf. blesan*.
BLAZE ABROAD, *blesan*.
BLEED, *blotan*(?).
BLEND, *blandan*.
BLIN† (cease), *af-linnan*.
BLIND, *vb.*, *gablindjan*.
BLIND, *blinds*.
BLITHE, *bleiths*.
BLOOD, *bloth*.
BLOOM, *bluma*.
BLOTAN* (to sacrifice), *blotan*.
BLOW (a hit); *cf. bliggwan*.
BLOW, *vb.*; *cf. blesan*.
BLUDGEON; *cf. bliggwan*(?).
BOARD, *baurd*.
[BOIL; *cf. wulan*.]
BOIL (*sb.*), BOLLED (swollen); *cf. uf-baulian*.
BOLD, *balths*.
BOND, *gabindi*, *bandwa*.
BOOK, *boka*.
BOOM; *see* BEAM.
BOOR; *cf. bauan*.
BOOT, *vb.*, *botjan*, *gabatnan*.
BOOT, *sb.*, *bota*.
BOROUGH; *see* BURGH.
BOTH, *bai*, *bajoths*.
BOURN, *brunna*.
BOW, *vb.*, *biugan*, *gabiugan*.
BRAID† (a twinkling); *cf. brahw*.
BRAND; *see* BREN.
BREADTH, *braidei*.
BREAK, *brikan*.
BREAST, *brusts*.
BREN† (burn), *brinnan*.
BRETHREN, *brothrahans*.
BRIDE, *bruths*.
BRIDEGROOM, *bruths* and *guma*.
BRIGHT, *bairhts*.
BRIGHTEN, *gabairhtjan*.
BRING, *briggan*.
BROAD, *braids*.
BROADEN, *braidjan*.

BROOK, vb., brukjan.
BROTHER, brothar.
BRUCAN* (to use), brukjan.
BUAN* (to build), bauan.
BULGE; cf. balgs.
BURDEN, baurthei.
BURGH, baurgs.
BURGHER, baurgja.
BURN, vb. act., gabrannjan.
BURN, vb. neut.; see BREN.
BURN, sb.; see BOURN.
BURY, bairgan.
BUXOM; cf. biugan.
BUY, bugjan.
BY, bi.
BYRNE* (breastplate), brunjo.

CALF, kalbo.
CAN; see KEN.
CARE, vb., gakaran.
CARE, sb., kara.
CHAPMAN; cf. kaupon.
CHEAPEN, kaupon.
CHILD; cf. kilthei (?).
CHIN, kinnus.
CHOOSE, kiusan.
CHOP (to barter), kaupon.
CLINK; cf. klismjan.
[COGITATE; cf. HOGIAN.]
COLD, kalds.
COM-, CON-, ga-.
COME, kwiman.
COMMON, ga-mains.
[COMMUNION; cf. gamainei.]
CON, kunnan.
CORN, kaurn, kaurns.
COULD, kuntha.
CROAK, hrukjan.
CROW, vb.; see CROAK.
CRUSH, gakroton.
CUFF, vb.; cf. kaupatjan.
CUNNING; cf. kunnan.
CWIð* (womb), kwithus.
CWYSAN* (to quash), kwistjan (?).

DALE, dal.
DAM, vb. faurdammjan.

DAPPER; cf. gadobs (?).
DARE, daursan, gadaursan.
DAUGHTER, dauhtar.
DAY, dags.
DEAD, dauths.
DEAF, daubs.
DEAFEN, gadaubjan.
DEAFNESS; cf. daubei, daubitha.
DEAL, vb., dailjan, gadailjan.
DEAL, sb., dails, daila.
DEATH, dauthus.
DEED, gadeds; cf. taui.
DEEM, domjan.
DEEP, diups.
DEEPEN, gadiupjan.
DEER, dius.
DEFT; cf. gadaban, gadofs.
[DEGREE; cf. grids.]
DEPTH, diupei, diupitha.
DERNE† (secret); cf. gatarnjan.
[DEXTEROUS; cf. taihsws.]
DIE, diwan.
[DIMINISH; cf. mins.]
DIP, daupjan, diupan.
DIPPING, daupeins.
DO; cf. taujan.
DOLE, dails, daila.
DOOM, doms, afdomeins.
DOOM, vb., gadomjan.
DOOR, daur, dauro.
[DOUBT; cf. tweifls, tweifleins.]
[DUBITABLE; cf. tweifjan.]
DOUGH, daigs.
DOUGHTY; cf. dugan.
DOVE, hraiwa-dubo.
DOW† (to avail), dugan.
DOWWNENN† (to smell); cf. dauns.
DRAG, dragan, gadragan.
DRAW; see DRAG.
DREE† (endure); driugan (?).
DRENCH, dragkjan.
DREOGAN*; see DREE.
DRILL; cf. thairko.
DRINK, sb., draggk.
DRINK, vb. driggkan.
DRIVE, dreiban, draibjan.
DRONE (a sound), drunjus.

DROSS; cf. driusan.
DRUNKEN, druggkans.
DRUNKENNESS, druggkanei.
DRY, thaursus.
DULL, dwals.
DUMB, dumbs.
DURST, daursta.
DWELAN* (to err); cf. dwals.

EA* (stream), ahwa.
EADIG* (happy), audags.
EAR† (to plough), arjan.
EAR, sb., auso.
EAR (of corn), ahsa.
EARFOð* (labour), arbaiths.
EARLY; cf. air.
EARM* (poor), arms.
EARN; cf. asans(?).
EARNEST, sb., cf. asneis(?).
EARTH, airtha.
EASY, azets.
EAT, itan.
EAVES, ubizwa(?).
EDDISH† (aftermath), atisks.
EIGHT, ahtau.
EITHER, conj., aiththau.
EKE, conj., auk.
EKE, vb. aukan, gaaukan.
ELD† (old age), alds.
ELEVEN; cf. ainlif.
ELL, aleina.
ELLEN* (vigour); cf. aljon.
ELSE, alis, alja.
END, andeis.
ENDLESS, andilaus.
ENLIGHTEN, inliuhtjan.
ENOUGH, ganohs.
ERE, air.
ERF† (inheritance), arbi.
ERN† (eagle), ara.
ERRAND; cf. airinon.
[ERRING; cf. airzis.]
[ERROR; cf. airzei.]
ESNE* (servant), asneis.
EST* (favour), ansts.
EVEN, ibns.

EVENLY, cf. ibnaleiks.
EVER, aiw.
EVIL, ubils.
EWE, awi.
EYE, augo.
EYND† (breath); see AYND.

FADE†; see FADIAN*.
FADIAN* (to dispose); cf. faths.
FAIN; cf. faginon.
FAIR, fagrs.
FANA* (a flag), fana.
FANG; cf. fahan.
FAR, fairra.
FARE, faran.
FAST, vb., fastan.
FASTEN, fastan, gathwastjan.
FATHER, fadar.
FATHOM; cf. fatha.
FAWN ON; cf. faginon.
FEAL† (to hide), filhan.
FEE, faihu.
FEED, fodjan.
FELE† (many), filus.
FELL† (hide), fill.
FELLMONGER; see FELL.
FEN, fani. [In O. E. fen means mud.]
FEORH* (life); cf. fairhwus.
FEUD, fiathwa.
FEW, faus, faws.
FIEND, fiands, fijands.
FIFTEEN, fimftaihun.
FIGHT; cf. waihjo(?).
FILL, fulljan.
FIND, finthan.
FINGER, figgrs.
FISH, fisks.
FISH, vb., fiskon.
FISHER, fiskja.
FIT, cf. fetjan.
FIVE, fif, fimf.
[FLACCID; cf. thlakwus.]
FLEE, thliuhan.
FLEKE* (hurdle); cf. flahta.
FLOOD, flodus.

FLOUT, *flautan* (?).
FOAL, *fula*.
-FOLD, *-falths*.
FOLD, vb., *falthan*.
FOOD, *fodeins*.
FOOT, *fotus*.
FOR, *faur*.
FOR-, *faur-*.
FORBID, *faurbiudan*.
FORE, adj., *frums*.
FORE-, *faura-*.
FOREMOST; cf. *frumists*.
FORE-RUN, *faurrinnan*.
FORGIVE, *fragiban*.
FORLORN; cf. *fralusnan*.
FORMER; cf. *fruma*.
FORSWEAR; cf. *ufar-swaran*.
FORWORHT* (malefactor), *frawaurhts*.
FORWYRCAN* (to sin), *frawaurkjan*.
FOUL, *fuls*.
FOUR, *fidwor*.
FOURTEEN, *fidwortaihun*.
FOWL, *fugls*.
FOX, *fauho*.
FRAIST† (to test), *fraisan*.
FRAYNE† (to ask), *fraihnan*.
FREA* (lord), *frauja*.
FREAK; cf. *friks*.
FREE, *freis*.
FREMED† (strange), *framatheis*.
FRET; *fra-itan*(?).
FRIEND, *frijonds*.
FRIGHT, *faurhtei*.
FROD* (wise), *froths*.
FROM, *fram*.
FROST, FREEZE; cf. *frius*.
FRUMA* (beginning), *frums*.
FULL, *fulls*.

GABLE, *gibla*(?).
GADELING† (a vagabond), *gadiliggs*.
GADFLY; see GOAD.
GAIN; cf. *ga-geigan*.
GAIT; see GATE.
GALLOWS, *galga*.
GANG, vb., *gaggan*.
GARDEN, GARTH; see YARD.
GATE, *gatwo*. [O. E. gate *means a way*.]
GAUM† (to consider), *gaumjan*.
GEDAFENIAN* (to suit), *gadaban*.
GENESAN* (to become well), *ganisan*.
GEOTAN* (to pour), *giutan*.
GET, *gitan*, *bigitan*.
GHASTLY; cf. *geisan*.
GIFT, *giba*.
GIN† (begin), *ginnan*.
GIRD, *gairdan*, *bigairdan*.
GIRDLE, *gairda*.
GIVE, *giban*.
GLAD, *hlas* (?).
GLEAM; see LEME.
GLEAW† (skilful), *glaggwus*.
GLITTER; cf. *glitmunjan*.
GO, *gaggan*.
GOAD, *gazds*.
GOAT, *gaitsa*.
GOD, *guth*.
GODFEARING, *gudafaurhts*.
GODLESS, *gudalaus*.
GOLD, *gulth*.
GOLDEN, *gultheins*.
GOME† (man), *guma*.
GONFANON; cf. *fana*.
GOOD, *gods*, *goths*.
GOSPEL, *gods* and *spillon*.
GOSSIP; see SIB.
[GRADE, *grids*.]
GRAME† (anger); cf. *gramjan*.
GRASS, *gras*.
GRAVE, vb., *graban*.
GRAVE, sb., *groba*, *graba*.
GREED, *gredus*.
GREEDY, *gredags*.
GREET† (weep), *gretan*.
GREFFTE† (herald); cf. *gagrefts*.
[GRIEF; cf. *gauritha*(?).]
GRIP, GRIPE, *greipan*.
GROOM, *guma*; see GOME.

GROUND, *grundus.*
GROUNDSIL; see SILL.
GUEST, *gasts.*
GUILD; cf. *gild.*
GUILT; cf. *us-gildan.*
GUND* (canker), *gund.*
GUSH; cf. *us-gutnan.*

HACELE* (cloak), *hakul.*
HAFT, HEFT; cf. *haftjan.*
HAIL! *hails.*
HAIRNS† (brains), *hwairnei.*
HALE, *ga-hails, hails.*
HALF, adj., *halbs.*
HALF, sb., *halba.*
HALS† (neck), *hals.*
HALT (lame), *halts.*
-HAM, *haims.*
HAMA* (covering, skin); cf. *hama.*
HAMLET; cf. *haims.*
HAND, *handus.*
HANDIWORK; cf. *handu-waurhts.*
HAND-WROUGHT, *handu-waurhts.*
HANG, *hahan.*
HANS† (a quantity); cf. *hansa.*
HARBOUR; cf. *harjis* and *bairgan.*
HARD, *hardus.*
HARDEN, *hardjan, gahardjan.*
HARDHEARTEDNESS, *harduhairtei.*
HATE, sb., *hatis.*
HATE, vb., *hatan.*
HAVE, *haban.*
HAY, *hawi.*
HEAD, *haubith.*
HEAL, vb. act., *hailjan, gahailjan.*
HEAL, vb. neut. *hailnan.*
HEAR, *hausjan, gahausjan.*
HEART, *hairto.*
HEARTH, cf. *hauri* (?).
HEAT, *heito.*
HEATH, *haithi.*
HEATHEN (woman), *haithno.*
HEAVE, *hafjan.*
HEAVEN, *himins.*
HEIGHT, *hauhei.*
HELE† (to hide), *huljan, gahuljan.*

HELL, *halja.*
HELM, HELMET, *hilms.*
HELP, *hilpan, gahilpan.*
HEN, *hana.*
HENDE† (urbane); cf. *handugs,* wise.
HENDEN†, HENTEN† (to seize), *us-hinthan, fra-hinthan.*
HEOFIAN* (to mourn), *hiufan.*
HEOR* (sword), *hairus.*
HERD (shepherd), *hairdeis.*
HERD (flock), *hairda.*
HERE, *her.*
HERE† (an army), *harjis.*
HERY† (to praise), *hazjan.*
HERYING† (praise), *hazeins.*
HEST; see HETE.
HETE† (behest), *haiti.*
HEVEDE† (head), *haubith.*
HIGH, *hauhs.*
HIGHT† (to be called); cf. *haitan.*
HINDMOST, *hindumists.*
HIP, *hups.*
HITHER, *hidre.*
HIVE; cf. *heiwa-frauja.*
HLUTOR* (clear), *hlutrs.*
HNIGAN* (to bow), *hneiwan.*
HOARD, sb., *huzd.*
HOARD, vb., *huzdjan.*
HOE, *hoha.*
HOGIAN* (to think), *hugjan.*
HOLD, *haldan.*
HOLD† (faithful), *hulths.*
HOLE, HOLLOW; cf. *hulundi.*
HOLLOW OUT, *us-hulon.*
HOME, *haims.*
-HOOD, *haidus.*
HORN, *haurn.*
HOUND, *hunds.*
HOUSE; cf. *gud-hus.*
HOUSEL† (to administer the communion); cf. *hunsljan, hunsl.*
HOW, *hwaiwa.*
HUE, *hiwi.*
HUGIAN* (to think), *gahugjan.*
HUNDRED, *hund.*
HUNGER, sb., *huhrus.*
HUNGER, vb., *huggrjan.*

HURDLE; cf. haurds.
HUT, hethjo(?). [But bethjo may answer better to A. S. heddern, a barn.]
HWEORFAN* (to turn), hwairban.
HYGE* (thought), gahugds.
HYNAN* (to humble), haunjan.

I, ik.
IF, ibai. iba, jabai.
IN, in.
INC* (you two), iggkwis.
INCER* (of you two), iggkwar.
INGOT; cf. in and giutan.
INNER, innuma.
[INVEST; cf. gawasjan, andwasjan.]
IRON, eisarn.
IT, hita.
IWIS† (certainly); cf. unwis.

KEN (to know), kunnan.
KENNE† (to make known), gakannjan.
KETTLE, katils.
KIN, kuni.
KISS, kukjan, gakukjan.
KNAP, dis-hniupan (?).
KNEE, kniu.

LAD, jugga-lauths (?).
LÆWIAN* (to betray), lewjan, galewjan.
LAMB, lamb.
LAND, land.
LARK (in vulgar phrase to lark about),; see LAYKE.
LAST (shoemaker's); cf. laists.
LATE, lats.
LAÐIAN* (to invite), lathon.
LAUGH, hlahjan.
LAVE† (remainder), laiba.
LAY, lagjan, galagjan.
LAY (song); cf. liuthon.
LAYING, sb., lageins.
LAYING-ON, sb., analageins.

LAYKE† (to play), laikan.
LAZY, lats.
LEAD, vb., cf. galeithan.
LEAF, laufs.
LEAN* (to reprove), laian.
LEAP; cf. us-hlaupan.
LEARN (to teach), laisjan, galaisjan.
LEASE† (to glean), lisan, galisan.
LEASING (lie); cf. lausawaurds.
LEAVE; cf. bilaibjan.
LEE; cf. hlija.
LEECH (doctor), leikeis.
LEFT-HAND; cf. hleiduma (?).
LEME† (gleam), lauhmuni.
LEND; see LENE.
LENE† (to lend), leihwan.
LERE† (to teach); see LEARN.
-LESS, -laus.
LET (permit), letan.
LET OFF (pardon), afletan.
LET (hinder), galatjan.
LIAR, liugnja.
LICH† (body), leik.
LICHAME† (body); cf. leik and hama*.
LICK, bilaigon.
LID; cf. hleithra (?).
LIE, ligan.
LIE (falsehood), liugn.
LIE (to speak false), liugan.
LIEF, liubs.
LIFE, libains.
LIFT† (air), luftus.
LIFT; cf. hlifan(?).
LIGHT, (not heavy), leihts.
LIGHT (bright), liuhadeins.
LIGHT, sb., liuhath, liuhadei.
LIGHTEN (illumine), liuhtjan, galiuhtjan.
LIGHTEN (shine as lightning), lauhatjan.
LIGHTNING, lauhmuni.
LIKE, adj., galeiks.
LIKE, vb., leikan, galeikan.
LIKEN, galeikon.
LINEN, lein.
LINN† (to cease), af-linnan.

LIST† (cunning), *lists.*
LITH† (limb), *lithus.*
LIÐAN* (to travel), *galeithan.*
LITTLE, *leitils.*
LIVE, *vb., liban.*
LOAD; *cf. aflathan.*
LOAF, *hlaifs.*
LOAFER; *cf.* LEAP.
LOAN, *laun.*
LOCK, *galukan.*
LONG, *laggs.*
LOOF† (palm of hand), *lofa.*
LOOSE, *laus; cf. lasiws (?).*
LOOSEN, *galausjan.*
LOSE, *fraliusan.*
LOT, *hlauts.*
LOVE, brotherly, *brothra-lubo.*
LOVELY, *liubaleiks.*
LOW† (tumulus), *hlaiw.*
LUST, *vb., luston.*
LUST, *sb., lustus.*
-LY, *-leiks.*
LYTIAN* (to deceive); *cf. usluton.*

MÆL* (a time), *mel.*
MAGGOT; see MAÐU.
MAID, *magaths.*
MAN, *manna.*
MANY, *manags.*
MANY† (a company), *managei.*
MAR, *marzjan, gamarzjan (?).*
MARCHES (borders), *marka; cf. gamarko.*
[MARGIN], MARGRAVE, [MARQUIS]; *cf. marka.*
MARRING, *sb., marzeins, gamarzeins (?).*
MAR-SHAL; *cf. skalkus.*
MAÐELIAN* (to speak), *mathljan.*
MAÐM* (a gift), *maithms.*
MAÐU* (maggot), *matha.*
MAY, *vb., magan.*
MAY† (maid), *mawi; cf. magus;* see MAID.
ME, *mis, mik.*
MEAL (repast); *cf. mel.*

MEAL (flour); *cf. malan, gamalwjan.*
MEALM* (sand), *malma.*
MEAN (common), *gamains.*
MEAN, *vb., munan.*
MEAT, *mats.*
MEAT-BAG, *matibalgs.*
MECE* (sword), *meki.*
MEED; see MEORD.
MEEK; *cf. mukamodei.*
MEET, *gamotjan.*
MELE† (to speak); *cf. mathljan.*
[MELODY; *cf. milith.*]
MELT; *cf. maltjan* (?).*
MEORD* (reward), *mizdo.*
MERE, *sb., marei.*
METE, *mitan, gamitan.*
MICKLE, *mikils.*
MID† (with), *mith.*
MIDDLE, *midja.*
MIDST; *cf. miduma.*
MIGHT, *sb., mahts.*
MIGHT, *vb., mahta.*
MIGHTY, *mahteigs.*
MILD; *cf. unmilds.*
MILDNESS; *cf. milditha.*
MILK, *miluks.*
MILL; *cf. malan.*
[MINCE; *cf. mins.*]
MIND, *muns, gaminthi.*
MIND, *vb.; cf. munan, gamunan.*
MINE, *meins.*
[MINIM, MINUTE, MINNOW; *cf. mins.*]
MIS-, *missa-.*
MISDEED, *missadeds.*
MISDOER, *missataujands.*
MIXEN; *cf. maihstus.*
MOLE (spot), *mail.*
MONTH, *menoths.*
MOOD; *cf. mods.*
MOODY, *modags.*
MOON, *mena.*
MOOT; *cf. gamotjan.*
MORE, *mais, maiza.*
MORN, *maurgins.*
MOST, *maist, maists.*
MOTH; *cf. matha.*

MOULD, MOULDER; cf. *mulda.*
MOULD-WARP (mole); cf. *mulda*
  and *wairpan.*
MOURN, *maurnan.*
MOUTH, *munths.*
MUCH; see MICKLE.
MURDER, vb., *maurthrjan.*
MURDER, MURTHER, sb., *maurthr.*
MYSE* (table), *mes.*

NÆTING* (a chiding), *naiteins.*
NAIL, vb., *ganagljan.*
NAKED, *nakwaths.*
NAKEDNESS; cf. *nakwadei.*
NAME, sb., *namo.*
NAME, vb., *namnjan, ganamnjan.*
NATTERJACK; see NEDDER.
NAY, *ni, aiw;* cf. *ne.*
NE†(not, nor), *ni, nih.*
NEDDER†(adder), *nadrs.*
NEED, sb., *nauths.*
NEED, vb., cf. *nauthjan.*
NEEDLE, *nethla.*
NEIGHBOUR; cf. *nehw* and *bauan.*
NEOTAN* (to enjoy), *niutan.*
NEPHEW, NIECE; cf. *nithjis, nithjo.*
NESH†(soft), *hnaskwus.*
NET, *nati.*
NEǷAN* (to dare); cf. *anananthjan.*
NEW, *niujis.*
NIECE; cf. *nithjo.*
NIGH, *nehw, nehwa.*
NIGHT, *nahts.*
NIM†(to take), *niman, ganiman.*
NIMBLE; cf. *niman.*
NINE, *niun.*
NINTH, *niunda.*
NIOTAN* (to enjoy), *niutan.*
NIǷ* (envy), *neith.*
NO, *ni, ne.*
NOT, NOUGHT; *ni* and *waihts.*
NOW, *nu.*
NUMB; cf. *niman.*

OATH, *aithis.*
OF, OFF, *af.*
OFT, *ufta.*
OIL, *alew.*
OKYRE†(usury), *wokrs.*
OLD, *altheis.*
OLFEND* (camel), *ulbandus.*
[OLIVE, *alewa-bagms.*]
ON, *ana.*
ONDE†; see AYND.
ONE, *ains.*
ONEFOLD, *ainfalths.*
ONWARDS; cf. *anawairths.*
OR, *aiththau.*
ORCHARD, *aurtigards.*
OTHER, *anthar.*
OUR, *unsar.*
OUT, *us, ut, uta.*
OVEN, *auhns.*
OVER, *ufar.*
OVERSHADOW, *ufarskadwjan.*
OWE†(to own), *aigan, aihan.*
OX, *auhsa.*

PAD* (undergarment), *paida.*
PLAIT, sb., *flahta.*
POUND, *pund.*

QUASH; cf. *kwistjan* (?).
QUEEN, *kwens.*
QUELL; cf. *ana-kwal* (?).
QUERN; cf. *asilu-kwairnus.*
QUICK (alive), *kwius.*
QUICKEN, *gakwiujan.*
QUOTH; cf. *kwithan.*

RÆSN* (roof), *razn.*
RAIN, sb., *rign.*
RAIN, vb., *rignjan.*
RAISE, *raisjan.*
RAISE UP, *ur-raisjan.*
RANSACK, *razn* and *sokjan.*

[RATIO; cf. rathjo.]
REACH, rikan.
READ; cf. garedan, fauragaredan, rodjan.
READY, raths, garaids.
READY (to make), raidjan, garaidjan.
REAP, raupjan.
RECKON, rahnjan, garahnjan.
[RECUMBENT; cf. anakumbjan.]
RED, rauds.
REDE† (advise), cf. redan.*
REMIND; see MIND.
REORD* (speech), razda.
REST; cf. rasta.
[REVOLVE; cf. walwjan.]
-RIC, reiki.
RICH, reiks.
RIGHT, adj., raihts, garaihts.
RIGHT, sb., garaihtei.
RIGHTING, sb., garaihteins.
RISE; cf. urreisan.
ROB; cf. biraubon.
ROOM, rums.
ROOMY, rums.
ROPE, raip in skaudaraip.
ROUPE† (outcry); cf. hropjan.
RUN, rinnan.
RUN, RUNNEL (stream), runs, garunjo.
RUNE, runa.
RUNG, hrugga.
RUSH, REED, raus.

SACAN* (to strive), sakan.
SACK, sakkus.
SACU* (strife), sakjo, sokeins.
SÆD* (sated), saths.
SÆNE* (sluggish); cf. sainjan.
SAL* (rope); cf. insailjan.
SALT, sb. & vb., salt, saltan.
SALVE, sb., salbons.
SALVE, vb., salbon, gasalbon.
SAM† (together), samath, samana.
SAME, sama.
SATE [SATISFY, SATURATE]: cf. gasothjan, saths.

SCALE, skalja.
SCATH, skathis.
SCATHE, skathjan, gaskathjan.
SCEALC* (servant), skalks, gaskalki.
SCEAT* (treasure), skatts.
SCHALK†.(servant), skalks.
SCOT-FREE; cf. SCEAT.
SCUCCA* (devil), skohsl.
SEA, saiws.
SEAL, sb., sigljo.
SEAL, vb., sigljan, gasigljan.
SEARO* (weapon), sarwa.
SEE, saihwan, gasaihwan.
SEED; cf. manaseths (?).
SEEK, sokjan, gasokjan.
SEEM; see SEMAN.
SEETHE; cf. sauths.
SEL* (a hall); cf. saljan, salithwos.
SEL* (good), sels.
SELF, silba.
SELL; cf. saljan, gasaljan; see SYLLAN.
SEMAN* (to appease, seem), samjan.
SEND, sandjan, gasandjan.
SENESCHAL; sineigs (superl. sinista) and skalks.
[SENIOR; cf. sineigs.]
SET, satjan, gasatjan.
SETTLE, sb., sitls.
SEVEN, sibun.
SEVENTY, sibuntehund.
SEW, siujan.
SHADOW, skadus.
SHADOWING, sb., gaskadweins.
SHALL, SHOULD, skal, skulda.
SHAME, vb., skaman.
SHAPE, vb., gaskapjan.
SHAVE, skaban, gaskaban.
SHE, si.
SHED†(to part), skaidan, gaskaidan.
SHEEN, adj., skauns.
SHEER, skeirs.
SHEET; cf. skauts.
SHELL, skalja.
SHEND† (to disgrace); cf. skanda.
SHIELD, skildus.

SHIMMER; cf. *skeima*.
SHINE, *skeinan, biskeinan*.
SHIP, *skip*.
SHOE, *skohs, gaskohi*.
SHOVE OFF, *abskiubjan*.
SHOW; cf. *skawjan*.
SHOWER; cf. *skura*.
SHRED, *disskreitan*.
SIB†(akin); cf. *unsibis*.
SICK, *siuks*.
SICKEN, *siukan*.
SICKNESS, *siukei, sauhts*.
SIDU* (a custom), *sidus*.
SIEN* (a vision), *siuns*.
SIFIAN* (to rejoice), *sifan*.
SIGE* (victory), *sigis*.
SIGH, SOUGH, vb., *gaswogjan*.
[SILENT; cf. *anasilan*.]
SILL; cf. *sauls*.
SILVER, *silubr*.
SILVERY, *silubreins*.
SIN* (his), *seins*.
SING, *siggwan*.
SINK, vb. act., *saggkwjan*.
SINK, vb. neut., *siggkwan, gasiggkwan*.
SISTER, *swistar*.
SIT, *sitan, gasitan*.
SITH† (since); cf. *seithu*.
SITHE† (a time), *sinth*.
SIX, *saihs*.
SIXTH, *saihsta*.
SLAUGHTER, *slauhts*.
SLAWIAN* (to be slow), *slawan*.
SLAY, *slahan*.
SLEDGE-HAMMER; cf. *slahan*.
SLEEP, sb., *sleps*.
SLEEP, vb., *slepan, gaslepan*.
SLIDE; cf. *afslauthjan*.
SLIGHT; cf. *slaihts*.
SLIP, *sliupan*.
SLOW; see SLAWIAN.
SMALL, *smals*.
SMEAR; cf. *smairthr*.
SMITH, *smitha* in *aiza-smitha*; cf. *gasmithon*.
SMUT, SMUTCH, *bismeitan, gasmeitan*.

SNARE; cf. *snorjo*.
SNIÐAN* (to cut), *sneithan*.
SNOTER† (wise), *snutrs*.
SNOW, *snaiws*.
SO, *swa*.
SODDEN; cf. *sauths*.
SOIL, vb., *bisauljan*.
SOILING, sb., *bisauleins*.
[SOLAR; cf. *sauil*.]
SOLE (of a boot), *sulja*.
SOME, *sums*.
SON, *sunus*.
SONG, *saggws*.
SOON, *suns*.
SOOTH (true); cf. *sunjeins, sunja*.
SOOTHE, *suthjon*.
SORE, sb., *sair*.
SORROW, sb., *saurga*.
SORROW, vb., *saurgan*.
SOTE† (sweet), *sutis*.
SOUL, *saiwala*.
SOW, vb., *saian*.
SPARROW, *sparwa*.
SPELL, sb., *spill*.
SPELL, vb.; cf. *gaspillon*.
SPEW, SPIT, *speiwan, gaspeiwan*.
SPIN, *spinnan*.
SPYRD* (a stadium), *spaurds*.
STAFF; cf. *stabs*.
STAMMER; cf. *stamms*.
STAND, *standan, gastandan*.
STAR, *stairno*.
STARK, STARCH; cf. *ga-staurknan*.
STEAD, *staths, stads*.
STEAL, *stilan*.
STEE† (a ladder). *staiga*.
STEER, sb. *stiur*.
STEER, vb.; cf. *stiurjan*.
[STERILE; cf. *stairo*.]
STEVEN† (voice), *stibna*.
STICK (to pierce); cf. *stiks*.
[STIGMA; cf. *staks*.]
STING; cf. *stigkwan, usstiggan*.
STODGE (to push), *stautan*.
STONE, *stains*.
STONE, vb., *stainjan*.
STONY, *staineins*.

STOOL, *stols*.
STREW, STRAW, *straujan*.
STRIKE † (a stroke), *striks*.
STROKE, *striks*.
STY † (to mount), *gasteigan*.
SUCH; *see* SWYLK.
SULLY; *see* SOIL.
SUN, *sunna, sunno*.
SUNDER; *see* ASUNDER.
SUNDRY; *cf. sundro*.
SWAB; *cf. swairban*.*
SWÆR* (heavy); *cf. swers*.
SWAMM* (toadstool); *cf. swamms*.
SWART, SWARTHY, *swarts*.
SWEAR, *sweran*.
SWEEP; *cf. sweipan*, swairban**.
SWEET, *sutis*.
SWEFEL* (brimstone), *swibls*.
SWEG* (musical sound); *cf. swiglon*.
SWEGER* (mother-in-law), *swaihro*.
SWELLING-UP, *uf-swalleins*.
SWELT † (to die), *swiltan, gaswiltan*.
SWIM; *cf. swimman*, swumsl*.
SWINE, *swein*.
SWING; *cf. afswaggwjan*.
SWIÐ* (strong), *swinths*.
SWYLK † (such), *swaleiks*.
SYLLAN* (to offer, sell); *cf. saljan*.

[TACIT; *cf. thahan*.]
TAIL; *cf. tagl*.
TAME, *gatamjan*.
TAN* (twig, basket), *tains, tainjo*.
TAWNEN † (to shew), *taiknjan*.
TEACH, *gateihan*.
TEAR, *sb., tagr*.
TEAR (a rent), *gataura*.
TEAR, *vb., gatairan*.
TEAT; *cf. daddjan*.
TEINE † (rod, ingot), *tains*.
TELL, *talzjan*.
TEN, *taihun*.
TENTH, *taihunda*.
THANNE † (when), *than*.
THARF † (need), *tharba*.
THAT, *thata, thatei*.

THEARFAN* (to need), *thaurban*.
THE † (to thrive), *theihan, gatheihan*.
THEE, *thus, thuk*.
THEN, *than*.
THEOD* (people), *thiuda*.
THEOW* (a serf), *thius, thewis, thiwi*.
THERE, *thar*.
THEY, THEM, *thai, thaim*.
THICK, *digrs*; *cf. digrei*.
THIEF, *thiubs*.
THIN; *cf. ufthanjan*.
THINE, *theins*.
THINK, *thagkjan, thugkjan*.
THIRD, *thridja*.
THIRL † (to pierce); *cf. thairko*.
THIRST, *sb. thaurstei*.
THIRST, *vb., gathairsan, thaursjan*.
THO* (clay), *thaho*.
THOLE † (to suffer), *thulan*.
THORN, *thaurnus*.
THORPE, *thaurp*.
THOU, *thu*.
THOUGH, *thau, thauh*.
THOUGHT, *thuhtus*.
THOUSAND, *thusundi*.
THREATEN, *us-thriutan*.
THRESH, THRASH, *thriskan*.
THREE, *threis*.
THRILL; *see* THIRL.
THRING † (to throng), *threihan*.
THRIST* (bold); *cf. thrasa-balthei*.
THRONG, *vb., threihan*.
THROUGH, *thairh*.
THRUST; *cf. trudan*.
THWART; *cf. thwairhs*.
THWEAL* (bath), *thwahl*.
THWEAN* (to wash), *thwahan*.
TILL, *vb., tilan*; *cf. tils*.
TIMBER; *see next word*.
TIMBREN † (to build), *timrjan, ga-timrjan*.
TINDER; *cf. tandjan*.
TO, *du*.
TOKEN, *taikns*.
TONGUE, *tuggo*.
TOOT, TOOTLE; *cf. thut-haurn*.

TOOTH, *tunthus.*
TOUCH, *tekan, teikan.*
TOW, TUG, *tahjan, tiuhan.*
TOWEL; *cf. thwahan.*
TOWN; *cf. tains* (rod, hedge).
TRAMPLE ON, *anatrimpan.*
TREAD, *trudan, gatrudon.*
TREE, *triu.*
TREEN† (*adj. from* tree), *triweins.*
TROW, *trauan.*
[TRUCE; *cf. triggwa.*]
TRUE; *cf. triggws, trauan.*
TRUST; *cf. trauan, gatrauan.*
TUG, TOW, *tahjan, tiuhan.*
TUNGEL* (star), *tuggl.*
TWELVE, *twalif.*
TWENTY, *twaitigjus.*
TWIN; *cf. tweihnai.*
TWIT, *idweitjan.*
TWO, *twai.*
-TY, *-tigus, -tigjus.*

UHTE* (early morn), *uhtwo.*
UN-, *-un.* [Prefixed to nouns, adverbs, and present participles, and to the verbs *unsweran, unthiuthjan,* and *unwerjan.*]
UNCOUTH, *unkunths.*
UNDER, *undar, undaro.*
UNDERMOST, *undaraists.*
UNDERN†; *cf. undaurni-mats.*
UNSEEN, *ungasaihwans.*
UNTO; *cf. und, unte.*
UNWITTING, *unwitands.*
UP, *iup.*

VANE, *fana.*
[VEST, VESTURE, *wasti.*]
VIE, *weigan* (?).
VINE, *weina-triu.*
VINEYARD, *weinagards.*
[VOGUE; *cf. wagjan.*]

WAFT (O. E. *waff*); *cf. waian* (?).
WAG, *wagjan, gawagjan.*
WAGE, WAGES, WAGER; *cf. wadi.*
WAIL; *cf. wai.*
WAKE, *vb. neut., wakan.*
WALE (in gunwale); *cf. walus.*
WALE, WHEAL; *cf. walus.*
WALE† (to choose), *waljan, gawaljan.*
WALLOW, *walwison; cf. walwjan.*
WALK, WAN; *cf. wans.*
WALTZ; *cf. waltjan.*
WAND, *wandus.*
WANE; *cf. wans.*
WANG* (field), *waggs.*
WANGERE* (pillow), *waggari.*
WANING, *sb., wanains.*
WANTING, *wans.*
WARDEN, *wardja.*
-WARDS, *-wairths.*
WARIE† (to curse), *gawargjan.*
WARINESS, *warei.*
WARM, *vb., warmjan.*
WARP, *hwairban* (?); but see next word.
WARP† (to cast), *wairpan, gawairpan.*
WARY, *wars.*
WAS, *was;* from *wisan.*
WATCH, *sb., wahtwo, wokains.*
WATER, *wato.*
WATERSHED; *cf. skaidan.*
WATTLE; *cf. waddjus.*
WAVE, *wegs.*
WAX, *vb., wahsjan.*
WAX† (growth), *wahstus.*
WAY, *wigs.*
WAYMENT† (to lament); *cf. wai.*
WE, *weis.*
WEAK; *cf. unwahs* (?).
WEALTIAN* (to reel), *waltjan.*
WEAPONS, *wepna.*
WEAR; *cf. unwerjan.*
WEAVE, *biwaibjan, weiban.**
WED, *vb., gawadjon.*

WED† (pledge), *wadi*.
WEEK, *wiko* (?).
WEEN, *wenjan, gawenjan*.
WEEP; see WHOOP.
WEIRD; *cf. wairthan*.
WELER* (lip), *wairilo*.
WELL, adv., *waila*.
WELL UP, vb., *wulan*.
WEM* (spot), *wamm*.
WEND, *wandjan, gawandjan*.
WER* (man), *wair*.
WEREGILD, WERWOLF; see preceding word.
WERE, *wesum;* from *wisan*.
WETHER, *withrus*.
WHARF; *cf. wairpan*.
WHEAT, *hwaiteis*.
WHEN, *hwan*.
WHERE, *hwar*.
WHETHER, *hwathar*.
WHICH; see WHILK.
WHID†(quick movement); *cf. withon*.
WHILE, sb., *hweila*.
WHILK† (which), *hwi-leiks*.
WHINE, *kwainon*.
WHIT, *waihts*.
WHITE, *hweits*.
WHITEN, *gahweitjan*.
WHO, *hwas*.
WHOLE, *hails, gahails*.
WHOOP, WEEP, *wopjan*.
WHORE, sb., *hors*.
WHORE, vb., *horinon, gahorinon*.
WHY, *du-hwe*.
WICK (town), *weihs*.
WIDOW, *widuwo*.
WIDOWED, *widuwairns*.
WIELD, *waldan, gawaldan*.
WIG* (war), *wigans*.
WIG* (holy), *weihs*.
WILD, *wiltheis*.
WILL, sb., *wilja*.
WILL, vb., *wiljan*.
WILLING, *gawileis*.
WIN; *cf. winnan*.
WIN† (joy); *cf. unwunands*.
WIND, sb., *winds*.

WIND, vb., *biwindan*.
WINE, *wein*.
WINNAN* (to toil), *winnan*.
WINNOW, *diswinthjan*.
WINTER, *wintrus*.
WIPE; *cf. swairban*.*
WISE, *weis*; cf. unweis*.
WISP, *waips, wipja*.
WIST (pt. t. of to wit), *wissa*.
WIT, vb., *witan*.
WIT* (we two), *wit*.
WITENAGEMOTE*; *cf. gamotjan*.
WITH- (in withstand), *withra*.
WITHY; *cf. gawidan*.
WITTY; *cf. unwits*.
WLITE* (face), *wlits*.
WLITAN* (to see), *wlaiton*.
WOCER* (usury), *wokrs*.
WOE! *wai!*
WOLF, *wulfs*.
WOMB, *wamba*.
WOOD† (mad), *wods*.
WOOL, *wulla*.
WORD, *waurd, gawaurdi*.
WORD, vb., *waurdjan*.
WORK, sb., *waurstw, gawaurki*.
WORK, vb., *waurkjan, gawaurkjan*.
WORKER, *waurstwa, waurstwja*.
WORM, *waurms*.
WORSE, WORSER, *wairs, wairsiza*.
WORT, *aurts, waurts*.
WORTH, WORTHY, *wairths*.
WORTH, sb., *wairthida*.
WORTH† (to become), *wairthan*.
WOT (from vb. to wit), *wait*.
WOUND, sb., *wundufni*.
WOUND, vb., *gawundon*.
WRÆD* (wreath, flock), *writhus*.
WRAK† (vengeance), *wraka, wrekei*.
-WRAY, BEWRAY, *wrohjan*.
WREAK, *wrikan, wrakjan*.
WREATH; *cf. writhus;* see WRÆD.
WRING; *cf. wruggo*.
WRITE; *cf. writs*.
WRY, *wraikws*.
WULDOR* (glory), *wulthus*.
WYRT* (root), *waurts*.

YARD, *gards, garda.*
YARD (of a ship), *gazds.*
YE, YOU, *jus, izwis.*
YEA, *ja, jai.*
YEAR, *jer.*
YEARN, *gairnjan.*
YEARNING, *gairnei.*
YEDE† (went), *iddja.*
YEME† (to regard), *gaumjan.*
YEOMAN, *gawi* and *manna.*
YESTERDAY; *cf. gistradagis.*
YIELD, *fragildan, usgildan.*
YOKE, *juk, gajuk.*
YON, *jains.*
YOND, YONDER, *jaind, jaindre.*
YOUNG, *juggs.*
YOUR; *cf. izwar.*
YOUTH, *junda.*
YRFE* (inheritance), *arbi.*

ERRATA, &c.

Ain-lif is out of place; look for it after Aine-hun.

Aith-thau should precede Aiw.

For Alabastraun read Alabalstraun.

The second reference under Ana-hnaiwjan belongs to Ana-hneiwan, for which see *Appendix*.

Under And-wairthi, *for* v. q. *read* v. 9.

For Audaugei read Audagei.

In col. 35, line 5, *read* gabaurjothus, *not* gabaurtjothus.

Under Basi, *for* weina-bazi *read* weina-basi.

For Bi-arbeidjan, read Bi-arbaidjan.

To the derivatives of Daur add "daura-warda, daura-wardo, daura-wards" for explanations of which see the *Appendix*.

Fra-liusan (col. 74) means *to lose*, not *to loose*.

For Ga-namjan read Ga-namnjan.

For Ga-tahrjan read Ga-tarhjan.

Jaindre (col. 143) occurs in Lu. 17. 37, not in Lu. 11. 37.

Under Mith (col. 173), for *prefix verbal* read *verbal prefix*.

For Naumbaimbair (col. 179) read Naubaimbair.

BERLIN.
Printed by A. W. Schade.

www.ingramcontent.com/pod-product-compliance
Lightning Source LLC
Chambersburg PA
CBHW032224230426
43666CB00033B/1274